WOMEN, CRIME, AND PUNISHMENT
IN ANCIENT LAW AND SOCIETY

WOMEN, CRIME, AND PUNISHMENT IN ANCIENT LAW AND SOCIETY

Volume 1
The Ancient Near East

ELISABETH MEIER TETLOW

continuum
NEW YORK • LONDON

Continuum

New York London

2004

The Continuum International Publishing Group Inc

15 East 26 Street, New York, NY 10010

The Continuum International Publishing Group Ltd

The Tower Building, 11 York Road, London SE1 7NX

Printed in the United States of America

Library of Congress Cataloging-in-Publication Data

    Tetlow, Elisabeth Meier, 1942–
        Women, crime, and punishment in ancient law and society / Elisabeth M. Tetlow.
          p. cm.
        Includes bibliographical references and index.
        ISBN 0-8264-1628-4 (hardcover vol. 1 : alk. paper) — ISBN
    0-8264-1629-2 (hardcover vol. 2 : alk. paper)
        1. Law—Middle East—History. 2. Law, Ancient. I. Title.
    KL147.T38 2004
    340.5'3—dc22

                                  2004022023

For my daughters

Tania
Maria
Sonia
Sarah

☙

And for my friend
Layla Haddo Khalaf,
proud daughter of Mesopotamia,
woman of compassion and of peace,
who died as this book was completed,
her heart broken by war in her beloved Iraq

Contents

PREFACE	ix
GENERAL INTRODUCTION	xi
INTRODUCTION TO ANCIENT NEAR EASTERN LAW AND SOCIETY	1
PART ONE: SUMER	5
The Law Reforms of King Uru-inimgina of Lagash	8
The Laws of King Ur-Nammu of Ur	10
The Laws of King Lipit-Ishtar of Isin	15
Sumerian Laws Exercise Tablet	18
Sumerian Documents and Inscriptions	19
Criminal Trials of Women	35
Art and Archaeology	37
Conclusion: Women, Crime, and Punishment in Ancient Sumer	40
PART II: BABYLONIA	47
Old Babylonia (1894–1595)	48
The Laws of Eshnunna	48
The Laws of Hammurabi	53
The Edict of King Ammisaduqa	73
Old Babylonian Documents and Inscriptions	74
Middle Babylonia (1595–627)	98
Late Babylonia (626–539)	100
Late Babylonian Laws	100
Late Babylonian Documents and Inscriptions	102
Conclusion: Women, Crime, and Punishment in Ancient Babylonia	112
PART III: ASSYRIA	119
Old Assyria I (2000–1814)	119
Old Assyria II (1814–1762)	124

Middle Assyria (1363–1057)   125
   The Middle Assyrian Laws   126
   The Middle Assyrian Palace Decrees   142
Late Assyria (934–612)   146
   Assyrian Documents, Inscriptions, and Art   146
   Royal Assyrian Conquest Annals   167
Conclusion: Women, Crime, and Punishment
   in Ancient Assyria   171

PART IV: KHATTI   177
   The Hittite Laws   178
   Hittite Documents and Inscriptions   189
   Conclusion: Women, Crime, and Punishment
   in Ancient Khatti   200

CONCLUSION: WOMEN, CRIME, AND PUNISHMENT
IN THE ANCIENT NEAR EAST   205

CHRONOLOGY AND NAMES   221
NOTES   237
PHOTO CREDITS   308
BIBLIOGRAPHY   309
INDEXES   329

Preface

Since this is a book about women, whenever the names of women are known, I have put them in the text, where they may become known in the light of scholarship. For the sake of space, I have often omitted the names of their husbands, fathers, and sons, many of which are known from other sources.

This book deals with three millennia BCE. The designation BCE will not be repeated after every date. All dates may be assumed to be BCE unless otherwise noted. In cases where confusion might arise, the correct dates are stated in the notes.

Since this is a book about the ancient Near East, I have used the spellings of names in their original languages as much as possible. The names of some Late Babylonian and Late Assyrian kings are familiar to readers who have studied the Hebrew Bible or ancient Near Eastern history. These versions of king names were often misspelled when used in the Hebrew Bible. For certain well-known kings, the common version of the name is given in the text and the Babylonian or Assyrian name is in the note. There are also charts at the end of the book that show both versions of these names.

I would like to thank Elisabeth Schüssler Fiorenza for her pioneering work in feminist studies and methodology. I am grateful to those who have read all or parts of the manuscript and have given me their critical suggestions. I am especially indebted to Professor William J. Fulco, S.J., of Loyola Marymount University, who promptly answered my numerous e-mails about linguistic questions, and Professor Robert Gnuse, of Loyola University New Orleans, and Professor Sean Freyne, of Trinity College, Dublin, for their sharing knowledge and insights about the greater world of the Hebrew Bible. I give special thanks to the patient and hardworking librarians at Loyola Law School and Holy Cross College, who went beyond the scope of their duties to provide me with innumerable books via Interlibrary Loan, and to the libraries of Tulane University in New Orleans, Union Theological Seminary and Columbia University in New York, and the Graduate Theological Union in Berkeley for giving me access to their collections. I would like to thank two exceptional editors, Maurya Horgan and Sonia Tetlow, for their corrections and improvements of the manuscript, and Frank Oveis at Continuum for shepherding the work to publication. Finally, I owe a great debt of gratitude to my husband, Mulry, for his endless trips to pick up and return library books, for proofreading texts, for prying definitions from English dictionaries, for drawing the map, and for providing great help with the indexes.

General Introduction

❦

T HE STUDY OF ANCIENT CIVILIZATIONS reveals the roots from which human beings and their history have sprung. The purpose of this work is to uncover pieces and fragments of that history in order to create mosaic portraits of women, crime, and punishment in the laws and societies of the ancient world.

The writing of history is not simply the collection of data about a subject and the placement of that data into a book. Historiography involves the selection, translation, presentation, and interpretation of the data and the underlying assumptions and reasons used in each process. In the past, most historians were men. Many equated humanness with maleness and ignored the existence of women, presenting them, if at all, as an appendage on the periphery of the "real" world of men. They assumed that the acts and roles of men were the norm and that those of women were a deviation from the norm. Male historians, both ancient and modern, viewed the data of history through male preconceptions and biases, of which they were often unaware. Many limited their accounts of history to political and military events, the accomplishments of men. Enormous amounts of information have been published about the history of men and their public roles and achievements. Unfortunately, such works have distorted the history they intended to communicate. This does not mean that all male historiography is false. Much can be learned from these histories, even as the data are expanded and reinterpreted and the preconceptions and assumptions brought to light, challenged, and corrected.

Authentic historiography communicates truth insofar as it is grounded in the reality of the past, which must include the history of women as well as that of men. Feminist historiography recognizes the fact that women constituted approximately half the population of every civilization. Therefore, history that does not take the lives of women into account cannot be accurate or complete. Feminist method expands the sources of history by the discovery and collection of new data that contain information about women, and it expands the tools of history to include contributions from other disciplines such as archaeology, art history, anthropology, sociology, political economy, law, and religious studies.

Feminist historiography operates with the fundamental assumption that history is not a fixed, static structure but a fluid process, in which new data are discovered and new insights reveal new meanings. The discovery of new material necessitates continuing reanalysis, reinterpretation, and revision of previous conclusions. Since history is mediated through both past and present cultures and beliefs, the subjectivity of both the ancient and the modern historian must be acknowledged and examined.

The purpose of feminist historiography is to reconstruct history to include all dimensions of the lives of women and men. In order to discover what it meant to be a woman or man in the historical past, the historian must first identify sources of information, collect all available relevant data, and then situate this material in its original context. The process begins with locating the data on the axes of time and place to establish the basic coordinates of the context. The historian must then study all aspects of the civilization of that time and place—its law, culture, language, literacy, religion, social classes, economic classes, and professions—and how these shaped the lives of women and men of that time and place. Next the historian must examine the categories that situated individuals within the context of the civilization, some of which were determined from birth, such as gender and nationality, and others that changed during the course of peoples' lives, such as age, marital status, economic status, social class, and slave status. The context of individuals also included relationships with other persons living in that civilization, time, and place, such as rulers, priests, parents, spouses, and children. Relationships change during the course of a person's lifetime, and many roles and relationships were not exclusive but were held concurrently. Understanding historical women and men requires knowledge of their roles and relationships within a specific civilization and awareness of the hermeneutics through which these have come to be known.

The subject of women, crime, and punishment begins with a study of ancient women, not in a vacuum but in the context of a specific civilization— its laws and the lives, roles, and relationships of women and men in that civilization. Each civilization must be studied individually, and it is precarious to generalize from one civilization to another. There may be similar data found in two or more civilizations, but the phenomena may have developed in different contexts and acquired different meanings. When there are areas of overlap, these must be studied first within each civilization, and only then compared with other civilizations to investigate whether the phenomena are indeed the same.

Crime is defined as a breach of the customs or laws of a society which causes harm to one or more persons of that society and for which the offender is punished. Crime has been part of human society since its beginning. Throughout history, women's lives have intersected with crime both as victims and as offenders. Women as well as men have been punished for crimes, and the forms of punishment have derived from the practical limitations, beliefs, and values of the civilization in which they have been imposed.

Crime and punishment, criminal law, and the administration of criminal justice have not been studied as extensively as the many noncriminal aspects of ancient civilizations. Since crime and its punishment have been present in all ancient civilizations, it is important to explore the impingement of crime and punishment on the lives of women and men in each civilization. At the same time, it is not possible fully and accurately to understand ancient women or men as victims and perpetrators of crimes without grasping the context of their lives and the societies in which they lived.

The subjects of crime and punishment fall within the larger category of law. In the ancient world, customary laws were created by men, formal laws were written by men, and both were interpreted and enforced by men. The study of women and ancient law must, therefore, seek to understand the roles of gender in the formation and administration of law. Many gender categories and relationships were established in law, including marriage, parentage, divorce, widowhood, adoption, inheritance, debt, liability, crime, and punishment. Gender was often a factor in the delineation of crimes and punishments, as well as in the enforcement of laws and administration of justice.

Civilizations have civil and criminal laws, with varied degrees of distinction between the two. Civil laws generally deal with persons, property, inheritance, contracts, sales, and suretyship, while criminal laws deal with offenses committed against individuals and against the society or state, which incur punishment. In ancient civilizations, the degree of distinction between these two categories varied.

Some crimes are found in most civilizations, such as murder and theft, whereas others are unique to one or more particular civilizations. The examination of a society's criminal law begins with the presupposition that criminal laws would not have been written to punish offenses that had never occurred, so that examination of the criminal laws of a society demonstrates what offenses were being committed by and against women.

Finally, in ancient thought, the name of a person was intrinsically connected to that person's existence on this earth. Whenever the sources reveal the name of a woman, even an insignificant woman, her name will be recorded in the text so that she may be remembered.

Women, Crime, and Punishment in Ancient Law and Society will discuss information about women, crime, and punishment that has been newly discovered, underreported, or omitted from previous works on ancient law and ancient civilizations and will reexamine and reevaluate prior interpretations and conclusions, in order to bring more facets of the lives of ancient women into the light of scholarship. The purpose of this work is to enable the silent voices of ancient women to speak and the invisible lives of ancient women to be brought into the light.

The great poet Adrienne Rich wrote of silence:

> It is a presence
> it has a history a form
>
> Do not confuse it
> with any kind of absence.*

HISTORIOGRAPHY OF THE ANCIENT NEAR EAST

The ancient Near East contained the oldest civilization known. It not only has a history but also a prehistory, some of which is accessible by means of archaeology. Much can be learned from the study of prehistoric cities, temples, houses, tombs, and art. For example, from the skeletons of women found in ancient tombs, scientists can determine the age, evidence of disease or deformity, and cause of death. From the art and artifacts buried with women, archaeologists and art historians can find information about their social status. Queens were buried with diadems, weavers with loom weights and spindle whorls. Excavated buildings contain information about how many people lived in them, and the purpose of specific rooms can often be determined by artifacts found lying on the floor. When there were reliefs or frescoes on the walls, the archaeologist can see, as through a window in time, the faces and activities of the people who lived there. Thus, archaeology extends the visibility of women into even earlier centuries.

Another source of prehistory is oral tradition, which is generally not accessible to historians until it was written down. Once written, however, it is no longer prehistory but history. There are many factors that determine the reliability of oral traditions. In some civilizations, especially when oral literature was sung, the oral transmission was more accurate than later written texts. The ancient Near East produced an abundance of written documents, even though those that have been discovered and published are but a fraction of those written. The historian must determine the context of each document and its reliability by analyzing the purpose and subjectivity of its author. Reliable empirical data situated in context are the starting point for historiography.

---

* Adrienne Rich, "Cartographies of Silence," in *The Dream of a Common Language* (New York: W. W. Norton, 1978), 17.

Introduction to Ancient Near Eastern Law and Society

CIVILIZATION AND ITS HISTORY began in the ancient Near East, a term that designates the geographical areas of western Asia including Mesopotamia, Asia Minor, and the Levant.* This area has been inhabited continuously from earliest prehistoric times to the present.[1] The earliest people in ancient Mesopotamia were nomadic hunters and gatherers.

In Mesopotamia there were two distinct ecological zones. In the south, prehistoric people could not live by hunting and gathering. The choice of where to settle depended to a great extent on the availability of water. In southern Mesopotamia, people settled near the Tigris and Euphrates rivers, which were a source of water for irrigation and a highway for trade. Since the rivers flooded before or during the time of crop harvest, the people had to build drainage canals to control the flood waters. Irrigation and drainage systems were well developed by the beginning of the third millennium BCE. The inscriptions of early Sumerian kings demonstrated their pride in building and improving irrigation channels, levees, and canals. As the environment forced the people to work together to construct irrigation systems and drainage canals, they soon began living together in towns. In northern Mesopotamia and Asia Minor, the climate was very different. There was sufficient rainfall so that prehistoric tribes could hunt and gather, and food was plentiful. When they settled on the land, they were able to grow crops without irrigation and

---

* *Mesopotamia* is a Greek word meaning "between the rivers," the Tigris and the Euphrates. Today Mesopotamia includes Iraq and parts of western Iran. Asia Minor, called *Anatolia* in Greek, is the Asian part of modern Turkey. The Levant includes Syria, Lebanon, and Israel/Palestine.

1

the rivers did not flood. The peoples of the north did not have to work together and so remained in tribal units for a significantly longer time.[2]

In the ancient Near East, the transition from prehistory to history occurred with the invention of writing, which could express and communicate human events. By the fourth millennium BCE, the need had arisen to create written symbols for numbers and representations of animals and other commodities for records of ownership and trade. At first there were symbols for numbers and pictographs of objects.[3] Then sounds were translated into written symbols that represented syllables, which in turn were combined into words. Grammar was developed to express relationships among words. History as such began when phonetic grammatical writing made it possible to express complex ideas and events, and thereby to record human events, literature, and law. This first took place in southern Mesopotamia in the late fourth millennium.[4]

The extant sources for the ancient Near East are abundant, but not complete. Ancient writers could not write everything in their remembered prehistory or their historical present. They first had to choose what to write down. The act of writing down an oral source did not generate an exact reproduction. The subjectivity of the writer interacted with the oral communication. New genres were created as different types of oral communications were written down. The modern historian only has access to written documents. The numbers and sophistication of written sources generally increased through the passage of time, although developments in ancient Near Eastern history were rarely linear and there were often exceptions to apparent trends.

The documentary sources of the ancient Near East were written in many literary genres. There were simple records of business transactions and ownership of commodities and land, as well as literary works of epic and myth. Later writers wrote political, military, administrative, legal, and scientific documents. Kings wrote laws and chronicles of their reigns. Religious writers wrote hymns, proverbs, incantations, and religious rituals. People from every civilization wrote letters, although the gender and social class of correspondents depended on the extent of literacy. Because of the complexity of the writing system, much of the actual writing was done by scribes. Many documents were written by male scribes commissioned by male officials for an upper-class male audience.

Many different ethnic groups settled in or passed through the ancient Near East. Some left no written records; others left written records that were destroyed or have not yet been discovered. The extant published documents represent only a portion of the documents written in the ancient Near East during the last three millennia before the common era. The incomplete nature of the documentation is due to many factors. Some documents were preserved in palace, temple, or family archives, and libraries.[5] Those that were not deposited in archives or libraries had more precarious chances of survival. Some sites yielded far more texts than others, for reasons that had nothing to do with their historical significance. Some sites have not yet been identified, such as Akkad. Other sites cannot be excavated because people live in modern cities on top of them. In some areas, documents were found by local villagers or herders and sold to antiquities dealers, thereby losing their connection to the site of origin and layer of deposit. Many documents are scattered in various museums or have disappeared into private collections, and many of these texts have not yet been translated or published. Many documents written on clay tablets have been damaged or destroyed, leaving tantalizing fragments from which crucial words are often missing. Other documents have not been published or have disappeared into private collections. The historian cannot infer that something did not exist or occur in the ancient Near East because he or she cannot find written evidence about it.[5]

Archaeologists excavated cities because there was visible evidence of urban sites, such as tells and stones. They did not excavate villages or agricultural settlements because there was no way to find them buried under the sands of the wide desert. Early archaeologists focused on excavation of temples, because they found more documents and artifacts within a smaller space. This led to an imbalance of documents that took years to correct. There were many texts relating to cultic activities at temples, but few from palaces or businesses.[6] Excavations of tombs revealed the bodies, jewelry, and musical instruments of women, when documents of the same time and place had little to say about those subjects. Art and artifacts serve to correct omissions or incorrect assumptions based only on documents or partial excavations.

In the first two millennia of ancient Near Eastern history, there was continual interaction between urban and tribal societies and laws. In urban societies, women had more rights and greater freedom, whereas in tribal societies the lives of women were generally restricted and controlled by the patriarchal authority of men. In cities, laws were collected, written down, and promulgated by kings, and courts existed for the administration of justice. Tribal societies retained their ancient oral tradition of customary law, which was administered by heads of families and tribal patriarchs.

The civilizations of the ancient Near East were not isolated settlements in the desert. Cities were built on rivers and trade routes. From prehistoric times, the peoples of Mesopotamia had trade relations with Greece and Egypt in the west, with Persia, Afghanistan, and India in the east, and with Arabia and the Gulf islands in the south.

This book concentrates on the major ancient Near Eastern civilizations that left written records with information about women and crime: Sumer, Babylonia, Assyria, and Khatti. Most of the extant writings are incomplete, and some are only brief fragments. No ancient document has been found that contains the entire civil or criminal law of a civilization or all of its laws affecting women. Each document or artifact contains a small piece of the puzzle. When put together with other writings, art, and artifacts, a general picture of the treatment of women, crime, and punishment of crime in each of these ancient civilizations begins to emerge. The picture is not complete and many questions remain unanswered. An element of mystery remains for continuing discovery and elucidation.

Part One

⌒∂

SUMER

THE EARLIEST KNOWN PEOPLE in the ancient Near East who left written records were the Sumerians.* There are traces of Sumerian culture before 5000 BCE. The Sumerians had built cities in southern Mesopotamia by 4000. The cities shared the same language, culture, and religion.[1] By the end of the fourth millennium, the Sumerians had developed a system of writing called *cuneiform,* using wedge-shaped characters made by a reed stylus pressed onto soft clay tablets which were then baked. The Sumerian writing system was sufficiently well developed to transmit complex historical, legal, and literary compositions. The Sumerians were the first civilization to write down their laws. The Sumerian writing system, laws, and legal terminology were later adapted and used by the Babylonians and other ancient Near Eastern peoples.[2]

By the third millennium, Sumer had become an urban society, a "civilization," marked by the existence of cities, which had kings, priests, judges, and soldiers, palaces, temples, communal buildings, large houses, and fortifications.* Urban people worked together to produce food, pottery, and textiles for trade. Sumerian cities became city-states, independent of other political entities, although linked to each other by common language, culture, and religion, and linked to foreign states by trade. At various times in their histories, the Sumerian city-states formed alliances, conquered or were conquered by other city-states, and became parts of empires.[3]

---

* The name *Sumer* means "from the south" and designates a place, southern Mesopotamia. The word *Sumerian* designates a people and a language. The Sumerian language is not related to any known language group. It was spoken through the third millennium BCE, but thereafter only written. Most other ethnic groups in ancient Mesopotamia spoke Semitic languages, including Akkadian, Babylonian, and Assyrian. In the Hebrew Bible, Sumer was called Shinar (Genesis 10:10; 11:2–4).

HISTORY OF SUMER	
Prehistory	Ubaid Period 4300–3500
Proto-history	Uruk Period 3500–3100

History	
Early Dynastic (ED)	3000–2371
Akkadian Dynasty	2371–2230
Second Dynasty of Lagash (Lagash II)	2230–2100
Third Dynasty of Ur (Ur III)	2112–2004
First Dynasty of Isin (Isin I)	2017–1794
Larsa Dynasty	2025–1763

Most Sumerian city-states were located near the lower Euphrates River in southern Mesopotamia. The principal city-states were Ur, Uruk, Eridu, Larsa, Shuruppak, Kish, Sippar, Adab, Isin, Umma, Girsu, and Lagash. Nippur was a religious center rather than a city-state in the political sense. The Sumerians identified themselves as citizens of a city-state, not as members of a tribe or clan. Each city-state had a patron god or goddess, a temple, and male and female priests. Each was governed by a king or, rarely, by a queen and had laws and judges. Early city-states had assemblies of citizens with political and judicial functions.[4]

In the ancient mythic literature of Sumer, goddesses were as important as gods. The divine world served as a paradigm for human society. Gods and goddesses came together in an assembly to make decisions. In early times, Sumerian cities were ruled by assemblies of men and women who made the important decisions for the city-state. Later, as men became more dominant in society, they created new myths about the gods to give divine approval to the power and authority of men. Ki, goddess of the earth, lost her title and her name when her functions were given to a male god. Inanna, goddess of heaven and highest deity in Uruk, was demoted by a new myth, in which she was raped by a gardener. Nidaba, goddess of writing, reading, and mathematics; Bau, goddess of medicine and healing; and Nanshe, the divine judge, lost their status and functions when men revised the old myths and gave the goddesses husbands.[5]

The stratification of classes in ancient Sumer included royal families, palace and temple officials, a large bureaucracy, skilled tradespeople, unskilled workers, and slaves. Social classes and slave status were not always determined by birth and were not immutable.

Women were highly visible in the history of ancient Sumer. There were few reigning queens in Sumer, but there was one important exception in the Early Dynastic period: queen Ku-Bau of Kish may have been the first woman ruler in recorded history. A few wives of later kings were called queen: for example, Tutasharlibish, wife of a late king of Akkad, and Shulgi-simti, wife of the Ur III king Shulgi. The wives of Sumerian kings exercised substantial economic and political power even without the titles and prerogatives of queens.[6] As the political power of royal men increased in Sumerian empires, so too did the religious and economic power of royal women.

In Sumer, as in most ancient societies, the institution of slavery existed as an integral part of the social and economic structure. Sumer was not, however, a slavery-based economy. There were more working-class free persons than there were slaves. Both men and women could be enslaved, but there were more women slaves than men. Slaves worked in households and in temples. Many were debt slaves of creditors or war captives. They were legally the property of their owners, but in Sumer slaves themselves could own property. Slavery was not a permanent status, and many slaves became free persons.[7]

There were a few wars among the Sumerian city-states, generally caused by kings attempting to bring other city-states under their own authority. The first king to unite the city-states of southern Mesopotamia was Sargon of Akkad, who was from the city-state of Kish on the northern frontier of Sumer. He built his capital, Akkad, nearby. Sargon spoke Akkadian, a Semitic language named for his capital. He consolidated his power and legitimized his kingship in Sumer by making himself king of Ur and Uruk, the two most important city-states in the south, and by making his daughter, En-kheduanna, high priest of the moon god at Ur and of the heaven god at Uruk. The Akkadian empire included all of Mesopotamia and parts of Syria, Asia Minor, and western Persia. It had a lasting influence on city-states of northern Mesopotamia and Asia Minor.[8] The Akkadian dynasty lasted for more than a century. Then nomadic Gutian tribes migrated into the area, and Sumer and Akkad refractured into independent city-states. During this time, a strong dynasty emerged in the city-state of Lagash.

A century later, king Ur-Nammu of Ur founded the third dynasty of Ur (Ur III) and peacefully reunited the city-states of Sumer into an empire. The next century was the golden age of Sumer; there was peace and prosperity, and the status of women was at its highest. By the end of the third millennium, however, the Ur III empire collapsed under the pressure of large migrations of Amorite tribes into Mesopotamia. Sumer again fractured into separate city-states.

The Amorites were nomadic tribes that came into Mesopotamia from the west. *Amorite* is a general term denoting a language and an ethnic group.

There were many Amorite tribes; some shared the same customs, and others had different customs. All were alike in relegating women to a low status and using harsh punishments for crimes. The tribes traced their genealogy back to a common ancestor, which gave them a common identity and basis for inter-tribal relations.

Some Amorite tribes had already settled in the Sumerian city-states, while others moved in at this time. In some city-states they assimilated the high urban Sumerian civilization, whereas in others they retained Amorite tribal traditions and customs. Contemporary cuneiform writers mentioned them with disdain for their lack of culture. The Ur III king Shu-Sin built a defensive wall between the Tigris and the Euphrates to hold the Amorites back, but they easily breached the wall. The last non-Amorite dynasty in southern Mesopotamia was founded in the city-state of Isin. It was later conquered by the Amorite dynasty of Larsa, setting the stage for the next epoch in Mesopotamian history.[9]

The Sumerians ruled southern Mesopotamia during the fourth and third millennia. Since they invented writing, they were the first people to record the memories of their lives and experiences, thereby creating history and literature. Sumer, though very ancient, was a highly developed urban civilization. Sumerians created the first known legal system with written laws and a system of administration of justice and a political system with defined structures of government. They are credited with the invention of the lunar calendar, the sundial, the water clock, indoor plumbing, the potter's wheel, the kiln, the plough, the chariot, and irrigation.[10]

The extant written documents and artifacts of Sumer paint a fascinating, albeit incomplete, picture of what life there was like, including the treatment of women, crime, and punishment. The extant laws of Sumer do not record all Sumerian law or all the crimes committed by and against women; yet each fragment is like a small stone, and when many such stones are put together, they begin to construct a mosaic picture of women, crime, and punishment in ancient Sumer.

THE LAW REFORMS OF KING URU-INIMGINA OF LAGASH

There are few extant sources of law from the Early Dynastic period. One exception was Uru-inimgina, king of Lagash in the late twenty-fourth century BCE. Only a few of his laws are known, but these provide the earliest access to laws on women, crime, and punishment in ancient Sumer. Inscriptions written on cones and an oval plaque document the reforms of this ruler. The texts described the abuse of power by the aristocracy and the priests, who were oppressing the poor and the powerless, including women. King Uru-inimgina stated his intent to protect the vulnerable, especially poor mothers and widows, from further oppression.[11]

Some of the laws of king Uru-inimgina raised the status of women, and others adversely affected women. He increased the rations of women priests, thus elevating their importance. He abolished an earlier law that had allowed the ruler and an official to take silver from a man seeking a divorce, thereby making it less expensive for men to divorce their wives and, consequently, making the position of wives less secure.[12]

Women had been victims of the abuse of power by men before the reign of king Uru-inimgina. Royal officials and male priests had misappropriated land belonging to temples and had used it to enrich themselves. They had reduced women priests to serfdom, working the fields for the rich. Uru-inimgina restored these lands to the temples, which enabled the women priests to return to the duties of their profession.[13]

Another abuse of power by the rich against the poor was committed by officials and priests who trespassed on the property of poor mothers and widows and stole the produce of their gardens and orchards. Such acts reduced the women victims and their families to destitution and starvation. King Uru-inimgina forbade his officials and priests to enter and steal from the gardens and orchards of women. Upper-class men and women were forbidden to steal fish from the ponds of commoners.[14]

The extant inscriptions of king Uru-inimgina described a few crimes committed by women. After stating that in previous times a woman could marry more than one husband, Uru-inimgina forbade the practice of polyandry henceforth and made it a capital crime.[15] Polyandry increased the power of wives over husbands, just as the opposite, polygyny, marriage between one man and more than one woman, increased the power of husbands over their wives.

King Uru-inimgina wrote that when a man and a woman loved each other they should live together. Her field and well would become his field and well. After they had been together for a time, if the woman had sex with another man, the first man could throw her out of his house.[16] The woman lost the property she had brought into the relationship. Since the text did not mention marriage, the offense was infidelity, not adultery.

The only evidence of corporal mutilation in Sumerian law was found in the early law of king Uru-inimgina as punishment for the crimes of theft of real estate and offensive speech by women. A contract for sale of real estate was attached with a peg to the wall of the building, with the stipulation that anyone who tried to take the property would have the peg driven through his or her mouth. When a woman said something offensive to a man, her teeth were crushed by burnt bricks on which her guilt had been inscribed. The bricks were then hung up in the city gate for all to see. Even in this early period in Sumer, crime and punishment were dealt with by the state.[17]

Polyandry and verbal offenses of women against men were harshly punished. In both women challenged and diminished the authority of men. Yet at the same time, laws were written to protect women against men who trespassed in their gardens and stole their food. Capital and corporal punishments were rare in later Sumerian laws.

Few laws of king Uru-inimgina have survived, yet these fragmentary laws afford a rare glimpse into the world of women, crime, and punishment in the laws of the mid-third millennium BCE.

THE LAWS OF KING UR-NAMMU OF UR

The third dynasty of Ur in the last century of the third millennium was the high point of the Sumerian empire and civilization. King Ur-Nammu created an empire that ruled all the city-states in Sumer and Akkad and many in northern Mesopotamia. Instead of military conquest, he formed his empire by building and restoring temples in cities which then acknowledged him as king in gratitude. He consolidated his authority through political marriages of his children and appointment of his daughters as high priests.[18] He married his son to Taramuram, daughter of the king of Mari, forming a political alliance to protect trade routes. His son and successor, king Shulgi, married two of his daughters to foreign kings to cement political alliances. Like Sargon of Akkad, Ur-Nammu made his daughter, En-nirgalana, high priest of Ur. King Shulgi later made one of his daughters, En-nirzianna, high priest of Ur.[19]

King Ur-Nammu founded the Ur III dynasty, which lasted more than a century. He established a large bureaucracy which generated thousands of clay tablets. He built canals for irrigation and travel and secured the trade routes. King Ur-Nammu made the first extant collection of laws in the ancient Near East.[20]

THIRD DYNASTY OF UR (UR III)	
Ur-Nammu (18)	2113–2096
Shulgi (48)	2095–2048
Amar-Sin (9)	2047–2039
Shu-Sin (9)	2038–2030
Ibbi-Sin (24)	2029–2006

The extant copies of the laws of Ur-Nammu, found in excavations of scribal schools in Ur, Nippur, and Sippar, were written in cuneiform script on clay tablets.[21] The extant text includes a prologue and thirty-four laws, some of which are brief fragments. The prologue described the ways in which king Ur-Nammu acted to establish justice in the land of Sumer and banish crime, violence, and strife. The stated purpose of the laws was to establish justice by correcting abuses prevalent at the time and by mandating the protection of widows, orphans, and poor persons against oppression by the wealthy and powerful.[22] Each law was written in the form of a conditional sentence with a protasis—if someone did "this"—and an apodosis—then the legal result would be "that."

Status of Women

In ancient Sumer, marriages were generally contracted between the bride's father and the groom or the groom's father. Each paid a certain amount of money or property: the prospective groom or his father paid "marriage gifts" to the bride's father, and the bride's father provided his daughter with a dowry. In civilizations that required marriage gifts from the groom, a daughter was an economic asset to her family. When the bride's family was required to provide a dowry as a legal requirement for a valid marriage and marriage gifts from the groom's family were not required, daughters were an economic liability to their families. In some societies this led to female infanticide. Since Sumer required both marriage gifts and dowry, the economic burden was relatively equal for both families. Sumerian families valued both their daughters and their sons.

After the marriage contract was signed and the marriage gifts delivered and accepted, a feast was held and the couple was considered betrothed. During the betrothal period, the groom generally lived in the household of the bride's family. After the marriage rites were completed and another feast was celebrated, the couple were legally married and the bride moved into the household of the groom's family.

The few laws of Ur-Nammu dealing with betrothal, marriage, divorce, and slavery reveal information about the status of women in ancient Sumer. The betrothal rite protected the bride and the groom. When a prospective groom had presented his marriage gifts and entered the house of his prospective father-in-law and the latter had then given his daughter to another man in marriage, the father-in-law had to give the rejected groom double the value of the marriage gifts he had brought.[23] This law penalized fathers who tried to marry their daughters to the highest bidder.

The frequent attestation of divorce indicates that Sumerian men dissolved one marriage before undertaking another, thereby avoiding polygyny. In the laws of Ur-Nammu, divorce was initiated by the husband, but he could not simply send his wife away empty-handed. He had to compensate her with sixty sheqels of silver. If the divorced wife was a former widow, the man had to pay her only half as much. But if the man had had sex with the widow before a formal marriage was contracted, then he owed her nothing if he later divorced her.[24] Prior marriage and sex outside of marriage rendered women less valuable to men and diminished the extent of women's legal and economic protection.

Slave marriages were legal marriages, but the rights of the slave owner took precedence over the marital rights of slaves. It was standard practice for a slave owner to give a slave woman to a male slave as a wife. The slave owner retained his ownership rights over the slave woman. If a male slave married a free woman, they had to give one male child of the marriage to the husband's owner to be a slave. The other children of the marriage were not enslaved. When a male slave married a slave woman whom he loved and later he was given his freedom, the slave woman had to remain in the household of her master. By mentioning the existence of love between slaves, this law suggested that slaves were regarded as human persons as well as property.[25]

The fragmentary text of another law dealt with an unnamed offense for which the penalty was to pay one slave woman. If the offender had none, then a fine was to be paid in silver or other personal property.[26] Thus, a slave woman was a commodity of property that could be replaced by another slave woman or by a sum of money.

Women Victims

The extant parts of the laws of Ur-Nammu mentioned only a few crimes against women. Two laws dealt with the rape of a virgin; both began with a clause stating that the rapist had violated the rights of another man. The first law dealt with the rape of a virgin who was betrothed. The penalty for the rapist was death, not because he had injured the woman but because he had injured the honor of her betrothed groom. The second law dealt with the rape of a virgin slave girl. A fine of five sheqels of silver compensated the slave owner for the diminished monetary value of his slave girl.[27] Both laws depicted men—the betrothed groom and the slave owner—as the victims of the rapes. No mention was made of a violation of the rights, much less the person, of the raped virgin women.

Women were frequently the victims of false accusation of various crimes. When the evidence in a trial was inconclusive, the guilt or innocence of the defendant was determined by the "river ordeal." The accused was thrown into the river. If she or he drowned, guilt was considered manifest. If the accused survived, she or he was presumed innocent and the accuser was then held guilty of false accusation. Although the river ordeal could result in the death of the accused, it was not intended to be a form of capital punishment. It was a tool used by courts to let the river god adjudicate cases when the evidence was insufficient for human judges.

When a man falsely accused another person of a minor offense and the accused was proven innocent by the river ordeal, the false accuser was fined three sheqels. If a man falsely accused another man's wife of adultery and the woman was proven innocent by the river ordeal, the accuser had to pay a fine of twenty silver sheqels to her husband. An allegation of sexual misconduct was worse than most other types of defamation, since it could destroy the honor of the husband and family of the accused woman.[28]

The laws of Ur-Nammu defined several crimes of assault, battery, and dismemberment: cutting off a foot or other limb, shattering a bone with a club, cutting off a nose with a knife, and knocking out a tooth. All were punished by fines.[29] The laws did not state whether the victims or the perpetrators were women or men, but applied to both. Women were more often victims.

When a person detained another person against his or her will, depriving the victim of his or her right to go elsewhere, the offense was false imprisonment. The offender was appropriately punished by imprisonment and incurred a fine of fifteen silver sheqels.[30] This law indicates that at least one place of detention existed in Sumer during the Ur III period.

Women Offenders

A woman or man who committed murder incurred the penalty of death. The crime of homicide was under the jurisdiction of the state, and the law stated that "they," meaning the state, would execute the offender. Private vengeance was not permitted.[31]

Another capital crime was one committed only by women. When a married woman intentionally approached and seduced another man, initiating adulterous sexual relations, the woman was put to death and the man was not penalized. The Sumerians believed that the woman's intent and initiative made the crime worse than simple adultery and therefore punished it by the death penalty. The man was viewed as the victim of the woman's offense.[32]

When a person committed perjury when testifying in a trial, the penalty was a fine of fifteen sheqels of silver. If a witness at trial refused to take the oath before the gods, it was presumed that he or she was giving false testimony. The penalty was the value of the matter in litigation.[33]

Slavery was an important institution in ancient Sumerian society. There were customary modes of speech and action expected between owner and slave. Even seemingly minor challenges to the authority of the slave owner by a slave were regarded as extremely serious. If a slave woman compared herself to her mistress or to one who had the same authority as her mistress and cursed or spoke insolently to that person, her mouth was scoured with a quart of salt. Another law described the offense of a slave woman who struck her mistress or "someone acting with the authority of her mistress. . . ."[34] Unfortunately the penalty clause is missing.

It was a serious crime for a slave to run away. When a slave woman crossed the border of the city-state attempting to escape, the man who caught her and returned her to her owner was paid a reward in silver by the slave's owner.[35]

Punishment

In the extant texts of the laws of Ur-Nammu there are twenty criminal laws. The death penalty was used four times, whereas fines were prescribed fourteen times. Capital punishment was used for homicide, rape, and seduction by a married woman resulting in adultery. False accusation of adultery was punished by a fine, which indicates that simple adultery was probably also punished by compensation. There was only one instance of corporal punishment—when a slave woman challenged the authority of her slave owner—but the law prescribed a mild symbolic punishment that did not involve mutilation, serious injury, or permanent damage. Even offenses of assault and battery that caused serious physical injury to the victim were punished by fines. In the laws of Ur-Nammu, compensatory penalties were preferred for most crimes.

Summary: The Laws of Ur-Nammu

The laws of Ur-Nammu are the oldest extant collection of laws from the ancient Near East. At the beginning the principle of justice was clearly articulated as the highest achievement of the lawgiver. Justice was effected by protection of the widow and the weak from oppression and by the abolition of enmity, violence, and injustice. The laws of Ur-Nammu generally treated women the same as men; daughters were valued as were sons. Women were, however, expected to be sexually faithful to their husbands and were punished if they were not. The death penalty was used for married women who seduced other men into adultery and for men who raped virgins. Most crimes were punished by fines. Slaves were expected to respect the authority of their owners. The laws of Ur-Nammu reflected a high urban civilization. Criminal offenders were tried and punished by the state. Private vengeance was not permitted, which avoided the blood feuds that erupted in tribal societies that sanctioned private executions.

The Laws of King Lipit-Ishtar of Isin

The last non-Amorite dynasty of ancient Sumer was the first dynasty of Isin, of which Lipit-Ishtar was the fifth king. He promulgated his collection of laws about 1930 BCE. A prologue, an epilogue, and thirty-eight laws are wholly or partially legible. In the prologue, Lipit-Ishtar stated that he was chosen king by the gods "to establish justice in the land, to eliminate cries for justice, to eradicate enmity and armed violence, to bring well-being to the lands of Sumer and Akkad." He called himself the "pious shepherd of Nippur," and the faithful garden-tender of Ur, both very peaceful and nurturing images. He wrote that he had liberated the sons and daughters of Nippur, Ur, Isin, and other city-states. In each of the four clauses, he repeated "and daughters." In the epilogue, the king proclaimed his accomplishments: the establishment of "fair judicial procedure"; the eradication of enmity and violence, weeping and lamentation; and the establishment of right and truth.[36] The laws contain considerable information on the status of women, but little on women as victims of crime or criminal offenders.

Status of Women

Women could be married or be priests or be married priests. Most women married, including many who held religious offices. The laws governing married laywomen and married women priests were similar. Women priests were so common that the Sumerians criticized less civilized foreigners for not having women priests.[37] Lipit-Ishtar's own daughter En-ninsunzi was a high priest, and he built her a residence.

The fathers of a prospective bride and groom negotiated the terms of a marriage and the amount of the marriage gifts. After the prospective groom delivered the marriage gifts to the bride's father, they held a feast, the couple was legally betrothed, and the groom entered the household of his intended bride. As in the laws of Ur-Nammu, if her father later evicted him and gave his daughter to another man, the betrothed bride's father had to pay the betrothed groom double the value of his marriage gifts. But the laws of Lipit-Ishtar added another clause, which made the law more effective: the betrothed daughter was not permitted to marry the second man.[38] This gave additional protection to the prospective groom against the machinations of the family of his betrothed, by removing the incentive for a father to look for a wealthier groom after his daughter was betrothed and "selling" his daughter to the highest bidder. The feelings of the prospective bride were not addressed.

A father had a legal duty to provide a dowry for his daughter when she married. The possession of the dowry gave a wife some measure of protection during marriage. If a girl was not yet married when her father died, her brothers had the obligation to give her in marriage and provide her dowry. Unmarried women priests were given dowries by their fathers or brothers when they left home for the temple.[39]

The laws of king Lipit-Ishtar gave greater protection to women within marriage. Polygyny was legal, but with restrictions. For example, if a man's wife became blind or paralyzed, thereby useless and unable to manage the household, he could not evict her from his house. The man could marry a second wife, but he had to support both wives and the second wife had to help take care of the first wife.[40]

The laws on inheritance encouraged a fair and consistent distribution of goods from one generation to another. When a mother died, her dowry was inherited by her own children. When a widower married a second wife, her dowry was inherited by her children of that marriage. When the father died, the children of both wives divided his property equally.[41]

The inheritance laws made distinctions on the basis of gender, age, and marital and religious status. When a father died who had no sons, his unmarried daughter could inherit his estate. If his eldest daughter had married and lived with her husband's family, her younger sister could inherit as long as she was still unmarried and lived at home. When a daughter left home and became a priest or other religious official in the temple during her father's lifetime, she could inherit with her brothers an equal portion of their father's estate.[42]

The inheritance laws also made distinctions on the basis of slave status. When a married man had children both by his wife and by his slave woman, only the children of his wife could inherit his estate; but after his death, the slave woman and her children were freed. However, if his wife died first and then the man married his slave woman, the children of his first wife remained his primary heirs, but the children of the slave woman could inherit a lesser portion.[43]

When a married man had no children by his wife, but a street prostitute bore him a child, he was obligated to support the prostitute with grain, oil, and clothing. Unless his wife subsequently bore a child, the child of the prostitute would inherit his estate. As long as his wife was alive, however, the prostitute could not reside in his house. In one case, a young married man had sex with a street prostitute and the judges ordered him not to do it again. Even if the man divorced his wife and returned her dowry, he was not permitted to marry the prostitute.[44] These laws protected legal wives who were barren and also gave some protection to prostitutes and their children.

King Lipit-Ishtar decreed that fathers must support their children and children must support their fathers. The laws enforced the obligation of fathers to raise and train children properly, including children not their own. If a man did not raise a boy as a son in accordance with an apprenticeship contract and this was proven before the judges, the boy would be returned to his birth mother. The next law dealt with girls. If a man did not raise a girl as a "daughter as he contracted to raise [. . .]."[45] The rest is missing, but the fragment suggests that girls also had legal rights to skills training and fair treatment under contracts similar to the apprenticeship contracts of boys.

Sumerian women owned real estate. With the right of ownership, however, came the obligation of paying property taxes. If the owner defaulted on tax payments and someone else paid the taxes, the owner could not be evicted for three years. After that time, if the owner still had not paid the taxes, the person who had paid them could take possession of the house or land and the original owner could make no claim against that person.[46]

Women Victims

The extant laws of Lipit-Ishtar described a few situations in which women were victims of crimes. When a man struck a married woman, causing her to have a miscarriage, he was fined thirty sheqels of silver for the life of the fetus. The offense was considered a loss of property for the husband. However, if the woman died as a result of the attack, the offense became homicide and the attacker received the death penalty. This law indicates that a wife had much greater value then a fetus, in part because she could bear more children. If a man attacked a slave woman, causing her to have a miscarriage, he was fined five sheqels of silver, which were paid to her owner.[47] The fine represented compensation for the property loss of a future slave to the slave woman's owner.

False accusation of sexual offenses also victimized women. When a man falsely claimed that the virgin daughter of another man was not a virgin and his claim was proven to be untrue, the false accuser was fined ten sheqels of silver.[48] According to the law, the injury was to the girl's father, not the girl. It was an affront to his honor as well as an economic loss, affecting his reputation in society and reducing his daughter's value and marriageability.

Women Offenders

Women and men owned houses and land. A property owner who had knowledge that a dangerous condition existed on his or her property had an obligation to repair it. When the owner made no repairs and a neighbor's property was damaged or lost because of the condition, the property owner had to pay compensation for the neighbor's losses.[49]

Men and women slaves were the legal property of their owners. Any free person who helped an escaped slave by letting the slave stay in his or her house was fined a slave for a slave. If the offender had no slave of his or her own, the alternative penalty was a fine of fifteen sheqels of silver.[50] The laws did not mandate the punishment of the slave, which was left to the owner.

Punishment

The penalties for crimes against persons were determined by the social status of the victim, free or slave, and the extent of the victim's injury, recovery or death. Battery on a pregnant woman causing miscarriage and death was the only crime for which Lipit-Ishtar prescribed the death penalty. The killing of a pregnant wife was homicide, a crime against a person, and was punished by death. The killing of a fetus was a crime against property, penalized by a fine. There is no indication in these laws of an awareness of the human personhood of the fetus or of the suffering of the woman. None of the extant laws mentioned corporal punishment. Theft was punished by restitution; false accusation was punished by the penalty of the case. In most cases, the penalties were fines.[51]

The laws of Lipit-Ishtar are fragmentary and incomplete. The extant laws did not prescribe harsh penalties for women or men; however, in the epilogue the king pronounced a curse upon anyone who in any way changed what he had written on the stone stela of his laws. The rhetoric of the curse invoked the complete obliteration of the offender and his city.[52]

Summary: The Laws of Lipit-Ishtar

The laws of Lipit-Ishtar provide an example of the laws of the Isin/Larsa period. Like the laws of Ur-Nammu, the laws of Lipit-Ishtar began with the principle of justice and the goal to end enmity and violence, adding the principle of truth and the goal of the well-being of the people. The legal position of women was basically the same as in the laws of Ur-Nammu. Husbands could not divorce sick wives but had to take care of them. Fathers had to support their children and train other boys and girls according to apprenticeship contracts. Adult children had to support their fathers. The state had jurisdiction over crimes and most punishments were fines.

SUMERIAN LAWS EXERCISE TABLET

A late Sumerian tablet containing ten laws was copied by students in a scribal school. None of the laws related specific information about the status of women, but seven of the laws dealt with women victims and offenders and their punishments.[53]

Women Victims and Offenders

Sumerian women were victims of assault and battery that caused miscarriage. This version of the offense took the intent of the offender into account. When a man accidentally injured a woman of the free citizen class, causing her to have a miscarriage, he was fined ten sheqels of silver. If he struck a woman intentionally, the fine was doubled.[54]

Two laws concerning rape have been interpreted very differently. According to one translation, in the first law, the attacker raped a virgin girl in the street and her parents could not identify the rapist. The attacker came to the parents and offered to marry the girl. The law mandated the marriage. In the second law, the parents identified the alleged rapist, but he denied his guilt. Then the accused had to swear a solemn oath at the temple gate that he was innocent. In another translation of these two laws, a man raped the daughter of free citizens in the street, when the girl's parents did not know she was outside in the street. The girl testified that she had been raped. The parents could force the rapist to marry her; however, if the parents knew their daughter was out in the street and the rapist denied under oath that he knew she was of the free citizen class, the rapist was not punished.[55] The first translation focused on the identity of the rapist; the second on the responsibility of the parents to keep their daughter in the house and the rapist's knowledge that the victim was a free citizen. The evidence consisted of oaths. Both state the same penalty: the forced marriage of the rapist and his victim.

There were two almost identical laws which stated that a mother or father who disowned his or her child was punished by forfeiture of all interest in the family estate.[56]

Punishment

A man who raped a virgin was punished by forced marriage to his victim. There may have been additional punishments that are missing from the extant text. A man who injured a pregnant woman causing a miscarriage was punished by fines, which were doubled if the injury was intentional. These laws shifted the basis of punishment from the class and extent of injury of the victim to the intent of the offender. The punishment for a son who repudiated his parents was forfeiture of all possessions and rights of inheritance and sale into slavery. Similarly, a parent who repudiated a child lost all rights to the family estate.[57] None of the laws prescribed death or corporal punishment.

SUMERIAN DOCUMENTS AND INSCRIPTIONS

Justice was a significant concern of the rulers of ancient Sumer. The Early Dynastic king Ur-Nanshe of Lagash built a temple and named it for the god of justice. Four centuries later, king Gudea of Lagash wrote that justice came from the gods and in practice justice meant protecting widows, orphans, and the poor from the rich and powerful. King Lipit-Ishtar of Isin proudly claimed that he established justice in Sumer and Akkad by implementing fair judicial procedure and by erecting a stela of his laws.[58]

Status of Women

Sumerian royal inscriptions and seals named many wives and daughters of kings. In the Early Dynastic period, Puabi, Ashusikidilgir, Nin-banda, Nin-Tur, and Gansamannu were wives of the kings of Ur. Menbara'abzu, Ashume'eren, and Nin-khilisug were wives of early kings of Lagash. Menbara'abzu had two daughters, Ninusu and Abda.[59] The name of another Early Dynastic queen was named Shu'am; her royal husband is known only from her seal.

In general, Sumerian queens did not rule. One exception, in the Early Dynastic period, was queen Ku-Bau, who ruled the city-state of Kish. She was named in the Sumerian King List as a king, a reversal of gender roles that was threatening to Sumerian men. The men diminished the reality and danger of a woman holding their sacred royal office by calling Ku-Bau a tavern keeper and a hermaphrodite.[60]

Tablets from Early Dynastic Lagash documented the households of queens. These were a major factor in the city-state's economy and employed thousands of people. Dimtur, Baranamtara, and Shagshag, wives of kings of Lagash, administered the royal household and its manufacturing and trade with other city-states. The queen's household owned much land, grew grain and other crops, and raised animals. It had a large textile manufacturing industry, processing wool into woven cloth. The household of the queen was an independent economy, completely separate from, and slightly smaller than, the household of the king, which had similar economic activities. The queen's office as administrator of the household did not necessarily end with the death of the king. Dimtur continued as administrator during the early part of the reign of the next king. Many wives of kings in the Early Dynastic period played a significant public role in the economy and acquired great wealth. Their position and wealth gave them some measure of political power.[61]

Less is known about the roles of kings' wives during the dynasty of Akkad. The few pertinent inscriptions demonstrated that they had male officials and scribes working for them. An administrator and scribe of Tashlultum, wife of king Sargon, dedicated an alabaster bowl to a temple. Tutasharlibish, wife of the fifth king of Akkad, was named on the seals of three of her administrtors: on two she was called queen, and "beloved of the king" on the third. Wives of the kings of Akkad held land and were involved in trade. Written documents show that Tutanapshum, daughter of the last king, conducted business transactions in dates, onions, cattle, and silver.[62]

In the second dynasty of Lagash, kings' wives had political influence, especially those who had made their husbands kings. Three kings held their office only because they had married daughters of a former king. A man wrote a petition to the wife of king Ur-Bau asking her to intercede with her husband to release his brother from prison, acknowledging that he had asked the king to put him in prison in the first place.[63] Such a letter presupposed that the queen had influence over her husband.

During the Ur III period, royal women exercised great administrative and economic authority in new ways. The people paid taxes in kind to support the ruler and the cult. Vassal states paid tribute in kind. The wives of the kings were in charge of the collection and distribution of tribute animals to temples and had other women officials working under them. The royal wives and the temples both profited from the arrangement. This high-level public role made queens wealthy and influential; however, the king appointed them to this position and ultimately had authority over it. The queens did not administer an independent economy as they had in the Early Dynastic period.[64]

Wives of governors had important administrative roles in the Ur III empire. Ninmelam, wife of the governor of Umma, supervised the gold, leather, wool, cloth, and grain transactions of Ninkala, consort of king Shulgi. Ninkhilia, wife of the next governor, supervised transactions in wool, leather, and perfume.[65]

Political marriage of royals began in the Early Dynastic period, and there were two types. In the first, a man of the same or a nearby city-state married the daughter of the king. When that king died, the husband of his daughter became king. One man became king of Umma by marriage to Bara'irnun, daughter of the previous king, granddaughter of an earlier king, and daughter-in-law of another king. In the second dynasty of Lagash, king Ur-Bau had many daughters. Several of them married men whom they thereby made kings of Lagash. Nin-alla married Gudea; Nin-inimgina married Ur-Gar; and Nin-khedu married Nammakhani, and all of these men subsequently became kings of Lagash.[66]

The second type of political marriage involved two separate states. Such marriages were common during the Ur III and Isin empires. King Ur-Nammu married a son to Taramuram, daughter of the king of Mari. King Shulgi married his daughters Liwirmitashu and her unnamed sister to kings of Markhashi and Anshan. Daughters of a king of Isin married kings of Susa and Anshan. Such practices created an international network of royal families related to one another. Wives of kings corresponded and exchanged gifts with wives of kings of other city-states. On the other hand, such political alliances created obligations. For example, Kunshimatum, daughter of king Shu-Sin, married the son of the ruler of Simmatum. Later the ruler was deposed in a revolt, and Shu-Sin took his army north and restored the ruler and his daughter to their positions.[67]

Three of the five kings of Ur III practiced polygyny, taking one or more wives and several consorts, but only one wife was designated as queen. The status of consort was slightly below that of wife. King Shulgi had a queen, Shulgi-Simti; two wives, Amat-Sin and Geme-Sin; and many consorts. Both wives and consorts supplied animals for religious rites. His consort Geme-Ninlila owned a herd of sheep and profited from the sale of their wool. In one list of the division of war booty, Geme-Ninlila and Eanisha, another consort of Shulgi, each received two ewes. In another list, Shulgi's consorts Geme-Ninlila, Ninkala, and Tadin-Ishtar all received precious stones and metals. Ninkala was a citizen of Nippur. Shulgi-Simti and Eanisha were traveling companions of the king. When king Shulgi died, Shulgi-Simti and Geme-Ninlila were buried beside him and women were released from work for seven days.[68] Abi-Simti was the queen of the next king, Amar-Sin, who also had several consorts. Kubatum was a wet nurse for the children of Amar-Sin and possibly also his consort. She later became the queen and consort of Shu-Sin, Amar-Sin's brother and successor as king. Shu-Sin had two other consorts, Tiamat-bashti and Ishdumkin. Ibbi-Sin, the last Ur III king, had one wife and queen, Geme-Enlila.[69]

Polygyny was practiced also in the Isin/Larsa period. King Sin-magir of Isin had a consort for traveling named Nutuptum, who was the mother of his first child. The Amorite king Rim-Sin of Larsa had three wives, Simat-Ishtar, Beltani, and Rim-Sin-Shalabastashu. Simat-Ishtar built temples, and she and another wife were praised for their humility, which made them "suitable ornaments for the king."[69] Their actions reflected the women of Sumer, but the complement reflected the status of women in Amorite kingdoms.

The fact that polygyny was practiced by royals and was not prohibited by law did not mean that polygyny was common among nonroyals. It was rare among ordinary people since it required considerable wealth to pay the marriage gifts and support for a second wife. When men had more than one wife, the status of all wives became lower and less secure.

From the Early Dynastic period on, wives of kings performed religious functions. In Ur, Nubanda was called both "queen" and religious officiant. In Lagash, queen Baranamtara presided at sacrifices during certain festivals. When she died, Shagshag, wife of king Uru-inimgina, organized a state funeral with hundreds of women mourners, despite the fact that Shagshag's husband had killed Baranamtara's husband. In Ur III, Shulgi-Simti was called both queen and priest.[71]

Throughout the history of Sumer and Akkad, royal men and women donated gold and silver, votive statues, and other gifts to the temples. The votive statues depicted women and men praying and were believed to make the donor continually present in the temple. The statues had inscriptions with the names of the donors and prayers for the donors' spouses and for themselves. In Lagash, Nin-niginesi, wife of king Ur-Ningirsu, dedicated a statue of a bull for the life of the king and for her own life. Nin-alla, wife of king Gudea, made dedications for the lives of her husband and herself. Nin-inimgina, wife of one king and mother or cousin of the next king, made dedications for the lives of both kings and for her own life. Nin-khedu, wife of king Nammakhani dedicated a stone slab for the life of the king and for her own life. Nin-metabare, daughter of the king of Mari, made a dedication to a god in Ur. In the Ur III dynasty, royal wives and daughters made many dedications. Siatum, wife of king Ur-Nammu, dedicated a bead for her son, Shulgi. The high priest En-nirgalana dedicated a bowl and a cone for her father, Ur-Nammu. Taram-uram made a dedication at Nippur for her father-in-law, Ur-Nammu. Eanisha, consort of Shulgi, dedicated a bead, Nin-kala dedicated a bowl, and Shuqur-tum, consort of Shulgi, dedicated a calcite vase. King Shulgi dedicated a bead for his daughter Ninturturmu and a bowl for his daughter Simat-Enlil. Wives and daughters of governors also made dedications. Khalalamma, daughter of the governor of Lagash, dedicated a diorite statue of a woman. Amanili, wife of the governor of Girsu, dedicated a plaque for the life of the king of Lagash, and Khala-Baba, wife of a scribe, made a dedication for the life of the king.[72]

Royal women also dedicated materials for the religious cult and festivals. In Early Dynastic Lagash, queen Baranamtara donated barley and grain for the feast of Bau. In the Ur III period, Geme-Ninlila, consort of king Shulgi, provided oxen for a festival and gave one oxskin, five sheepskins, one goatskin, one eweskin and several cattleskins to make the boat that would carry the statue of the god An on the river during his festival. She also gave three sheep-skins as a prayer offering.[73]

King Sargon of Akkad began the custom whereby kings made their daughters high priests of Ur, one of the most ancient and the most symbolically important of the city-states of Sumer. This legitimized and provided divine protection for their rule. King Sargon of Akkad, who claimed that his mother had been a high priest, appointed his daughter, En-kheduanna, high priest of the moon god at Ur and of the heaven god at Uruk. Sargon spoke Akkadian and his power was greater in the north. En-kheduanna spoke Sumerian and helped her father control the city-states of the south. En-kheduanna, a trained scribe, has been called the "first known author in world literature." She wrote literary works about gods and kings and two long cycles of hymns; she also wrote and collected other hymns. She lived in the residence of the temple of Nanna in Ur. Archaeologists excavating the residence found a translucent alabaster disc that portrayed four persons facing the locus of a god. The dominant figure was En-kheduanna, dressed in the garb and headdress of the high priestess. The size, dress, and detail of relief emphasized her importance. In fron of her, a person poured a libation, and two attendants followed her. En-kheduanna was the overseeing authority, in charge of the libation. The inscription on the reverse of the disc stated: "En-kheduanna, high priestess, wife of the god Nanna, daughter of Sargon, king of the world, in the temple of the goddess Inanna in Ur, made an altar for the god An." En-kheduanna performed religious functions, including purification rites, sacrificial offerings, and the singing of hymns and lamentations. There were women high priests before the dynasty of Sargon, but no evidence that such women were daughters of kings. Sargon made a strategic move to legitimize his dynasty by inserting his daughter into the preexisting religious tradition of Sumer.[74]

King Naram-Sin, the grandson of Sargon, appointed three of his daughters high priests. He made En-menana high priest of Ur, Tutanapshum high priest of the god Enlil in Nippur, and Shumshani high priest of the god Shamash in Sippar. His granddaughter, Lipushia'um, who played the lyre, was a lamentation singer of the moon god.[75] The Ur III kings Ur-Nammu, Shulgi, and Amar-Sin made their daughters, En-nirgalana, En-nirzianna, and En-makhgalana, respectively, high priests of Ur.[76] King Ishme-Dagan of the first Isin dynasty appointed his daughter En-anatuma high priest of Ur. King Lipit-Ishtar made his daughter En-ninsunzi high priest of a different god in Ur. King Sumuel of Larsa made his daughter En-shakiag-Nanna high priest of Nanna in Ur. The father of the last two kings of Larsa appointed his daughter En-anedu high priest in Ur.[77]

The appointment of royal women as high priests was for life and did not terminate with a change of king or even of dynasty. En-kheduanna retained her office during the reigns of four kings of Akkad: her father, two brothers, and her nephew. King Ur-Bau of Lagash did not appoint his own daughter, En-annepadda, high priest of Ur until after the high priest daughter of the last Akkadian king had died. When Larsa conquered Isin and Ur, the daughter of the last king of Isin was high priest of Ur. She remained in office until her death, and then En-anedu, sister of the king of Larsa, became high priest of Ur. Ninshatapada, daughter of the ruler of Uruk and Durum, wrote a long letter to the king of Larsa, praising him for sparing the people of these cities when he conquered them and asking him to let her return to her rightful position as high priest in Durum, which he did. Ninshatapada, a professionally trained scribe, wrote the letter herself. She composed it in vivid literary imagery, in the style of the royal letter-prayer. The first fifteen lines praised the king, and the next fifteen lines pleaded her case. The letter was preserved in the royal archives of Larsa, which demonstrates that it had reached the king and that it was perceived as favorable to the king.[78]

Women high priests were wealthy and made donations of money and land to the temples. In the reign of Uru-inimgina, women high priests held a very high position in Lagash and helped the king's wife administer the temple estates. In the Isin/Larsa period, En-anatuma of Isin dedicated a statue, offering it for her own life, and gave sesame oil to the temple. En-shakiag-Nanna and En-anedu of Larsa donated gold and silver. En-anedu was honored for her restoration of the residence, decoration of the temple, and repair and development of the irrigation works. At least two of the women high priests, En-anatuma and En-megalana, were deified after their deaths. Offerings were made to them and a small cult established. The fact that En-anatuma had a son was not an obstacle to her deification.[79]

In ancient Sumer, each city-state had its own god or goddess. Women high priests generally served male gods and male priests served female gods. More Sumerian city-states had male gods and women priests than the opposite. Women high priests played a significant political role, bound city-states together through a common cult, and reinforced the authority of their royal fathers. For more than six centuries, the kings of Sumer and Akkad appointed their daughters to positions of high priesthood.[80]

Throughout the history of Sumer, women priests were respected and supported by kings. The early king Uru-inimgina of Lagash returned lands and houses to the women priests and the temples they served. Later women priests owned their own houses and administered large estates with a few men and numerous women working for them. Women *naditu* and *ugbabtu* priests were prominent; they performed sacrificial rites and were usually wealthy. For example, inscriptions from the reign of the Ur III king Shulgi mentioned two women *ugbabtu* priests, Tulid-Shamshi and Geme-Lama. The latter was wealthy and had many employees working on her estate. The *qadishtu* women were religious officiants who were often members of the royal family or other prominent families. At the end of the Ur III dynasty, a *qadishtu* woman wrote a lamentation over the destruction of Ur. After the wives of kings, the most active, influential, and best-documented women in the early history of Sumer were women priests and religious officials.[81]

Women priests performed religious functions, the most important of which was offering animal sacrifices to the gods. King Gudea described part of the ritual of sacrifice. The woman priest sang a hymn and put a special mark on a pregnant black ewe, which she then lifted up to the gods. Women priests also offered libations. Other women were basket bearers, carrying implements for the sacrifice. Women priests, but not other women, could partake in the sacred meal that followed the sacrifice.

Women musicians reached their highest status during the Ur III dynasty, working with and under women priests. Women musicians were on temple ration lists. The temple archives of Lagash named more than two hundred women musicians.[82] They donated animals to the temple, witnessed legal documents, sang incantations at the sacrifices, and composed and sang hymns to the gods. Women were singers, dancers, and players of musical instruments. At funerals, women served as mourners and sang laments. Women musicians were held in great esteem in ancient Sumer.

Ancient Sumerian myths told stories about the sexual escapades of the gods. Inanna, goddess of fertility and procreation, was the queen of heaven and patron god of Uruk. Poems recited her sexual relations with two pre-historic rulers of Uruk. By Ur III, the stories were reenacted annually in the rite of sacred marriage at the festival of the new year. A woman priest enacted the role of the goddess. The rite began with a procession of virgin priestesses, singers, clappers, and instrumental musicians before the statue of Inanna. The temple had a special room with a bed. First there were purification rites for the king and the priestess. Then the king had sexual relations with the woman priest who represented the goddess, and afterward there was a great banquet with music.[83]

Children born of the rite of sacred marriage were considered special and quasi-divine. King Shulgi claimed to have been born of the union between his father, king Ur-Nammu, and the goddess Inanna, represented by a priestess.[84] In the sacred marriage rite, the king entered the divine realm through his union with the "goddess." The king was thought to become a god at that moment. Since wives of kings could be priests, kings could consummate the sacred marriage rite with their own wives. When the queen enacted the role of the goddess and the king "became a god" through his union with the "god-dess," the rite provided the rationale for the deification of both. After their deaths, many Sumerian kings and sometimes also their wives were deified and given votive statues. Even in the Early Dynastic period, Nubanda, the wife of a king of Ur and Kish, was called "divine priestess," and Baranamtara, wife of a king of Lagash, was called a "living goddess." The people made offerings to them as to gods.[85]

Women with special gifts were called "wise women." In an ancient Sumerian story, Enmerkar, a prehistoric ruler of Uruk, refused to pay tribute to another city-state, Aratta. The ruler of Aratta sent a sorcerer to conquer Uruk. The sorcerer was defeated, after a series of contests, by a wise woman named Sagburru.[86]

During the Akkadian dynasty, which differed from the rest of Sumer in speaking a Semitic language and exhibiting customs found in other Semitic tribes, marriage customs were more conservative. The family of the prospective groom made an agreement with the parents of the bride, who was often still a child. She remained with her family until she was of age. Then the groom "took possession" of her and, after a marriage ceremony in which he veiled her, brought her into his family's household. The bride remained in his household for the rest of her life. The husband was considered master of his wife, and she was expected to be submissive and obey him while doing her domestic chores and bearing him children. Married women were veiled at marriage and remained veiled thereafter. The veil was a symbol of their subordination to their husbands. In theory, married Akkadian women were supposed to remain inside the houses of their husbands. The roles of women in marriage were more restrictive during the Akkadian dynasty.[87] These practices stood in sharp contrast to Sumerian law, literature, and art, both before and after the Akkadian dynasty, where women were not veiled or confined to the house but were very active in all aspects of their society, including high offices, with the exception of kingship.

In the Sumerian city-states, marriage required a contract between two families, which included marriage gifts and a dowry, a ritual and feast at the house of the bride's family, and the transfer of the bride and her dowry to the household of the groom. Dowries of wealthy families could be quite extensive, and the contents were written down at the time of the marriage. The dowry of the bride Rubatum included three minas "of silver, five slaves, three tables, two copper kettles, one copper bowl, ten bronze vessels, two bronze mirrors, two storage vessels, two pestles, four chairs, one bed, and ten spoons."[88]

Marriage established a household. Husbands were responsible for providing grain and wool, which the women processed into food and clothing. Wives were the administrators of their households and the mediators of conflicts within the household. After the death of her husband, a widow could be head of the family.[89]

There is evidence that Sumerian husbands and wives had loving, caring, and compassionate relationships. Husbands kissed but also beat their wives. Mothers had loving relationships with their children. They had more effective authority over daughters than over sons. Mothers were exhorted not to scold or beat their children and children to speak respectfully and truthfully to their parents.[90]

There is some evidence that Sumerian children were raised according to expected gender roles. An incantation sung at birth stated that a boy was born holding a weapon and an ax, whereas a girl was born holding a spindle and comb. Girls were supposed to be quiet, while boys were allowed to talk. Girls had their own special room in the house, their own domain where they felt safe. When their city was conquered, girls expressed grief for the loss of their special rooms. Girls had close relationships with their brothers, who were their best friends. Older siblings were more like parents than friends. Younger siblings were taught to respect and obey older siblings as their parents.[91]

Sumerian husbands and wives both could initiate divorce. If a married man came to despise his wife, he could not simply throw her out but had to give her a divorce settlement in silver. After a husband divorced his wife, she could remarry and her first husband had no further claim on her as his wife. Sumerian contracts and court records show that women could initiate divorce. In the

Ur III period an official testified under oath that a wife had "taken her stand." She had made a formal demand for divorce and for the sum of ten sheqels of silver. In return she promised to make no further claim against her husband. The husband paid the sum, and the divorce was made official and recorded.[92] These texts depict divorce proceedings as occurring amicably between reasonable adults.

In the Ur III period, Sumerian women of the upper class were financially independent and had almost the same status, privileges, and duties as men. Women had their own money and could make and guarantee loans. Legal documents show that women bought and sold houses, fields, orchards, and slaves. In Nippur, a man and his wife, Metug, sold a house; and a man, his wife, Geme-Enlila, and their two sons bought a house and lot. In Umma, another man and his wife, Ishagani, sold a house to the chief constable.[93]

In the Early Dynastic period, men and women priests, their spouses, and their daughters were active in buying, selling, and leasing real estate. One of the earliest legal documents known, recorded on stone, was a contract for the sale of land. The principals were a priest and his daughter, Shara'igiziabzu; the buyers; and the unnamed daughter of a priest of a different temple, who was the seller. Another early inscription recorded the sale of a large house to a priest for the lady Ashag, the wife of another priest. She was also given 4,500 liters of grain, garments, lard, beer, food-grain, meal, and a slave woman. The lady Igidingirnaesu received 300 liters of meal and a mina of wool. Baranamtara, daughter of the priest-husband of Ashag, received 3,000 liters of meal.[94]

Women bought and sold slaves. In Nippur, the woman Geme-Abzu sold the woman slave Nina and took the oath not to contest the sale. The woman Shat-Sin sold the slave woman Ennilas to the woman Geme-Nanna and swore the oath not to contest. The woman Ninkare sold the woman Ninshesh and sealed the document. A man and his wife, Nindubsar, sold a slave woman who later escaped. Nindubsar swore to replace her with another slave woman.[95]

Destitute women and men sold themselves into slavery. In Nippur, a man; his wife, Dingirbuza; his daughters, Nindada and Ninurani; and his son sold themselves. In Ur, the woman Ninagrigzi sold herself as a slave to a brewer. The woman Ennimami sold herself into slavery and swore not to contest the sale. The woman Shatirra was guarantor of the sale and swore to take the place of Ennimami if any claims arose against her.[96]

Poor families sold their children into slavery. In Nippur, Waruru sold her daughter, Nizatia. Another mother, Zanka, sold her daughter, Geme-ezida. Both women swore not to contest the sales and sealed the documents with their seals. A mother, Alibashti, and her son sold another son into slavery. They swore not to contest, and Alibashti sealed the sale document. In Lagash, a father sold his daughter, Inmuasi, into slavery. Another father sold his daughter, Agatima, to a shepherd. In Nippur, two brothers sold their sister, Alane, and promised to serve as slaves in her place if she ran away.[97]

Slave women and unwanted women, such as widows without children, orphans, and the handicapped, were often given to temples. Many such slave women were captives of war. Some women slaves were taught to read and write and served as scribes for the temple or household of their owners.[98]

Women were parties and witnesses to legal transactions, such as contracts of sale. In some slave sales, women sealed the sale documents with their own seals. In Nippur, the woman Ninkare sold the woman Ninshesh and sealed the document. The witnesses to the sale included two women, Ningudku, a wife, and Amakala, a midwife. In Ur, a woman Nineana and a man jointly sold a slave boy; both sealed the document with their own seals. The seal of the man listed his name, occupation, and patronymic. The seal of Nineana was inscribed "daughter of Umma, the female mill-worker of Ningal." In Lagash, the woman Geme-lama was one of four witnesses to the sale of a slave woman. In Umma, the woman Mama and her son sold a slave. Two of the witnesses were women: Ninkagina and Ninukkine. In a fragmentary document of the sale of a slave woman, at least one of the witnesses, Shigitum, was a woman. The witnesses to the sale of the woman Shiquradat included the woman Mama-sharrat.[99]

Women had legal rights and could go to court to exercise and defend their rights. Women personally appeared in court and swore oaths by the gods and by the lives of the king and the queen. The names of women were found on records of witnesses for trials.[100]

The ownership of real property and slaves by women was sometimes challenged by men. Ur III court records show that the widow Innasaga was sued by the heirs of her late husband concerning ownership of a house and a slave woman named Ninana. Innasaga proved by her own sworn testimony and the written act of sale document that she had bought the house with her own money. She proved by the testimony of three eyewitnesses that her husband had given her the slave woman as a gift. In addition, she manumitted the three daughters of the slave woman before the court. She won the case, and the judges made the heirs swear an oath never again to challenge her ownership.[101]

There is considerable evidence that women worked outside of the household in ancient Sumer. Non–ruling-class women were classified as skilled or unskilled workers. Throughout the third millennium women worked as weavers, spinners, and potters. Documents attest more than thirteen thousand women weavers at Ur and more than seven thousand in Lagash. Other women worked as millers, leather workers, oil pressers, laundresses, nursemaids, hairdressers, and cooks. Women frequently made beer from dates and made wine once a year at the grape harvest. Women tavern keepers often sold beer on

credit and were paid in grain at the harvest. Women were midwives and practiced herbal medicine. They worked in irrigation and agriculture, winnowing,
carrying harvested grain, and cutting thorns. Not all working women were
poor; some owned land. A wet nurse, Ummeda, rented her field to two men
and each cultivated half.[102]

Workers were paid in rations of barley and oil, and detailed records were
kept. Skilled workers were paid more than unskilled. The pay of women was
from thirty liters of barley up to a hundred liters with skill and experience.
Men who performed the same work earned from sixty to three hundred liters.
Men could earn two to three times as much as women for the same or similar
work.[103]

Older women and widows without support could continue to work, but
they were given unskilled jobs and fewer rations. Older persons were put in a
separate category in the ration lists, subdivided by gender. Older women were
paid twenty liters of barley per month; younger women were paid thirty to a
hundred; and older men received fifty. The clothing ration for older women
was less than that for younger women but more than that for children.[104]

Widows of families with means were able to survive financially. While husbands were alive, they provided for their wives' future support by giving them
property, such as real estate, slaves, animals, furniture, millstones, and jewelry.
Such gifts were made by written document with witnesses to avoid later challenges in court by male heirs. Widows inherited property and retained possession of their dowries. Widows could sell and lease property without male
representation; one woman, Baramezida, sold her field for silver, barley, wool,
and donkeys. Widows could rent out their fields for money and fulfillment of
the obligations that went with the fields. When the widow Geme-Sin rented
her field, the lease was signed by nine witnesses, four of whom were officials.
On the negative side, widows were liable for the debts of their late husbands.
The widow Nintu was responsible for her deceased husband's debts, even after
all the property in his estate had been sold. Widows who remarried lost their
rights to inherit from their late husbands' estates.[105]

In ancient Sumer, parents had the duty to support their minor children,
and adult children had a legal obligation to support their parents. Support due
to parents consisted of housing, food, and clothing. If the parents had no
house, their adult children were obligated to provide them with shelter. One
act of sale documented a temple gardener buying a house for his parents. The
obligation of support was so well established that a man who did not support
his parents was regarded as abnormal. Widows with children were thus protected from destitution in old age.[106]

The high point of Sumerian empire and achievement was the third dynasty
of Ur. In this period women had the highest status and the most extensive
rights. In addition to wealth and power, Sumerian women were valued for

their wisdom and knowledge, and men came to them for advice. Sumerian women were praised also for their compassion.[107]

When the Amorite tribes in southern Mesopotamia disrupted communications between Ur and the other cities of its empire, the other cities asserted their independence. After the collapse of Ur III, power shifted to the dynasties of Isin and Larsa. The first dynasty of Isin ruled parts of the land of Sumer, including the two most politically and religiously important cities, Ur and Nippur. There was considerable continuity between Ur III and Isin I in the roles of women, especially in religion. Kings of Isin appointed their daughters high priests of Ur and other cities of Sumer. Women of Isin made dedications to the gods of Sumer. Women were still active in business as partners with their husbands. For example, Nutuptum, wife of a prosperous merchant of Ur, corresponded with her husband on business matters, such as trading in wool, lending silver, and leasing real estate. Some women invested in trade and became wealthy.[108]

Documents from the Amorite dynasty of Larsa, which was concurrent with and successor to the non-Amorite first dynasty of Isin, illustrate the increasing restriction of women. The meticulously kept economic records of Larsa demonstrate the decline in the status of women under Amorite rule. Women could still own property, but few women did. Only one out of numerous records of real estate transactions mentioned a women, Daqqatum, who sold a house lot that she owned jointly with her sons. Another woman, Nanna-lamassi, owned the grain that was distributed on the ration list. Business records that mentioned wom2en became increasingly rare. Women made business transactions with their husbands or sons, but not without male representation. Women were named in the records of the distribution of rations in Larsa, but less often than men. Barley was distributed to the women Belis-sunu, Nuduhtum, and Ishtar-ummi; dates to Nanna-lamassi and Nanna-ummi; and flour to Taribatum. The records also show that fewer women worked outside of the household.[109] The Larsa dynasty served as a transition from Sumerian civilization to the Amorite empires of Babylonia and Assyria.[110]

Women Victims

Sumerian women were victims of rape. When a man seized and raped a virgin slave girl, her owner brought charges before the assembly of Nippur. The rapist denied the accusation, but witnesses confirmed the accusations of the owner. The rapist was fined thirty sheqels of silver because he raped the slave girl without the owner's consent. A young man was exhorted not to rape the daughter of a free man, for she would cry out and he would be publicly shamed.[111]

The practice of using women as pledges for debts often resulted in abuse of the women. When a woman pledge died, became ill, fled, or disappeared, the debtor had to pay compensation for her work quota.[112] The law punished the debtor, not the creditor, even when the creditor's abuse caused the sickness or death of the woman pledged.

Women were illegally distrained and held by men in various situations. The women distrained were frequently the wives of other men. Many letters were written asking that distrained women be released. One such letter was written to the wife of king Ur-Bau, asking her to persuade her husband to release an illegally distrained woman. In the Ur III period, creditors took the wives and daughters of debtors who did not make their payments.[113]

Freed slave women were easily victimized by men, even if they had wealth. For example, the reputation of a freed slave woman, Khala-Bau, was destroyed by slander, leaving her ostracized from society. She was called a camp follower, liar, double dealer, quarrelsome, worthless nymphomaniac. Even her own mother, Ninurrani, rejected her. She owned considerable assets, yet because of her reputation, only a scoundrel would take her into his household, along with her slaves, garments, boat, and forty-five sheqels of silver, which she had inherited from her father. One such man and his daughter lived off the woman's assets for six months. When her assets had been depleted, all three became destitute, and the man was described as wandering homeless on the streets of Borsippa.[114] Khala-Bau was the victim of slander and theft.

Since women owned property, they could be victims of theft. A king of Akkad restored to a woman priest the house and land that had been taken from her and two slaves who had not been delivered to her. A letter protested the seizure of a field belonging to a widow. Another letter ordered a man to pay back to a man and a woman money that he had taken from them.[115]

Women Offenders

In ancient Sumer, for wives to refuse to have sexual relations with their husbands was considered a grave offense against the city and against the goddess of love and birth. The goddess imposed catastrophic punishment on the whole city. Since wives were supposed to produce children, barren wives had no place in Sumerian society. In literary sources, husbands and wives accused each other of adultery, with or without evidence. No punishment was mentioned.[116]

A contract for the sale of real property, from the Early Dynastic period, was attached to the property by a peg. It specified the criminal penalty for anyone who took the property: the peg would be driven through the mouth of the offender.[117]

A fragmentary law text from Ur stated that the wife of a slave voluntarily pursued the slave owner and they had sex. The slave wife was put to death and her slave husband was set free.[118] The husband was the victim of his wife's offense but was well compensated for his injury.

Other Sumerian documents relate little about the offenses of women until the Isin/Larsa period. The state regulated intrafamilial relationships, and the breach of such relationships was criminalized. The penalties indicated how the types of breach were made dependent on gender. When a wife repudiated her husband or committed adultery, she was punished by death. Both offenses challenged the authority of her husband. When a husband repudiated his wife, he was merely fined thirty sheqels of silver.[119]

Punishment

In ancient Sumer the state decided and carried out punishment of crimes. Sumerian documents attested the existence of the death penalty but not its use. Corporal mutilation was found only in the earliest period. Most crimes in ancient Sumer were punished by restitution or fines. Sumerian laws punished the property crime of theft by double restitution. Letters, which often better reflect actual practice, showed theft punished by simple restitution of the object or amount stolen. Sumerian law distinguished between intentional and unintentional crimes. The fines prescribed for intentional offenses were double those for the same offense when it was not intended.

King Gudea of Lagash declared a moratorium on punishment of household offenses in a document that revealed what sort of domestic punishments were being used. The overseer was to stop using the whip on workers; a mother was not to chide her children; a mistress was not to strike her slave, even when the latter committed a great wrong; and no one was to report offenses to the king. After the moratorium, the overseer was told to bind ewe's wool onto the whip, so that it would not cause as much pain or injury.[120] This text indicates that corporal punishment was used in private, to uphold authority and punish minor domestic offenses within the household, even though it was not a penalty prescribed by the laws or the courts.

A major innovation in the theory of penology occurred in the nineteenth century with the composition of the "Nungal Hymn" by an unknown writer. Nungal was a goddess who had the roles of judge and prison warden. According to the hymn, after criminal offenders were tried, convicted, and sentenced to death, Nungal, who prided herself on being compassionate, did not allow the executions to take place. Instead she brought the condemned into her prison, where she first discerned those who were hopelessly evil, whom she sent down into eternal darkness, and those of truth, whom she rehabilitated into wholeness. She called the prison her "house of life," a womb from which the offender was reborn a new person. Although the goddess Nungal had the male roles of judge and prison warden, her policy of compassion exhibited her feminine nature. The poem indicated that at least one place of detention existed in ancient Sumer.[121] The poem demonstrates a sophisticated understanding that the most important function of a prison should be the rehabilitation, not warehousing, of offenders.

Texts from the late Isin/Larsa period reveal Amorite beliefs and practices. Some laws based the severity of punishment on the gender of the victim or the offender. Offenses against men were punished more severely than offenses against women. When a son repudiated his mother, the city officials removed him from his household, shaved half of his head, and paraded him around the city. The state mandated and carried out the punishment because the mother did not have the authority to punish her son. If the son committed the same offense against his father, the father had the authority to administer the punishment himself. The penalty, sale into slavery, was greater because the victim was a man. Women offenders were punished more severely than men for the same offense. The punishment for the repudiation of a spouse was death by drowning when the offender was the wife, but a small fine if the offender was the husband.[122]

Adultery was punished by impalement, one of the cruelest forms of the death penalty and highly symbolic of the sexual control of women by men. A long pole was thrust up through the body of the woman, then fixed in the ground where she was left to a slow and painful death. In Amorite thought, offenses such as adultery were perceived to be very serious because they challenged the authority of fathers and husbands over their wives and children.[123] The practices of determining punishment on the basis of the gender of the victim and offender, and the use of the death penalty, especially by cruel forms of execution, indicate Amorite influence.

A late, brief, and very fragmentary law collection ended with an epilogue in which the writer invoked a curse on any person who erased his name and substituted his or her own name in the inscription. The penalty in the curse was the not only the obliteration of the offender; it was extended to innocent inhabitants of the offender's city—that all the young men become blind and all the young women become barren.[124] The extension of penalties to innocent persons was not found in Sumer, but such texts provided a literary rationale that would later be used to justify collective punishment in other societies.

Summary: Sumerian Documents

At least one Sumerian queen ruled, while others administered large estates, becoming wealthy and powerful. Daughters of kings married other kings or became high priests of major gods in the most important cities. Many women were priests and held other religious offices. Most women married, after an exchange of marriage gifts and dowry. Women could divorce, and husbands who divorced had to give a settlement to their ex-wives. Women owned, bought, sold, and leased property. Transactions in property, including gifts, were written and recorded. Women could inherit. They could sue and be sued in the courts. Women were weavers and potters, midwives and wet nurses.

Although Sumer was not an especially violent society, women were victims of rape, assault, and battery—crimes punished by fines. Women were also given over as pledges to creditors, who sometimes abused them. Sumerian documents show that throughout most of the history of Sumer, especially in the centuries when the position of women was very high, few crimes were committed by women. Only in the very early and very late documents is there evidence that women committed offenses that challenged the authority of men. The punishment for such acts was corporal in the Early Dynastic period, and capital and corporal in the Larsa period. At that time, as Amorite influence began to appear, punishments were determined on the basis of the gender of the victim and the gender of the offender. Women generally received harsher punishments than men. Such laws illustrate the widening gap between the increasing power and authority of men and the decreasing power of women in the late Isin/Larsa period, which developed parallel to the decreasing influence of the law and culture of the high urban civilization of Sumer and the increasing influence of Amorite tribal customs.

CRIMINAL TRIALS OF WOMEN

The administration of justice of a state is revealed not only by its written laws and records, but also by accounts of actual cases and trials. The two trials described below occurred in the Isin/Larsa period.

The record of a murder trial held in Nippur has been found on three clay tablets dating from the early second millennium. The case was first brought before the king of Isin, who referred it to the assembly of Nippur.[125] The order of the trial record is detailed and includes a summary of the facts of the case, a procedural history, statements of the prosecution and the defense, the summation and opinion of the assembly, and the pronouncement of judgment and sentence by the assembly.

The facts of the case were simple and undisputed. Three men had murdered a religious official in Nippur. After the murder, the men told the victim's wife that her husband was dead; she kept silent and did nothing. The three men who had murdered the man were found guilty and sentenced to execution in front of the chair of the victim, a symbol of the victim's presence and office.[126]

The difficult issue in the trial was the guilt or innocence of the widow, Nindada, whether she was an accomplice to the murder because of her silence. There was no evidence that she was present or actually took part in the murder. There was an underlying assumption that all persons had a legal duty to report to the authorities their knowledge of crimes committed. The nine prosecutors asked the assembly to convict Nindada along with the three men and to execute all four. The two men who defended Nindada did not discuss whether or not she was guilty of murder, but argued, on the basis of the presumption of the weakness of women, that a woman was not capable of committing a capital offense. The assembly did not accept the "weaker sex" argument and applied a harsher standard to the woman. It inferred, without evidence, on the assumption that wives could not be trusted, that Nindada must not have valued her husband and therefore must have had an adulterous relationship with an enemy of her husband, who then killed him, informed Nindada of the murder and ordered her to keep silent.[127] Without evidence of adultery or evidence that Nindada participated in any way in the murder of her husband, the assembly found her guilty of his murder. Furthermore, it pronounced Nindada more guilty than the men who had actually killed him, because she had violated her marriage vows by committing adultery. The assembly sentenced Nindada to death, and all four were delivered up for execution.[128]

The record of an adultery case tried before the assembly in the same period begins with a statement that the couple were married, followed by a narrative of the facts, judgment, and sentencing. In this case, a man caught his wife, Ishtar-ummi, committing adultery in his bed with another man. He tied her and her paramour onto the bed and had the bed carried to the assembly. In the trial before the assembly for adultery, other alleged and unrelated offenses were used to persuade the assembly of the wife's moral turpitude. The wife was accused, without evidence, of breaking into her husband's locked grain storeroom and opening a jar of oil, stealing some and covering it up with a cloth. Then the charge of adultery was presented. Since her credibility had been destroyed by the other allegations, she was presumed guilty of adultery. The penalties were corporal mutilation and public humiliation: her pubic hair was shaved, her nose was pierced by an arrow, and she was thus led through the city in shame and humiliation.[129]

The penalties in these two examples of criminal trials of women in the Isin/Larsa period were severe. The penalty for the woman in the murder trial was death. The Sumerians did occasionally use the death penalty, and homicide was an appropriate crime for imposing it. In the adultery trial, the guilty woman was sentenced to corporal mutilation and public humiliation. These penalties are not found in Sumerian legal documents but were common in Amorite practice. Both trials took place during the Isin/Larsa period.[130] The prescribed penalties show the influence of Amorite Larsa, and the trials, dominated by men, providing minimal due process to the women defendants, reflect the transition between Sumerian law and Amorite custom.

ART AND ARCHAEOLOGY

From proto-historic times, persons of property had seals, which were used to authenticate documents and transact business. Large numbers of seals were found in archaeological excavations of Sumerian cities. The more elaborate seals were inscribed on cylinders made of metal or stone, which, when rolled across soft clay, displayed impressions of names and pictures of persons and their activities. Seals are the earliest concrete evidence of the names and roles of women in ancient Sumer.

The existence of seals of women throughout the history of Sumer attests to women's legal rights to own and use seals and to certify legal transactions, such as the sale or acquisition of property. The seals of the wives, daughters, and sisters of kings were inscribed with their own names, and some even included the woman's picture. In the Early Dynastic period, Puabi was called queen of Ur on a cylinder seal made of lapis lazuli. Ashusikildingir was called wife of a king of Ur; Baranamtara was named wife of the king of Lagash; and Nin-banda was called queen on one cylinder seal and queen mother on another. During the Akkadian dynasty, Tutasharlibish was called queen on two seals and "beloved of the king" on a third. Archaeologists found seals of the Ur III period, which named Eanisha and Geme-Ninlila, wives of king Shulgi; Simat-Ishtara, sister of king Shu-Sin; Ana'a, wife of an official of Shu-Sin; and Ninkhilia, wife of the governor of Umma.[131]

Seals of women priests contained their names and portrayed their activities. The seal of the scribe of the high priestess Geme-Lama named her and the god she served. Seals depicted women priests under kings Shulgi and Shu-Sin. Tiamat-bashti and Kubatum were priests "beloved of Shu-Sin," who sang to him. Seals had pictures of women in processions, in front of temples, and carrying religious symbols and offerings. Other seals depicted women priests of different ranks performing various religious functions. Many seals portrayed presentation scenes, in which women priests led male or female worshipers to a seated god or goddess, and other seals showed women making libations, bringing animals for sacrifice, and carrying cultic objects. Seals depicted women playing musical instruments, including lyre, harp, flute, pipes, and drum. One seal named the woman Ninkinda, the chief *qadishtu* of Ur. The seal of the priestess Khekunsig had two tiers: the top tier showed two women eating; the bottom tier, a procession to the temple. In addition to royal and religious women, a few seals depicted women working as weavers and potters and in agriculture.[132]

Many wives of Early Dynastic kings were named in inscriptions on objects that they dedicated to the gods. Pakalam and Akalam, wives of early rulers of Nippur, dedicated stone vessels; Bara'irnun, wife of the king of Umma and daughter of a former king of Umma, dedicated a gold plaque; Megirimta, daughter of a king of Uruk, dedicated a stone bowl; and Khesamanu, wife of a king of Ur, dedicated a stone vessel. A dedication was made for the life of the king of Kish, for his wife, Nin-banda, and for his son. In Early Dynastic Lagash, Geme-Bau, the daughter of a temple administrator who later became king of Lagash, dedicated a statue. An early king of Lagash dedicated a stone statue for his father and his mother, Ashume'eren. Another king of Lagash, Ur-Nanshe, made a stone plaque to commemorate his building of temples; the relief portrayed the king, his daughter, Abda, and his four sons. During the second dynasty of Lagash, many dedications were made by wives of the kings. Nin-niginesi, wife of king Ur-Ningirsu of Lagash, dedicated a stone bull with a human head. Nin-alla, daughter of king Ur-Bau and wife of king Gudea, dedicated a bowl, a macehead, and a statue to the gods. Nin-inimgina, wife of king Ur-gar, dedicated maceheads and statues, a bull with a human head, and an alabaster vessel. Nin-khedu, also a daughter of Ur-Bau and wife of another king, dedicated a marble slab and a macehead. In Isin, Lamassatum, the mother of king Lipit-Ishtar, built and dedicated a storehouse to a goddess for the life of her son and for her own life. In Larsa, Rim-Sin-shalabashtashu, wife of king Rim-Sin, dedicated a stone basin for the life of the king and for their daughter, Lirishgamlum.[133]

Archaeologists found the Sumerian royal tombs at Ur filled with bodies of women and men surrounding the remains of deceased queens. The tomb of queen Puabi contained the bodies of three attendants with her body in one room and the bodies of twelve women and fourteen men in a large adjacent pit. Some of the women were musicians, buried with their lyres, and others were women of the royal court. Another royal grave contained the bodies of seventy-four attendants, of whom sixty-eight were women. These attendants represented the court of the royal decedent. The women attendants were "sacrificed," killed or induced to commit ritual suicide, to accompany the deceased in death. Since their bodies showed no evidence of the use of force, the deaths of the attendants probably involved taking hashish, opium, or poison. Someone neatly arranged the unconscious bodies, and then the tomb was sealed and the pit filled with dirt. The men were guards and charioteers, the women were court attendants and musicians. Some carried their musical instruments, including three with lyres, inside the tomb, suggesting that there may have been a funeral ritual before the deaths occurred. The rank of the decedents can be determined by their jewelry and clothes. Queens, princesses, and high priestesses were dressed in special clothes and wore a great amount of jewelry. Examination of the bodies of the primary deceased showed that the life expectancy of royal women was about forty years.[134] Yet the nature and meaning of the deaths of so many attendants remain a mystery.

Music was prominent in Sumerian art. Beautiful lyres and parts of lyres have been found by archaeologists in the royal Sumerian tombs at Ur and in excavations of other city-states. Sumerian lyres had different numbers of strings and different sizes and shapes. Some were inlaid with mother of pearl, lapis lazuli, and gold. Women were depicted playing the lyre, the harp, the flute, single and double pipes, and percussion instruments. Women were singers, musicians, dancers, and clappers, serving in temples and palaces in festivals, funerals, and other religious rites.[135] There is evidence of women musicians in every period of Sumerian history.

Stone and terra cotta reliefs portrayed Sumerian goddesses, queens, high priests, priests, and ordinary people. A stone plaque from the Early Dynastic period found at Ur in the residence of the women high priests depicted a woman high priest wearing a rolled hat like that of En-kheduanna. She was preceded by a libation bearer. The plaque indicates that there were women high priests in Ur before En-kheduanna. A relief on an alabaster disc from Ur pictured the high priest En-kheduanna, daughter of king Sargon, with three attendants, one in front pouring a libation and two behind carrying objects. Her hand was raised in a ritual gesture, and she was wearing a much more elaborate dress than the others. They faced a small altar. An inscription on the disc called her "wife of the god."[136]

Statues of women high priests are rare, but several have been found in the area of Lagash dating from the Akkadian and Ur III dynasties. The women were wearing long dresses and had their hair in a chignon held by a band. The dress and hairstyle differ from those of other women priests of the time, who were depicted wearing a cloak with one shoulder uncovered and having long hair down their backs.[137]

Stone plaques depicted women priests serving the goddess Inanna. Women priests were portrayed carrying cultic objects, drinking from cups, and making offerings and libations to the gods. The head of a woman priest was sculpted in white marble. Reliefs on alabaster and silver vases showed women priests receiving offerings from the people and making offerings to the gods. Votive statues of queens and other women with folded hands, praying, have been found in temples. These statues were not intended to be exact portraits of the donors, but were representatives of the donors, making them continuously present in the temples. One statue, found in a temple, portrayed a woman, tall and thin, with her hair braided and wrapped around her head, wearing a floor-length robe.[138]

Portrayal of a male or female figure seated denoted the importance and authority of the person. Sculptures of the goddesses Bau and Ningal seated on thrones were found in Ur. Queens and women priests are shown seated. A three-tiered plaque with scenes of a banquet was found in a temple. At the top, a woman of authority was seated on the left, while a seated man and standing woman on the right were drinking from cups. They were served by male and female attendants. The musicians were male.[139]

Many statues of women have been found. Some had only the head only; others only the torso. A few statues of standing women remain intact. The majority were sculpted in the Early Dynastic period.[140]

There are many beautiful reliefs and statues of ordinary women and men, most of which were created in the third millennium BCE. A few stone reliefs depicted women working as weavers and potters. In one such relief, a woman was seated on a stool spinning wool, while her attendant fanned her with a large fan. In another women were depicted harvesting dates.[141]

In a stone relief of a couple, the man and woman stood gazing into each other's faces. Several reliefs depicted couples embracing. A beautiful stone sculpture portrayed an older couple seated, with their arms around each other, facing forward.[142]

These artifacts provide concrete visual access to the lives of Sumerian women, the works in which they engaged, and even the affection that existed between older married couples. Some Sumerian works of art are greatly superior to those of later civilizations. Art and artifacts serve to correct the historian. For example, documents have provided much evidence of the existence and activities of women priests, whereas the art of the Early Dynastic and Akkadian periods portrayed more male priests than women. The male priests were depicted totally naked, with no question as to their gender.[143]

CONCLUSION: WOMEN, CRIME, AND PUNISHMENT IN ANCIENT SUMER

Royal Sumerian lawgivers expressed their goals of justice and protection of the poor and oppressed, including women, especially vulnerable women such as widows without children. They believed that these goals could be achieved through written laws, impartial courts, and a workable system for the administration of justice. The city-states of Sumer developed judicial systems early in the third millennium. First the assemblies of the city-states functioned as courts and later there were panels of judges. Trials were conducted in a formal manner: facts were gathered in evidence, the arguments of both sides were heard, guilt was deliberated by the assembly, and, in the case of conviction, sentence was handed down. Defendants had the right to appeal, generally to their ruler or to the king of the dominant city-state in the area. Women were treated the same as men under the laws and in the courts of Sumer.

In ancient Sumer, upper-class women approached equality with men in most areas, with the exception of kingship. Kings ruled the city-states of ancient Sumer. Only in the earliest period did a woman rule alone as queen. But the wives of kings and governors exercised important roles, administering large royal and temple estates. Daughters of kings were high priests in the most important cities of Sumer. Women served as priests and other religious officials in the temples. Since women owned and inherited property, some women became wealthy, and wealth gave them power. Thus, many Sumerian women exercised political, economic, and religious authority. Lower-class women were singers and musicians in the temples and palaces. Some women were professional scribes, while others were skilled weavers, potters, millers, brewers, and tavern keepers.

Sumerian laws protected marriage, family, and property. Marriage required both marriage gifts and dowry, creating economic equality between spouses. Polygyny was legal, practiced mainly by royals and the very wealthy. Laws protected first wives if their husbands married second wives. A sick wife could not be thrown out but had to be cared for by her husband and any subsequent wife he married. Men could not divorce their wives without giving them a property settlement and returning their dowry.

Women were victims of the crimes of rape, assault and battery, and false accusation of serious crimes. Men who raped women were punished by death when the victim was a betrothed virgin, but only by a fine or forced marriage to the victim if she was not betrothed. Assault and battery severe enough to cause miscarriage were punished by death only when the woman victim died and in other cases by fines to compensate for the loss of the fetus. False accusation of women was often punished by the penalty of the case, which was generally a fine.

Women who committed crimes were tried in a court and punished by the state if convicted. The Sumerians distinguished between intentional and unintentional offenses, and adjusted the penalties accordingly. They developed the concept of liability for negligence, which was punished by compensation for loss. There were few capital crimes. Men and women who committed murder were executed by the state, and wives who repudiated their husbands were put to death by drowning. Seduction by a married woman leading to adultery was punished by the death of the woman; adultery without seduction by the woman was not a capital offense and was merely punished by a fine in Ur III. Other offenses that occurred within the family and threatened to tear it apart, such as children disowning their parents or parents disowning their children, were punished by loss of possessions and inheritance, symbols of being part of the family, and, in the Isin/Larsa period, by sale into slavery, a radical cutting off from the family. In the extant laws of Sumer, there were only two references to corporal mutilation in the very earliest period. A mild corporal penalty appeared late in the Isin/Larsa period and reflected Amorite influence. A literary document expressed the radical idea that prison in an environment of reform and rehabilitation was better than punishment for turning offenders into good citizens.

Ancient Sumer was a highly developed urban civilization. The legal status of Sumerian women, their access to courts, legal rights, and protection by law were greater than those of women in most later ancient Near Eastern civilizations. The treatment of women who were victimized by crime or who committed crimes in ancient Sumer was generally better than in other ancient civilizations.

There was discernible change and development in the criminal law of ancient Sumer. The death penalty and corporal punishment were attested in the very earliest laws. Capital punishment was rare in later Sumerian laws, and corporal punishment was not used at all. By the end of the third millennium, the majority of crimes were punished by fines.

During the transitional Isin/Larsa period in the early second millennium, capital and corporal punishment became prominent. Amorite tribes had settled in the city-states of Sumer, where some lived for years and even generations. When Amorite rulers took over the government of these city-states, the earlier Amorite settlers had already assimilated much of Sumerian civilization, law, and culture.

Sumerians had lived in cities for several millennia. They identified themselves as citizens of their city-state and never alluded to a tribal past. The Amorites, on the other hand, had been tribal nomads in their recent past and still identified themselves by their tribal kinship group and retained the memory of their tribal traditions and customary laws.

In southern Mesopotamia, where Amorite settlement was gradual and there was a strong and cohesive civilization in the cities, Sumerian laws and culture had a great and long-lasting influence on the laws and civilization of the emerging Amorite empire of Babylonia. A symbol of the transition from the relative equality of women in Sumerian society to the disenfranchisement and disappearance of women from the public arena in Amorite societies was the change in gods. The Sumerians had a large pantheon of male and female gods. Each city-state had a goddess or god as its patron. Amorite Babylonia and Assyria had one or more dominant male gods, who were later given a subordinate consort. Amorite influence was most visible in the treatment of women, the use of private administration of justice, and the types of punishment of crimes.[144]

1. Map of Ancient Near East

SUMER

2. Greenstone cylinder seal rolled and unrolled. Sumer, Ur III Dynasty. Presentation scene: women priests present local governor to seated king Ur-Nammu. About 2100 BCE. British Museum, London.

3. White marble head of woman found near temple of Eanna in Uruk. Originally it had a stone wig and inlaid eyes and eyebrows. 3100 BCE. National Museum of Archaeology, Baghdad, Iraq.

4. Alabaster statue of woman. Ur, about 2700 BCE. National Museum of Archaeology, Baghdad, Iraq.

5. White limestone head of woman found at Tell Agrab, Diyala River region. 2600 BCE. National Museum of Archaeology, Baghdad, Iraq.

6. Stone head of woman priest, inlaid with plaster, asphalt, and shells. Found in temple in Mari. About 2400 BCE.

7. Seated woman holding vase. Alabaster. Early Dynasty. Louvre

8. Steatite statue of seated woman priest. Found in temple in Mari, about 2500. Early Dynasty. Damascus Museum.

9. Alabaster disc relief of the high priestess En-Kheduanna performing a religious rite. Ur, about 2350 BCE. Akkadian Dynasty. University of Pennsylvania Museum.

10. Clay relief of nursing mother. Girsu. Lagash II. Louvre.

11. Steatite statue of royal woman. Found in Girsu, Lagash II (2145 to about 2130). Louvre.

12. Terracotta relief of couple embracing. Girsu, Lagash II (about 2100). Louvre.

13. Seated old woman. Found in Ur, Ur III Dynasty. National Museum of Archaeology, Baghdad, Iraq.

14. Diorite statue dedicated to goddess by En-annatumma, high priest daughter of King Ishme-Dagan of Isin. About 1950. University of Pennsylvania Museum.

Part Two

∽

BABYLONIA

BABYLONIA AS A GEOGRAPHICAL ENTITY comprised the southern part of Mesopotamia. As a political entity, Babylonia was a nation state with its capital at Babylon, which ruled the other cities of southern Mesopotamia, and an empire, which ruled the city-states of northern Mesopotamia as vassals. The history of Babylonia is divided into three very different periods. Old Babylonia was ruled by the Amorite Old Babylonian dynasty. Its sixth king, Hammurabi, conquered the Old Babylonian empire and compiled a collection of laws that dominated Babylonian legal tradition for centuries. The Middle Babylonian period was a dark age of foreign occupation, which left few written sources. Late Babylonia had strong kings who conquered and ruled an even greater empire, including all of Mesopotamia as well as much of Syria and Canaan. Since the differences are very great, each period must be treated separately.[1]

HISTORY OF BABYLONIA	
OLD BABYLONIA (OB)	1894–1595
MIDDLE BABYLONIA (MB)	1595–627
Kassites	1595–1158
Isin II	1158–1027
Assyria	1026–627
LATE BABYLONIA (LB)	626–539

OLD BABYLONIA (1894–1595 BCE)

By the early second millennium, after the collapse of Ur III and the first dynasty of Isin, Sumer ceased to exist as a power or even as an entity. Amorites who had settled in the fragmented city-states of Sumer had risen to positions of power. At the beginning of the Old Babylonian period, Amorite kings ruled the three most powerful city-states in central and southern Mesopotamia: Larsa, Eshnunna, and Babylon. By 1762, Babylon had conquered Larsa, Eshnunna, and the other cities of Sumer and Akkad and had formed the Old Babylonian empire.

THE LAWS OF ESHNUNNA

Eshnunna was a small Amorite kingdom in the Diyala valley, located north of Sumer and east of Babylon. It became independent after the fall of Ur III and had its own dynasty of kings during the first quarter of the second millennium. In 1762 the Babylonian king Hammurabi conquered Eshnunna and annexed it to his capital at Babylon.[2]

The Laws of Eshnunna were written in the early second millennium. Like the Sumerian laws, the extant copies of the Laws of Eshnunna were written in cuneiform script on clay tablets by later scribes. The lack of order and fragmentary content indicate that these laws were not intended to represent a law code containing all of the laws of Eshnunna, but were a collection of laws dealing with specific subjects.[3]

Status of Women

Many of the laws of Eshnunna were about marriage. It is significant that legal marriage required the permission of the bride's mother as well as her father. A valid marriage required a formal written marriage contract between a prospective groom and the bride's father and mother, delivery of marriage gifts by the groom, a nuptial feast, and the transfer of the bride to the house of the groom. If a man took a woman without the permission of her father and mother, with no marriage contract or nuptial feast, even though they lived together in his house for a year or more, it was not a valid marriage and the woman did not have the legal rights and protection of wifehood.[4]

When a father accepted marriage gifts from a suitor of his daughter, the couple were considered betrothed. In one case, when the betrothed groom arrived to claim his bride, he found that her father had given her to someone else. The bride's father had to refund twice the value of the marriage gifts to the betrothed suitor.[5]

When a couple was betrothed but the bride died before the marriage took place, the marriage gifts reverted to the groom. When the wife died after the marriage was completed, the husband could not get back the marriage gifts he had given to her father but only the fruit or interest that had accrued since the gifts were delivered.[6]

Eshnunna was a feudal society, and the king gave possession of land to men in exchange for military service. This system excluded women from possession of feudal lands, since they did not serve as soldiers. Some men became prisoners of war in foreign lands for a long time. When a soldier returned home and found that another man had married his wife, even if she had a child by him, the wife had to return to her first husband. However, if a man had left home voluntarily because he hated his city and his feudal lord, he had no claim for the return of his wife if she had remarried during his absence.[7] The laws were silent about the preferences of wives in such situations.

One law protected wives from abandonment by their husbands. If a man divorced his wife after she had borne children and took another wife, he had to leave his house and his possessions and go into exile. The rest of the law is broken off. Since the husband left everything, it is possible that his first wife retained his house, possessions, and the children. The law is unusual and appears to be an attack on polygyny, unless the missing parts of the text referred to a special situation.[8]

A profession dominated by women in the ancient Near East was that of tavern keeper. The Laws of Eshnunna regulated women tavern keepers and the price they could charge for foreign beer. Foreign merchants could not sell their beer in Eshnunna. Women tavern keepers had to sell it for them at the legal price.[9]

A slave woman or man was legally the personal property of the owner. Slaves were regarded as chattel, the same as oxen or donkeys. Slave men and women had to be visibly identifiable as slaves by wearing fetters, shackles, or the slave hairlock.[10] Slave men and women were not legal persons and had no legal rights.

Women Victims

When a man kidnapped a betrothed girl without the knowledge or consent of her parents and took her virginity, the rapist was punished by death. Although the crimes of kidnapping and rape after betrothal had unavoidable property implications involving marriage gifts and contracts, the law treated the rape of a free betrothed virgin not as a property offense but as a capital crime of violence against a person. In contrast, when a man raped a virgin slave girl belonging to another, the rapist had to pay a fine of twenty sheqels of silver and return the girl to her owner. Since slave women were not legal persons but property, the rape of a virgin slave girl was a crime against the owner of the property, which had been diminished in value, and was punishable by a fine.[11]

Women and men were victims of assault and battery causing injury and dismemberment. The Laws of Eshnunna specified fines depending on the nature and severity of the injury. When an offender bit or cut off the nose or put out the eye of another, the fine was sixty sheqels. If an offender knocked out a tooth, cut off an ear, or caused a broken arm or leg, the fine was thirty sheqels. When a person cut off a finger or broke the collarbone of another, the fine was twenty sheqels. The fine was ten sheqels for a slap on the cheek or general injuries.[12]

Women could be distrained and held by creditors to compel payment of debts incurred by their husbands. But when a man had no claim against a free commoner and illegally seized the man's wife or child, took the wife or child into his house, and caused her or his death, the penalty was death. The prescription of the death penalty indicates that an offense causing the death of a free woman or child, even though of commoner class, was treated as the capital offense of homicide.[13]

The same offense was treated differently when the victim was a slave. If a citizen who had no claim against another citizen illegally distrained his slave woman, took her into his house, and caused her death, he had to pay double restitution, that is, two slave women, in return. If a citizen illegally seized a slave woman belonging to another citizen and the slave owner swore an oath that the first man had no claims against him, the first man had to pay the owner the value of the slave woman in silver.[14] The lives of slaves were exchangeable for silver or other slaves. Although the slave woman was the actual victim, the legal victim was her owner.

Since slaves were objects of property, they could be stolen just as other property could be. If someone claimed to have bought a slave woman or an ox but was unable to identify the seller, the alleged buyer was considered guilty of theft. When a man was caught with a stolen slave woman, the penalty was double restitution. He had to return the slave to the owner and bring another slave of the same gender to the owner as well. If an official seized an escaped slave woman, stray ox, or donkey and kept her or it in his house for more than a month, he was charged with the crime of theft.[15] These precepts illustrate that the Laws of Eshnunna protected the rights of the slave owner. The feelings of the slave women stolen, seized, or used to pay a criminal penalty were not considered.

Women Offenders

Only a few criminal offenses committed by women were mentioned in the extant legible parts of the Laws of Eshnunna. The most serious crime treated was adultery. It was dealt with under private jurisdiction by the husband as in tribal custom. If a married woman was discovered "in the lap of" a man other than her husband, a euphemism for sexual relations, the crime was adultery and the penalty for the woman was death. Since the law stated that she was caught in the act and executed the same day, there was no necessity or time for a trial. Such cases were left to the husband, who was permitted to punish his wife by summary execution. The law did not state whether there was a penalty for the male accomplice.[16]

Women tavern keepers and merchants were prohibited from accepting anything of value, such as silver, barley, wool, or sesame oil, from male or female slaves. Since slaves could not own property, whatever they had in their possession was presumed to be stolen property.[17]

The crime of trespass involved entry into the house or field of another without permission. If a citizen was caught in the house or field of a commoner in the daytime, the penalty was a fine of ten sheqels. If the trespass occurred at night, the penalty was death.[18] It is unlikely that women were out at night, but they could have trespassed in the field or house of another in the daytime.

The Laws of Eshnunna considered the negligent failure to prevent injury a crime. In one case, the wall of a building was unstable and the owner of the property was given notice of the danger but failed to fix it. The wall fell down, killing a citizen. The property owner was arrested, and the case was decided by the king. The penalty for such negligence was death.[19] A second type of negligence involved animals. The district authorities gave notice to the owners of oxen or dogs that their animals were dangerous. If the owner did nothing to restrain the animal, which then killed a citizen, the owner was fined forty sheqels; if it killed a slave, the fine was fifteen sheqels. Insofar as women could own buildings and animals, these laws applied to them.[20]

When a slave woman gave her child to a free woman of the upper class with the intent to defraud her master, the slave owner could take the child back and reclaim it as his property. This law applied even after the child became an adult. Likewise, if a slave woman of the palace gave her son or daughter to a free commoner to raise, a representative of the palace could take the child back. Neither law explicitly mentions a formal punishment of the mother, even though the first law noted the mother's intent to defraud.[21] Yet the seizure of the child by the slave owner did in effect punish the mother, since her child was returned to slavery.

Punishment

In the extant Laws of Eshnunna, the death penalty was prescribed for the crimes of kidnapping, rape of a betrothed virgin of citizen class, adultery, distraint without cause when the victim died, trespass in a field or house at night, and negligent failure to repair a dangerous condition in a building which caused the death of a citizen. The form of execution was not stated. No cases of corporal punishment or mutilation are found in the extant laws.

Most other crimes were punished by fines or restitution. It is significant that crimes involving injury to persons were punished by fines, as in Sumer, not by corporal mutilation, as in Amorite custom and Babylonian law.

Punishment for crimes was often determined by the social class of the victim. Rape of a free virgin was punished by death. Rape of a virgin slave girl was punished by a fine. Illegal distraint of a free woman resulting in death was a capital offense. If the victim was a slave woman, the same offense was punished by a fine. When the penalty for a crime was a fine, the amount was much larger when the victim was a free person than when the victim was a slave.

The punishment for negligence was contingent on the nature of the proximate cause of the death of the victim. When a building collapsed and killed a free person, the proximate cause was the failure of the owner to repair the building. In this case, the penalty was the death of the owner. When a vicious animal was the proximate cause of the death of a victim, even though its owner was negligent in not keeping it locked up, the penalty was a fine.

Summary: The Laws of Eshnunna

The Laws of Eshnunna prescribed marriage gifts given by the prospective groom to the father of the bride as a necessary requirement for legal marriage and did not mention dowry. This made daughters an economic asset to their families. Women were still considered legal persons in the Laws of Eshnunna. When a free woman was killed, the offense was treated as a crime against a person and punished by death. On the negative side, women were held vicariously liable for the debts of their husbands, for which they were distrained, held, abused, and sometimes even killed by the creditors of their husbands.

The extant Laws of Eshnunna are fragmentary and incomplete. The laws show some influence of Amorite customary law in the decline of the right of women to own property, the increased use of the death penalty, and the tolerance of private jurisdiction over sentencing and execution of punishment of certain crimes. Yet there is no evidence of the use of corporal punishment or mutilation. The Laws of Eshnunna serve as an example of the transition between the laws of Sumer and the laws of Babylonia. Amorite influence was much more pronounced in the Laws of Hammurabi.

The Laws of Hammurabi

At the beginning of the second millennium, the city-state of Babylon was small and unimportant, although it was geographically close to and in communication with the great city-states of ancient Sumer and had been part of the Akkadian and Ur III empires. The city became prominent when the Euphrates river changed its course and ran through Babylon, making it a center for trade.[22]

In 1894, an Amorite sheikh made himself king of Babylon and established the Amorite Old Babylonian dynasty, which ruled for three centuries and established an empire. The first five kings concentrated on infrastructure, building fortifications and digging canals.* When Hammurabi acceded to the throne of Babylon in 1792, he spent the early years of his reign continuing to improve the infrastructure and the canals, thereby enhancing trade and building up the wealth of his kingdom. At this time, the Amorite king Rim-Sin of Larsa ruled southern Mesopotamia and the Amorite king Shamshi-Adad I of Asshur controlled the north. Relations among the three Amorite kings were amicable. Amorite kings, although from different tribes, were related by genealogy, custom, and language, and often gave each other political, military, and economic aid. After the death of King Shamshi-Adad I in 1781, Hammurabi became the strongest king in northern Mesopotamia, and he lived in peace with the kings of Larsa and Mari for many years. In 1763, however, Hammurabi conquered Larsa, thereby gaining control over all of southern Mesopotamia. Two years later, he conquered Eshnunna, which gave him the trade routes of the Diyala region, the northern city-states of Mari on the Euphrates, and Asshur and Nineveh on the Tigris. By 1760, Hammurabi ruled all of Mesopotamia. The king recorded twenty-five cities that he had conquered. He incorporated the nearby cities of Sippar and Eshnunna into the city of Babylon and integrated the cities of south and central Mesopotamia into one nation, with Babylon at its center. The conquered city-states of the north became his vassals, paid tribute, and provided troops. He ruled the empire himself for forty-two years, controlling minute details of political and judicial administration in the south. The empire lost the north soon after his death but retained control of southern Mesopotamia. The Old Babylonian empire lasted almost two centuries.[23]

---

* Communication and trade among the city-states occurred mostly by water, although there were roads where there was no water. Each emperor dug and improved the system of canals. The rivers ran north to south; canals ran east to west, connecting the rivers to each other and to land routes.

The laws compiled by King Hammurabi constitute the most extensive extant collection from the ancient Near East. The Laws of Hammurabi were engraved on a stone pillar that was taller than any human person. The stela was made of diorite, a hard black stone used for important royal inscriptions. On the top is a relief depicting Hammurabi receiving the commission from the god of justice to promulgate the laws. The stela contains a nearly complete text of 282 laws, written in the Old Babylonian language in cuneiform script.[24] Many historians consider the laws to be Hammurabi's greatest achievement, greater even than the empire he built.

The Laws of Hammurabi consist of a prologue, the laws, and an epilogue. The prologue and epilogue were written in semipoetic style in the first person. In the prologue Hammurabi listed his accomplishments and the titles by which he was known. The most frequent title he used was "King of Justice." He also called himself the shepherd of his people, using the maternal image of holding Sumer and Akkad safely in his lap, giving them peace and protection. The prologue began and ended with the divine commission "to make justice prevail in the land," to abolish evil and evildoers, and "to prevent the strong from oppressing the weak."[25]

The epilogue is an encomium of praise to Hammurabi for bringing justice to the people of the Babylonian empire through his "just decisions," which taught the people the way of truth and proper behavior. Hammurabi wanted to establish justice for the weak and the widowed; he had his laws inscribed on a stela which he set up at the center of the empire in front of his statue in Babylon, where it could be read by all. Thus, Hammurabi, the "king of justice," made justice a reality both by his written laws engraved on the stela and by his person and actions, represented by his statue.[26]

King Hammurabi stated the purpose of his laws: to do justice, render just judgments, and make justice prevail in the land. The Babylonian concept of justice included economic sufficiency, public safety, order, and peace, and the abolition of crime, oppression, and injustice. Hammurabi was proud of his establishment of peace among city-states. Peace was a prerequisite for justice, and justice was a gift of the gods, immutable, conformed to nature and truth, with everyone and everything in the right place, on the right road, in balance and harmony. Hammurabi himself considered justice his greatest achievement.[27]

The laws have been called the "code" of Hammurabi. Despite the fact that there are almost three hundred laws and the extant texts are almost complete, the Laws of Hammurabi do not constitute a law code. The essence of a code is its comprehensiveness. A law code articulates principles that systematically cover every area of law. The Laws of Hammurabi were not systematic or complete and did not consist primarily of principles, but were rather a collection of laws and legal decisions properly entitled "Laws of Hammurabi."[28]

King Hammurabi promulgated a series of amendments to and restatements of existing laws, such as were needed to do justice in the empire during his reign. Some of the laws responded to new situations and issues that had arisen and were not covered by existing laws. Other laws resolved differences and conflicts between Sumerian law and Amorite customary law. Hammurabi was a law reformer and a master of jurisprudence.[29]

King Hammurabi standardized laws in written form for the empire. He told future kings not to alter, but to be guided by, the laws he had written on his stela, and he cursed at great length anyone who might change or rescind his laws. Hammurabi established precedents in his laws that affected judicial decisions in Mesopotamia for the next thousand years.[30]

King Hammurabi had a well-developed system for the administration of justice. The king appointed royal judges for the major cities of the empire. The laws were administered in courts where panels of three or more professional judges heard cases. They were assisted by scribes, who made records of the cases and judgments. Judicial decisions were handed down in writing, recorded, and sealed. A judge who attempted to reverse his own decision was fined and permanently removed from office. The king himself judged serious capital cases and heard appeals.[31]

The people of Babylonia were divided into distinct classes. At the top of the social class structure were the king and the royal family, then free citizens and free commoners. Below these classes were the slaves. There were also special classes of people who crossed social class divisions and were categorized by their function in society, such as royal officials and their staff who worked in the palace, priests and other religious officials who worked in the temples, merchants, craftspersons, and farmers.[32]

Status of Women

The Laws of Hammurabi contain extensive provisions regulating marriage and family; they specify four formal legal requirements for marriage: marriage gifts given by the groom to the family of the prospective bride, dowry provided by the father of the bride, a written contract of marriage, and a marriage feast.[33] Marriage gifts paid by the groom made daughters an economic asset to their families. On the other hand, the requirement of dowry made them an economic hardship for their families, although it gave them a better economic position in marriage. Since the Laws of Hammurabi required both marriage gifts paid by the groom or his father and dowry paid by the father of the bride, the economic relationship of bride and groom was more egalitarian.

When a suitor had delivered his marriage gifts to his proposed father-in-law, but then decided to marry someone else, the father of the rejected bride could keep all the marriage gifts. However, if the intended groom had given his marriage gifts to his prospective father-in-law but the latter then refused to let his daughter marry him, the father had to pay the rejected suitor twice the value of his marriage gifts. When a suitor had delivered his marriage gifts to his prospective father-in-law, but later someone slandered the suitor's reputation, so that the bride's father no longer wanted his daughter to marry him, the bride's father had to return twice the value of the marriage gifts, but the slanderer was not permitted to marry the girl.[34]

A couple could make a written prenuptial contract to protect each against premarital debts incurred by the other. If the husband incurred a debt after marriage, both the husband and his wife were responsible on the basis of community property.[35]

Marriages according to the Laws of Hammurabi were monogamous, with three exceptions: when the first wife became seriously ill and was not expected to recover; when the first wife was a *naditu* priest who could not bear children; and when the first wife tried to obtain a divorce by means of public scandal.[36] In these three situations, the husband could take a second wife. There were no situations in which a wife could take a second husband.

The laws protected wives who became sick or disabled during the marriage. If a man married a woman who became seriously ill, he could marry another woman without divorcing his first wife; but he had to house and support the first wife and care for her until she died. If the first wife chose not to remain, the husband had to restore her dowry and allow her to leave.[37]

The primary duty of a wife was to bear children for her husband. When the wife was unable to do this because she was a priest, the law gave the couple other options for having children, so that the husband would not discard his wife. The wife could provide a slave woman to her husband. Once a slave woman bore children, the husband could not take a second wife. But if the wife did not provide a slave woman, the husband could marry a lower-level religious functionary as a secondary wife to bear children and bring her into his household, but the second wife was not allowed to seek equal status with the first wife.[38] Adoption was another solution and was regulated by law. There were laws that protected the child and others that laid duties upon the child, such as respect and gratitude to his or her adoptive parents, with harsh penalties for their transgression. Parents had to treat adopted children the same as their own children, and they were prohibited from disinheriting an adopted child.[39]

The third exception was when a wife left her husband, stole and then squandered his property, and disparaged his reputation. The city court tried the wife. If she was convicted, the husband could choose either to divorce her, giving her nothing, or keep her in his house as a slave while he married a new wife.[40] By her own public acts, the wife effectively destroyed the marriage.

The Laws of Hammurabi protected widows after the deaths of their husbands. If a man gave land, a house, or goods to his wife while both were still living, and gave her a sealed document as proof, then after his death the widow was protected against any claims regarding her ownership of such property. The widow had the legal right to give the property to any of her children, but not to anyone outside the family.[41]

When a widow with minor children wanted to remarry, the case went before the judges, who investigated the value of the estate. The widow and her second husband had to make a written contract promising to take care of the estate, raise her children, and not sell any part of the estate, which belonged to her children.[42]

When a husband died, the widow kept her dowry and his personal gifts and had the use of her husband's house as long as she lived. She could not sell the house, because the ownership of it belonged to their children. If the children tried to make her leave the house, the city court could enforce her right to stay. If her late husband had not given her any gifts during the marriage, the widow could receive the full portion of an individual heir from his estate. When a widow voluntarily left the house of her late husband, she had to leave her husband's gifts with her children, but she could take her dowry, which would make it possible for her to remarry. If she remarried and had more children, after her death the children of both marriages divided her dowry. If a widow remarried but had no children in the second marriage, her dowry went to the children of her first marriage at her death.[43]

The principles were the same when the wife died first. In one case, a man married a woman who bore him children and then died. The man then married another woman, who also bore him children. The children of the deceased first wife divided their mother's dowry. The children of the second wife divided their mother's dowry after her death. When the man died, the children of both marriages divided their father's estate equally.[44]

Once a wife had borne children, ownership of her dowry belonged to her children, although she retained the possession and income of the property during her lifetime. When a married woman died without bearing children, her father had to return the marriage gifts to her husband and her husband had to return the dowry to her father. If her father did not return any or all of the marriage gifts, the husband had the right to deduct their value from the dowry before he returned it to her father.[45]

Many women became priests. Most fathers gave their daughters a dowry in land when they became priests or other religious officials and recorded the donation in a written document. If a father did not give his daughter written permission to sell or transfer the property, then after his death her brothers took ownership of the land, but not possession, which she had for life. Her brothers were required to give her sufficient food, oil, and clothing to live comfortably. If they did not, the woman had the right to hire a tenant to work

her land to provide her with income. She could not sell the land, since it ultimately belonged to her brothers. However, if the father of a woman priest had
given her a dowry and a sealed written document containing permission to do
whatever she wished with her estate after his death, she could sell or give it to
whomever she pleased and her brothers had no claim against her.[46]

Women priests and other religious officials generally either received a
dowry or inherited part of their father's estate, but not both. When the father
of a daughter who became a lower religious officiant gave a dowry, recorded
the transaction in a sealed document, and gave her in marriage to a husband,
after her father died she had no claim to inheritance from his estate. If the
father had given his daughter no dowry and no husband, then when he died
her brothers had to provide her with a dowry proportionate to the value of the
estate and find her a husband.[47] When a father dedicated his daughter as a celibate *naditu* priest and did not give her a dowry, after his death she received
possession and use of one-third of his estate as long as she lived. When she
died, her portion reverted to her brothers. However, if a woman was a *naditu*
priest of Marduk in Babylon, who could marry, and her father died without
giving her a dowry, she took full ownership of one-third of her father's estate,
even without a document of donation or will written by her father. She owned
the land and had the right to dispose of it any way she chose.[48]

Divorce was legal in ancient Babylonia and was generally initiated by the
husband. The Laws of Hammurabi protected wives by requiring a property
settlement and by placing some restrictions on the circumstances under which
a man could divorce. If a man of the upper class wanted to divorce his wife and
she had not borne any children, he had to give her the full value of his marriage gifts in silver and return her dowry.[49]

It was more expensive for a man to divorce a wife who was a priest. If his
priest wife had borne or provided him with children, he had to return her
dowry and also give her half of their fields, orchards, and goods so that she
would have the means to raise the children. After the children were grown, she
and the children could divide the property into equal shares. The mother's
share would enable her to remarry if she chose.[50] Women priests had a higher
level of legal personhood than ordinary women in the areas of divorce, possession of feudal property, and inheritance.

It was very difficult for a wife to initiate divorce. Her husband could refuse
to divorce her and not permit her to take any property if she left. If the wife
made public charges against her husband, the district authorities investigated
the case. If they found the husband at fault and the wife above reproach, they
permitted the wife to leave with her dowry. But if they found any fault on the
part of the wife, she was put to death.[51] This law discouraged many women
from attempting divorce.

Land tenure in ancient Babylonia was organized in a feudal system. The king was the owner of feudal lands. Men were given tenancy of land in exchange for military or other service to their king. If the king gave tenancy of field, orchard, house, cattle, sheep, or goats, to a soldier, fisher, or other feudal subject, none of these properties could be legally sold. A feudal subject could not assign any feudal property to his wife, daughter, or creditor.[52]

Women were excluded from the system of feudal land tenure because they could not perform the obligation of military service. Women priests, however, were exempt from feudal duties, so they could use, lease, and transfer feudal property. Any nonfeudal land or house that a man himself had bought, and thereby owned in his own person, could be assigned in writing to his wife or daughter.[53] Free women could own and transfer nonfeudal real property and woman priests could also possess and transfer feudal property.

The Laws of Hammurabi contain laws on debt servitude. When the debt of a citizen came due, he could satisfy it by selling the labor of his wife, son, or daughter, who then had to live and work in the house of the creditor for up to three years. In the fourth year, the law mandated their release. When male or female slaves were put into debt servitude, the creditor could make them work longer than three years or could sell them. The debtor had no right to reclaim them, unless a female slave had borne him children. Then he had the right to repay the money and redeem his slave woman.[54]

In Old Babylonia, slaves of both genders were the personal property of their owners, with the same status as money and livestock. A woman could become a slave by birth, through the debt of her father or husband, or as a captive of war. Only a minority of slaves were slaves from birth. Many had been free and even upper-class citizens until poverty or war had taken their freedom and transformed them into slaves. Babylonia was not a slavery-based economy, and many were slaves only for part of their lives.

Marriages between slaves and free persons were permitted. When a male slave married the daughter of a free citizen, she remained free. She came to live with him in the palace or house of his master, bringing her dowry, and together they acquired possessions. If the slave died, the widow took her dowry and half of the community property acquired during the marriage. The slave's owner took the other half. The owner of the slave had no claim on their children as slaves.[55]

A man's wife and his slave woman could both bear him children. If the man acknowledged paternity of the children of the slave woman during his life-time, then after his death all his children shared equally in his estate, except the firstborn son of the wife, who received a double share. If the man never admitted his paternity during his lifetime, then after his death only the children of his wife divided his estate. The slave woman and her children did, however, receive their freedom.[56]

Several laws about the purchase of slaves protected the buyer. If a slave man or woman contracted epilepsy within a month after purchase, the buyer was entitled to a refund of the full sale price. When claims arose pertaining to a slave recently purchased, the seller, not the buyer, of the slave was responsible for paying the claims.[57]

There were laws about the wives and children of soldiers taken as prisoners of war. If a soldier was captured in war, his son was responsible for his land and the performance of his feudal obligations. If the son was still a minor, possession of one-third of the field and orchard was given to his wife so that she might have sufficient income to raise the son.[58]

When a soldier was taken captive in war and had left his wife sufficient means to live, she was expected to remain faithful. This was symbolized by her not leaving his house or entering the house of another man. However, if the husband taken captive had not left his wife enough to live on in his house, she was free to enter the house of another man without any stigma. If she bore children to the second man, and her first husband eventually returned, the wife had to return to her first husband and leave the children with their father. However, if the husband had deserted his city, the wife was free to enter the house of another man; and if her first husband returned, she did not have to go back to him.[59]

Women Victims

The Laws of Hammurabi attempted to protect women against crimes, especially in situations where they were weak and vulnerable. The laws prescribed the death penalty for the crimes of rape and incest. For example, a man was caught forcibly raping a betrothed virgin who still lived in her father's house. Since the rapist was caught in the act, no trial was deemed necessary. The penalty for the rapist was death because the victim was betrothed. The text stated that "they" would put the rapist to death, without indicating the antecedent of "they." "They" generally denoted the state, but here it is unclear since the crime took place in the house of the victim's family. If it meant those who caught the rapist in the act, the girl's father, brothers, or betrothed, they could have exercised private jurisdiction and summarily executed the rapist in accord with Amorite tribal custom.[60] The woman was the victim of forcible rape, the loss of her virginity and her chance for a good marriage.

The Babylonians believed that certain crimes were so terrible that they created pollution and infuriated the gods. Pollution, which denoted impurity and separation from the gods, was a danger to the state and to its religion. Pollution was overcome through the annihilation of the source and the purification, by fire, water, or blood sacrifice, of what had been polluted—the state, the temple, persons, or objects. Offenders who committed crimes that engendered pollution were generally put to death by fire or water.

Incest was believed to cause dangerous pollution to the state, and therefore it was a public crime, punished by the state. The crime of incest was considered much more serious when the parties were related by blood than by marriage. The blood relationship between mother and son was considered more profound than that between father and daughter because it began nine months earlier inside the womb. Therefore the worst form of incest was believed to be sexual relations between a son and his mother. Both the mother and son were condemned to death by fire. This was considered an offense against the gods that defiled the land and could be purified only by fire. Both parties involved were polluted and had to be destroyed, even if the mother was completely innocent and had been taken by force. If a father had sex with his daughter, he was banished from the city. Exile included loss of his property, as well as the loss of protection of his person by the laws and might of his city. The male offender was considered the source of pollution, and his exile took the pollution away from the city.[61]

Incest between persons related by marriage was less serious. The laws generally punished the male perpetrator and treated the woman as a victim. For example, a father-in-law who was caught having sex with his daughter-in-law after her marriage to his son had been consummated was executed by the state by drowning. There were two capital offenses in this case: adultery, since the marriage had taken place, and incest, because the two parties were then related through marriage. However, if the marriage had not yet been consummated, the woman was not legally married and the same act was fornication or rape, not adultery or incest. No pollution was involved, and the penalty was a fine of thirty sheqels of silver and the return of the daughter-in-law's dowry. The woman was then free to marry a man of her own choice.[62] The law did not represent the reality of the woman's situation; she had become damaged merchandise. She was discarded and sent away with a small sum of money and her dowry. It would be very difficult for her to find a husband since she had lost her virginity. The woman victim suffered the consequences of the crime of the man.

When a son had sex with his stepmother after his father's death, even if she had been his father's chief wife and had borne him sons, the act was not considered incest because the parties were not related by blood or marriage. The offense therefore did not incur pollution. The act was not adultery, because the stepmother was no longer married. Thus no capital crimes had been committed. The penalty for the son was loss of his inheritance from his father's estate.[63] The stepmother was the victim of a sexual act that may have been imposed without her consent.

The fear of pollution is demonstrated in other laws. Women priests were not permitted to enter a tavern. The penalty for this offense was death by fire, since fire was the most potent instrument of purification and was also the necessary medium for sacrifices that placated the gods. The severity of the penalty suggests that entering a tavern implied contact with men and possible sexual relations, which would have destroyed the purity required for the women's duties as priests.[64] If a woman priest returned to the temple in an impure state, she could thereby pollute the other priests, religious officials, and the whole temple, making religious rites impossible until all the persons and the temple itself were purified. Interruption of the cult was perceived to be very dangerous to the well-being of the city.

The Laws of Hammurabi included many laws on assault and battery. There were laws that dealt explicitly with assaults and batteries committed against women. The offender was generally a member of the upper class, and the penalties were based on the social status of the victim. If a citizen struck the pregnant daughter of a citizen, causing her to have a miscarriage, the penalty was compensation for the life of the unborn child, which was given a monetary value of ten sheqels of silver. If the victim died, the offense became homicide, a crime of violence against a person. Since the offender and the legal victim, the father of the dead girl, were both of citizen class, the penalty was based on the principle of *talion:* a daughter's life for a daughter's life. Thus the offender's daughter, not the offender, was put to death. This was a form of vicarious punishment, whereby someone other than the offender suffered the punishment for the offender's crime. When the victim was of a lower class, such as the daughter of a commoner, the value of her lost fetus was five sheqels. If she herself died, the penalty was a fine of thirty sheqels of silver. If the victim was a slave woman, the value of her fetus was two sheqels, and if she died, her life was valued at twenty sheqels. The death of the daughter of a commoner was not treated as homicide; she had less value than the daughter of a citizen. The daughter of a slave was merely property, so her death was easily compensated by money paid to her owner.[65]

In other assault and battery laws, penalties based on *talion* were imposed when the offender and victim were of the same class. The victim's loss of an eye was punished by removing one eye of the offender, a broken bone by breaking the same bone of the offender, the loss of a tooth by the extraction of a tooth of the offender. When the victim was of a lower class or a slave, the penalties were fines. But when the victim was of a higher class, the offender was flogged in front of the assembly, thus publicly humiliated. A crime against a member of a higher class constituted a challenge to authority.[66]

Women were victims of false accusation of crimes. The Laws of Hammurabi strongly proscribed false accusation and made it a capital offense when the accusation was of a capital crime. When a citizen brought a charge of murder against another citizen but could not prove it, the accuser was put to death. If a citizen brought charges of sorcery or witchcraft against another person of the citizen class without sufficient evidence, the guilt of the accused was determined by the river ordeal. If the accused drowned, guilt was presumed to be proved and the estate of the accused went to the accuser. If the accused survived, he or she was presumed innocent. The false accuser was then put to death and the accuser's estate went to the falsely accused victim, leaving the accuser's wife and family destitute.

Women were likewise victims of perjured testimony. The penalties for both false accusation and perjury were the penalty of the case. Thus, the penalty for perjury in a capital case was death.[67] The operative principle was that the penalty for false accusation or perjury should be the same penalty to which the false accuser or false witness exposed the accused. These laws protected women who were falsely accused of crimes or prosecuted for crimes based on perjured testimony.

The Laws of Hammurabi offered some protection to women who were falsely accused of sexual offenses. If a person "pointed the finger"at a celibate woman priest or the wife of a citizen, thereby accusing the woman of prohibited sexual conduct, but was unable to prove his allegations against her, the false accuser was flogged in front of the judges and had half of his hair cut off.[68] A wife accused of adultery by her husband when there was no concrete evidence of her guilt was entitled to trial by oath. The Babylonians took the oath very seriously. Oaths were solemnly sworn before the statue or symbol of the god in the temple. By swearing the fearful oath, the woman proved her innocence and was permitted to return to her home. When someone made a public accusation of adultery against a wife without evidence, she had to undergo the river ordeal "for the sake of her husband," to restore his honor if she survived and proved her innocence.[69] In both cases the wife had not been caught in the act of adultery and the only evidence against her was the word of the accuser. It is significant that the word of an accuser alone was insufficient for the Old Babylonian judges to convict a woman in a capital case, yet the law placed the burden on the woman to prove her innocence by oath or by the river ordeal.

Robbery was the theft of property from a person with violence or threat of violence. As property owners, women could be victims of robbery. The penalty for robbery was death if the robber was caught in the act. When the robber was not caught in the act or in possession of the stolen property, the victim of the robbery had to swear an oath as to the value of his or her loss and the city district where the victim lived paid restitution to the victim. If the victim was killed during the robbery, thus making identification of the robber improbable, the city district paid sixty sheqels of silver to the victim's family.[70] State compensation of victims was a unique manifestation of Hammurabi's pursuit of justice for his people.

In ancient Babylonia, men, women, children, and slaves were held as pledges or security for debts. The Laws of Hammurabi made abuse of a pledge of the citizen class a criminal offense. If a person held as a pledge died a natural death, there was no penalty. But when a debtor proved in court that the pledge had died from beating or abuse at the hands of the creditor, and if the pledge was the debtor's son or daughter, then the son or daughter of the creditor was put to death. This law used the principle of *talion*, a son or daughter for a son or daughter, rather than punishment of the actual offender. If the pledge victim had been the debtor's slave, *talion* did not apply and the penalty was merely a fine.[71]

Women were incidental victims of the criminal penalties of their husbands and fathers. The primary obligation of a feudal tenant was to give military service to his king. The Laws of Hammurabi prescribed the death penalty for a man who refused to take part in a military campaign of his king or who hired a substitute to take his place. The person who informed on him was given his property.[72] The offender's widow and children were left destitute, without husband or father or property.

Women Offenders

In ancient Babylonia women committed many of the same crimes as men and incurred the same penalties. There were certain offenses, however, that could be committed only by women. Of the many capital crimes in the Laws of Hammurabi, the one considered most heinous of all was when a wife was involved with another man and caused her husband's death. The penalty for the woman's offense, which involved two capital crimes, murder and adultery, was death by impalement.[73] This crime was the ultimate challenge to the authority of men in marriage.

When a son committed incest with his mother, both parties were condemned to death by fire.[74] The law did not state that the woman was culpable. The son committed the crime, but both had incurred pollution. The pollution involved the state and thus required ritual purification by fire, which cleansed the city by incinerating the polluted pair. This is the only one of the laws against incest that penalized the woman.

Witchcraft was a crime more often attributed to women than to men. When a citizen accused a person of witchcraft without sufficient evidence to prove the charge, the court ordered the accused to undergo the river ordeal. If the accused drowned, the accuser was given the property of the accused. But if the accused survived, the false accuser was executed and his estate was given to the person falsely accused.[75]

The death penalty was imposed in some cases of adultery. The law in the case of a wife of a citizen caught in the act of committing adultery with another man had two parts. The first could use either private or state jurisdiction. The couple was caught in the act, so no trial was deemed necessary, and they were summarily bound and thrown into the river to drown. There was no mention of a trial or conviction. The plural "they" was used, and, although it designated the state in other laws, including execution by drowning, here "they" could have been male members of the victim's household. In the second part, the state was involved, but jurisdiction was hybrid. The husband still had jurisdiction over the sentencing of his wife. If he decided to spare his wife, then the king spared her accomplice. At this point, it is clear that the state was involved in the case. At the end of the law, an Amorite image was inserted: the husband was master of his wife as the king was master of his subject. In this law Hammurabi combined two traditions of jurisdiction over and punishment of adultery, which shows that the tension between Sumerian and Amorite law had not yet been resolved.[76]

When a husband had been taken as a prisoner of war, as long as he had left sufficient provisions for his wife, she was supposed to remain inside his house. If it was proved at trial that the wife of a prisoner of war had entered the house of another man, the state put her to death by drowning.[77] It was presumed, without evidence, that she left her house and entered the house of another man in order to commit adultery.

When a wife was imprudent, went out of her husband's house, squandered his property, and disparaged his reputation, the state executed her by throwing her into the river to drown.[78] This was a public offense against the honor and reputation of a husband, and Babylonian men valued their honor more than the lives of their wives. When honor was lost, the alternative was to live in shame, which Babylonian men found intolerable. Honor could be restored through the death of the person who had taken it away.

The property crime of theft covered a wide spectrum of offenses committed by women and men. Theft of property from the temple or the palace, which belonged to the gods or the king, was punished by death. The property that was located within the temple or palace was sacred. The crime was a sacrilege because it involved violation of a sacred place as well as theft of sacred property. Theft of animals or boats belonging to the temple or palace but kept outside was punished by a fine of thirty times the value of the property. In this case, neither the property nor its location was sacred, although the theft was still serious because the property belonged to the temple or the palace. If the thief did not have sufficient means to pay the fine, the penalty was death. The penalties were the same for anyone to whom the thief conveyed the stolen property.[79]

When a wife left her husband seeking divorce and took anything with her from his house, she could be prosecuted for the crime of theft. If she was convicted, the husband could either divorce her and make her leave his house with nothing, or refuse to divorce her and keep her in his house as a slave while he remarried. When a wife seeking divorce publicly repudiated her husband and accused him of denying her conjugal rights, the district authorities investigated the case. If they found the husband at fault, a divorce was granted and the ex-wife could take her dowry and return to her father's house. But if they found the wife at fault, she was executed by drowning.[80] The water that drowned the wife restored the husband's tarnished honor.

The crime of theft from a burning building was punished by death by fire, although it did not involve pollution. For example, when a house was on fire, a friend of the owner came to help put out the fire but instead stole his property. Since the offender did not help put out the fire because he or she was busy looting, the fire burned longer, causing more damage. Trial was not necessary because the offender was caught in the act. As punishment, the offender was summarily thrown into the fire.[81] In this case death by fire was not for purification, but was simply a convenient and appropriate way to execute punishment.

When a man or woman, without witnesses or a written contract, purchased property or received it for safekeeping from a minor or a slave, who could not legally own or transfer property, it was presumed that the buyer or receiver knew that the property was stolen. The act was considered theft, and the possessor of the stolen property was subject to the death penalty.[82]

Even lost property was protected by law, and false testimony claiming lost property was a serious offense. An example is the case of a person who claimed to have lost property and the property was found in the possession of another, who claimed to have bought it. When both the owner and the buyer produced witnesses who supported their claims, the judges examined the witnesses for both sides under oath and reviewed the evidence. If the alleged seller of the property to the possessor was identified and found guilty, the penalty for the seller was death, the lost property was restored to the owner, and the buyer took the price he or she had paid for the property from the condemned offender's estate. If the alleged buyer could not produce witnesses as to the purchase of the property and the owner could prove that the property was originally his or hers, then the alleged buyer was considered a thief and was sentenced to death and the property was returned to the owner. If the alleged owner of the property could produce no evidence that he or she owned it, the crime became false accusation of the capital crime of theft and the penalty for the alleged owner was death.[83]

The Laws of Hammurabi included a number of laws regulating offenses that occurred in trade, most of which imposed monetary penalties. The only trade laws that explicitly involved women were also the only trade laws that prescribed the death penalty. One subsection of a law punished dishonesty and immoral behavior in taverns. In ancient Babylonia, taverns were run by women, who prepared and sold liquor, and the reputation of such women was not the best. A woman wine seller who accepted silver in payment for liquor and used a false measure to weigh the silver, or one who reduced the value of the liquor by diluting it with water, was tried and, if convicted, sentenced to death. If criminals gathered in a tavern to conspire and the woman tavern keeper did not have them arrested and taken to the palace, then she herself was subject to the death penalty. This was a capital crime because of the danger to public security if taverns became the locus for criminal conspiracies.[84]

There were cases of women being accessories to crimes committed by slaves. Although it was the slave who committed the crime of escape, the law made giving aid to an escaped slave a very serious crime. Free persons who helped slaves escape or gave shelter to escaped slaves were severely punished. The Laws of Hammurabi prescribed death for any free man or woman who helped a slave belonging to the state or to an official escape through the city gate. A free man or woman who harbored a fugitive slave belonging to the state or to an official in his or her house and did not bring the slave forth when called on by the police was also subject to the death penalty. When a person found an escaped slave in open country, the person was obligated to return the slave to his or her owner and a reward was prescribed for so doing. If the slave refused to name his or her owner, the finder had to take the slave to the palace to ascertain the identity of the owner and then return the slave to the owner. However, if the finder kept the slave in his or her own house, and the slave was discovered in his or her possession, then the finder was subject to the death penalty. If the slave escaped from the finder, there was no penalty.[85] These laws made the rights of slave owners paramount. Citizens who infringed on those rights by harboring or otherwise helping a slave escape were punished by death. The slave was punished privately by his or her owner when returned.

When a slave woman challenged the authority of a free woman, it was perceived as a threat to the social structure supporting slavery. For example, a man married a woman priest and she provided him with a slave woman to bear him children. When the slave woman later tried to claim equality with the priest-wife because she had borne children, the priest-wife was not permitted to sell her, but could brand her, put the slave hairlock on her and relegate her to the slave quarters. If the slave woman had not borne any children, the wife could sell her.[86]

There is a single law about the profession of wet-nursing. A wet nurse had contracted to feed and take care of a child and the child died while in her care.

If she contracted to nurse the child of another family without telling them about the child who had died, the penalty was amputation of her breast.[87]

Repudiation of adoptive parents by adopted children was considered a very serious crime. If an adopted child said to the adoptive father or mother, "you are not my father," or "you are not my mother," the penalty was to cut out the child's tongue. If adopted children found out who and where their real parents were, and ran away to find them, the penalty was to pluck out their eyes.[88]

Punishment

In the earlier civilization of Sumer, most offenses had been punished by fines. The criminal penalties of Amorite tribal law influenced Old Babylonian law. Punishment of crimes was significantly harsher, and the death penalty was prescribed for many offenses and corporal mutilation was widely used. The principle of *talion* and the practice of vicarious punishment were employed.[89]

In the Laws of Hammurabi the death penalty was prescribed in thirty-six laws. Special forms of the death penalty were written in some of the laws. The most painful and cruel form of execution was death by impalement. It involved thrusting a long pole up through the body of the convicted offender and propping it upright so that the offender died slowly and painfully in public view. Impalement was prescribed only for women and only for one crime: when a wife who was in an adulterous relationship caused the death of her husband.[90] The extreme severity of this form of execution was determined by the nature of the offense. For an unfaithful wife to cause the death of her husband was the ultimate challenge to patriarchal authority over women in marriage. Although the penalty could not help this victim, through it other men took revenge through the intense suffering of the woman and retrieved their "honor" by the symbolic thrusting of a pole up through the woman's body.

Another harsh form of execution was burning the offender to death. Fire was the strongest means of purifying a city that had been polluted by a crime which offended the gods. Death by fire was prescribed for the crime of incest between a son and a mother and for a woman priest who entered a tavern. Both crimes engendered pollution, creating the danger to the state, the temple, and the people.[91]

Another type of execution that also effected purification was death by water. This was applied to certain forms of incest, which caused pollution and required ritual purification. The offenders were bound and thrown into the river. The use of binding made it impossible for the offender to turn over or swim away and distinguished drowning as capital punishment from accidental drowning in the river ordeal. Death by drowning was also used as a symbolic punishment for tavern keepers who watered the wine.[92]

Crimes committed by women that challenged the authority and honor of their husbands were also punished by death by drowning. For example, when the wife of a prisoner of war, who had left sufficient provisions for his wife and family, entered the house of another man, adultery was presumed, and the husband was dishonored. When a wife squandered her husband's possessions and publicly disparaged his name and reputation, she destroyed his honor. After trial and conviction, these crimes were punished by death by drowning.[93] The offender who had shamed her husband by public derision or by committing adultery was eliminated by water. Water cleansed the husband from shame and restored his tarnished honor.

Many laws prescribed the death penalty without indicating the method of execution. Some of these laws illustrate the transitional process of integrating Sumerian written law and Amorite customary law. Laws which dealt with the capital crimes of rape, adultery, kidnapping, and robbery did not mention trial or conviction when the offender was caught in the act, but simply stated that the offender was put to death. These laws reflect tribal customary laws, which permitted private jurisdiction and summary execution by the victim's kin. However, in other laws on rape and adultery, the use of the plural "they" for the disposition of the offenders shows that more people than just the representative of the family of the victim were involved. In laws concerning both rape and adultery, the two people were caught in the act and neither law made mention of trial. Summary execution was permitted, although the agent was plural: "they shall bind them and throw them into the water," and "they shall seize him lying with her, that man shall be killed." The state was generally the antecedent of "they" in such laws. However, the adultery law stated that the husband could rescind the death penalty for his wife, in which case the king would do the same for the male offender.[94] These laws illustrate the coexistence of two legal traditions for the punishment of adultery: private summary execution by the husband as in tribal custom and state jurisdiction, involving courts and due process. The Old Babylonian state was increasing its jurisdiction over crimes that affected the well-being of families and thereby also of the state.

Some capital crimes specifically involved the state. Women tavern keepers who allowed criminals to gather in their inns and did not report them to the authorities were executed by the state. Citizens who helped slaves escape or harbored fugitive slaves were put to death.[95] The first crime was a threat to state security. The second was a threat to the importance of slavery in the economic order. Trial, conviction, and punishment of both crimes were administered by the state.

False accusation and perjury in capital cases were punished by the penalty of the case, which was death. False accusation of a crime bearing a penalty of corporal punishment or a fine was punished by the same corporal punishment or fine prescribed for the crime falsely alleged.[96] The concept of equity in prescribing the penalty of the case for false accusers was introduced by the Sumerians.

The property crimes of theft and possession and sale of stolen or lost property were sometimes punished by death or corporal mutilation, which reflected Amorite custom. Other laws prescribed restitution and fines for theft offenses, as in Sumerian law. In the Laws of Hammurabi, the death penalty was reserved for the two most serious types of theft: of sacred objects from the temple or of royal property from the palace. These acts also constituted the capital crimes of sacrilege and treason.[97] Most other cases of simple theft were punished by restitution and fines.

The Laws of Hammurabi used corporal mutilation in many of its laws, which was rare in ancient Near Eastern law before this time.[98] In the Laws of Hammurabi corporal mutilation was administered under three principles: functionality, *talion,* and retribution.

Under the principle of functionality, professional doctors, barbers, and wet nurses were expected to perform their work lawfully and professionally. A surgeon who performed major surgery on a citizen causing the death or blindness of the patient was punished by the amputation of his hand. Thenceforth it was much more difficult for the physician to perform surgery, and patients who noted the missing hand would likely seek another surgeon. If it happened twice, the doctor could never practice surgery again. A barber who removed a slave hairlock without authorization had his hand cut off, which would similarly limit his ability to work as a barber. A wet nurse, who had a child die while in her care and took another nursing position without informing the parents about the death, was punished by the amputation of her breast.[99] This limited her ability to nurse children and reduced the number of families who would hire her. If a second child died in her care and her remaining breast was cut off, she was permanently excluded from her profession.

The principle of functionality was used in the prescription of corporal mutilation for other crimes, including those of children. If a child struck his father or mother, the punishment was to cut off his or her hand. This would make it more difficult for the child to strike a parent or anyone else in the future. If an adopted child said to his or her adoptive parents, "you are not my father," or "you are not my mother," they could cut out the child's tongue, ensuring that neither these words or any other words could be repeated. If a child repudiated his or her adoptive parents and left to find his or her birth parents, the adoptive parents could "pluck out" his or her eye, making it more difficult for the child to find anyone in the future.[100] Functional corporal mutilation did prevent recidivism.

The second operative principle for corporal mutilation was the rule of *talion*, an eye for an eye, a primitive attempt at equity by equivalence in punishment. It was only applied when the offender and the victim were of both of the citizen class. When a citizen put out the eye of another citizen, the penalty for the offender was the loss of an eye. When a citizen broke the bone of another citizen, the penalty was to break the same bone of the attacker. *Talion* limited the penalty through proportionality. If the offense was a broken bone, the punishment could not be blinding or death. On the other hand, unless the victim and the offender were the same in all categories, including gender, age, and relationship, the application of *talion* often led to vicarious punishment of the innocent. When a citizen struck the daughter of a citizen, causing miscarriage and death, the punishment was not the death of the guilty offender, but the death of his innocent daughter. Thus, the principle of *talion* resulted in the vicarious punishment of innocent women for the crimes of men. If a builder did substandard work on a house, resulting in the collapse of the house and the death of the owner, the builder was put to death. The punishment was the death of a citizen for the death of a citizen. But if the same negligent construction caused the death of the owner's son, the penalty was the death of the builder's son, under *talion,* the death of a son for the death of a son.[101] Thus, the principle of *talion* limited the penalty so that it could not be greater than the injury inflicted, but at the same time it caused the vicarious punishment of innocent persons.

Vicarious punishment was tolerated in a society that regarded men as full persons and citizens and relegated wives and daughters to the category of the property of men. An offender could be punished for a crime by having to give up his wife or child, ox or a slave. Such penalties were imposed on male offenders; there is no evidence of any law that required a woman offender to give up her husband.

The penalty for certain offenses was determined by the social class of the victim. Offenses committed against persons of the upper class received greater penalties and were punished in public. *Talion* was used only when the offender and victim were of the same social class. When offenders committed the same offense against victims of a lower class, the penalties were merely fines.

Challenges to the authority of those of higher station received severe capital and corporal penalties as retribution. Capital punishment was used when wives challenged the authority of their husbands, because this offense jeopardized the authority of all husbands over their wives. The worst was the adulterous wife who had her husband killed; she was punished by death by impalement. When a wife challenged the authority of her husband by committing adultery or publicly disparaging his reputation, it tarnished his honor, which was restored by her obliteration through death by drowning.

The act of "striking the cheek" of a person of higher status challenged the victim's honor and authority. When a citizen struck the cheek of a citizen of higher rank, the penalty was flogging: sixty lashes with an ox whip in the public assembly. If a citizen or commoner struck the cheek of someone of the same rank, the penalty was a fine. When a slave struck the cheek of a citizen, the penalty was the amputation of one ear. The act of striking the cheek of a person of higher authority was a challenge to that person's authority and caused the person public humiliation and loss of honor. The penalty for a slave who challenged the authority of her or his owner physically or verbally was amputation of an ear, because the act shamed the owner and challenged the institution of slavery. The severity and public nature of the corporal penalties shamed the offender and helped restore the honor of the victim.[102]

The prominent use of capital punishment, corporal punishment, corporal mutilation, *talion,* and vicarious punishment in the Laws of Hammurabi demonstrates the influence of Amorite customary law. The harsh forms of execution and corporal mutilation and the use of corporal and vicarious punishment in the Laws of Hammurabi were not found in Sumerian law. Capital and corporal penalties provided simple and immediate resolution of criminal cases, which was necessary in tribal milieux. Although Babylonia became an urban empire, Amorite tribal customs of capital and corporal penalties, *talion,* and vicarious punishment became standard in ancient Mesopotamian law.

Summary: The Laws of Hammurabi

The Laws of Hammurabi are the longest and most detailed collection of laws yet discovered from the ancient Near East. The laws show two strains of influence: the high urban civilization and laws of Sumer and the tribal traditions and customary laws of the Amorites, who at this time ruled Babylonia and most of the other city-states of Mesopotamia. Hammurabi himself was the son of an Amorite, although his highest articulated goal, the pursuit of justice for all people, including the poor and the weak, reflected Sumerian influence and values.

Under the Laws of Hammurabi, women retained some of the rights they had had under Sumerian law. Monogamy was the rule, and exceptions were limited. Marriage required marriage gifts, a dowry, and a written contract. Women could be free of obligation for their husbands' premarital debts by inserting a clause to this effect in the marriage contract. Husbands made *inter vivos* gifts of property to their wives by sealed document. Women inherited property from their husbands' estates and owned nonfeudal property in land. Women priests owned and inherited nonfeudal property and possessed feudal property. Husbands could divorce, but had to return the dowry and give their ex-wives a settlement, which, if there were children, was half of the husband's estate. When a woman attempted to initiate divorce, her own character was put on trial and, unless she was found above reproach, she was put to death.

Crimes committed against women, such as rape, robbery, the killing of a pledge, false accusation, and perjury, incurred the punishment of death. Crimes committed by women, including certain types of theft and offenses that challenged male authority, were also punished by death.

The expansion of the death penalty, the use of corporal punishment and many forms of corporal mutilation, the principle of *talion,* and vicarious punishment in the Laws of Hammurabi are evidence of the influence of Amorite customary law. So too were the focus on illicit sexual acts and female gender as sources of impurity and pollution. After Amorite tribes settled in the city-states of Mesopotamia, they assimilated the law and culture of the existing urban civilization to varied degrees. Yet even in the urban city-states of southern Mesopotamia their memory of tribal customs was still operative. King Hammurabi himself was a product of both the assimilation and the memory.

THE EDICT OF KING AMMISADUQA

Ammisaduqa was the tenth king of the Old Babylonian dynasty. He ruled for twenty years during the seventeenth century BCE. It was customary among Sumerian and Old Babylonian kings to publish an edict at the beginning of their reigns and some kings issued subsequent edicts at seven-year intervals. Such edicts, which declared the remission of debts, obligations, and taxes, were called "acts of justice" and had the force of law.[103]

Debt remission affected business women in two ways. When women tavern keepers were behind in their payment of taxes to the king, the tax collector could not sue for the arrears. On the other hand, if women tavern keepers had sold beer or barley on credit, they could not collect what was owed.[104]

The edict decreed the release of citizens of dependent cities who had given themselves, their wives, or their children to creditors as pledges for loans or who had been seized and held in debt servitude by creditors because of debt foreclosure. Women slaves who had been born into slavery in the same dependent cities, whether sold, pledged, or held in debt servitude, were not released by the edict.[105]

Although the edict dealt primarily with debt remission, there were a few provisions that were phrased as laws and prescribed criminal penalties.[106] One such law dealt with the crime of fraud. A woman tavern keeper or a merchant who used false weights or measures was subject to the penalty of death.[107] The reliability of weights and measures was essential to the trade of the empire.

This brief document is an example of decrees that were periodically issued by Old Babylonian kings. The effect on women was generally economic, although this decree contained a capital law specifically affecting women tavern keepers.

OLD BABYLONIAN DOCUMENTS AND INSCRIPTIONS

Tens of thousands of documents have survived from the Old Babylonian period, most from the palace and temple archives. There were also court records, archives of a few wealthy families, contracts, letters, rituals, and hymns.

Babylonian documents contain information on the administration of criminal justice. The prosecution of an alleged offender began with the issuance of an arrest warrant. King Hammurabi wrote letters and sent arrest warrants to his officials in various parts of the empire. A warrant contained the name and occupation of the alleged offender, but generally did not state the crime of which he or she was accused. An arrest involved two officials, one to identify the accused, the other to make the arrest and transport the accused to the king. When the king's court accepted a civil case, the king's runner was sent to summon the parties and witnesses.[108]

There were both city judges and royal judges. Judges were trained in the scribal schools. Two qualifications for judges were wealth and the respect of the people. Wealth was believed to prevent temptation to bribery. Court was held in the primary temple of a city. Cases were judged by panels of judges. The panels consisted of four judges before Hammurabi. During his reign there were five to ten judges on a panel. Sometimes there were judges from two or more cities on a panel in cases concerning intercity questions such as citizenship, slaves, and property of murder victims. The judges read evidentiary documents and heard testimony of witnesses. They also required fearful oaths before the gods, which eliminated much false accusation and perjury. The temple was the location of the symbols of the gods and was thus the most convenient place for oaths. The courts had scribes to record trials and decisions.[109]

Old Babylonian kings and judges shared information on cases. The king exercised supervision of courts in other cities of the empire. Sometimes a king ordered a case to be tried before him in Babylon. For example, a king wrote to the judges of Sippar that he was ordering the removal of a case about an escaped slave woman to Babylon. When an official informed him of a serious crime, such as bribery, King Hammurabi instructed the local authorities to investigate the case, and, if they found that bribery had occurred, to send the accused, the witnesses, and the evidence to him and he would try the case. At other times, kings delegated cases to local officials.[110]

King Hammurabi wrote to the mayor of a town, asking him to hear a case about a pledge, to examine the case and the parties, and to give judgment "according to the yoke." A judgment made by the judges of Babylon stated that it was according to the "ordinances of the king."[111] The meaning of "yoke" is unclear; it could designate written laws or criminal laws that prescribed harsh forms of punishment.

There were two types of appeal. In one the local court refused to hear the case at all; the other was after the trial and verdict in the lower court. In an example of the first type, two men appealed to the king that their brother had been illegally held as pledge for two years. During that time they had filed petitions in their city court but the judges had done nothing. The king ordered the judges of the city court to send the pledge and the witnesses to Babylon, so that he could judge the case. In the early years of the dynasty, all parties had the right to appeal the verdict of a local court to the king in Babylon. Later, as the volume of cases and appeals increased, kings limited their jurisdiction to the most important cases, such as those that involved pollution and national security.[112]

Status of Women

In the Old Babylonian empire, kings wrote detailed chronicles about buildings, temples, and fortifications they built, canals they dug, and wars they won. But there was no mention of women in these chronicles, not even of the wives of the kings. Old Babylonian women did not hold political office or high priesthoods.

Other documents reveal that Old Babylonian kings used marriage to cement political alliances. The second king of the dynasty married his daughter to the king of Uruk. King Hammurabi married his daughter to the king of Eshnunna. An early king of Eshnunna had married the daughter of an Amorite sheikh. He married his daughter Mekubi to the king of Elam, where she built a temple and was called a great queen.[113]

The wives of kings and governors did not have official status or authority, but they did have some influence. In one case, for example, two men wrote a petition to Akhatum, the wife of a provincial governor, asking her to plead with her husband and son for their pardon. One king of Eshnunna gave a seal to his wife, and two kings gave seals to their daughters, Mekubi and Inibshina. This indicates that in Eshnunna, some royal women did transact business.[114]

During the Old Babylonian period, men and women wrote thousands of letters, many of which have survived, at least in fragments. These letters open a window into the daily lives of people in ancient Babylonia. Letters were written by women, to women, and about women. Literate women wrote them themselves; nonliterate women hired a scribe, who might be a woman. Old

Babylonian women also wrote contracts, were parties to contracts, and signed and witnessed contracts. Court records provide information about women victims and offenders.[115]

The question of the literacy of women is very important in determining their status. One Old Babylonian woman, Beltiremenni, was a scribal scholar who wrote a vocabulary text. In general, only men attended scribal schools, but daughters of scribes learned the profession from their fathers.[116]

Women worked for the palace and for temples as administrators of manufacturing and sheep raising. Women also worked as artisans, spinners, weavers, fullers, millers, bakers, tavern keepers, and scribes. Poor women gleaned barley in the fields. Women owned and possessed real property and rented property to tenants.[117]

In an Old Babylonian hymn, a goddess recounted the stages of a woman's life: "I am daughter, I am bride, I am spouse, I am housekeeper." The stage of daughter lasted all too briefly. Fathers sometimes gave gifts to their daughters and recorded the donation in writing. One father gave his daughter Ninkuzu a house lot. The ruler of Eshnunna gave his daughter Inibshina a duck weight on which the donation was inscribed.[118]

In the Old Babylonian period, the majority of women were married, including women priests. Marriage required marriage gifts from the suitor's family, a dowry from the bride's family, and a marriage contract. Married women were protected by their dowries and marriage contracts. Old Babylonian marriage contracts generally specified the content of the dowry and the conditions for divorce, which could differ greatly from one contract to another. In one marriage contract, the father of the bride gave his daughter, Sabitum, a dowry consisting of "two beds, two chairs, one table, two baskets, one millstone, one mortar, one measure, and one grinding bowl." The father had received marriage gifts of ten sheqels of silver, which he gave to Sabitum, tying it into the hem of her garment. This signified that the principle sum ultimately belonged to her, although her husband could use it. The second part of the contract concerned divorce. If Sabitum ever tried to initiate divorce, she would be bound and thrown into the river to drown. If her husband initiated divorce, he had to give her twenty sheqels of silver. Sabitum's brother represented her, swearing assent to the contract.[119] This contract shows that women owned personal property, that their fathers sometimes gave them the marriage gifts instead of keeping them for themselves, and that marriage contracts could require husbands to compensate ex-wives in divorce, although wives could be executed if they initiated divorce. It also shows that men were representing women in some legal transactions.

Another Old Babylonian marriage contract sets forth the conditions for the marriage of the male high priest. The bride, Amasukkal, brought nineteen sheqels of silver as a dowry. If her husband later divorced her by saying, "you are no longer my wife," he had to return the silver of her dowry in full and pay her an additional thirty sheqels compensation. However, if the wife initiated divorce by saying, "you are no longer my husband," she forfeited her dowry and had to pay her husband thirty sheqels of silver. The contract was a mutual agreement, sworn to by both parties, signed, witnessed by eight men and two women, notarized, and twice sealed.[120] In the first marriage contract, the wife could not initiate divorce under penalty of death. In the second, the wife could initiate divorce, although she forfeited her dowry and had to pay compensation to her husband. In the second contract the penalties for divorce were almost identical for both spouses.

There is one document from Old Babylonian Ur that attests to polygyny. A woman, Mattu, adopted a girl, whom she gave to her husband as a secondary wife. The contract stated that the husband had to remain married to both of them or divorce both of them.[121]

Children were required to support their parents in old age, especially when their mothers did not inherit. Support generally consisted of at least a certain quantity of barley each month, several liters of oil, and enough wool to make one garment each year. Sons who divided the support likewise divided the inheritance. Mothers and daughters had possession of the family home and the right to receive support until death or marriage. Sometimes sons provided female slaves to their mothers for physical care or male slaves who were put out to work to earn the cost of support for the parents. Many such slaves were freed after the parent died. When both parents died, their sons had the legal duty to support their unmarried sisters.[122]

Women wrote many letters about the support men were legally obligated to send them, especially letters of complaint when the rations were not received, were insufficient, or were of poor quality or spoiled. One woman wrote a letter complaining about the quality of the sesame oil she had received and told her agent to be present when they were extracting the oil to make sure she got the best quality. The support rations consisted of oil, barley or flour, beer, wool, and sometimes a little money. Women also asked for other things, such as baskets, a copper kettle, and a measure. One woman asked for a slave girl to grind her flour and a slave boy to wash her feet. Rations were generally transported by riverboat and some were delivered by women. The requests of women for their rations often were ignored or shipments were delayed or stolen en route, so that the women were left with little or no food. Men wrote letters ordering rations to be sent to women in need.[123]

When a husband died with no adult male children, his widow became head of his household. An Old Babylonian will made the decedent's widow the head, literally the "father," of the household. If the son of her late husband repudiated her, the will gave her the authority to disinherit him by a symbolic slap on the cheek and by putting him out of the house. If the widow chose to leave, she could not take anything with her but was free to go wherever she wanted and to remarry. She had only to put her cloak on the stool and leave the house. The leaving of the cloak was a public act demonstrating that the widow took nothing with her.[124]

Adoptions were formalized by contract. Some contracts added penalties to enforce a good relationship between parents and children. According to one such contract, if the father and the mother ever said to their adopted son that he was not their son, they would forfeit their house and possessions. If the son ever said to the adoptive father and mother that they were not his real father and mother, they could shave his hair and sell him into slavery.[125] It is significant that both clauses mention both the father and the mother. The mother in this contract was named Alitum.

Adoption was often used to provide someone to support and care for a childless woman or man in old age. In return, the adopted person inherited the estate of the adoptive parent. When married couples adopted, the names of the wives were generally given: Elmeshum, Kuritum, Tappiya, Beltiya, Akhatum. A man and his wife, Mukhadditum, adopted a man as their son. The contract of adoption specified that the adopted son had to provide them with 360 liters of barley, six liters of sesame oil, three kilograms of wool, and one half sheqel of silver each year, as long as they lived. After both had died, the adopted son would inherit their house, orchards, slaves, prebends, and all other possessions. Adoption contracts generally contained lists of the quantities of barley, oil, and wool to be provided for support and the obligation of respect to be shown at all times to the adoptive parent. If the adopted person did not support or show respect to his or her adoptive parent, according to the terms of the contract, he or she would not inherit the neglected parent's estate. The Old Babylonians believed that true respect for parents was impossible without supporting their needs. Failure to support destroyed the parent–child relationship, and the "unnatural" child therefore could not inherit.[126]

Another means of support was through prostitution. Shallurtum bought a girl, Apirtum, from her father and her mother, Ribatum. The contract stated that Apirtum would be made a prostitute and from her earnings provide for Shallurtum, her adoptive mother. If Apirtum should ever say to Shallurtum, "you are not my mother," she could be sold into slavery. If Shallurtum said Apirtum was not her daughter, she would be fined ten sheqels.[127]

Adoption was also used in marriages when one spouse already had children from a previous marriage. The other spouse then adopted the children as his or her own. For example, a man married Salkala and adopted her three children. If he ever repudiated her, he had to pay twenty sheqels. If she and the children repudiated him, they would be sold. Naramtum adopted her husband's three sons. The husband of Mukhadditum adopted her three sons.[128]

Slave women and men were objects of property, not legal persons. In sales, they were categorized with oxen and donkeys. Slaves were named as assets of estates. There were frequent disputes over ownership of slaves. They were bought and sold, given as gifts, and bequeathed in wills throughout Babylonia. Men wrote letters to agents in other cities to buy slave girls. Slaves were transported from one city to another by boat, yoked together, under guard. A document from the Old Babylonian period illustrates the sale of a slave woman. The price of the slave woman, named Ina-Eulmashbanat, was fifty-one and two-thirds sheqels of silver. Three days were allowed from the date of sale for examination of the slave woman and one month to ascertain that she did not have epilepsy. Estate inventories listed male and female slaves by name; for example, two slave women were named Ilidumqi and Ali'abusha.[129]

The city and cloister of Sippar are well documented and serve as a microcosm of the lives of women, especially women priests, in the Old Babylonian period. Sippar consisted of three parts: the city, the temple compound, and the cloister of women priests. After Babylon took control of Sippar, King Hammurabi shifted the administration of the city to the kings in Babylon, who ruled it directly for two centuries. Thenceforth Sippar had no king, no palace, and no army of its own. Instead it had a mayor, an overseer of merchants, and an assembly.[130]

The archives of one family of Sippar document seven generations. In the Old Babylonian period, men of the third through seventh generations were lamentation singers in the temple. The women were just as active in the temple and cloister. Waqartum, of the third generation, and Eli-eressa and Inim-Aya, of the fifth generation, were *naditu* priests of Shamash in the cloister. Nakkartum, of the fifth generation, and Lamassani, of the seventh generation, were *naditu* priests of Marduk. A daughter-in-law of the sixth generation, Ilshakhegalli, was a *qadishtu*. The women sealed documents when they sold houses and land, and they were witnesses to contracts in which the parties were women.[131]

Sippar had both city and royal judges. Disputes between women priests of the cloister were heard by royal judges. The court had scribes to record the proceedings. Most were men, but there was at least one woman scribe, Inanna-amamu, the daughter of a judicial scribe. If the parties were not satisfied with the judgment of the local court, they could appeal to the king.[132]

The temple of Shamash was the most prominent building in Sippar, and the chief administrator of the temple was a male priest. There were male overseers who kept records of everything that went into and came out of the temple compound and a male steward who oversaw the agricultural business of the temple. Male priests served in the temple. They could own property, and some were quite wealthy. They could marry and have children, and sometimes their sons and daughters became priests. One male priest gave his daughter, a *naditu* priest, four fields and a house as a gift. There were men and women singers and musicians in the temple and an overseer of the women who played musical instruments. The wives of male priests and of other male temple functionaries also served the goddess in the temple. The wives were not wealthy and sometimes borrowed barley or money from the women priests of the cloister. The income of the temple was derived from sheep raising, agriculture, lease of fields, interest on loans, payments for religious rites, and donations.[133]

The cloister of Sippar, which flourished during the Old Babylonian period, was a place of security for women *naditu* priests and women holding other religious offices. It was surrounded by a wall, enclosing the houses of the women priests and their employees, the administration building, and a granary. There were generally about two hundred celibate *naditu* priests of Shamash living in the cloister at a given time. The women priests who lived there were not poor; many owned houses, land, and slaves.[134] Only women could be *naditu* priests. Young women entered the cloister to become *naditu* priests at the age for marriage and remained there for life. The entrance requirements resembled those for marriage: the cloister gave the woman's family "marriage gifts," and the families of the young women provided them with dowries, which often included houses and land.[135]

The *naditu* priests of Shamash did not marry or have children. The word *naditu* means "fallow," like a field unplowed, kept fallow for the plough of the gods. Most were from royal or upper-class families. Some were daughters or sisters of kings. The first royal *naditu* may have been Aya-latum, daughter of King Sumulael. Women priests often adopted names of gods. There were a limited number of such names, so many women in the cloister and in temples had the same names. Such women could be distinguished by the name of their father, which was often included on documents and seals. There were at least three *naditu* priests named Iltani: the sister of King Hammurabi, the daughter of King Sin-muballit, and the sister of King Ammiditana. Others were daughters of palace or temple officials. They lived in their own houses and were permitted to visit with their families. They performed religious rites, including the funeral rites for their parents, and also conducted business in real estate, textile manufacture, and agriculture. *Naditu* priests of Shamash had to provide animals for sacrifice and bread and beer for festivals. Iltani, the *naditu* priest sister of King Hammurabi, made offerings of date cakes at festivals.[136]

Naditu priests bought, owned, inherited, sold, and leased houses and land. The majority of extant contracts for the sale and lease of real property in Sippar named women priests as the buyers or lessors. For example, *naditu* priests of Shamash were sixty-six of ninety-seven documented buyers of fields. *Naditu* priests named Iltani, Lamassi, and Mannashi bought houses and fields, and a *naditu* priest named Khuzalatum bought ten fields, as well as houses, plots of land, and threshing floors. Some *naditu* priests bought land next to land owned by their families. A *naditu* priest named Lamassi bought two properties adjacent to her family estate, thereby enlarging it and helping to keep it intact.[137] Sometimes *naditu* priests were given properties by their fathers. The father of one *naditu* priest gave her a large house, a tavern, and several shops. Another father gave his *naditu* daughter a house, half of a shop, and half of a tavern, which was the inheritance of her mother. The *naditu* priests could not personally administer a tavern or a shop, so they leased them to tenants. Another father gave his *naditu* daughter an orchard and a tower.[138]

Women priests owned and used personal seals. Women who sold property sealed the contracts of sale, whereas the buyers or beneficiaries of contracts did not. For example, Eli-eressa, a *naditu* of Shamash, sealed the contract when she sold a house.[139]

Women priests were the owners of the properties in the majority of extant lease contracts from Sippar. They owned and rented out houses and fields. Lease contracts were written down, dated, and signed by multiple witnesses. A *naditu* named Ribatum owned and leased several houses and a shop. The *naditu* Taribatum, daughter of the king of Larsa, rented out parts of her house and leased her field. The owners of leased fields received one-third of the produce of the field, unless specified otherwise by contract. The *naditu* Mellatum rented her field to a scribe, who paid one sheqel of silver in advance, the rest to be paid in grain after the harvest. Iltani, sister of King Hammurabi, leased her orchard for payment of back taxes and leased her field to a scribe.[140]

The cloister was administered by the overseer of the *naditu* priests. In the early Old Babylonian period, this office was held by *naditu* women, but later overseers were men. Women scribes lived and worked in the cloister. Some were themselves *naditu* priests, and some were daughters of male temple scribes. The cloister had women servants, weavers, and cooks, but men were in charge of the agricultural workers, both free and slave.[141]

Women holding other religious offices also lived within the cloister. The *ugbabtu* was another type of woman priest. They too could own and inherit property. One *ugbabtu* priest, Yakhilatum, inherited two orchards and a field. Another *ugbabtu*, Sippiritim, had a sister, Damiqtum, and a niece, Munawwir-tum, both of whom were *naditu* priests of Shamash. There were other women who lived within the cloister and performed religious functions, including the ritual to undo witchcraft.[142]

Celibate women who lived in cloisters had no one to care for them in old age. It was common for such women to adopt an heir, sometimes a niece, often another woman holding religious office. After a formal adoption by written contract, the two were legally related as mother and daughter. The daughter then had the legal obligation to support her "mother" and to provide her rations during her lifetime. The *naditu* priest Erishti-Aya adopted a slave woman, Surratum, and her infant daughter, purifying them in the rite of adoption. After the death of Erishti-Aya, Surratum and her daughter were free and no family member of Erishti-Aya could make any claim against them.[143] The *naditu* Belessunu was supporter and heir for two other women priests, Eli-eressa and Iltani. Beltani, heir of another *naditu*, acquired her estate after she paid its debts. A *naditu* priest named Amat–Shamash adopted four other *naditu* women as daughters and heirs. *Naditu* priests who supported and inherited from several other *naditu* priests could become very wealthy, but they also had to be relatively wealthy in the first place to provide support to several *naditu* "mothers." *Naditu* priests also inherited property from their families. They bequeathed property to other *naditu* priests or to family members by will.[144]

The god of Sippar and its temple was Shamash, the sun god, and the god of Babylon was Marduk. There were two types of *naditu* priests: those of Shamash, who were celibate and lived in the cloister, and those of Marduk, who could marry and did not live in the cloister. The *naditu* of Shamash ranked higher than the *naditu* of Marduk.[145]

King Hammurabi brought the cult of Marduk to Sippar. Before Hammurabi there were *naditu* priests of Marduk in Babylon. *Naditu* priests of Marduk owned land and slaves. The first known *naditu* priest of Marduk in Sippar, Khaliyatum, owned a house, a field, and a fig orchard. Another *naditu* priest of Marduk, Arnabum, bought a field. Sometimes sisters or other members of the same family became *naditu* priests of Shamash and *naditu* priests of Marduk. Arnabum, a *naditu* priest of Marduk, had a sister, an aunt, and a cousin who were *naditu* priests of Shamash.[146]

Naditu priests of Marduk were permitted to marry but not to have children. Parents gave their priest daughters large dowries when they married. In one case, the dowry of Liwir-Esagila, a *naditu* of Marduk, on her marriage to a priest of Ishtar, consisted of two slave girls, money, jewelry, clothes, furniture, dishes, pots, two cows, thirty sheep, and many other things.[147] Marriage contracts indicated that these marriages were far from conventional. Although they lived in their husbands' households, the priest-wives had to spend a significant amount of time in the temple. Since *naditu* priests of Marduk were not permitted to bear children, they provided children to their husbands by adoption or by giving them slave women or low-level religious officiants as secondary wives. One couple had three marriage contracts. The first simply stated that the husband had to pay thirty sheqels of silver if he divorced Taramsagila, his priest-wife. The second contract added a woman named Iltani as a second, but inferior, wife. Iltani had to wash the feet of Taramsagila and carry her chair to the temple of Marduk. The third contract indicated that Iltani had been adopted by Taramsagila's father, making them sisters, and stated that the children of Iltani would belong to both. If Iltani denied that

Taramsagila was her sister, she could be sold into slavery. Another *naditu* priest of Marduk, Akhatum, adopted the slave girl of her sister Sanakratum, a *naditu* priest of Shamash, and gave the slave girl to her husband. Akhassunu, a *naditu* priest of Marduk, adopted a slave girl to serve her and to bear children for her husband. If the girl ceased to please Akhassunu, she could sell her.[148]

Other women held religious offices and lived outside the cloister. *Kulmashitu* women sang hymns during religious rituals. The *kulmashitu* could marry, although most did not. Some *kulmashitu* women were also *naditu* priests of Marduk. Other *kulmashitu* had sisters who were *naditu* priests of Shamash. Erishti-Shamash was a *naditu* priest of Shamash, and her younger sister, Beltani, was a *kulmashitu*. Beltani was wealthy and left an estate of three slave girls, a house, and a number of fields.[149]

Qadishtu women were not cloistered. They could marry and have children, but many did not. They were generally less wealthy than the *naditu* priests and received smaller dowries from their families. Some owned a house or a field; others rented houses from *naditu* priests.[150]

The *shugitu* women were often younger sisters or adopted sisters of *naditu* priests of Marduk. They served as secondary wives to bear children to the husbands of *naditu* priests of Marduk. The *shugitu* Damiqtum received a dowry from her parents, consisting of one slave girl, millstones, furniture, and household utensils. A diviner gave his *shugitu* wife, Khuggultum, two slave girls, millstones, and furniture. Her estate passed to her sons after her death.[151]

Women priests were wealthy, independent, and held in high esteem in Old Babylonia. Women captives of war were used for slave labor in the palace or temple. Women priests in captured cities fared considerably better than other captive women. For example, when King Hammurabi conquered a city, he sent the statue and priestesses of the god or goddess of the city back to Babylon. The "goddess" was placed in a boat made into a shrine. The captive women priests followed in other boats with ample provisions.[152]

In the north there were two kingdoms, Mari and Karana. The archives of these kingdoms have yielded numerous documents about women, many of which were written by women. During the first four decades of the eighteenth century, the city-states of the north, including Eshnunna, Asshur, Mari, and Karana, were ruled by Amorite kings. Many Amorite tribes shared genealogy and traditions and made political and military alliances with one another, but there were fundamental differences among them as well. By 1760, all were under Babylonian rule. Mari had been an ally of King Hammurabi, although he later conquered and destroyed it. Karana was a vassal kingdom of the Old Babylonian empire, which paid tribute to Hammurabi. In both, geographical distance diminished the influence of Old Babylonian law. Both were ruled by Amorite kings, but of different tribes, which had very different customary law.[153]

Mari was located on the Euphrates River in northern Mesopotamia at an important crossroads of major trade routes between the east and the Mediterranean. In the third millennium women of Mari were depicted in statues, reliefs, and mosaics of queens, women priests, and women spinners and weavers.[154] In the second millennium, Mari was ruled by its own Amorite dynasty, which was deposed by another Amorite king of the Asshur region, Shamshi-Adad I, after whose death, Zimri-Lim, the son of the former king of the Mari dynasty, returned as king of Mari.[155] The lives of royal and upper-class women in the kingdom of Mari are well documented in the royal archives on thousands of clay tablets found in the excavation of the royal palace. The majority of these documents are from the reign of Zimri-Lim.[156]

The father of Zimri-Lim was king of Mari before the Assyrian interregnum. He had at least eighteen daughters, of whom one, Inibshina, was a priest. On her seals, she is called both "wife of the god" and "servant of the god." She wrote letters to her brother, Zimri-Lim, informing him of prophecies that he should not trust a peace offer from Eshnunna. Another daughter, Yamama, was married to a diviner. The seal of his daughter Nagikha was found in Asia Minor. Another daughter, Ishtar-tappi, borrowed ten sheqels from the temple and, as interest, promised to sacrifice two rams. When the Assyrians conquered Mari, they put most of the former king's daughters into their harems.[157]

During the Assyrian interregnum, the status of women was much lower than under the Mari dynasty, and there are fewer documents from that time that mention women. According to one document, Izamu, a secondary wife of the Assyrian viceroy, was also a religious official and dedicated a statue to Ishtar. The inscription stated that she made the prayer of the viceroy find favor with the goddess.[158]

After King Zimri-Lim regained the throne of his father in Mari, he married Shibtu, the daughter of the king of Aleppo. She ruled as queen and had extensive administrative responsibilities. She wrote numerous letters to her husband—some personal, but most official reports about the city, the palace, and the temple. She also forwarded military and intelligence reports to him. In the king's absence she was responsible for administering the city, the palace, and the temple, including the construction of a reservoir. She had authority over the king's highest officials, all of whom were men. Her seal validated official documents and entry into the royal archives, which she opened for the king's auditors and resealed after they finished. The king was officially head of the cult, but delegated the duties to his wife and to governors in the provinces. He specifically instructed Shibtu to offer sacrifices, the characteristic duty of a priest. In the king's absence, she was in charge of overseeing the offering of sacrifices and the taking of omens. Shibtu had authority over governors of cities dependent on Mari, and governors and other officials wrote letters asking for her help in various matters. One official wrote asking her to obtain the release of a woman distrained by another official, who would not release her because the distraint order had come from the provincial governor. Shibtu had the authority to override the official and the governor. Another governor responded to a letter from the queen, stating that he would personally take charge of a case concerning a woman named Partum. The king and queen exchanged frequent letters, keeping each other informed about the latest developments. Sometimes the king gave his wife specific assignments. Shibtu was in charge of the king's harem. In one letter, he instructed her to choose thirty of the most beautiful war captives for his harem and to assign the rest to work in the textile factory. In another, he told her to put the harem woman Naname, who was sick with a fever, in quarantine and not to let other women use her cup, chair, or bed, which could be instruments of contagion.[159] Shibtu often wrote asking about his health. She sent him clothes she had made herself. In one letter she announced to him that she had given birth to twins, a boy and a girl. The letters give the impression that the king and queen had great respect for each other. Shibtu had substantial power and influence whether or not the king was present in Mari. In the last year of their reign, Zimri-Lim wrote to Shibtu, asking her to obtain two oracles on the intentions of Hammurabi as to whether he would attack Mari. Shibtu made a point of consulting both a male and a female prophet for reliability and forwarded the oracles, which said that Hammurabi would not return the soldiers Zimri-Lim had lent him and he would try to take Mari but Zimri-Lim would defeat him. This oracle proved wrong on the last point. Zimri-Lim believed the prophecy and did not prepare to defent Mari. Hammurabi defeated him and destroyed the city.[160]

King Zimri-Lim had secondary wives as well as a harem, at least part of which he inherited from the previous ruler. The two were very different. His primary wife, Shibtu, had her own palace in Mari, and the secondary wives lived in and often administered the king's other palaces in different cities dependent on Mari. Secondary wives of Zimri-Lim named Yatar-aya and Umumtabat had seals. The harem was confined inside the king's palaces. Harem women had no legal status or roles other than sexually pleasing the king.[161]

Damkhurasi, a secondary wife, was administrator of the palace at Terqa. She supervised the women and some male personnel of the palace and the local harem. She had some authority in the local cult, in which she was active, praying for the king. She wrote many letters to the king and received many from him, which document her authority and her close relationship with the king. She also made administrative reports to the king. In one letter, she promised to deal personally with a woman doctor, whom she called "idle."[162]

Ten daughters of King Zimri-Lim were named in one palace list and another ten were mentioned in other documents found in the archives. Daughters Ibbatum and Inibsharri received greater rations than their sisters. Zimri-Lim had put most of his daughters into political marriages in other towns. Thus they wrote many letters home to their father in Mari.

Ibbatum was married to the ruler of a town after he became a vassal of Zimri-Lim. He was already married and had grown children. Yet Ibbatum managed to become his primary wife. When her husband went to Babylonia, Ibbatum functioned as queen and ruled the state, just as Shibtu had ruled Mari when Zimri-Lim was away. Her marriage was happier than those of most of her sisters.[163]

Inibsharri wrote many letters to her father complaining about the conditions of her marriage and her husband's household. Her father had made her, against her will, marry the conquered ruler of a vassal state as part of a political alliance. Zimri-Lim had demanded that his daughter be principal wife and queen. Although the ruler already had a wife, he agreed to the marriage and sent marriage gifts to Zimri-Lim. When Zimri-Lim left the area, the ruler restored his first wife to her position as queen. Inibsharri was unable to prevail over the first wife. She wrote to her father that the restored queen took all the tribute gifts and made her sit in a corner doing nothing "like a simpleton." She complained that she did not have enough food or firewood and was kept under guard. Zimri-Lim wrote back, telling her to manage her household, but if the situation was totally impossible, she could cover her head and return to Mari. Instead she fled to nearby Nakhur, where the governor protected her against her husband, who eventually abandoned her there. Her sister Naramtum had been put in a similar political marriage. She wrote bitter letters home about being kept prisoner in the ruler's harem.[164]

Zimri-Lim married his daughter Kiru to the prominent ruler of a vassal town to solidify a political alliance. Her father had made her mayor of the town, which resulted in conflict with her husband, who was the ruler of the town, over their respective authority. The husband threatened to kill her if she tried to exercise her authority. He suspected that she was more loyal to her father than to him. Some officials brought political messages to Kiru rather than to her husband. She had greater influence as the daughter of Zimri-Lim than as the wife of the local ruler. She sent reports to her father about the local political situation and urged him to listen to her political advice, since she was usually right, even though she was only a woman. She wrote to her father complaining that he had put her into a miserable marriage. A complicating factor was that Zimri-Lim had married another daughter, Shimatum, to the same ruler. Shimatum became the principal wife and queen. There is an extant list of her dowry, the details arranged by category: gold and silver jewelry, bronze utensils, clothes, furniture, and servants. She wrote to her father about her travels with her husband and invited him to visit her. The final break occurred when the husband rejected and humiliated Kiru in the presence of other rulers. Kiru threatened to leave, but her husband said he would kill her with a bronze dagger if she did. Kiru wrote to her father, begging to come home. In one letter she even threatened to jump off the roof. Zimri-Lim sent a messenger to assess the situation. He sent a woman back to Mari to tell the king that false rumors were being circulated in the town putting Kiru's life in jeopardy. The husband still refused to let her go. In the end, her husband himself wrote to Zimri-Lim, asking him to take Kiru back. The king wrote to his wife Shibtu, telling her to bring Kiru back to Mari. The marriage was dissolved. Kiru returned to Mari and Shimatum remained in the town.[165]

Zimri-Lim had married his daughter Tizpatum to the ruler of a town in the north to concretize a political alliance. She became principal wife and queen. When Zimri-Lim ignored a request from her husband to send troops to defend their town, Tizpatum wrote to her father, begging him to send the troops and giving him reasons why it was necessary.[166]

When Zimri-Lim married his daughter Khazala to the ruler of another town, the wedding took place in Mari, without the presence of the groom, although he sent representatives and wine. Zimri-Lim married another daughter, Dukhshatum, to a high official of the palace of Mari. Since she lived in Mari, she did not write letters. No letters have been found of her sisters Qikhila or Akhatum, although they were put into political marriages.[167]

Political marriage was a common custom in this period, but it was uncommon for married daughters to be able to send written complaints to their fathers about the conditions of the marriage. Zimri-Lim allowed his daughters to do so and responded to their complaints. Thus, the princesses of Mari had a means of protection in political marriage and did not simply become defenseless victims of their husbands.

The letters attest to the lives of other women of political importance. Inibshina was the wife of the mayor of Mari. Four of her letters have been preserved. The king had given her authority to open and reseal the royal archives. She sent the king a chair and a footstool as gifts. She also sent the king notice of oracles that the religious sources had delivered to her personally. For example, she transmitted to the king the content of a prophecy given to her by a woman from the temple at Terqa that the peaceful gestures of the king of Eshnunna were a trick and that he was really planning to attack and destroy Mari.[168]

Addu-duri was a woman official in Mari who exercised authority over the palace, the temple, and the city and reported on them to the king. She was one of the highest royal officials in the kingdom and lived and worked in the palace. Persons who worked in the palace or temple brought their complaints, such as unfair treatment of elderly servants, to Addu-duri, who forwarded them to the king. She investigated and reviewed cases involving property disputes and then sent them to the king for judgment. The king gave her responsibility for the function of the cult in his absence. She mediated a conflict over a project of the king in the temple. She offered sacrifice and took omens to discern the decision of the god. She transmitted prophecies and oracles, including her own dreams, to the king, who put her in charge of making all the preparations for ceremonies and sacrifices during the state visit of another king. She was wealthy and gave her own stores of grain to the palace.[169]

Amadugga was a servant of Yasmakh-Addu whom Zimri-Lim kept on. She was in charge of palace food supplies, as attested by her seal on receipts for grain and oil, and was a supervisor of men.[170]

The Mari letters document the same religious offices of women as those found in Sippar and Babylon. There is one mention of women *en* high priests, in the context of divination. Two women contended for the office of *en* high priesthood. The oracles of a woman dream prophet named Aya-la and a diviner were sent to the king so that he could decide the case. Another document mentioned a *qadishtu* women who served in the Annunitum temple.[171]

There were many women *ugbabtu* and *naditu* priests in Mari. The women priests were celibate and sometimes lived within a cloister. They were daughters of the highest classes. Some were members of the royal family. The *naditu* priest Erishti-Aya was the daughter of Zimri-Lim and Shibtu. She lived in a cloister of *naditu* priests of Shamash far from Mari, probably the cloister in Sippar, which served the god Shamash. Her parents decided that she would be a *naditu* priest; it was not her own decision. Her most important role was to pray for her father, which she did diligently. She wrote many letters complaining that she had not received provisions of food and clothing from Mari. She owned slaves, whom her father had trained and given to her. When one died, she wrote and asked for a replacement.[172] Bakhlatum, daughter of the king, was an *ugbabtu* priest. Inibshina, the sister of Zimri-Lim, was also an *ugbabtu* priest, serving the god Dagan. She was supported by rations from the palace in Mari.[173]

The temple of Dagan in Terqa was served by a single *ugbabtu*. At some point after the end of the Assyrian occupation, the residence had fallen into disrepair and the office was vacant. Zimri-Lim and the governor of Terqa had the residence restored and brought a young *ugbabtu* priestess from Mari to serve the temple in Terqa. The shrine of Adad in Kulmish was served by a number of women *ugbabtu* priests. During a war, they were taken with other women to Mari as booty. Zimri-Lim felt that this had displeased the god, and he ordered his wife Shibtu to separate the priestesses, see that they were well treated, and send them back to their shrine.[174]

There were female and male prophets in the city-state of Mari in the decades before it was conquered by Hammurabi. They served the king by providing oracles from the gods to advise him on important decisions. Some prophets were professional, attached to specific gods and temples, but ordinary persons sometimes spontaneously prophesied, often through dreams. There were three types of prophets: the speaker, the respondent, and the ecstatic. One of each type, regardless of gender, served on the staff of each temple. A woman respondent, Innibana, was named in the Mari documents. A daughter of the king wrote to her father: although I am a mere woman, may my father listen to "my words. I will constantly send the word of the gods to my father."[175] This letter suggests that she exercised a prophetic role.

Ration lists and lists of palace personnel provide some information about lower-class women. Approximately four hundred people worked in the palace of Mari. Among these were twenty-seven female weavers and fifty-eight male weavers. Both men and women ground grain, but women were given millstones as part of their dowries, a symbol of their work after marriage. A woman named Ashumiyalibur was a baker for the palace, and both men and women were cooks. Women were pastry chefs, and two women, Bekhi and Abishamshi, drew water. Under the supervision of queen Shibtu, women dried garlic on the palace roof and then placed the dried garlic in storage jars. Women brought their children to work and were given extra rations to feed them. Women also worked as wet nurses and governesses for the children of the royal family. There were women singers and players of musical instruments. At least nine women scribes worked in the palace, and one letter mentioned a woman physician.[176]

The royal archives of Mari provide still more information on royal and upper-class women. The legal status of such women in many areas was almost equal to that of men. Women owned property and slaves and made legal transactions, such as contracts, loans, and pledges. They sealed official documents. Women brought legal actions in court, where they also were witnesses. Some women were literate and wrote many letters. There was no tabu against women holding authority over men. Women served as royal administrators and officials and in the highest levels of priesthood and cultic office. They could travel inside the kingdom without their husbands. The status of upper-class women at Mari was among the highest in ancient Near Eastern history. It was comparable to that of women in Sumer and higher than that of other women in Old Babylonia. The letters provide a vivid glimpse into the lives of the women of Mari.[177]

Karana was north of Asshur, between the two rivers but closer to the Tigris. It had a large palace, in the excavation of which the archive of queen Iltani was found, containing some two hundred documents. Iltani was the daughter of the previous king and the sister of the ruling king, when her husband, a divination priest, usurped the throne and made Karana a vassal state of Hammurabi. The archive contains correspondence between the king and queen, other letters to the queen, and administrative records. Iltani was the chief administrator of the palace, with responsibility for its food supplies and textile manufacturing. She processed fish and fish roe, chickpeas, oil, lard, and beer. She received gifts of fruit and pistachio nuts, and her husband sent her wool, which she made into garments. He had to send cloth and garments as part of his tribute to Babylon. Iltani employed fifteen women and ten men in making cloth and garments, as well as two millers, a brewer, a doorkeeper, and twenty women with other jobs. Iltani supported her sister, Lamassani, who lived in Asshur, with grain and oil rations and a slave girl. Lamassani wanted to buy a lapis lazuli necklace to send her in return. Iltani had another sister, Amat-Shamash, a *naditu* priest of Shamash in Sippar, who sent her a basket of shrimp but complained that Iltani never wrote or sent her anything, although her husband, the king, had sent her two slaves. Iltani even had authority to order judgment of a dispute between workers over ownership of a garment, after the parties had sworn the oath of the god.[178] The documents illuminate only a brief point in time in the life of one woman, Iltani, yet demonstrate that it was not very different from the lives of ruling-class women in Mari. The vassal status of Karana to Babylonia did not change or restrict her life as queen.

These documents, from different times and places in Old Babylonia, demonstrate that women, especially women priests and women in other religious offices, had many rights. They owned, rented, and inherited real property, transacted business, initiated litigation, and served as legal witnesses in court. Women legally adopted daughters and sons. Some women were literate, and some were professionally trained to work as scribes. Women were able to travel between cities and towns. Sons wrote respectfully to their mothers and offered them their help and support. A man who honored his daughter was praised by the people of his city.[179]

Yet restrictions were beginning to encroach upon the freedom of women. Men whose sisters inherited part of their father's estate challenged them in court, arguing that "custom" dictated that men should be the primary heirs. Men were raising questions about the propriety of women going outside of the houses of their husbands or fathers. One man asked another man why a certain woman went out into the country. The second man replied that she went to visit the shrine of a god. The first man declared with authority that women should not go out of the city for any reason, even for a religious purpose. Women were no longer permitted to go onto the roofs of their houses to look at people below or to approach the city gate.[180] City gates were more than just openings in the city wall. Many city gates were enclosures containing shops and offices. In some cities, judges assembled at a city gate to hold court. The city gate was a place where women would inevitably be in contact with men.

Women Victims

In the Old Babylonian period, women were victims of crimes and of false accusation of crimes. Many cases were documented in letters and court records. Women were physically beaten by men. A woman bore witness that her brother had beaten a servant woman to death. She underwent the river ordeal to prove she was telling the truth.[181]

A *naditu* priest appealed directly to the king when a man refused to pay for a garment she had sold to him. When she approached the man asking for payment, he beat her and boasted that he had beaten five other women priests whom he had also cheated by refusing to pay what he owed them.[182] Thus, six women priests were victims of battery and theft by a man who thought he was above the law.

Women were kidnapped and held hostage. The woman Zunana sent her servant girl Kittumshimkhiya to another town and men kidnapped her on the way. Zunana herself arrived safely, which she attributed to the god. The girl let her know where she was by sending her shallots. Zunana confronted the man who held her. He admitted his offense, but would not release the girl. Zunana had to petition the king to retrieve her servant girl.[183] In another case, some men had seized a servant woman, but the text is broken off where it said what they did to her.[184]

Women were used as pledges for the debts of men. Some women were illegally taken as pledges or distrained. A man had paid his rent to the woman owner of the house in which he lived as she had instructed. Another man came to the house claiming to be a rent collector. The tenant explained that he had already paid the rent to the owner, but the man attacked him and illegally took a pledge. In a different case, a man wrote a letter telling the recipient to release a woman who had been distrained and kept in a storehouse, and to let her stay in his house as a guest. Another man wrote to a friend, telling him that if he did not trust a third man, he should have other men write and seal documents about the third man, but he should not detain the third man's wife. A man wrote that he had brought the silver to repay a debt, but his distrainees were still being held in confinement.[185]

Mari was involved in frequent, but generally small wars. In a tribal attack on Karana, the enemy seized men, five women, and six boys from their villages and killed them.[186] An unnamed woman of Nawar commanded an army. Her own general betrayed her, bound her, and gave her to the enemy.[187] The mother of a ruler wrote to her son that a general had taken away all her women servants and those of her sisters.[188]

Kings took servant women from the households and husbands either for themselves or gave them to others. A man communicated to the king the complaint of a man that "they" took his woman, whom the king had given to him, and gave her to another.[189] In another case, the king took a woman, Khazz-ikannum, who was young, beautiful, and a weaver, and ordered his official to substitute another woman, Ekallatani, who was old, to give to the messenger of another ruler.[190] A royal official serving in a border town complained to the king that "they" had taken his house in Mari, for which he had paid five sheqels, and had given it to someone else. Two other men had moved into his father's house. As a result, his own family and household members were homeless.[191]

A mother had come with her daughter-in-law and family before the ruler to plead her case. An official was afraid that if she testified that he had taken some of her slave women and put them in the ruler's household, he would be shamed before the whole city. So the official countersued the woman with false accusations about missing money and barley. She denied the charges before the officials and the assembly. Then the official wrote directly to the ruler, informing him that he would bring many more witnesses to discredit the woman on the charges about the money and barley the next day and asking him to interrogate these witnesses himself. After the assembly ruled on the charges against the woman, he would present his defense against the main charges.[192]

Women who owned or inherited valuable property were often victimized by others, inspired by greed to commit fraud, file false accusations against them, and make false claims to their property. Women had to appear in court to defend or retrieve what was legally theirs. The records of lawsuits provide considerable information about such cases. In one Old Babylonian case, a woman named Khamazirum brought a fraudulent lawsuit against another woman, Manutum, challenging her ownership of a house. The judges held the trial in the temple and put Manutum under oath. After Manutum swore by the goddess that her ownership was true, Khamazirum dropped the case. The court declared that henceforth Khamazirum could never again file suit against Manutum regarding her ownership of the house, her other possessions, or her inheritance. The judgment was signed by two judges, two witnesses, and a woman scribe.[193]

Another Old Babylonian document recorded litigation over the ownership of a house lot within the cloister in Sippar. A woman priest, Amat-Shamash, had bequeathed her property to her adopted daughter. After her death, two men challenged the adopted daughter's inheritance before the mayor and judges of the city. The men alleged that Amat-Shamash had not executed a written document during her lifetime and that her adopted daughter had drawn up the document after her mother's death. Standards of the gods were brought in before which male and female witnesses testified that Amat-Shamash had executed the document herself during her lifetime. The judges affirmed the adopted daughter's inheritance and forbade the men and anyone else who had an interest in the estate to challenge her inheritance.[194] Later, however, one of the original plaintiffs in the case above filed suit again despite the court order. The judges said that having "forgotten" the initial decree was no excuse. As punishment for his attempt to relitigate a case already decided, the authorities shaved half his head, pierced his nose, "extended his arm[s and] marched him around the city." The original decree was restated, that never again could anyone challenge the inheritance of land or personal property by the adopted daughter of the priestess.[195] The prescription of corporal penalties made criminal the relitigation of a case in violation of the judgment of the original trial court.

In another case over inheritance, a *naditu* of Shamash and her two brothers filed suit contesting the inheritance of twelve acres of land by their cousin. The court found that they had suffered no harm or injustice and imposed punishment on them for filing a frivolous lawsuit. They were forbidden ever to relitigate the matter.[196]

There were many lawsuits over sales of land. One man, for example, sold a plot of land to the *naditu* priest Manassi. A year later he filed suit against her, alleging that she had taken more land than what she had paid for. After the trial, the judges found that she actually had less than the amount of land for which she had paid.[197] Manassi won the case, but lost time and resources defending her property against a frivolous lawsuit.

The *naditu* priests of Sippar owned land in villages outside the city. It was difficult for cloistered women to defend their property outside the cloister. This made them easy victims of those who would steal their property. Disputes were generally resolved by the village mayors and elders, but many court cases also dealt with fields owned by *naditu* priests that had been taken over by men of a village.[198]

In an Old Babylonian suit over payment of the sale price of a house, the plaintiff seller, Ilushakhegal, was a religious official, and the defendant buyer, Belessunu, a *naditu* priest. She was represented in court by her husband. Since the seller had no witnesses, the judges admitted the document of sale into evidence and called the original witnesses to the act of sale, who testified that Belessunu had paid in full. At this point, Ilushakhegal conceded. The judges continued to examine the case and made Ilushakhegal write a tablet renouncing her claim. They imposed a penalty on her for putting her seal on a false claim. In another case, a *naditu* priest had sold real estate, but had not been paid. This case was heard before the king in Babylon.[199]

The rules for divorce were established in marriage contracts; however, when a husband initiated divorce, he did not always return the dowry or give other compensation to his ex-wife, as promised in the marriage contract. If he put his ex-wife out with nothing, she became destitute as a result of his unlawful breach of the marriage contract.

Men further victimized their ex-wives by using up their dowry before a court could adjudicate their claims. Mattatum, the mother of an ex-wife, sued her former son-in-law over the return of the dowry after the end of the marriage. The judges of Babylon instituted proceedings according to the king's ordinances. The court ordered that the dowry that Mattatum had given her daughter be returned to Mattatum, and they sent a soldier with her to recover what remained of it.[200]

Brothers frequently tried to take the inheritance of their sisters. One father made his will under oath before the standard of the god. When he died, his sons still tried to take the whole estate, including the portion, two orchards and a field, their father had left to their sister Yakhilatum, an *ugbabtu* priest of Shamash. In another case, Amat-Shamash, a *naditu* priest, was the caretaker and heir of Iltani. Nine years later, her sister, Taramulmash, a *kulmashitu*, made Amat-Shamash her primary heir. Their brother filed suit against them, arguing that by custom a man should be the primary heir.[201]

In the vassal kingdom of Karana, the queen, Iltani, was falsely accused of theft of oxen and sheep by her husband, who threatened to cut her into twelve pieces. She wrote back, proclaiming her innocence of taking anything without his permission and asked him why he would accuse her and threaten to put her to death.

Belassuna was the wife of an official who abused her. A letter from her adult son stated that he was coming to take her home. Another woman named Belassuna wrote to the queen that she had been falsely accused and detained. The king had said he would adjudicate the case but had not done so. Belassuna appealed for a statement of the charges against her and for due process to plead her innocence.[202]

Women Offenders

Witchcraft was a capital crime committed by women. Old Babylonian witches were believed to cause physical illness, such as skin disease and paralysis, by use of the evil eye, tongue, and spittle. Religious incantations were used to inform the gods of acts of witchcraft and to ask the gods to undo them. In one example of an anti-witchcraft ritual "trial," the witch was accused of causing illness by putting her spit into food and beer. She was also accused of kidnapping children. Witchcraft was overcome by turning it against the witch by a curse. Three terms of the curse attacked the witch's mouth, to destroy her ability to speak; her womb, that it drip beer; and her acts of sorcery, that they would dig into her flesh like a stake. Her male victim was purified by water.[203]

Since witches brought evil magic into the human world, it was believed necessary to destroy the source, the witch, by death, using fire or water to purify the persons and city affected.

An official wrote to the king that Shimatum, either the king's daughter or another woman of that name, had sent herbs used for sorcery to the king.[204] The king instructed the governor of a vassal town to investigate an accused witch. He enlisted a male servant to gather evidence, but he did not.[205]

Soldiers had arrested a woman, Marat-Eshtar, with her daughter and son, on charges of sorcery and delivered them to take the river ordeal. The young woman's mother heard about the arrest and came to defend her daughter. The mother swore that her daughter was innocent of all charges and underwent the river ordeal to prove the truthfulness of her testimony. Unfortunately, the mother drowned, which legally proved just the opposite, that her statements had been untrue, and that her daughter was guilty and subject to the death penalty.[206]

Two Old Babylonian documents reported a case in which two women were accused of witchcraft. A father brought suit against his son, his son's wife, and her mother. He accused the three of eating the seed barley he had entrusted to them instead of planting it, with the result that there was no barley harvest; and he accused his son's wife and her mother of witchcraft. In the first document, the village judges wrote a statement of the facts on a tablet and sent it to the mayor and elders of a larger city, asking them to return the son, his wife, and her mother to the village so that they could render judgment. The second document was written by the plaintiff father to the mayor, who had granted bail for the three accused, asking him to return the three to their village so that the local court could give judgment.[207] This case shows that charges of witchcraft were tried in courts.

Adultery was a crime in all ancient Near Eastern civilizations. Mari provided a unique statement by a woman. This was a formal public statement, made just before undergoing the river ordeal. The unnamed woman, designated by the male writer as the wife of her husband, had had sex with a father and his son before her marriage to the father. When her husband was away, his son tried to make her have sex with him. The woman described the episode in graphic detail: he verbally demanded sex, kissed her, and touched her genitals, but did not penetrate her with his penis. She stated that she would never betray or shame her husband and that she had prevented a crime from taking place in her husband's house. She went through the river ordeal and vindicated her innocence.[208]

A wife charged the woman Rumatum with adultery with her husband. The king ordered that the accused undergo the river ordeal and be sent to him. The officials found no woman of that name in the city quarter of the accuser, but finally found a woman named Rumatum elsewhere in the city and sent her to the king. There was no mention of any form of investigation to ascertain whether this was the same woman.[209]

A letter implicated Shimatum, daughter of Zimri-Lim, in a conspiracy against a vassal supporter of Zimri-Lim, who was arrested, imprisoned, and his property confiscated. The writer noted that Shimatum had spoken insulting words about her father. As a result the god had punished her with mutilation of her fingers and seizures.[210]

A woman could put herself under the threat of criminal penalties by signing a marriage or other contract that stipulated such penalties if she broke the contract. Some Old Babylonian marriage contracts contained provisions that specified capital punishment if the wife initiated divorce proceedings. The wife would be bound and thrown into the river to drown or thrown off the city wall or tower to her death.[211] In such cases, the crime of the wife was not just breach of contract, but was challenging the authority and power of the husband.

There is one reference in the Mari documents to a woman religious officiant who was the daughter of a vassal king. She had been accused of an unnamed offense and was kept under surveillance.[212]

Punishment

In the Old Babylonian period, the river ordeal was used in place of formal trial to determine the veracity of witnesses and defendants and to determine the guilt of accused offenders. The ordeal contained its own automatic form of punishment: if the accused died, he or she was presumed guilty of the offense charged. In Mari, which was situated on the Euphrates, the ordeal sometimes took place in the river, but other times the accused was thrown into a bitumen well, where the accused could also die from inhalation of toxic fumes.[213]

A slave woman of the household of the king was first made to swear oaths as to whether her mistress had performed witchcraft, treason, or any other offense against the king, or revealed any palace secrets, or that any other person had opened the letters of her mistress. The slave swore the oaths but drowned in the river.[214]

False accusation of witchcraft was punished by death by fire, the penalty of the offense falsely alleged. The death penalty was used in Old Babylonian documents for crimes involving threatening forces, such as evil magic. Death of an offending witch by fire or water purified the state and kept it safe.

Capital punishment was also used for offenses that challenged the power and authority of men. Women who breached their marriage contracts by leaving their husbands were executed by being thrown into the river to drown or by being thrown off a high wall or tower. The latter form of punishment was unusual and not mentioned in other documents or laws. Not all Babylonian cities were situated on rivers, but most were fortified by high walls and towers.

Contracts could mandate corporal mutilation for breach of the contract. Some of the penalties were amputation or piercing of the nose, shaving off half of the offender's hair, stretching out the offender's arms and parading the humiliated offender around the city.[215]

Summary: Old Babylonian Documents

Laws expressed the ideals of the lawgiver for the conduct of the people of his state. Other documents, especially letters and records of court proceedings, illustrated how the laws were applied in the real lives of the people. In many areas the laws and the other documents coincided, but not in all.

Women priests and other women religious officials held positions of importance in the cloister and in temples, both as religious officiants and as administrators of large businesses in textiles and wool. Many of these women owned houses and lands and were quite wealthy. Women worked as professional scribes, skilled artisans, and tavern keepers. Women did not, however, hold positions in the secular government.

Wealth had positive and negative consequences for women. Wealth was a source of protection and influence. On the other hand, wealth held by women elicited the greed of men. Many of the law court records showed men trying to take wealth, generally in the form of land, away from women, often by dishonest and illegal means, such as false accusation of crimes, fraud, perjury, illegal distraint, breach of contract, frivolous lawsuits, and outright theft.

Amorite influences on Old Babylonia were in evidence. Restrictions on the freedom of women outside the household were beginning to appear. So too was a growing awareness that women could contaminate men through impurity, pollution, and witchcraft. This, in turn, generated in men feelings of fear of women and speculation about how to minimize contact with women. One way was to confine women to the house. The father was the highest authority in the patriarchal family structure, and husbands had authority over their wives. When women challenged the authority of men, the penalty was death. These changes demonstrate the influence of Amorite thought and customs.

Old Babylonian documents indicate that many crimes were punished by death. The forms of capital punishment were burning, drowning, and throwing the offender off a wall or tower. Fire and water were used to obliterate polluting offenders and at the same time to purify the city and temple from the pollution generated by the offender. Corporal mutilation was rarely mentioned in the documents, and most forms were mild compared to those in the Laws of Hammurabi. Thus, although the influence of Amorite customary law is evident in the documents, there is far less than in the laws.

Middle Babylonia (1595–627)

During the middle period of Babylonian history, Babylonia was ruled by three foreign nations. It was conquered by the Hittites, who quickly withdrew, leaving a political vacuum. The Kassites, nomadic tribes of traders and mercenary soldiers, moved into Babylonia and ruled for more than four centuries. There are few documents extant from this period, with the exception of boundary stones. These recorded grants of land by kings to their subjects, including one to a royal princess. The Kassites were absorbed into Babylonian culture. They facilitated the collection and preservation documents of literature, law, and religion written in Sumerian and Old Babylonian times. The Kassite dynasty was a time of stability and continuing unification of southern Mesopotamia into one nation.[216]

Kassite kings continued the practice of political marriages. One such marriage was between the daughter of the Kassite king of Babylonia and Pharaoh Amenophis III of Egypt. Political marriage was developed beyond the earlier practice of formation of political alliances. The royal parents of the couple were expected to send valuable gifts to each other. Embassies were sent back and forth to deliver and receive such gifts and to find out how the married daughter was being treated.[217]

Some families sold their young daughters as brides. One document described such a sale, in which Kassite parents sold their young daughter to a Babylonian merchant for two garments, worth two sheqels of gold, and food for an unspecified period of time.[218]

There were few schools in the ancient Near East for boys and almost none for girls. Yet a letter from Nippur revealed the existence of a boarding school in Nippur for the sons and daughters of political officials and diplomats who traveled or lived outside Babylonia.[219]

There is very little information about crime and punishment during the Kassite period. One writer of Middle Babylonian wisdom literature described a sick man who blamed a woman sorcerer for his mysterious illnesses. But this was written in a literary genre, not as a report of an actual case of witchcraft.[220]

A Middle Babylonian text documented part of the procedure for the release of a prisoner on bail. A friend put up bail for a man who was in prison. He arranged that the bail money be given through an intermediary to the man and his wife. Then they took it to the governor who had imprisoned the man.[221]

In the second part of the Middle Babylonian period, Babylonia was ruled by the Second Dynasty of Isin. There are few documents extant from this period, but one important event was recorded. King Nebukhadrezzar I revived the custom of Akkad, Sumer, Isin, and Larsa by making his daughter high priest of the moon god at Ur.[222] This action put a woman in a high and influential position after centuries of male control of such offices. It demonstrated that this king was cognizant of Sumero-Akkadian history, and that there was a remembered past that relocation of peoples and rule by different ethnic dynasties had not erased.

The last part of the Middle Babylonian period took place under the domination of Assyria. It was a time of frequent incursions by tribal groups. Aramean tribes lived in small settlements and periodically raided the cities, and Chaldean tribes had built fortified cities in the south. Some Chaldeans lived in Babylon and aspired to its kingship.[223] An early Chaldean ruler noted that he adorned several of his palace women and sent them as gifts to the lands of Khatti and Elam. He also sent citizens of Babylon as gifts to the same lands.[224]

Since Babylon was an important trade center, Assyrian control over Babylonia grew tighter. The Late Assyrian king Sennakherib made his son ruler of Babylon, but the Elamites captured and killed him. Then, according to his own account, he destroyed and burned the city and deported and enslaved its people. His son and successor, King Esarhaddon, rebuilt Babylon and returned the statues of the gods to their temples. He brought back the deportees, released the enslaved, and restored their property and privileges.[225]

The Assyrian king Esarhaddon made one of his sons, Asshurbanipal, king of Assyria and another king of Babylonia. The latter rebelled and his brother laid siege to Babylon. Famine in the city grew so bad that parents sold or reputedly ate their children. When the Assyrians broke through, the Babylonian king died in the fire that destroyed his palace. Asshurbanipal then installed a puppet ruler of Babylonia. When both died in 627, Assyrian control over Babylonia came to an end.[226]

During Assyrian rule of Babylonia, few women were mentioned in Babylonian documents. One exception concerned the propriety of the dedication of a tiara for the statue of a goddess in Babylon sent by Naqia, the mother of the Assyrian king. Another exception was a letter written by the Assyrian commander of Babylon to the wife of a judge, telling her to keep her husband under house arrest because he was accused of inciting a protest demonstration. That a woman was asked and had the power to do this was significant in the light of the low status of women under Assyrian rule.[227]

During the war for independence from Assyria, the date palm trees of Babylonia were destroyed by the Assyrians. Dates were a staple of Babylonian diet and were harvested by women. It took six years for new trees to bear fruit.[228] This had a serious effect on one source of employment for women and on the diet of all the people of Babylonia.

LATE BABYLONIA (626–539)

During the power struggle between Assyria and Babylonia, Assyria was the greater military power, but Babylonia emerged the greater economic power, especially through the wealth of its temples.[229] The first Late Babylonian king, Nabopolassar, with his Mede allies, defeated the Assyrian army, freed Babylonia, and, by 610, had destroyed the Assyrian capitals of Asshur, Nimrud, and Nineveh, after which Assyria ceased to exist. Nabopolassar consolidated Babylonian control over north and south Mesopotamia and founded the Late Babylonian dynasty. His son, king Nebukhadrezzar II, conquered the Levant, including the kingdom of Judah. He devoted much of his reign to rebuilding Babylon as a magnificent and beautiful city, using temple slaves and war captives as forced laborers. The Late Babylonian period was a time of prosperity, which lasted until 539 when the Persians defeated the Babylonians and took Babylon.[230]

LATE BABYLONIAN LAWS

There is only one collection of laws known from this period. The extant text of the Late Babylonian Laws consists of fifteen laws on one damaged clay tablet, a fragmentary copy of a larger work. The date of the laws is uncertain, but they were probably collected during the earlier part of the period, in the late seventh century.[231] The laws are incomplete and fragmentary, but shed some light on the lives of women.

Status of Women

Marriage in Late Babylonia generally required marriage gifts from the groom's family and a settlement from the bride's, but the difference from the marriage gifts and dowry of previous laws was that these were given directly to the betrothed couple. The father of the bride gave his daughter a settlement, and the father of the groom transferred property to his son. The two fathers made a written contract, the terms of which could not be changed. However, if the father of the bride later suffered financial adversity, he could reduce the settlement in accordance with the reduced assets of his estate.[232] This law made it possible for a family with financial problems to retain its honor and status in the community.

The laws on marriage also dealt with inheritance. For example, a man gave a marriage settlement to his daughter, but she bore no sons or daughters.

When she died, the settlement reverted back to her father.[233] This law explicitly mentioned "daughters," indicating that if the deceased wife had a daughter, the settlement would have gone to her daughter, not to her father. The law made no mention of the husband or the family of the husband.

Late Babylonian women had broad inheritance rights. For example, the case of a couple who married but had no children. When the husband died intestate, the wife was entitled to a sum equivalent to her settlement out of the husband's estate. If her husband had given her gifts, she also kept these. If the wife had no settlement, the case went before a judge, who determined the amount of her inheritance based on the size of her late husband's estate.[234]

In the case of a couple who married and had sons, when the husband died, the widow married a man of her own choice. When she moved to the house of her second husband, she was permitted to take her settlement and any gifts her first husband had given her. As long as she lived, she and her second husband had the usufruct of her property. If she bore sons in the second marriage, after her death the sons of the first and second marriages were entitled to equal shares of her estate.[235]

In another case, a couple married and had sons, but then the wife died. The man remarried and his second wife also bore sons. When the man died, the sons of his first wife inherited two-thirds of their father's estate and the sons of his second wife, one-third. This disposed of the whole estate. But the next sentence began: "their sisters, who are still residing in their father's house...," which was followed by a large lacuna in the text.[236] The missing lines most probably contained provisions for the support and marriage settlements of unmarried sisters.

Slaves were considered a commodity of personal property, and their lives were at least partially regulated by the laws of property. For example, if a man or woman sold a slave woman and later a third-party claim against the slave woman arose and the claimant took her in satisfaction of his claim, the seller had to refund the full purchase price to the buyer, although the buyer had to pay a half sheqel for each child the slave woman had borne while in his or her possession.[237]

Women Offenders

In the Late Babylonian Laws only one law survived on a crime committed by women. The law proscribed two offenses of witchcraft. The first offense was against property. A woman had performed a magic ritual on the field, boat, oven, or kiln belonging to another person. The penalty was a fine of three times the value of the losses her magic had caused to the property. The second offense was against persons. A woman was caught in the act of performing a magic ritual at the door of a free man's house, thereby directly threatening the man and the members of his household. Her penalty was death.[238]

The punishments were made appropriate to the offenses. Witchcraft used against persons was a capital offense. Theft and property damage were punished by multifold restitution.

LATE BABYLONIAN DOCUMENTS AND INSCRIPTIONS

The sources for this period are royal chronicles, royal inscriptions, temple archives, religious rituals, literary texts, legal documents, family business archives, ration lists, marriage contracts, and letters. There are works by almost contemporary historians, which described the period, although the descriptions were filtered through the writers' interpretations and biases. Many more documents have been found that are not yet published.[239]

Status of Women

Late Babylonian kings practiced political marriage. Nebukhadrezzar II was reputed to have married a Mede princess. His eldest daughter, Kassh-Aya, married a general, Nergal-sharr'usur, who thereby became king of Babylonia. Late Babylonian kings had a principal wife but also a harem with many women. A building text for the palace mentioned the "House of Palace Women."[240] Wives of kings did not rule as queens in the Late Babylonian period.

Most marriages were arranged by the parents. If the father of a young unmarried woman died, her marriage was arranged by her mother or brother. A daughter was under the authority of her father, mother, or brother until she married and left their household. If both her parents and her brothers died, the young woman could arrange her own marriage once she was old enough. In some cases, the bride accepted the groom's offer and became thereby a party to the marriage contract. A groom could choose his bride but had to have his father's permission to marry. If a man married without his father's permission, this was grounds for annulment of the marriage. Grooms were generally ten years older than their brides.[241]

The groom or his father asked permission of the father, mother, brothers, or the bride herself for permission to marry, and then the person asked gave his or her permission. Issues that were subject to negotiation, such as the amount of the bride's settlement, were agreed upon and written down in the marriage contract, which generally began with request and permission clauses, and often included clauses pertaining to virginity, divorce, and adultery.[242]

Late Babylonian laws and documents demonstrate a change in the practices of marriage gifts and dowry. Fathers gave assets to their sons when they married. The bride's father gave a marriage settlement to the bride, not to the groom's father or family. It was for the couple and later for their children. Thus, fewer assets were transferred between families, and the assets given to the bride and groom remained their own. Newly married couples were able to set up their own households and become independent of their families.

Bridal settlements included houses, orchards, fields, money, and slaves. Since the couples were setting up their own households, most settlements included practical necessities, such as linens, bedding, cloth, furniture, lamps, and kitchen utensils. For example, a bride named Kabta was given a settlement consisting of an orchard and a field, three slave women, "a bed, two chairs, a table, three bronze goblets, a bronze bowl, one copper cooking vessel, and one lamp." A certain amount of money was set aside for the bride's spending money. In another settlement, the father of Khipta, the bride, freely gave her and "five minas of silver, two slaves, thirty sheep, two oxen, and household utensils" to his new son-in-law as a "wedding gift." If the settlement contained money, the husband could use or invest it, but had to return it to the settlement. Some fathers gave part of their inheritance to their sons when they married, which could be used to support the couple and later the widow and children if the husband died first. Wealthy families gave smaller settlements to their daughters, and the brides of their sons received larger settlements because of the prestige of marrying into a prominent family. For example, daughters of the wealthy Egibi merchant family named Tashmetutabni, Ina-Esagil-belat, and Nana-etirat were given settlements of a field, a few slaves, and household goods. Daughters-in-law of the same family, Amat-Bau, Erishtu, and Shushanni, brought settlements with gold and silver, several fields, orchards, slaves, and household goods.[243] Sometimes women relatives of the bride gave her slaves, land, money, or things for the house, but such gifts were not written down in the marriage contract.

Most nonroyal marriages in the Late Babylonian period were monogamous. Only rarely did a very wealthy man take a second wife, and he had to obtain permission for reasons such as the first wife's failure to produce a son. For example, a marriage contract for a second marriage stipulated that if the first wife, Esagil-banata, who was barren, eventually gave birth to a son, that son would inherit two-thirds of his father's estate, whereas if the second wife, Kulla, bore a child, she and her child would share the other third. If the first wife never bore any children, and the second wife did, the entire estate went to the second wife and her children.[244]

Wealthy merchant families used marriage to cement economic alliances and by practicing endogamous marriage to keep land and other property within the family. For example, a man married Nupta, the daughter of his cousin. Her settlement consisted of a date palm orchard, land, and slave women. She died soon after the marriage, and her settlement was returned to her father. The widower, not wanting to lose the assets of his late wife's settlement, married her sister, Kabta, and got it back. They had two daughters. When the husband died, Kabta did not inherit, but her daughters and her deceased husband's brother inherited his estate. Then Kabta married her late husband's brother and they had two sons. Although she had other alternatives, Kabta played a major role in preserving the estate within the family. The two husbands in this case had a married sister named Khubbusitu. When she died, her husband married her niece, Amtisutiti, a daughter of Kabta. Endogamous marriages kept property within families.[245]

Divorce was addressed in many marriage contracts. Husbands generally initiated divorce because they wanted to marry another woman. In such cases, the husband had to give his wife a large sum of money and return her settlement. Theoretically a wife could initiate divorce, but if she did, she forfeited her settlement and any future support from her husband.[246]

Widows were legally independent. They had a legal right to the full amount of their settlement from the estate of their deceased husband, and they had the possession and use of their settlement for life. This made them financially independent, although they had to support their children. They could transact business, make loans, lease land, or use their settlement to remarry.[247]

The reign of the last Late Babylonian king, Nabu-naid, was a high point for women. Women again could hold religious offices. Adad-guppi, the mother of Nabu-naid, arranged the funeral for the deceased previous king, which was normally done by the king's male heir. She also asserted that Sin, the moon god of Harran, had chosen her son to be king. These actions helped legitimize Nabu-naid's claim to the throne.[248]

Late Babylonian kings were heads of the religious cult. This office had serious political implications. King Nabu-naid and his mother worshiped the moon god, Sin, in Babylon. Many questioned the legitimacy of his kingship because of this, since Marduk was the traditional god of Babylon. In response, King Nabu-naid made his daughter high priest of the moon god, Nanna, at Ur, the oldest cult in ancient Sumer. He legitimized his act by attributing it to a request of the moon god, Sin, which coincided with a lunar eclipse. The moon god was called Nanna in Ur and Sin in Babylon. He combined the two gods as one god with two names. He gave his daughter a Sumerian name: En-nigaldi-Nanna. He researched the rituals and dress of the women high priests of Ur from a stela of the Middle Babylonian king Nebukhadrezzar I and other documents he found in the old temple at Ur, which he rebuilt and restored. These acts legitimized his allegiance to the cult of the moon god Sin and connected him back to the kings of Sumer and Akkad. It is not known to what extent En-nigaldi-Nanna performed the religious functions of high priest.[249]

According to extant documents, the woman who came closest to exercising the role of priest was Adad-guppi, the mother of King Nabu-naid. She wrote her own autobiography, an act previously reserved to kings. She declared that she had spent her whole life serving the gods. Whatever she had, she considered a gift of the gods, and she dedicated all her valuable possessions to the gods. She performed cultic rituals for the god Sin. In return, the god gave her "an exalted position and a famous name in the country." She had made her son an official of two previous Late Babylonian kings, who, she said, had treated her like a daughter and had given her an important position. In gratitude she made funerary offerings for them and instituted and performed perpetual incense offerings.[250]

When his mother, Adad-guppi, died, Nabu-naid wrapped her body in fine linen and laid it in a tomb decorated with gold and precious gems. He summoned kings, princes, and governors to attend the funeral. He sacrificed fat rams. For seven days they made lament, put dust on their heads and walked about. On the seventh day, they bathed and put on new clothes given by the king. They feasted and returned home with ample food and drink provided by the king.[251] The king functioned as a priest in this long and elaborate ritual, performed in honor of a woman, the queen mother.

A very intriguing witness to the religious roles of Late Babylonian women in the temple cult is the text of a ritual performed in the Esagil temple in Babylon, the most important temple in Babylonia. Several male priests, including the high priest and the king, performed various acts. Toward the end there was a section where the principal officiant was a woman *naditu* priest. She was seated, which denoted high rank and authority. She put down a drum beside the barley beer and wrote seven inscriptions. Then she held the inscriptions in her left hand and the drum and barley beer in her right hand in front of the palm frond.[252] In the Old Babylonian period there had been many women *naditu* priests of Marduk who served in the Esagil temple in Babylon. This is a rare piece of evidence that a woman *naditu* priest functioned in this temple in the Late Babylonian period.

Elsewhere in Babylonia, the archives of temples, especially those in Sippar and Uruk, rarely mentioned women in this period, and then only weavers, artisans, and temple slaves. One exception was a text that mentioned a woman, called a *sagittu*, who performed cultic functions. The administrators and high officials of temples in Late Babylonian documents were men. After the priests, the lower cultic personnel included lamentation chanters, liturgical singers, and exorcists. The temples had numerous workers and suppliers, but in the Late Babylonian period most of these were men.[253]

The purity of women who had any contact with a temple was a serious issue. Persons who held temple offices were first checked by temple officials as to the purity of their mothers, which was believed to affect the applicant's purity. The widow of a priest was forbidden to remarry until her sons reached adulthood, suggesting that there may have been special purity requirements for the wives of priests, which extended even to their widows.[254] If the priests or the temple became impure, the cult could not be performed. This was believed to endanger the security of the state.

There were other religious functions that women performed outside of the male-dominated temple cult. Women were prophets and were consulted by kings in making major decisions. At least one woman prophet performed a significant role in an important ritual in Babylon.[255]

In a Late Babylonian case, a brother adopted his sister's infant son. His sister, Balta, was a prostitute. The brother had the adoption recorded and made the adopted son his heir after his natural son. As long as Balta practiced prostitution, she continued to pay the expenses of rearing her son. But when Balta entered the house of a free citizen, becoming a concubine and ceasing to earn wages, her brother then had to pay for the care, food, and clothes of his adopted son. The brother swore an oath that he would never give the boy away and that he would raise the boy to serve the king and the goddess alongside his natural son. This document demonstrates that prostitution was a legal and accepted profession.[256]

Late Babylonian women owned and inherited property. Women received land and other property in their marriage settlements and through inheritance. Women leased real property. The lady Sikkuti leased a house for one and three-fourths sheqels per year, half paid at the beginning, the other half at the middle. She was responsible for maintenance and repair of the roof. The woman Amata owned and leased three houses. The rent was twelve meals per day and one-half sheqel per year, with four years paid in advance. The lessee had to pay ten sheqels for anything broken. The transaction was witnessed by Amata's daughter, Kulla. All property transactions were written, usually in duplicate, with a copy for each party, and recorded.[257]

Women sold the fruit of their agricultural property. Documents showed, for example, that a woman named Banitu-banat had to deliver an order of barley to a buyer by a certain day. Another woman, Nidintumbelit, and three men had to deliver their date harvest in certain baskets on a specified date to a specified place.[258]

Husbands and wives jointly made loans. A man and his wife, Nada, loaned thirty-five sheqels of silver on a promissory note. Another document stated that a man made a loan, but it was repaid to his wife, Bazitum, and son. An unmarried woman of Sippar, Busasa, made and recorded a loan of barley to a man.[259]

Sometimes husbands represented wives in legal transactions, but their wives were present. There were fewer seals and signatures of women as witnesses to legal documents, but some women did possess and use seals. One woman witnessed and sealed a property transaction between men. Free women filed lawsuits and took oaths. Women appeared in court as litigants and witnesses. Women posted bail for male relatives. On the other hand, women were held liable for the debts of men.[260]

Temple benefices provided an income to their owners, without the obligation of temple service. Such benefices were broken up into shares and sold, given, or bequeathed. Ownership of these shares was a sign of wealth and status in society. Only those whose father and mother had been free persons could own temple benefices. Women who owned temple benefice shares elevated their family's social status and their own marriageability.[261]

Wives were expected to care for their husbands in old age. However, care for elderly parents was not required of their children in Late Babylonian law. As a result, even widowed parents who had children were sometimes left without care and support in old age. Parents could, however, arrange to receive care from their children or others by contract. For example, an elderly man asked his daughter to care for him. They made a contract whereby he would continue to receive the income from his temple office shares for life. He promised not to alienate them so that his daughter would inherit his shares in full when he died as recompense for her care. A sick man wrote to his daughter, Tabata, that he had been abandoned by his brother and son, and begged her to take care of him, promising her his estate after his death. Another man manumitted his slave to care for him, but the slave ran away. Esagil-ramat, the widow of his deceased son, took care of her father-in-law with respect and honor. The manumiaaion of the slave was revoked and he was given to Esagil-ramat and her daughter, Nubta.[262]

A woman of some wealth, Khanna, owned seven slaves. She had a friend, Gigitu, who was free but poor because she had married a slave. Khanna adopted Gigitu's son and freed him from slavery. She arranged that her seven slaves would take care of her during her life, but would become the property of Gigitu and her adopted son on her death. Khanna had wealth but no family. This transaction ensured that she would be cared for in her old age. When she inherited the slaves, Gigitu's economic status would change from poor to wealthy.[263]

Slavery was common in the Late Babylonian period, and slave ownership was not limited to the wealthy. Many documents showed husbands and wives jointly owning and selling slaves. One man and his wife, Ilsunu, owned and sold a slave for one mina of silver to the son of a blacksmith. A mother, Rimat, and her two sons jointly sold a slave man and three slave women for two minas of silver. A woman, Belilitum, sold her slave, and her son assumed liability for any claims that later arose. Another woman named Belilitum bought a slave man and his wife, Nana-risuni. Her son had the right to make claims against the seller for a limited period of time. One contract stated that the lady Nupta would sell and deliver one slave man and two slave women on a certain date. If she did not return the purchase price by the end of the month, the slaves would be inscribed as the property of the buyer. A man and his wife, Khanashu, gave a slave to their son-in-law as a wedding present. Later the son-in-law and his wife, Khipta, sold the slave, in the presence of the wife's parents. The buyer paid both couples. There are also many records which show that slave families were sold together.[264] Soldiers were often paid with war booty and thereby came to own slave women. Some they used or sold, and others they rented out as prostitutes.

Women slaves were rarely given a profession, although at least one became a tavern keeper. Few women slaves owned property, while many male slaves did. No seals of women slaves have been found, although seals belonging to male slaves have. Women and men slaves were used as pledges for their owner's debts. Some women domestics and temple slaves were hired out for salaried jobs. Their income went to their owner or to the temple.[265] Privately owned slaves could be sold or given away at the will of their owners.

Both men and women were temple slaves. Their slave status was for life and was inherited by their children. Slaves of the temple of Uruk were dedicated to the goddess Ishtar and were tattooed with a star on the back of the hand. In the law courts, a temple slave was identified by his or her star and by other temple slaves who had known the person's mother and grandmother. In one case, a brother testified that Khussa, who had the star mark, was his sister. Temple slaves held offices and worked as skilled artisans.[266] Their status was higher than and preferable to that of other slaves.

In times of famine and siege, some women sold themselves or their children into slavery to get food. During the siege of Nippur, mothers sold their young sons and daughters into slavery in order to keep them alive, hoping that as slaves they would be fed. A widow sold her two sons as slaves to a temple because she could not feed them or herself in a time of poverty and famine. Temples accepted the children of poor families as slaves.[267] But temple slavery was for life, and parents could not reclaim their children when their financial situation improved.

Mothers exposed children they could not feed. Small girls found abandoned could be taken in by families, raised, and made their slaves. One such girl was named Shepitta. When she came of age, her "family" filed a legal document recording her status as a slave.[268]

The legal status of women in the Late Babylonian period was lower than in the Sumerian and Old Babylonian periods, but considerably higher than in Assyria. Women were not secluded, and they assembled at the city gate, where business was transacted and cases were adjudicated. Women owned and inherited real property and slaves. Women were legal persons; they made contracts and appeared in court. Business records show that a few women were administrators of family businesses and engaged in international trade. Some women officiated in the temple cult.[269]

Women Victims

Late Babylonian documents portrayed women as victims of customs as well as of crimes. Daughters of free families could be used as pledges and sold as slaves if parental debts were not paid. However, men could no longer use their wives as pledges or sell them as slaves. Mothers could hire out their daughters for wages. One daughter was sent out to work as a wet nurse for a year. In a written contract, Urkisharrat promised to nurse the daughter of a man. Her mother witnessed the contract, which stated that her wages were to be paid to her father.[270]

Some Late Babylonian widows were victims of the theft of their dowry and inheritance. When such cases resulted in litigation, a record was preserved. Bunanitum claimed that her stepson had taken the record of her dowry and refused to give her anything. Finally the dowry contract was produced and the court rendered a decision in her favor.[271]

Women who served as domestic slaves were often used as sex slaves by their owners. The children that resulted added to the owner's property. Slave women who were young and beautiful had a higher value than those who were old and ugly. Some slave owners hired their slave women out as prostitutes, both in brothels and to individuals.[272] Since prostitution was legal, it was not a crime. But insofar as prostitution forced women into unwanted sex, it victimized women.

The owner of the slave woman Nubta dedicated her to the temple and had her marked with a star. When he died, his brother illegally took Nubta with his inheritance and made her bear him three children. Nubta herself brought her case to court. The judges ruled that she had to stay with her brother-in-law until he died, but he was forbidden to have sex with her again or to sell her. After his death, Nubta would belong to the temple. Nubta was the victim of her brother-in-law's illegal use of a temple slave for sex. Nannaya-khussinni was a slave of the temple of Ishtar in Uruk. A man bought her as a domestic slave, but she ran away from his house. A trial ensued in which the issue was the date of the star mark on her hand. Experts testified that it was old. The court returned the woman and her son to the temple and told the buyer to collect what he had paid from the guarantor of the sale.[273] Nannaya was the victim of abduction from the temple and fraudulent sale.

Women Offenders

Witchcraft was a capital crime in Late Babylonia. Witches were believed to cause disease, miscarriage, abnormal infants, impotence, contamination of a house by touching its door, and crimes of false accusation, while rendering their victims unable to speak in their own defense. Anti-witchcraft rituals were conducted in the format of a trial. The falsely accused victim first had to prove her or his innocence. Then the status of the parties was reversed and the witch became the defendant. After conviction, witches were condemned to death by fire or water.[274] Since the crime of witchcraft made evil magic manifest, death of the witch by fire or water was considered necessary to purify the state and make it safe.

Women committed crimes in Late Babylonia, as attested in a document which states that married women who were in prison for unnamed offenses could be hired out for wages.[275] Sometimes the courts were called on to intervene in family matters. A mother brought her daughter, Tabat-Ishtar, to court. The daughter was accused of going out with a young man without the knowledge or consent of her father. The girl was officially warned that if she continued to see the young man or married him without her father's consent, she would be sold into slavery.[276]

Many Late Babylonian marriage contracts contained a clause that prescribed the penalty of death by the iron dagger for a wife caught in the act of adultery. The iron dagger was a common weapon in the Late Babylonian period and men wore them at the waist in their belts.[277]

A woman named Gague sold her marriage settlement without the permission of her husband, a descendant of the merchant house of Egibi. Her penalty was forfeiture of her interest in any property they held in common.[278]

In a quasi-civil trial in Uruk, the woman Innana-eterat was the defendant. She and her husband had bought a wife for their slave and had written and sealed a contract giving the slave and the children of the marriage the status of oblates of Ishtar. The slave couple had three children. After her husband died, Innana-eterat sold the slave man to a man who branded him as a slave. The slave took the matter to court, before the governor and judges. Innana-eterat testified that a creditor had put a lien on her property without authorization, claimed to be her husband's creditor, and forced her to give him the man. The judges relied on the initial written contract and confirmed the status of the man and his children as oblates.[279]

Punishment

Women witches were outside the sphere of official religion and society, as well as of marriage and household. Thus, they were not under the control of men, and men believed that this threatened the male dominated social order. Men perceived women witches as dangerous and threatening, and punished them by death to eliminate the sources of their fear.

Adultery also threatened male authority and control. Many Late Babylonian marriage contracts prescribed the penalty of death by the iron dagger for adultery. The penalties for other offenses were fines for most, sale into slavery for a few, and prison for one.

In the Late Babylonian empire, there were harsh penalties for vassal kings who rebelled and broke their vassal oaths. King Zedekiah of Judah had rebelled. When the Babylonians caught him, they killed all his sons, then blinded him, and took him bound in fetters to Babylon.[280]

Summary: Late Babylonian Documents

Among the extant published documents of the Late Babylonian period, certain subjects are missing and others are strikingly different from those of the Old Babylonian period.

Several Late Babylonian kings were powerful warriors and empire builders. Their wives did not rule and were scarcely mentioned. One exception was queen mother Adad-guppi, who played an active and influential role in the reign of her son, Nabu-naid, the last king of Babylonia.

Men had taken over most of the positions held by women in the Old Babylonian period, such as temple offices and the collection and distribution of tax and tribute animals. These positions had given Old Babylonian women power and wealth. Late Babylonian women had little role in the religious cult, except for two isolated texts that mention a woman *naditu* priest and a woman *sagittu*, both temple offices. There were many woman prophets. There is little evidence of other professional women.

The use of royal marriages to concretize political alliances was fading, but those royal daughters given in political marriages received better protection through frequent contact with their families. Late Babylonian marriages between wealthy merchant families to cement economic alliances were well documented. The wealthy merchant and banking families married off their daughters for financial or social gain. Many such marriages were endogamous, preserving the assets within the family.

When a couple married, the parents of each gave a settlement to their child, and the couple was then able to set up their own household. Thus, adult children became independent of their families at a much earlier age. There is no evidence of a legal requirement for children to support their parents in old age. Even elderly parents with children had to contract with their child or another person for care in their old age. The status of older women, especially those without property, was quite insecure.

A small but wealthy middle class of merchant and banking families emerged in this period. Women owned and inherited property; they could litigate and testify in courts. But there is evidence that men were representing women in legal transactions.

Slavery and forced labor increased, especially during the building projects of King Nebukhadrezzar II. Women slaves could be used for sex by their owners or hired out to work as prostitutes in brothels to earn money for their owners. Temple slaves were more prosperous and could not be used for sex; however, they were slaves for life, whereas privately owned slaves were often manumitted.

There are few extant Late Babylonian documents that deal with crime and punishment. The sources are inadequate to make a definitive assessment of women as victims of crime or as perpetrators of crimes. Few forms of punishment are known, except death for adultery and witchcraft, restitution for property crimes, and sale into slavery. It is significant that the extant documents make only rare mention of capital punishment and none of corporal punishment or corporal mutilation.

The lives of Late Babylonian women were somewhat more restricted than those of Old Babylonian women. Yet Late Babylonian women were legal persons with legal rights and had a much higher and more public position in society than the women of Assyria.

CONCLUSION: WOMEN, CRIME, AND PUNISHMENT IN ANCIENT BABYLONIA

The civilization of Babylonia lasted for fifteen hundred years. The status of women, their experiences as victims of crime, and their commission of and punishment for crimes changed in the early second millennium as Amorite men took over the political leadership of southern Mesopotamia. The lives of women became more restricted and consequently less exposed to crime. Punishment of crime became harsher, and for the first time innocent women could be vicariously punished for the crimes committed by others.

The laws of Old Babylonia showed both continuity with those of ancient Sumer and influence of Amorite customary law. The written laws embodied Sumerian ideals of justice and equity and Amorite punishments for crimes. The documents revealed more of the daily lives of the people. Each law and document refracted another sliver of light, revealing new pieces of the puzzle about how women were treated in Babylonian society, victimized by crimes and punished when they committed crimes.

In Old Babylonian laws there was a strong focus on the concept of justice and integration of justice into the formulation of law. King Hammurabi stated that the purpose of his reign and of his laws was to bring justice to his people and empire by protecting the weak against the oppression of the strong. His laws reflect the seriousness of his goal. He introduced the concept of community property in a law on divorce, whereby the ex-wife would receive half of the husband's real estate and custody of the children. When a robber killed a person, the state provided compensation to the victim's family. Old Babylonian kings issued edicts called "acts of justice," which redistributed wealth more equitably by remission of debts.

The status of women was relatively high in Old Babylonia, although not as high as in Sumer. Women owned and inherited property. Marriage required transfer of marriage gifts and a dowry. Marriage contracts were written down, signed, witnessed, and sealed. Old Babylonian marriage law was moving away from polygyny toward monogamy. The Laws of Hammurabi allowed second wives in only three cases and in each the first wife was protected. The laws prevented husbands from abandoning wives who were barren or who became seriously ill or injured during the marriage. Husbands could divorce their wives, but had to provide them with a monetary settlement and return their dowries. It was difficult for women to initiate divorce, and it could be very risky if the marriage contract contained a clause making it a criminal offense. Wives of prisoners of war who were absent for long periods of time were allowed to remarry if their husbands had not left them sufficient provisions. A widow in the Old Babylonian period had a legal right to possess and use her late husband's estate as long as she lived in his house, and she had the right to leave and remarry, although she could take nothing with her.

Old Babylonian women did not hold political offices, but they were priests and held many religious offices. Such women became very wealthy. Women priests could own feudal land, but ordinary women could not. Large communities of women priests in Sippar and Nippur lived independently of men. Women administered textile manufacturing, and they were professional scribes, tavern keepers, and artisans. Women inherited, bought, owned, rented, and sold real property; they signed contracts, gave evidence as witnesses, sued and were sued, and defended themselves and their rights in court.

Laws protected slave owners from loss of property caused by theft or escape of slaves. Slave women and men were chattel, not legal persons. They were bought and sold just as were donkeys and oxen.

Old Babylonian women were victims of the capital crimes of murder, rape, kidnapping, incest, robbery, and assault and battery causing death. Wealthy women were often victims of the crimes of fraud, false accusation, perjury, and theft. However, creditors who abused or killed women in the vulnerable status of pledges and illegal distraint were subject to criminal penalties.

Old Babylonian women committed crimes, such as murder, sacrilege, treason, and witchcraft, which were punished by death The most heinous offense a woman could commit was to cause the death of her husband when involved in an adulterous affair with another man. This crime threatened the very roots of male authority over women in marriage, and the penalty was death by impalement. Incest between mother and son incurred the penalty of death by fire, because the act engendered pollution, which was a threat to the whole populace. Adultery was usually a capital offense for both the man and the woman involved, but the law permitted a husband to forgive his wayward wife or give her a lesser punishment, in which case the state did the same for the male adulterer. Witchcraft was a capital offense because it threatened the well-being of the people.

Some crimes were committed only by women. Women priests who opened or entered a tavern became impure sources of pollution, dangerous to the religious cult, and therefore were put to death. Women tavern keepers who gave false measure were a threat to trade, and those who did not report criminal conspiracies were a threat to state security. Both crimes were punished by death.

Challenges to the authority of the king, state institutions, courts, social classes, and men in general were serious, and frequently capital, crimes. Married women who challenged the domestic authority of their husbands by disparaging their reputations in public were punished by death. Litigants who failed to obey the judgment of a court incurred the death penalty. Free persons who helped escaped slaves were put to death. Slaves who defied the authority of their owners had their ears cut off.

Old Babylonian punishments for crimes illustrated the influence of Amorite custom. Capital punishment was used frequently, and new harsh forms of execution, including impaling, burning, drowning, and throwing offenders from a tower, were employed. The fear of pollution led to the use of fire and water to eliminate the source and effect purification. Corporal punishment and corporal mutilation were used, but were not as frequent or as harsh as in Assyria. The Amorite principle of *talion* and practice of vicarious punishment of innocent persons were employed.

Old Babylonian law continued to proclaim the Sumerian ideal of justice for the weak and oppressed, including women. But restrictions on the activities of women outside the household began to appear. The Old Babylonian dynasty marked the first stage in the amalgamation of Sumerian civilization and law, which had given women extensive legal rights and personhood and had punished most crimes by compensation, with Amorite tradition and customary law, which regarded women as fearful sources of impurity and pollution, took away their legal rights, legal personhood, and access to wealth and punished their offenses by death or corporal penalties. Old Babylonian law and practice maintained a certain balance between the two systems and cultures.

For the next thousand years, Middle Babylonia lived under foreign occupation. Under the benign rule of the Kassites, the legal, literary, and religious works of Sumer and Old Babylonia were collected and preserved. During the rule of Isin, there was a brief revival of the ancient Akkadian and Sumerian custom of the king making his daughter high priest of Ur. Under Assyrian rule, the city of Babylon was destroyed after a long siege, which caused a great famine, but the city was later rebuilt. Babylonian men and women were killed, deported, and enslaved, but later were allowed to return.

Although nearly a millennium under foreign rule had passed between the Old and Late Babylonian periods, there were signs of continuity amidst the differences. Late Babylonian kings had libraries and were familiar with Old Babylonian history and the Laws of Hammurabi.

The status of Late Babylonian women was higher in some areas. In marriage, for example, women could accept marriage proposals, be active parties to marriage contracts, and receive marriage settlements themselves. Late Babylonian women were legal persons who had legal rights, owned property, and inherited. But their status was lower in areas such as personal wealth, influence, independence, and training for professional work outside the household. Few religious or literary texts were written by women, and fewer women were represented in art. In religion, men had taken over most of the important offices, and the extant sources document only a few women who played roles of any significance in the religious cult. Communities of women priests had long ceased to exist, and there were no comparable institutions in which women could live and work independently of men. One mother of a king had a position of influence, but her son was the last king of Babylonia.

Late Babylonian women were victims of crimes such as theft and false accusation, and of abuse of pledges, sale into slavery and prostitution. They committed capital crimes such as witchcraft, adultery, and theft. Late Babylonian criminal law and practice had grown beyond the residual influence of Amorite customs on criminal punishment. There were few references to capital punishment and no mention of corporal punishment or mutilation, of collective or vicarious punishment.

During the Late Babylonian dynasty, the empire was prosperous and great cities were built. Women were regaining rights and legal personhood. Unfortunately, the Late Babylonian kings were the last independent rulers in Mesopotamia for the next two and a half millennia.[281]

15. Torso of woman. Ur, Larsa
Dynasty. Nineteenth century.
British Museum.

16. Bronze statue of kneeling
woman. Found in Eshnunna, Old
Babylonian Period. National
Museum of Archaeology, Baghdad,
Iraq.

17. Stone statue of woman priest or
goddess. Mari, palace of King
Zimri-Lim, about 1780-1760 BCE.
Damascus Museum

18. Gypsum bas-relief of woman priest
or goddess smelling a flower. Mari,
palace of King Zimri-Lim, about 1780-
1760 BCE. Aleppo Museum

19. Ceramic mask of woman, with eye makeup and hair braided with beads. Mosul. National Museum of Archaeology, Baghdad, Iraq.

20. Phoenician ivory relief of woman priest looking out of window. Nimrud, eighth century. National Museum of Archaeology, Baghdad, Iraq.

Photo credit: Erich Lessing/Art Resource, NY

21. Bronze relief of Queen Mother Naqia and son King Esarhaddon. Asshur, about 650. National Museum of Archaeology, Baghdad, Iraq.

22. Phoenician ivory of enthroned queen or goddess. Nimrud, eighth century. National Museum of Archaeology, Baghdad, Iraq.

23. Basalt grave stele relief of child scribe with writing tools standing on mother's lap. Bird indicates falconry. Marash, eighth–seventh century. Louvre.

24. Basalt grave stele relief of woman spinning with child-scribe. Marash, eighth–seventh century. Adana Museum.

25. Alabaster relief of banquet scene. Asshurbanipal reclining with seated wife Esharra-khammat, both drinking. On the left, the head of the defeated king of Elam hangs from a tree. Servants are fanning the king and queen; other servants are playing musical instruments. North palace of Asshurbanipal in Nineveh. Later part of his reign (653-645). British Museum.

Part Three

ASSYRIA

ASSYRIA DERIVED ITS NAME from the ancient city-state of Asshur, located on the Tigris River in northern Mesopotamia. There had been agricultural settlements in the region since 6000 BCE. Towns and cities developed much later.

The Old Assyrian I period was very different from subsequent Assyrian history. The dominant population consisted of a merchant middle class. There were laws and a system for the administration of justice, and women had full legal rights.

In the Old Assyrian II, Middle Assyrian, and Late Assyrian periods, kings were warriors and builders. Middle and Late Assyrian kings built magnificent cities, palaces, and temples, conquered other cities and states, and created a great empire. The middle and late periods of Assyrian history were predominantly a history of conquest and construction, the achievements of men. Women were, for the most part, irrelevant in Assyrian imperial history.

HISTORY OF ASSYRIA	
Old Assyria I (OA I)	2000–1814
Old Assyria II (OA II)	1814–1762
Middle Assyria (MA)	1363–1057
Late Assyria (LA)	934–612

OLD ASSYRIA I (2000–1814)

The Old Assyria I period began in the second half of the third millennium and lasted through the nineteenth century BCE. At that time Asshur was still a small northern Mesopotamian city-state, not unlike those in the south, except smaller and less important. The Assyrian people were primarily merchants and textile manufacturers. The higher civilizations of the south had some limited influence on Asshur through trade and brief rule by the Akkadian and Ur III empires.[1] Asshur did not have a high urban culture comparable to Sumer and Babylonia.

In the Old Assyrian I period, Asshur was a city-state with a flourishing trade and merchant middle class. The merchants exercised great influence over the economy of Asshur. They had established a large trading colony in the city of Kanish in Asia Minor, which was self-governing by assembly and administered its own courts. A document from Kanish describes court procedure. It stated that one-third of the citizens served as judges for trials and more than half were required for appeals. The assembly of citizens included both the important and the unimportant, the rich and the poor. Mediation of conflicts was preferred over litigation. A document from Asshur described the administration of justice there. Seven judges sat together at the Step Gate and heard cases. The judges had a variety of symbolic names, such as "Justice," "He Heard the Prayer," "Get Out Criminal," "Extol Justice," "Watch Over the Downtrodden," "His Speech is Upright," and "God has Heard."[2]

Status of Women

In the Old Assyrian I period, the legal rights of women were not very different from those of women in Sumer and Babylon. The status of women was unique: they were literate professional business administrators. Assyria grew in importance and wealth through trade. Many Assyrian men lived and worked in trading colonies in Asia Minor, while their wives were their agents in Asshur, sending and receiving shipments of goods, paying taxes, and running the business in the capital on their own. These Assyrian women were literate, competent professionals, who represented their husbands and their companies in the capital. More than twenty thousand clay tablets have been discovered in the archives of the Old Assyrian I merchant colony at Kanish. Men and women merchants wrote volumes of correspondence concerning their trading business, and other documents recording legal transactions. Although most of the documents dealt with business matters, there were also a number of court decrees and marriage contracts. Such documents shed valuable light on the lives of the women of Assyrian merchant families in the nineteenth century. This was the time of greatest literacy among nonroyal women and men in the history of ancient Mesopotamia.[3]

Women had a significant role in business. For example, Taramkubi, the sister of a merchant, married the son of another merchant and became a professional businesswoman. Taramkubi worked in Asshur, and her husband worked in Kanish. Taramkubi collected textiles and sent them to her husband, who, in return, sent her silver and gold. She was responsible for paying taxes to the city-state and the temple. In some of her letters, she complained that her husband should send more silver, since, after buying textiles and paying taxes, she did not have enough left for food.[4]

Marriage was a problem when the spouses lived in different cities. The problem was most often resolved by written contracts for marriage and concubinage that allowed the husband to take a secondary wife or concubine in the city where he lived and worked. According to one Old Assyrian I contract of concubinage, a merchant man took Ishtar-lamassi to be his concubine wherever he went in Asia Minor and to reside with him in Kanish. If she did not produce a child within three years, he was entitled to obtain a slave woman for that purpose. If he left her, he promised to give her five minas of silver. If she left him, she had to give him five minas of silver. In addition to these arrangements, the man promised that his wife in Asshur was his only true wife and that he would not take another. An Old Assyrian I marriage contract stated that the husband married Khatala as his legal wife and that she would reside with him in Asia Minor. The merchant promised not to marry another woman in the trading colony, although in Asshur he could take a *qadishtu* woman as a secondary wife. If his primary wife, Khatala, did not bear a child within two years, she would have to purchase a slave woman to bear a child for her husband. After a child was born, the slave woman could be sold. If the husband later divorced his wife, he would have to pay her five minas of silver. If Khatala chose to divorce her husband, she had to pay him five minas of silver. The document was signed by four witnesses.[5] Some Old Assyrian I marriage contracts illustrate that women and men had the right to initiate divorce and the obligation to pay compensation to their ex-spouses. Although polygyny was practiced among merchants, it was generally restricted by contract to one additional and inferior wife or one concubine.

Old Assyrian I law required families to take care of their elderly. Merchants who retired from trade in Kanish went home to Asshur to spend their old age cared for by their families. Such men generally had two wives and many children. Husbands provided care for their wives and unmarried daughters in their wills. Assyrian documents used two words, one meaning "support" and the other, "respect, fear, serve and obey." The second word characterized the proper attitude of people to the gods, children to parents, and wives to husbands. The duty of sons and daughters to care for their mothers and fathers continued after a parent's death and included mourning rituals, burial, and funeral rites.[6]

In the Old Assyrian I period women were beneficiaries of wills. Many women holding religious offices inherited from their parents' estates. For example, a father wrote a will, providing for his daughter, Akhatum, an *ugbabtu* priest, who could not marry but had to maintain her own household. Her father left her many debt-claims owed to him and a full share in his estate. He also mandated that her two brothers give her annual monetary support and provide animals for temple sacrifice. He left to his wife, Lamassi, a house in Kanish and a large debt-claim. The husband of another woman named Lamassi, who held the religious office of *qadishtu*, left her a house in Kanish, slave girls, and other property. In his will, he admonished his sons to respect and support their mother, and he gave her the authority to eject them from the household if they did not do so.[7] In a fragmentary will, a man left his estate to his sons, but made a special bequest to his widow, Buza, although she had to leave the family house. A man who was not married made a will in which he left his house, furniture, and slave woman in Kanish to his half-sister, Shat-Adad, and two shares of the remainder of his estate to Shat-Adad and her mother, and he stipulated that his brothers support the two women.[8]

In Old Assyria I, women made wills and left their property to their chosen beneficiaries. Lamassatum, widow of a merchant, left silver, debt-claims, textiles, and slaves in Kanish, to be transported to Asshur and there divided among her priest-daughter and her sons according to the shares she had specified in her will. Another woman, Ishtar-lamassi, declared her intended bequests on her deathbed, with her sister as witness. She left her daughter, an *ugbabtu* priest, gold, silver, her seal, and a share with her brothers in her estate.[9] These wills indicate that Assyrian women of the merchant class in the nineteenth century were priests and other religious officials in the Old Assyrian religion and that these women were supported by and inherited from their families.

Old Assyrian I women were not, however, very well protected in divorce. In one case, the court of Kanish decreed that a husband divorced his wife, Zibe-zibe. He had to pay her one mina of silver as a divorce settlement, and he kept their three sons. After the divorce was final, the ex-wife had no further claim on her ex-husband or their sons.[10] The fact that men who divorced their wives had to give them fair compensation affirmed the status of women as legal persons with some rights in the Old Assyrian I period. Yet the situation of the ex-wife was precarious. The loss of the relationship between mother and sons meant destitution for the woman in her old age, when she would otherwise have been supported by her sons. Since she had some money, and if she were not too old, she might remarry and then be supported by her second husband and children borne of that marriage.

In Old Assyria, judgment on debts was rendered by the court of Asshur. One case concerned a dispute over the repayment of a debt of forty minas of silver owed to the father of the sons and daughter who brought the action. Another son had gone with a bailiff and recovered the money. The court held that the siblings who had brought the suit had no claim to the money. Instead they were ordered to return the tablet that recorded the debt, since the debt had been repaid. The plaintiff brothers and the sister had to acquiesce in the decision of the court of Asshur. The brothers were not named, but their sister, Akhakha, a religious official, was named. She was represented by a man; her brothers were not.[11] This case provides evidence that, in the Old Assyrian I period, women held religious offices, were parties to lawsuits, at least through a representative, and were entitled to a share of their father's property.

Another Old Assyrian I court decision from Kanish dealt with the dissolution of a partnership. When one partner died, his children brought suit against the children of the other partner. The son of each partner represented his own interests and those of his sister, Abshalim and Akhakha, respectively. Both women were religious officials and could own property. A panel of judges was assembled to decide questions of the obligations of each of the partners. When these issues were resolved, the decree forbade any further litigation on this matter by any of the parties.[12] This document confirmed that women held religious offices and that these women owned and inherited property in this period.

In Old Assyria I, many women were wealthy, and some made dedications to temples. For example, a woman named Khaditum made a dedication to the goddess Ishtar in the main temple of Asshur for the life of her husband, her own life, and the lives of her children.[13]

Women of the Old Assyrian merchant class had far more freedom and wealth than later Assyrian women. Through marriage contracts, Old Assyrian I husbands and wives had almost equal rights in marriage. The quantum of support and the penalties for violation of the marriage contract were the same for men and women. Women made wills and loans, owned and inherited property, and bought and sold slaves. Old Assyrian widows of the merchant class were provided with sufficient property by their deceased husbands that they could live their lives financially independent of men.[14]

This was a unique time and a unique class of women in ancient Near Eastern history. Assyrian merchant women were wealthy, even though they were middle-class, not royals or aristocrats. The very existence of a strong middle class was unusual in ancient Near Eastern history. Many women were literate and experienced professional businesswomen, trusted partners and representatives of their husbands. These women were the most literate professional women in Assyrian history. Yet even so, husbands practiced polygyny and had final authority over their wives. Representation of women by men was beginning to appear in court cases.

Women Victims and Offenders

Women in the Old Assyria I period were strong and well protected by the laws. There is little evidence of women being victims of crimes or committing crimes at this time. Women had status and wealth and were busy running trading companies. There was little time or motivation for criminal activities.

There were, however, a few crimes that women did commit. For example, violation of a court judgment was a capital offense. An Old Assyrian I court decreed the divorce of a man from his wife, Taliya. It stated that if Taliya tried to reclaim her ex-husband, she would be fined two minas of silver and be put to death in a public place. If her ex-husband or his father tried to reclaim the ex-wife, they too would be fined two minas of silver and be put to death in a public place. Perjury was also a capital offense.[15] Truthfulness was very important in a merchant society.

Punishment

An Old Assyrian I royal decree pronounced the penalty for perjury in the language of a curse. The offender would be lifted up and thrown down so that his or her head would be smashed "like a shattered pot" and water would run out of his or her mouth. The gods would then obliterate out the offender's household and descendants.[16] There is no evidence that such a penalty was actually executed.

OLD ASSYRIA II (1814–1762)

In northern Mesopotamia there was neither a strong, well-established civilization nor a gradual settlement of Amorites. There the Amorites took the city-states quickly by force and ruled by might, with little assimilation of the indigenous culture. The Amorites perceived their identity as tribal even after they settled in cities. Amorite tribal custom had a much greater influence on law and society in northern Mesopotamia.

At the end of the nineteenth century, the status of women changed radically when an Amorite chief, Shamshi-Adad, conquered Asshur and founded a new dynasty. Amorite society in northern Mesopotamia was patriarchal, and the primary role of women was to bear children. The legal system of the merchant middle class disappeared and was replaced by Amorite tribal customs and edicts of kings.

Shamshi-Adad I consolidated power in the person of the king, calling himself "king of the universe." He built temples, united the city-states of Asshur, Nineveh, and Arbel, all of which were situated on important trade routes. He conquered the powerful city-state of Mari and created a small empire in northern Mesopotamia.[17]

During Old Assyria I, husbands and wives had a basic equality and mutual respect in marriage. In the Old Assyria II period, class stratification and gender distinctions drew people apart. Shamshi-Adad I reduced women to sex objects and began the Assyrian custom of collecting a harem. Like later Assyrian kings, he and his sons had collections of women as objects for their pleasure. Shamshi-Adad I gave the daughters of the conquered king of Mari to the harem of his son, the governor of Mari. Some of them he kept in his own palace, for his son's use on visits. Others were taught singing, and some were traded for slaves.

Shamshi-Adad I arranged a political marriage for his son with Beltum, the daughter of the king of Qatna, who agreed on condition that his daughter would be queen. There could be only one queen at a time, and she had influence on the king, thus providing an advocate for her family's interests. The bride brought fifteen talents of silver as a dowry. The groom's family paid only four talents. The son already had a principal consort, a daughter of the previous king of Mari, as well as secondary wives and a harem. He did not want to change and considered building a house for Beltum outside the palace, or relegating her to the harem. Either action would have provoked scandal and threatened the political alliance. Shamshi-Adad wrote to his son and forbade him to do either. He ordered his son to give her a suite in the palace and see her frequently. Beltum was very young when she came to Mari, but she gradually learned her way as she grew into adulthood and became a correspondent with and an advocate for her father. Her husband had another secondary wife named Kunshimatum, who resided in Terqa. One letter from her has survived. In it she complained that she had been slandered by unnamed persons, causing the loss of her husband's trust. She defended her performance of her duties of maintaining the household and praying for her husband. She challenged the king to send auditors to inspect her management of the palace.[18]

In Old Assyria I, many middle-class women had been priests. In the Old Assyria II period, Shamshi-Adad I personally took over the priesthood and made himself chief priest.[19] In Old Assyria I, nonroyal women had been - powerful literate professionals working in international trade. Shamshi-Adad I destroyed the city of Kanish and the merchant middle class. The legal and social position of women in the Old Assyria II period under the first Amorite Assyrian dynasty was radically different from their status in the Old Assyria I period, but it was consistent with the Middle and Late periods of Assyrian history.[20]

MIDDLE ASSYRIA (1363–1057)

There was a gap of more than three centuries between the Old and Middle Assyrian periods. This was a time of migrations and conquests when little was written down. Amorite, Aramean, and Chaldean tribes roamed through Mesopotamia and settled in various areas. The Hittites made incursions into Mesopotamia from Asia Minor.

By the fourteenth century, Assyria ruled northern Mesopotamia, and Kassite Babylonia ruled the south and was its rival for trade routes. The Assyrians had friendly relations with those states which agreed to be their vassals and to pay annual tribute. States that rebelled and refused to pay tribute to Assyria were punished by war and destruction. Middle Assyrian kings conquered all of Mesopotamia and began the deportation of war captives to distant parts of the empire. Deportation was a common practice among Assyrian kings. They resettled conquered peoples far from their homelands, providing them with clothes, food, equipment, and wives. Assyrian kings wanted the resettled peoples to make a viable and contented life in their new location so that they could provide labor for the empire, create new farmlands and not rebel or cause trouble as they had in their previous location.[21]

Middle Assyrian kings wrote laws and annals of their conquests and accomplishments; yet, in the end, Assyria became weaker and the invading tribes grew stronger.

THE MIDDLE ASSYRIAN LAWS

In the first quarter of the eleventh century, the Middle Assyrian king Tukulti-apil-Esharra I sent out jurists to collect the laws of Assyria. He assembled the laws they found, added his own to those of his predecessors, collated and redacted them. The Middle Assyrian Laws were a mixed collection of Old Babylonian law, Amorite customary law, and decrees of Assyrian kings. The Middle Assyrian Laws did not constitute a law code, but contained commentary on, additions to, and amendments of earlier laws about various subjects, written and collected by jurists and legal scholars, edited and promulgated by the king.[22]

Many copies of the Middle Assyrian Laws have been found in the excavations of ancient Asshur. The tablets are broken and fragmentary, leaving many lacunae in the text. Tablet A is the longest and best preserved of the tablets. Many of the laws in tablet A dealt with issues affecting women: marriage, divorce, and inheritance; crimes of which women were victims; and criminal offenses committed by women.[23]

The laws demonstrate that Middle Assyria was still in a time of transition from the tribal custom of private jurisdiction over crimes such as murder and adultery by the head of the victim's kinship group to the administration of justice by the state, which conducted trials and carried out the punishment of those convicted of crimes.

Status of Women

In the Middle Assyrian period, the status of women was considerably lower and more controlled by men than it had been in the earlier civilizations of Sumer and Babylonia. The Middle Assyria Laws demonstrate the influence of northern tribal customary law, especially in the areas of the legal status of women and the penalties for crimes.

The primary role of women in Middle Assyria was to marry and bear children. Marriages were arranged by contract between the father of the groom and the father of the bride, after negotiation of the marriage price. Once the prospective groom delivered the agreed marriage price to the father of the bride and it was accepted, the couple was betrothed and a feast was held. When the bride moved into her husband's house, with ceremony and feasting, the marriage was complete. The change of the residence of the bride signified the final step in marriage and ended the rights of her family of birth to her person or property. The procedure in Assyria was more like a sale than a mutual exchange of gifts.[24] Married women were the legal property of their husbands.

The Assyrians had a custom of pouring oil on the head of a prospective bride to signify her betrothal. For example, the father of a prospective groom brought food for the betrothal feast, during which he poured oil on the head of the prospective bride. When a betrothed son died or ran away before the marriage, his father had the right to marry any of his other sons who were at least ten years old to the betrothed bride. If both the father and his betrothed son died, and the latter had a son ten years old or older, then that son could marry the prospective bride. If the deceased only had sons younger than ten years old, the father of the prospective bride could decide whether to give his daughter to one of them or to return the marriage price.[25]

In one case, a couple was betrothed but not yet married, and the groom's brother died, leaving a widow. The groom's father gave the widow into the protection of his betrothed son. If the prospective bride's father then changed his mind about the marriage, since the groom's circumstances had been altered by his new responsibilities to his brother's widow, he had to return the marriage price, except what had been consumed at the betrothal feast. Then the father of the prospective groom had the right to marry his no longer betrothed son to his widowed daughter-in-law.[26]

In another case, after a suitor had delivered the agreed marriage price to the house of his prospective father-in-law, his prospective bride died. He could choose either to marry another daughter of the same family or take back the marriage price. If he chose the latter, he could only take back the silver. The father of the deceased bride could keep the grain, sheep, and anything that was edible.[27]

Assyrian women owned only small amounts of personal property, generally gifts from their husbands. Women had no inheritance rights in intestate succession. When a married man died without a will, without having made written donations of property to his wife during his lifetime, and without sons, his brothers had the right to divide all his property, including anything of value he had given to his widow. However, if the deceased husband had sons by his present or a former marriage, the sons took the estate and whatever gifts their father had given to his wife or wives. According to this law, if her late husband had no sons, the widow could keep his gifts.[28]

Other laws concerning inheritance did not mention women at all and stated that the estate of a deceased father was to be divided among his sons. One fragmentary law stated that women did not receive shares of silver. There is nothing in these laws to indicate that any portion of a man's estate was given to his widow or daughter.[29]

All of a deceased man's sons had the obligation to support his widow. The sons would draw up a contract whereby they provided her with food and drink. The widow resided with one of her sons. If she were a second wife and had no sons of her own, she could reside with one of her husband's sons from a previous marriage. But as long as she had sons, they had to provide for her and, in return, she had to serve them. This requirement of service was unique in ancient Near Eastern law. It underscored the Assyrian view of women as commodities that men controlled and used to their advantage.[30]

When a widow remarried, her new husband had to support her, and her sons were discharged from their obligation of support. If a widow had no sons, her father-in-law could give her in marriage to another of his sons or to a son of her late husband by a previous marriage. Her own father could give her in marriage to her father-in-law. If both her husband and her father-in-law had died, and her deceased husband had no brothers or sons, she was considered a legal or true widow and could go wherever she pleased.[31]

A widow who was pregnant when her husband died could remarry, but her child would not inherit from the estate of her new husband or be liable for his debts unless the child was formally adopted by the new husband.[32]

When a man lived with a widow without a written marriage contract for two years, the widow became his wife and could not leave his house. If a widow remarried and moved into her new husband's house, whatever property she brought with her became the possession of the husband. On the other hand, if a man entered a widow's house to have sex with her, whatever he brought with him was considered a gift and became the possession of the woman.[33]

Several laws dealt with absent husbands, but these were not consistent and thus were from different sources and time periods. In one, a man left the country without providing his wife with food, oil, wool, or clothing and did not send her anything. He did leave his wife a house where she could live. She had to remain in her husband's house for five years, after which she could remarry.

When her first husband returned, he had no claim to her. When the husband had been detained more than five years through no fault of his own, and he could prove this, even if his wife had remarried, he could take her back, but had to provide a comparable woman to his wife's second husband. If the husband was away more than five years in the king's service, his wife was supposed to wait for him indefinitely. If the wife remarried before five years had elapsed and had children by her second husband, when her first husband returned, he had the right to take back his wife and take the children.[34]

According to another law, when a man was taken prisoner in war and his wife did not have a father-in-law or son to support her, she had to remain faithful to her husband for two years. If she had nothing to eat, she was permitted to work for food If she was destitute during the time of his absence because her husband's field did not yield enough to support her, she could appeal to the judges of the city, who then provided her with a house and field for two years. After the two years, the state granted her the legal status of widow and she could marry a husband of her choice. If her first husband later returned, he could reclaim his wife, but not the children of the second marriage. He also had the obligation to repay the city for the house and field leased for his wife's support.[35] Under the first law, the wife had to wait five years, or longer if her husband was in the king's service, and her sons, if she had any, were her only means of support. In the second, the wife was obligated to wait only two years, and she could work or the state would support her if she became destitute.

There were two laws that treated divorce. In both, the husband initiated the divorce. Women had no right to any compensation if their husbands divorced them. When a man decided to divorce his wife, he could give her something if he chose, but he was not obligated to give her anything. He could simply turn his wife out of his house empty-handed. If a wife resided in her father's house when her husband divorced her, he could take back whatever personal gifts he had given her, but not the marriage price, which belonged to her father.[36] There is no indication in the Middle Assyrian Laws that women could initiate divorce.

Several laws dealt with women given as pledges for debts. A debtor gave his daughter as a pledge to his creditor. The creditor wanted to give the daughter in marriage, but he had to ask permission of the girl's father before he could do so. If the father did not give permission, the creditor could not give the girl in marriage. If her father died, then the creditor had to ask permission of her brothers, who had the right to redeem their sister by paying off the debt within one month. If they did not do so, the creditor then had the right to give the girl in marriage.[37] It was to the advantage of the creditor to give a girl in marriage if he could negotiate a marriage price greater than the amount of the debt.

A man who was in debt to another man gave his daughter as pledge for the debt. The creditor gave the girl in marriage. When a prior creditor came to collect his debt, the first creditor had to pay the prior creditor the full value of the girl. If he could not pay, the prior creditor could take the man himself.[38] The pledge laws treated women as commodities with a specific monetary value.

In the Middle Assyrian Laws, there are two laws governing the veiling of women. One law stated that wives, widows, daughters, and other respectable Assyrian women should not go out of their houses into a public street with heads uncovered. A concubine who went out with her mistress could wear a veil. Prostitutes and slave women were not permitted to wear the veil. The second law required a married *qadiltu* woman to be veiled, while an unmarried *qadiltu* woman was not permitted to be veiled.[39] The veil was perceived as a symbol of respectability and signified that the wearer was not available for sexual relationships. Veiling was another way men exercised control over women any time they went out in public. The veil was ultimately a symbol of the domination of men over women.

Polygyny was legal in Assyrian law. If a man wanted to raise the status of his concubine to that of secondary wife, he had only to summon six witnesses and in their presence veil her and state that she was his wife. A concubine who was not thus formally veiled was not a wife.[40]

Women Victims

The Middle Assyrian Laws on homicide were deeply rooted in Amorite tribal custom. The laws explicitly stated that the victim and the perpetrator could be either male or female. If a man entered the house of another and killed a woman, the murderer was handed over to the head of the victim's household or clan, who could choose either to put the offender to death or take compensation from the murderer's property. If the murderer had no property, the head of the victim's household could take the murderer's son or daughter instead. The text is fragmentary, and it is unclear whether the son or daughter was put to death, taken into servitude, or sold into slavery.[41] This law reflects the tribal custom of private resolution of capital cases. Women were victims of homicide, and daughters of murderers could be victims of vicarious punishment for the parent's crime.

Assyrian women were victims of rape. There are five different laws pertaining to rape in the Middle Assyrian Laws. Three laws dealt with rape of married women. In the first, the rapist seized a married woman by force in public and stated his intention verbally; the woman refused consent, protested, and tried to protect herself. The state held a trial, heard eyewitness testimony, and convicted the rapist. The death penalty was mandatory for a man who took a married woman by force and raped her despite her protest and struggle. The state executed the rapist. There was no blame or punishment for the woman. In this law, the adjudication of the offense of rape was completely under the jurisdiction of the state.[42]

In two older laws, the women victims were married, and the line between rape and adultery was blurred. The laws used hybrid jurisdiction and treated both offenses more as adultery, and the women victims were punished by their husbands. In the first, a man raped a married woman in public or in an inn. This law did not mention non-consent or resistance by the woman, but focused on the offender's knowledge of her marital status. If the offender knew the woman was married, the state gave him whatever punishment the husband chose to inflict on his wife. If he did not know that she was married, he was not punished. The husband had to prove charges against his wife in court, but then he could punish his wife however he wished. In the second law, the husband caught the rapist/adulterer in the act. The subjects of the verbs are unclear. "They" had to prove him guilty and then "they," including the husband, could put both to death. If the husband brought the male offender to a formal court, and "they" found him guilty, then the husband decided and executed the penalty for both: death, corporal mutilation, or no penalty at all.[43]

Other rape laws dealt with the rapes of unbetrothed virgins, which were considered crimes against the property rights of their fathers. In one law, the rape of the virgin daughter was dealt with privately by her father. A man forcibly seized and raped a young virgin who lived in her father's house and was not yet betrothed. It was irrelevant whether the rape took place in the city or the countryside, during the day or at night. The father of the victim had the right to take the wife of the rapist and hand her over to others to be raped. The father could keep the rapist's wife and make the rapist marry his daughter. If the rapist had no wife, he had to pay the victim's father three times the value of a virgin daughter in silver and marry the victim. The father of the victim could, however, accept the silver but give his daughter to another man in marriage. In this situation two innocent women were the victims of a crime committed by one man. A young girl who was raped could be forced to live the rest of her life with the rapist, and the wife of the rapist could be gang raped as punishment for the crime of her husband. In another law, jurisdiction was hybrid. The rapist was tried by oath and the state administered oaths. He swore that the girl had consented. In this case the wife of the rapist could not be punished. The rapist still had to pay the same triple fine, and the father had the authority to punish his daughter however he chose.[44]

These two laws perceived the rape of a virgin in terms of property damage, economic loss to the father because of the diminished value of his no longer virgin daughter for sale into marriage. The first rape was dealt with in private between the family of the victim and the offender. The penalty was the infliction of equivalent property damage on the rapist that he had inflicted on the father of the victim, which resulted in the vicarious punishment of an innocent woman for the crime of her husband. In both laws, the young virgin girls could be punished for having been raped.

Most of the rape laws were hybrid, combining summary procedures and punishments at the discretion of the patriarch, father, or husband with state judicial procedures including charges, evidence, trial, conviction, and sentencing. The rape laws treated fathers and husbands as victims because the women raped were their property and the rape diminished the value of their property. They were also victims insofar as public knowledge of the rape diminished their honor. Even if a married woman was exonerated by the court, her husband could still punish her however he wished. Women victims of forcible rape were punished for having been raped, making them twice victims.

Several laws dealt with other sexual crimes against women, in which the offending man was punished. Sexual battery was punished by corporal mutilation. When a man laid his hand on a woman, "attacking her like a rutting bull," and formal charges were brought against him and proven in court, the state cut off one of the man's fingers. If the attack included a forced kiss, the state cut off the offender's lower lip with the blade of an ax.[45] When women were victims of sexual battery, the state punished their attackers.

There were many cases of false accusations of infidelity made against married women. Different laws dealt with the offense in different ways. For example, in one law a man made slanderous statements to a husband, accusing his wife of having had sex with many men, but the accuser had no witnesses. The wife had to undergo the river ordeal to determine the truth or falsehood of the slander.[46] The wife could die in the process of proving her innocence. In another law, a man told a husband that many men were having sex with his wife. He made public charges and said that he had proof, although he did not. When he failed to prove his accusations in court, the court subjected the false accuser to multiple penalties: forty blows with rods, one month of penal servitude, the cutting off of his hair, and a fine of one talent of lead.[47] The state handled the case, and the woman accused was not involved.

Women were victims of assaults and batteries that were sometimes so severe that they caused miscarriage or the death of the woman. Two laws treated the same crime differently. In both cases, an upper-class man struck a woman of the upper class, causing her to have a miscarriage. In the first, the offender was charged and proven guilty in court, and the penalties were imposed and carried out by the state on the offender: fifty blows with rods, one month's penal servitude, and a fine of two and a half talents of lead. In this law, the mother did not die of her injuries. The second law did not mention a court or a trial, but used the plural "they" in the penalty clause, implying state jurisdiction. The crime was the same, but the penalties were different. If the woman did not die, "they" treated the wife of the offender as he had treated the victim. Thus the offender's wife, not the offender, was vicariously punished for the crime of her husband. She was beaten in proportion to the extent of the original assault. This punishment was based on the principle of *talion*: a beaten wife for a beaten wife, a dead fetus for a dead fetus. In this law, the attacker was punished vicariously through his innocent wife, creating a second victim. The offender had to pay compensation for the life of the fetus. If the initial woman victim died, the state put the attacker to death for the life of the woman, and his estate had to pay for the life of the fetus. If the victim's husband had no sons and the aborted fetus was a boy, the offender was put to death for the life of the fetus. If the fetus was a girl, the offender had to pay the monetary value of her life in compensation to the father of the fetus for his property loss.[48] The laws show that innocent women and their unborn children were beaten to death by men. The death of an upper-class wife was treated as homicide, but the death of the fetus was a capital crime only if the fetus was male. The same offense was considered merely a property loss if the fetus was female. The second law included penalties based on tribal customary law: *talion* and vicarious punishment of an innocent woman. In both laws, punishment was under the jurisdiction of the state.

In another case, a man beat the pregnant wife of another man, causing a miscarriage. But since the woman did not raise her own children, the fetus was considered of less value to her and her husband and the penalty was reduced to a fine of two talents of lead.[49] The husband received monetary compensation for his property loss. The real victims of the battery, the wife and the unborn child, were not compensated for their losses.

When a man struck a pregnant prostitute, causing miscarriage, the offender was punished by the same number of blows he had inflicted on the victim, and he also had to pay full compensation for the life of her fetus.[50] The number of blows was an attempt at equity, making the quantity of the punishment fit the crime, but it was not based on *talion*, which would have required the equivalent beating of a pregnant woman. Since a prostitute belonged to no man, the monetary compensation was paid to the prostitute herself.

In earlier laws on assault and battery causing miscarriage, some cases were resolved by the husband of the victim, others by the state. The line of transition was crossed when the state realized that both feticide and homicide were crimes against itself, which caused the loss of future citizens and the mothers of future citizens.

The practice of holding women as pledges for the debts of men created situations in which women were very vulnerable. Women of the upper class had greater legal protection. According to one law, if a woman of the upper class held as a pledge was treated with cruelty, she was free of any further obligation to the man who abused her. Other laws made it a crime for a creditor to sell a pledge who was the son or daughter of a citizen. After trial and conviction, the penalty was forfeiture of the sale price, public flogging, and penal servitude. If the creditor sold the pledge into foreign servitude, the penalties were the same, but the length of penal servitude was doubled. If the pledge died in the foreign land, the penalty was the death of the creditor.[51] The Middle Assyrian Laws increased the penalties for men who abused pledges, yet the existence of these laws demonstrates that pledges were cruelly abused in the Middle Assyrian period.

The laws were different, however, when the value of the pledge was the same as the amount of the debt. In this case, the debt was discharged and ownership of the pledge transferred to the creditor, who then could do whatever he wanted with the pledge. The creditor could beat the pledge, pull out his or her hair, mutilate or pierce his or her ears, or sell the pledge into slavery in a foreign land.[52] Assyrian women given as pledges for the full value of the debts of men could be victims of abuse, mutilation, and sale into foreign slavery.

Married women, even though they did not possess any property, were held legally responsible for the debts of their husbands and for any criminal penalties to which their husbands had been sentenced. If the husband had been sentenced to death, for example, and died before he could be executed, his widow could be executed in his place.[53]

The fact that wives could satisfy debts and criminal penalties, when slaves could not, indicates that free women had some legal personhood, at least when it was to the advantage of men. The practice of vicarious liability and punishment of women for the debts and crimes of their husbands was a significant factor in the victimization of women in Assyrian law and society.

Women Offenders

The first eight of the Middle Assyrian Laws dealt with crimes committed exclusively by women. The first law treated the crime of sacrilege. A woman of the upper class "entered a temple" and stole something belonging to the temple, that is, to the god of the temple. If the woman was caught in the act or with the stolen property, or was prosecuted and found guilty, her punishment was decided by the god of the temple. The priests presented the evidence, the stolen property, to the god to determine sentence. The god's will was communicated to the priests by divination. The sentence was carried out by the priests of the temple. Sacrilege was the only crime in the Middle Assyrian Laws that fell under religious jurisdiction. Since women could not casually enter a temple, the woman offender probably lived or worked inside the temple. In the Middle Assyrian period, few women were priests or held other religious offices, but some women still worked and resided in temples as servants, artisans, musicians, pledges for debts, and temple prostitutes.[54] When a married woman or the daughter of an upper-class family spoke words of blasphemy or sedition, she alone was punished, not her husband or sons and daughters.[55]

The Middle Assyrian Laws may be the first legal system to deal with assault and battery committed by women against men. Such acts were considered a very serious challenge to the authority of men over women and consequently were severely punished by the state. If a woman laid a hand on a man and a formal charge was brought, two punishments were imposed: a fine of thirty minas of lead and a beating of twenty blows with a rod. Both punishments were severe. The penalty indicates a presumption that a woman would be able to obtain sufficient funds to pay the fine and that she would have sufficient strength to undergo such a beating.[56]

When a woman crushed one of a man's testicles in a fight, one of her fingers was cut off. However, if she crushed both testicles in the fight, or if the second testicle became infected after she crushed the first one, the penalty was more invasive mutilation: both of the woman's breasts were torn off.[57] Both crime and punishment involved the loss of organs that were part of the person's sexual identity and functioning.

In a male dominated society, adultery was a serious crime. When a married woman went to the house of a man who was not her husband and he had sex with her, even though he knew that the woman was married, the state imposed the death penalty on both the wandering wife and the man.[58] The crime of adultery affected the state because it could result in confusion about the legitimacy of its citizens.

Two laws treated rape of a married woman as adultery by punishing the woman as well as the male offender. When a man had sex with a married woman in a public street or an inn with knowledge that the woman was married, the crime was considered adultery. Both parties were tried and found guilty or innocent. If the offender had no knowledge that the woman was married, he incurred no penalty. If the wife was found guilty by the court, the husband could punish her however he chose.[59] If a husband caught another man on top of his wife and the state tried and convicted the man, the state put both the wife and the adulterer to death. In the second part of this law, jurisdiction switched from state to hybrid. When a husband caught a man having sex with his wife, he could bring the male offender before the judges or the king. If the court found the adulterer guilty, the husband had the right to determine and execute punishment on both parties. The husband could kill his wife and the convicted adulterer. If the penalty chosen was mutilation, the husband cut off his wife's nose, but castrated the male adulterer, while others slashed the man's face. If the husband did not want to punish his wife, he was barred from punishing the male offender.[60] The issue of the woman's consent, which would legally distinguish rape from adultery, was not mentioned.

When a married woman invited a man to have sex, the man was not punished and the woman was punished by her husband, who could impose whatever penalty he chose upon his wife. Since the wife initiated the crime, she was
presumed guilty and no trial was held. But if a man had sex with a married
woman by force, the charges against the man had to be proved in court. If the
man was convicted, his punishment was the same as that of the wife, even
though, in this case, she was an innocent victim and was not tried or convicted
by a court. The punishment of the woman was left to her husband, since she
was his personal property. The punishment of the man, who was a legal person, was carried out by the state.[61] The second crime was really rape, but the
law treated it as adultery.

When a virgin consented to sex with a man, she committed the crime of
fornication. The man had to swear an oath that the girl had consented. Even
so, he still had to pay three times the value of a virgin girl in silver to her father
for his property loss. The father could punish his daughter however he
pleased.[62] The prescription of the monetary penalty for the man indicated that
his action was perceived as wrong.

Married women committed offenses through contact with men outside
their husbands' households. If a married woman traveled with a man who was
not a relative, the man had to swear an oath that he did not know that the
woman was married, but he still was fined two talents of lead. If he did know
that she was married, he had to swear that he did not have sex with her and
pay damages. If the wife contradicted his testimony, then the man had to
undergo the river ordeal. If he refused, the state punished him in the same way
as the husband punished his wife.[63]

There were sexual implications whenever a woman entered the house of a
man other than her husband or her father. When a married woman took
another man's wife into her house and brought a man to have sex with the
wife, if the man knew that the woman was married, the state prosecuted him
for adultery. The state gave the woman procurer the same punishment that the
husband inflicted on his wife. If the husband did not punish his wife, then the
state would not punish either the man or the woman procurer. However, if the
wife did not know what was intended and the woman procurer brought the
man in by deceit, and when the wife left the house she immediately declared
that she had been raped, she was not punished. The woman procurer and the
rapist were put to death by the state. If the wife did not declare that she was
raped, her husband could punish her in any way he chose. The woman procurer and the adulterer were still executed by the state.[64] The wife was under
the authority of her husband, so he had the right to choose and carry out her
punishment. The woman procurer and the adulterer were not subject to the
authority of the husband, and they were sentenced and punished by the state.
This case moved one step beyond the earlier hybrid jurisdiction. The state

chose and carried out punishment without regard to the punishment chosen by the husband for his wife.

In one case, a wife left her husband and went to the house of another man, staying there with the man's wife for three or four nights. The host did not know that the guest was a married woman. When the runaway wife was caught, her husband could punish her by mutilation and take her back as his wife. The wife of the man in whose house she stayed was presumed to have knowledge that her guest was married and had left her husband. Under the law, the state could cut off her ears and take her away unless her husband exercised the option of paying a ransom and taking her back. If the host knew that the fugitive was a married woman, he had to pay a fine. If he denied having such knowledge, he had to undergo the river ordeal, and if he refused, he had to pay the fine. But if he was exonerated by the river ordeal and the husband refused to take the river ordeal and took back his wife without mutilating her, then none of the parties was punished.[65]

Another way Assyrian men exercised control over women was by requiring that married women and widows be veiled in public. The Middle Assyrian Laws made it a crime for certain women to wear a veil and for other women not to wear a veil and prescribed harsh penalties. A prostitute was forbidden to wear a veil and could be arrested for going about with her head covered. The person who arrested her was given her clothing. The prostitute received fifty blows with rods and had hot pitch poured over her head, causing disfiguration and thereby jeopardizing her livelihood. On the other hand, if a man who saw a prostitute veiled did not turn her in to the palace, he received fifty blows with rods. Further, they pierced his ears, tied them together with a cord at the back, and made him perform penal servitude for the king for one month. The person who informed on him got his clothing.[66] Respectable married women had to wear veils in public, whereas prostitutes and slave women were not permitted to be veiled. This made it very easy for men to tell the status and sexual availability of the women they encountered.

The practice of witchcraft was considered a serious crime, and it was dealt with directly by the king. Any person who witnessed or heard about the crime was obligated to inform the king. The king could interrogate the eyewitness by any method he chose. If a woman or man was caught in the act of practicing witchcraft or with magical potions in her or his possession, formal charges were brought in court. If the charges were proved and the court found the defendant guilty, the penalty was death. In the ancient Near East, women were more often accused of witchcraft, magic, and sorcery than men. The same laws applied to both.[67] In extant Assyrian literature, there are far more written incantations and rituals to undo witchcraft than evidence of the apprehension, trial, or execution of witches.

The most serious crime committed by women in ancient Assyria was abortion. Abortion was viewed as a public offense against the state, which took jurisdiction, not as a private offense against the husband or the fetus. The primary reason abortion was an offense against the state was the terror of blood in ancient societies, the fear that innocent blood shed would pollute the state and cause a calamity. Families and tribes were connected by blood. If an outsider shed the blood of a family member, the family had to respond by blood revenge. It was a worse offense when a family member shed the blood of another family member. The worst form of homicide was when a mother killed her child. The blood relationship between mother and child was the most profound that existed, beginning nine months before the child was born, during which time the child was nurtured through the blood of the mother. Another reason was practical: the state's need for replenishing the population to replace soldiers killed in its constant wars. This reason applied only to male fetuses, but the abortion law did not distinguish on the basis of gender. A woman who aborted her fetus by her own act was formally prosecuted by the state. If the charge was proven and she was found guilty, the penalty was death by impalement and denial of burial. Even if the woman had died during the abortion, her body was still impaled on a stake and denied burial. Her body could not be buried because it would pollute the earth. The punishment was carried out by the state, not by the husband, because her crime affected the whole state. The final line of the law is fragmentary, but it indicated that anyone with knowledge of an abortion who concealed the offender or failed to report the offense also committed a serious crime.[68] The penalty of impalement caused bleeding, which served to purify the state from pollution. Denial of burial avoided pollution of the land.

The laws concerning theft and stolen property generally required trial, conviction, and sentencing by a court. Several laws dealt with specific thefts in which the offender was a women. When a wife stole any property from her husband when he was sick or had died and gave it to another person, both the wife and the receiver of the stolen property were executed by the state. The penalty was severe because it involved a threat to the dominance of men if women could take advantage of them when they were weak or sick. When a husband was alive and well and his wife stole something from his house and delivered it to another person, the husband could file charges against his wife. Then, if her guilt was proven, he had the right to decide and carry out the punishment of his wife. The receiver of the stolen property had to return it, and then the court imposed the same punishment on the receiver as the husband had inflicted on his wife.[69] This law is in the same hybrid form of state and private jurisdiction that was used for crimes against persons.

When a married woman stole anything of value from the house of a man other than her husband and the man charged her with theft, the woman's husband had the duty to return the stolen property and the right to ransom his wife and punish her by cutting off her ears. If the husband did not ransom and punish his wife, the owner of the stolen property could "take her" and cut off her nose.[70]

Since women did not have the legal capacity to own or transfer property, there was nothing in a husband's household that a wife could have legally taken or deposited outside the house. The wife could have stolen something from her husband or from a third party, but she could not keep stolen property in the house; she would have to leave it with someone outside her house. When a married woman deposited property outside of her house with a third party, that person was expected to notify the state or the property owner. If the third party failed to make a report and was found in possession of the property, he or she was presumed guilty of possession of stolen property. When the receiver of property stolen by a wife was a male or female slave, the state punished the slave by amputation of his or her nose and ears and restored the stolen property to the husband, who could then amputate his wife's ears. If the husband chose not to punish his wife, then the state did not punish the slave.[71]

Punishment

The penalties for crimes in the Middle Assyrian Laws were harsh and primitive. Death was the penalty for the crimes of sacrilege, blasphemy, sedition, witchcraft, homicide, assault and battery causing miscarriage and death of the woman, forcible rape, adultery, procurement of a married woman for sex, and theft from a weak or sick husband. The most severe penalty, death by impalement and denial of burial, was reserved for the crime of abortion.

The Middle Assyrian Laws introduced combinations of several noncapital penalties for a single offense: corporal punishment, corporal mutilation, penal servitude, and fines. Penal servitude was generally imposed only on men. Corporal punishment usually consisted of public flogging. Assaults and batteries on women that caused miscarriage but not death were punished by public flogging and penal servitude. Public flogging and fines were rarely imposed on women. However, when a woman committed the crime of a man, such as physically attacking a man, she was punished like a man, beaten with rods and fined. One attempt at equivalence of punishment and injury was when the victim of battery was a prostitute; the assailant was given the same number of blows he had inflicted on the woman victim.

Corporal mutilation was common in crimes against persons. When a man and a married woman were convicted of adultery, the husband cut off his wife's nose and castrated the man, while others slashed the man's face. This was an early law, since the husband still had the right to punish both offenders. A man convicted of sexual battery of a woman had his finger cut off. A man who forced a kiss on a nonconsenting woman had his lower lip cut off with an ax. A wife who ran away from her husband to another person's house was punished by mutilation. The wife of the man in whose household she stayed was punished by amputation of her ears. A woman who fought with a man and crushed one of his testicles was punished by amputation of one finger. If she crushed both testicles or if the second testicle became infected, the penalty was cutting off her breasts or gouging out her eyes.

The Middle Assyrian Laws also used corporal mutilation as punishment for property crimes. A wife who stole property from a man was punished by her husband by amputation of her ears. But if her husband refused, the owner of the stolen property could cut off the woman's nose. When a wife gave stolen property to a slave, the husband cut off the ears of his wife and the state cut off the nose and ears of the slave.

False accusation of sexual activity against a wife was punished by forty blows with rods, cutting off the accuser's hair, and penal servitude. A prostitute who went outside veiled was punished by fifty blows with rods and by pouring hot pitch over her head, disfiguring her face for her profession. A man who saw a prostitute or slave woman veiled and did not report her was punished by fifty blows with rods, the piercing of his ears with a cord tied around his back, penal servitude, and loss of his clothing. A husband could punish his wife by beating her, striking her, pulling out her hair, and mutilating her ears.

The Middle Assyrian Laws prescribed collective and vicarious punishment of women for crimes committed by men. Rape of a virgin was punished by rape of the offender's wife. Under the principle of *talion*, a man who beat the wife or child of another was punished by the beating of his own wife or child. A betrothed or married woman was punished for the crimes of her betrothed or husband. Yet when a woman committed a serious crime, she alone was punished. Her husband and children were not punished for her crime, which demonstrates a double standard for punishment of crimes in the Middle Assyrian Laws.[72]

The final legible law listed additional punishments that husbands had the right to execute upon their wives. A husband was permitted with impunity to whip his wife, strike her, pull out her hair, and mutilate or destroy her ears. No specific offense on the part of the wife was mentioned. This law may be a list of acceptable punishments for offenses that had no set penalty in the laws. The law also put a limit on the husband's range of punishment by omitting those that were unacceptable, such as death or gross mutilation.[73]

The punishment of crime in the Middle Assyrian Laws was in transition. Only two crimes were still completely under private jurisdiction: homicide and rape of an unbetrothed virgin. Nine laws had hybrid jurisdiction. When crimes were committed by wives or daughters, the role of choosing and carrying out the punishment of the woman offender was still held by the offender's husband or father, but the state was in charge of the trial and conviction of other offenders. The state imposed and carried out on other offenders the punishment the husband chose for his wife. If the husband declined to punish his wife, the state generally did not punish other offenders. The majority of crimes were punished by the state. The Middle Assyrian Laws had fifty-six criminal laws. Of these forty-two were punished by the state, nine were hybrid, two were under private jurisdiction, and one was under religious jurisdiction.

Summary: Middle Assyrian Laws

The Middle Assyrian Laws reveal how, in this period, the status and roles of women were being increasingly limited. Women could own only minimal personal property. Women rarely inherited property—only when their deceased husbands had no brothers and no sons. Men could divorce their wives without giving them anything, and wives could not initiate divorce. Men veiled women and segregated them from the world outside the household. Marriages, both royal and nonroyal, could be polygynous. Women were liable for the debts and were punished for the crimes of their husbands, but husbands were not punished for the crimes of their wives. Women who challenged the authority of men were put to death. Women were increasingly controlled by men in a society based on male dominance. The status of women under the Middle Assyrian Laws was far lower than in other ancient Near Eastern societies and legal systems.

At the time the Middle Assyrian Laws were compiled, the administration of criminal justice was still in transition. The state criminal justice system was taking over the prosecution and punishment of additional crimes, thereby limiting the private execution of justice within the family. Yet the latter still existed, centuries after other ancient Near Eastern civilizations had abolished it, illustrating how profoundly Assyrian law had been influenced by tribal customary law and how deeply the domination of men over women and husbands over wives was embedded in Assyrian law.

The greatest influence of tribal law was on the types of punishment for crimes. The Middle Assyrian Laws contained sixty-three criminal laws, of which forty-eight prescribed capital or corporal punishments. There was little information about the forms of execution, except for the use of impalement for the crime of abortion. Corporal punishment was generally public flogging with rods. Corporal mutilation was most often the amputation of ears, nose, eyes, breasts, and fingers, although the Assyrians also castrated men, poured hot pitch over the heads of women, and cut up the faces of offenders. Innocent women were vicariously punished for the crimes of their husbands and fathers.

THE MIDDLE ASSYRIAN PALACE DECREES

The Middle Assyrian Palace Decrees present a different type of law source, consisting of decrees written by nine Middle Assyrian kings between 1363 and 1076. The last king collected the decrees of his predecessors and promulgated them as one document. The subject of all the decrees was quite narrow: rules and regulations for the behavior of women and men in the palace harems where the king's women resided. Each decree addressed a specific problem. The decrees remained in effect long after the deaths of the kings who issued them.[74]

These decrees are valuable for providing a glimpse into the lives of the king's palace women. The Middle Assyrian Palace Decrees illustrate the degree of control over the king's women, the low status of women, and some of the harsh penalties of Middle Assyrian law.

Status of Women

The Assyrian king had a primary wife who had a visible position in society. Kings also had numerous other women whom they locked up in the harem. Management of the king's women was a major enterprise and required its own collection of laws and regulations. The decrees were enforced by harsh penalties for anyone who violated them. Witnesses to infractions had to report them to the palace commander or they would be severely punished.

The earliest decree described how the building in which the royal wives and concubines were housed was equipped with many locks to keep women in and men out. Entry into the women's quarters without permission of the palace commander was a serious crime, as was going out onto a roof of the palace, from which men could look down into the women's quarters and look at the women. The same decree noted the presence of two professional women, a midwife and a *qadiltu* woman, who worked inside the harem.[75]

Another decree prescribed the procedures when one of the king's women, his sons, or his brothers died. If the king was in the Inner City, an official had to report the death to the palace overseer, who would then report it to the king. When the king was less than twelve miles away, the palace overseer sent written tablets. If the king was more than twelve miles away from the palace, the overseer allowed the palace women to begin the mourning rites.[76]

One of the ways Assyrian kings protected the sexual purity of their women was by the requirement that all male officials who worked in the women's quarters be castrated. Palace officials and a physician inspected all the royal eunuchs to make sure they had been properly castrated. If they were not, the officials reported them and had them castrated a second time. Any official who allowed a non-castrated male attendant to enter the palace was punished by the amputation of one foot.[77]

If the king sent a eunuch to the women's quarters when the women were present, the eunuch had to report first to the palace commander, who then stood at the entrance while the eunuch was inside. The women had to leave while the eunuch was there. It was a criminal offense for a eunuch to enter women's quarters without the permission of the palace commander.[78]

If a eunuch eavesdropped while palace women sang or quarreled, the penalty was amputation of one ear and a hundred blows with rods. When a court attendant spoke with a palace woman, he had to stay seven paces distant from the woman. If a palace woman summoned a court attendant and they spoke longer then necessary to give an order, the attendant was flogged with a hundred blows, his clothes were taken, and he was dressed in sackcloth.[79]

The Middle Assyrian Palace Decrees revealed the growing importance of the blood tabu in controlling and denigrating women. Blood was thought to render a woman unclean and was a source of pollution that would contaminate anyone with whom she had contact. When the time for offering sacrifices was near, a menstruating woman could not enter the presence of the king. Any contact with a menstruating woman would render the king unclean and unfit to offer sacrifices or enter the presence of the god.[80]

One decree dealt with married women who worked in the palace but resided with their husbands outside the palace. On holidays they could not go back or forth to their homes without the permission of the king.[81]

Women in the women's quarters in the palace were generally protected from any contact with men, with the exception of the king and his eunuchs. The rationale was to keep their bodies pure from sexual contact with anyone other than the king and thus to prevent any possibility of illegitimate offspring.

Women Victims

The Middle Assyrian Palace Decrees did not contain laws that specifically described women as victims of crimes. Since these regulations concerned the women's quarters of the palace, women there were well protected against most crime. Yet the women were victims of the institution of the harem, confined under lock and key, sex objects belonging to the king, sequestered in one part of the royal palace with no contact with people outside except eunuchs and the king. Insofar as these restrictions were perceived by the women as negative, they were victims of the harem system.

If harem women were falsely accused of capital crimes, such as looking at a man or speaking a few words to a man, they had no recourse or means to defend themselves. Innocent wives or daughters of palace officials who committed crimes under these laws were victims of vicarious punishment.

Women Offenders

The Middle Assyrian Palace Decrees contain laws and regulations in which palace women were forbidden certain acts and punished if they committed these acts. If the women fought or quarreled with each other, they were punished. A woman who blasphemed the name of the god Asshur, a capital crime, had her throat cut. Improper swearing in the name of the god was a capital offense. If a palace woman cursed the king or his descendant, a member of the royal household, an official of the royal bedroom, a woman who was beneath her in station, or a pregnant woman, the royal officials pierced her nose and beat her thirty blows with rods.[82]

It was a capital offense for a palace woman and a man to stand by themselves talking with no third party present. If a court attendant or another palace woman saw this and did not report it to the king, the witness was thrown into an oven. If a palace woman summoned a court attendant and he stayed longer than necessary speaking with her, even though the woman initiated the conversation, the man was punished by a hundred blows with rods and the loss of his clothes to the person who reported him.[83] No punishment was stated for the women, but this did not mean she was not punished.

There were decrees that dealt with the relationship between palace women and their slave women. If the slave woman of a wife of the king or of another palace woman committed an offense that challenged the authority of her mistress, the mistress could punish the slave woman by thirty blows with rods. If the same slave woman committed a second offense, her mistress brought her to the king, who decided the punishment and had it carried out in his presence. He then returned the slave woman to her mistress. But if a palace woman beat her slave woman so violently that the slave died, even though the beating itself was permitted by the king, by her excess the woman committed a punishable offense against the king.[84]

The crime of theft was mentioned frequently in the decrees. It was a capital crime for anyone to take anything out of the palace without the express permission of the palace commander. When the king left the palace, the palace commander and doorkeepers searched the containers of jewelry, clothes, and oil of everyone who traveled with the king. If the king summoned women from the palace, the palace commander and the doorkeepers inspected their clothes as they left. When the king stayed at a different palace within the city, palace women who were with him could not send for anything from the main palace, not even a cloak, a veil, or a pair of boots, without the express permission of the king or the palace commander.[85]

Palace women were forbidden to give gold, silver, or precious stones to palace slaves. Slaves who accepted such valuables from palace women were punished by amputation of their noses and ears. An official who knew about the crime but did not report it was doused with hot oil and his sons were made slaves to the palace. The extant text is fragmentary and does not contain the punishment for the woman who initiated the offense.[86]

Palace women who committed crimes were not tried before a court, since they could not leave the harem or be seen by men. Without the ability to confront their accusers and without any means to mount a defense, palace women were convicted by the reports of eyewitnesses or hearsay witnesses, and punishment was summarily executed.

Punishment

The royal palace decrees did not contain as great a variety of punishments as the Middle Assyrian Laws, but both collections prescribed the use of capital punishment, corporal punishment, corporal mutilation, and vicarious punishment.

The two forms of execution referred to in the Middle Assyrian Palace Decrees—throat cutting and the oven—were not mentioned in the Middle Assyrian Laws or earlier Sumerian or Babylonian laws. Execution by throat cutting was the penalty for the crime of blasphemy, which was committed by the larynx. The death penalty by unspecified means was prescribed for improper swearing, theft from the palace, close contact with a man, and failure to report a capital offense.

Most other penalties were physical. They included corporal punishment, by beating with rods and corporal mutilation, by piercing the nose, amputation of the nose, ears, finger, foot, or breasts, and pouring hot oil over the offender's head.

Lesser penalties included giving an offender's clothes to the witness who reported him or her and making the offender wear sackcloth. The penalty for an official who did not report a crime was vicariously imposed on the official's innocent children, who were enslaved to the palace for their father's crime.[87]

The penalties used in the Middle Assyrian Palace Decrees were harsh but easily carried out without having to leave the women's quarters. The forms of punishment used in the Palace Decrees illustrate the same influence of earlier tribal customary law as did the criminal penalties in the Middle Assyrian Laws.

Summary: Middle Assyrian Palace Decrees

The Middle Assyrian Palace Decrees stem from the same milieu and time period as the Middle Assyrian Laws. The Palace Decrees, however, were addressed to a small specific group of persons who lived and worked in the women's quarters of the palace. Every aspect of the lives of royal wives and concubines was regulated by men. It was almost impossible for these women to challenge either the regulations or the power of the men who made and enforced them. If a woman crossed over any of the boundaries of law that confined her, the penalty was generally death.

Late Assyria (934–612)

There is a time span of more than a century from which almost no Assyrian inscriptions have survived. The Late Assyrian empire began in the tenth century when Assyria grew strong again and economic prosperity returned. The first king consolidated control over the cities of Assyria. His successors were strong and capable kings and generals. Late Assyrian kings restored the old empire of Assyria and expanded it to include, at its greatest extent, all of Mesopotamia, western Asia Minor, the Phoenician coast, Syria, and Palestine.[88]

One example of a Late Assyrian conquest was the kingdom of Israel, which had initially been an Assyrian vassal but later had switched its allegiance to Egypt. Then the Assyrian army besieged the capital at Samaria for three years until it surrendered. The Assyrian emperor deported the entire population of Israel to the far northern and eastern regions of the empire.[89]

King Sennakherib conquered Babylonia and put all of southern Mesopotamia under Assyrian rule. He sacked and destroyed the city of Babylon. His son and successor, Esarhaddon, rebuilt Babylon and its temples and made one of his own sons its king. His other son, Asshurbanipal, was the last effective Assyrian emperor. He was harsh and cruel, burning and mutilating his enemies and destroying their cities. After his death, Babylonia regained its independence and conquered the remnants of the Assyrian empire. The axis of power in Mesopotamia then shifted back south to Babylonia.[90]

Assyrian Documents, Inscriptions, and Art

Numerous ancient Assyrian documents of various types have been found, written on clay and on stone. Inscriptions on stone were primarily royal, religious, or funerary documents or boundary markers. Clay tablets contained court documents and cases, contracts, business transactions, and letters. From the time of Shamshi-Adad I, Assyrian kings kept archives of documents from their reigns. Middle and Late Assyrian kings wrote annals about the military achievements of their reigns. Some kings set up libraries in their capitals.[91] Assyrian art depicted kings and conquests, gods and animals, but very few women and ordinary people.

Status of Women

Women's names and information about women are noticeably rare in Assyrian art and royal inscriptions. No Assyrian women were portrayed in the stone reliefs in Assyrian royal palaces until the reign of Asshurbanipal at the end of the Late Assyrian period. Middle and Late Assyrian kings embodied and increased male power and dominance. The ninth-century king Asshurnasirpal II frequently recited his royal titles in his documents. He wrote, "I am king, I am lord, I am exalted, I am important, I am magnificent, I am foremost, I am a hero, I am a warrior, I am a lion, and I am virile." Elsewhere he described himself as a "strong male, who treads upon the necks of his foes."[92] The use of the titles "virile" and "strong male" was not accidental, but part of the ideology of kingship, which defined itself in terms of masculinity, virility, superiority over and otherness from women. The connotations of this machoistic ideology affected the lives and status of women.

Some Assyrian kings used political marriages of their children to children of other kings to strengthen political alliances or treaties of vassalage and to acquire large dowries as a form of tribute. King Shamshi-Adad I married his younger son to Beltum, the daughter of the king of Qatna. Her father gave her on the condition that she would be the queen, a condition the prince was reluctant to perform, since he already had a principal consort. Although very young at the time of her marriage, Beltum eventually achieved influence and carried out political and military correspondence with her father. King Tukulti-apil-Esharra I had his son marry the daughter of an Aramean prince, an Assyrian vassal, who gave Assyria his daughter and a very large dowry. When King Sargon II conquered Tabal in Asia Minor, he gave his daughter, Akhatabisha, to the old king's son and made him king. King Esarhaddon gave his daughter in a political marriage to a polygynous Skythian ruler when the Skythians were still nomadic tribes. Later he expressed uncertainty whether that had been a good decision.[93]

Comparatively little is known about most of the wives of Assyrian kings, even their names. However, excavation of tombs under the royal palace at Nimrud have revealed the identity and names of four Late Assyrian queens: Mullissu-mukannishat-Ninua, wife of King Asshurnasirpal II and mother of King Shalmaneser III; Yaba, wife of King Tiglathpileser III; Banitu, wife of King Shalmaneser V; and Atalia, wife of King Sargon II. Each was buried in a sarcophagus, with gold crowns, jewelry with precious stones, and ivory figurines.[94] A row of stelae in Asshur contained only the names of kings, with three significant exceptions: Sammu-ramat, Naqia, and Libbalisharrat, all wives of Late Assyrian kings. In the inscriptions, they were called "Ladies of the Palace," a title that implied authority and status superior to that of the palace women.[95]

Sammu-ramat was the wife of King Shamshi-Adad V and the mother of King Adad-nerari III. She was active and influential in political affairs, but did not rule officially as queen. It is possible that she reigned as regent for four years until her son was old enough to be king. The power and influence of Sammu-ramat were greater as queen mother than as the wife of the king. A boundary stone marking the border between two vassal kingdoms was inscribed by her son and stated that she rode out with him and crossed the Euphrates, where he fought a battle defending his vassal states. The district governor dedicated two statues in the temple, one inscribed for the life of the king, the other for the life of Sammu-ramat.[96]

The most important of the these royal women was Queen Naqia, the wife of King Sennakherib, mother of King Esarhaddon, and grandmother of King Asshurbanipal. There are numerous royal inscriptions, economic and administrative documents, building inscriptions, dedications, letters, succession treaties, seals, queries to gods, and oracles that were written by, addressed to, or mention Naqia. She had been a secondary wife of Sennakherib while he was still crown prince. After his eldest son and designated heir was killed, King Sennakherib left the succession open for eleven years before he chose Esarhaddon, his youngest son, to be his successor. This act brought Naqia, as mother of the crown prince, to prominence and to wealth, when Sennakherib transferred the estate of the previous queen mother to Naqia. When another son of Sennakherib killed his father in 681, Esarhaddon defeated his brothers in a brief civil war and became king.[97]

As queen mother, Naqia played a significant role in the reign of her son. Since his own accession had involved a civil war, Esarhaddon and Naqia planned ahead so that this would not happen again. Their strategy was for Esarhaddon to make a written document of succession and to increase public awareness of the stature and accomplishments of Naqia so that when the king died, the aristocracy would know and respect her royal position and authority and she could maintain control of the empire during the interregnum.[98]

Sennakherib had destroyed the city of Babylon; his widow and son rebuilt it. Naqia built a palace for Esarhaddon at Nineveh. That such a project could be accomplished by a woman was without precedent in ancient Assyria. The building inscription used the form and terminology of royal Assyrian building inscriptions, except the builder was not a king but a queen. Naqia was called "queen of Sennakherib, king of the world" and "mother of Esarhaddon, king of the world." Her acts and the inscriptions that recorded them increased her royal stature and authority and effectively communicated both to the people.

Naqia contributed to the rebuilding of temples and endowed religious festivals. She made dedications of jewelry and gold to temples and donations of animals and supplies for sacrifices. Her temple dedication inscriptions began with the standard words: "for the life of Esarhaddon and for herself," but hers added: "for her own life, the stability of her reign and her well-being."[99]

Naqia was active in religious rites and temple administration in five of the most important cities of the Assyrian empire. Esarhaddon included his mother in religious rituals at a time when most other women were excluded. Esarhaddon commissioned statues of himself and of Naqia for a temple. Previous Assyrian kings had often placed statues of themselves in temples, but not statues of their wives. A bronze relief depicted Esarhaddon with a scepter in his hand, followed by Naqia with a mirror in her hand, performing a religious ritual. This was part of their strategy to elevate the position of Naqia by showing her devotion to the gods and the gods' approval of her. Many letters were written to Naqia by priests answering questions she had asked about the necessary implements and rituals for various sacrifices.[100]

Administrative letters reveal the political importance of Naqia as queen mother. The king himself wrote frequently to his mother, telling her, for example, that he had done what she had asked him to do concerning various matters. The governor of the Sealand province in the south wrote to the queen mother concerning an Elamite border raid, asking that the king send him troops. The letter ended with a statement of his loyalty to the household of the king, rather than simply to the king. A fragmentary letter stated that certain persons had appealed to the queen mother and that she wrote to the person in charge of the matter. Such letters indicate that officials and the people knew that Naqia had influence and that the king would listen to her. She received letters from Assyrian and Babylonian officials, including two written when the king was away at war. It is probable that Naqia ruled during the king's absences. One letter from an Assyrian official stated that the decisions of the queen mother were "as final as the gods."[101]

During Esarhaddon's last years, he survived an attempted coup, but his health was very poor, and Naqia may have ruled during his illnesses. When Naqia herself was ill, she was treated by the king's exorcists and physician, because her recovery was crucial to their plans for the succession. A year after she recovered, Esarhaddon died. Naqia immediately took charge and instituted a loyalty oath to her grandson, Asshurbanipal. It was styled as a treaty between the queen and the people. It required anyone learning of a plot or conspiracy against Asshurbanipal to report it to the queen and anyone with knowledge of an armed rebellion to kill the conspirators and bring their corpses to the queen. Six times, the queen was named first. As queen and sole ruler she enforced the succession treaty and held the empire together for twenty days until the coronation of her grandson. The succession was peaceful and the political situation in Assyria remained stable for the next forty years, until a successful Babylonian revolt brought the Assyrian empire to an end.[102]

Although she was not mentioned on the stelae, King Esarhaddon loved his principal wife, Esharra-khammat, very much. She was the mother of the next kings of Assyria and Babylonia. When she predeceased her husband, her daughter and her daughter-in-law prepared her for burial. Esarhaddon so revered her that her death was mentioned in his annals, which was very unusual.[103]

There is less documentary evidence about the last queen, Libbalisharrat. When Asshurbanipal was still crown prince, his sister, Sherua'eterat, wrote a letter to his wife, Libbalisharrat, scolding her for not practicing her writing skills, which could cause embarrassment to the royal family, and reminding her that she was merely a daughter-in-law, whereas the writer was the eldest daughter of king Esarhaddon. The fact that this letter remained in the archives and was not destroyed after Asshurbanipal became king, thereby making Libbalisharrat queen, is remarkable. Libbalisharrat made dedications to temples. She was portrayed in a stone relief sitting in a chair beside her husband, who was reclining on his dais. Both were drinking from bowls.[104]

Although their own wives were not officially ruling queens, Late Assyrian kings had mixed reactions when foreign or vassal states were ruled by queens. Tiglathpileser III frequently mentioned Zabibe, queen of Arabia, in his tribute lists. When she broke her oath of vassalage, the king pursued her into the desert and captured her. He appointed an Assyrian officer to monitor her but allowed her to retain her throne. Later, he conquered the Arabian army led by queen Samsi and took much booty. Afterward, she became a vassal and paid tribute. King Sargon II had the woman ruler of a town in Urartia killed and blamed it on the Urartians, attributing to them a principle that an Urartian woman could not occupy a throne.[105]

The titles used by Assyrian kings represented their ideology of kingship and their roles and functions as emperors: military commander in chief, highest judge, and high priest. Kings held the highest political office in the state and empire. As commanders in chief of the army, Middle and Late Assyrian kings rode at the head of their armies, destroyed their enemies, and created a large empire. Assyrian kings took the titles "judge" and "highest judge." Two Middle Assyrian kings used the term "just scepter," which is believed to have originally belonged to the gods, who gave it to the kings to rule the people with justice. Kings appointed judges and heard the most important cases and appeals themselves.[106] Kings called themselves high priests and functioned as priests, offering sacrifices to the gods. Thus, kings controlled the political, military, judicial, and religious systems from the top, and the officials who served under them in all four areas were almost exclusively male.[107]

Despite male control of all the power structures of the state and the empire, there were a few exceptions. Although there were no defined political roles for queen mothers, exceptional women such as Sammu-ramat and Naqia gained power, wealth, and influence, not because their sons were kings, but through their own abilities. The king's wives and palace women had to please both the king and his mother. The queen mother had a large staff, many of whom also became wealthy. Queen mothers had treasurers and stewards of their possessions. Letters recorded horses sent to a king by the treasurer of the queen mother. The scribe of the queen mother bought a large estate in land. Queen mothers owned towns and had managers of those towns. They even had a chief confectioner. Queen mothers had eunuchs and bodyguards. Some queen mothers had their own troops, under a personal cohort commander, as well as chariot drivers. Queen mothers were assigned a certain amount of money from taxes and tribute, which they could lend at interest. They also donated money to temples.[108] Queen mothers were quite wealthy and exercised influence on their king-sons, on other members of the royal family, and on palace personnel.

Queens held a position much higher than that of the women of the king's harem. Queens owned gold, silver, jewelry, land, and slaves; they had their own staff, including troops under their own cohort commander, chariot drivers and eunuchs. Some queens had women scribes. Queens had their own cup-bearers. The royal gardeners delivered baskets of fruit and bowls of wine to the queen. Queens made offerings of oxen, sheep, lambs, and ducks to the temples for sacrifice and received meat from the ceremonies.[109] The queen's administration was parallel to, but smaller than, that of the king.

Royal women bought land and slaves. Shadditu, the daughter of Sennakherib and the sister of Esarhaddon, bought a house and land along the river for eight minas of silver. Another daughter of a Late Assyrian king owned a whole town. Abirami, the sister of a queen mother, leased land that had been pledged, although the debtor could redeem it by repaying his debt.[110]

Archaeology has shed light on the lives of royal women. Excavations of the royal palaces demonstrate that the open part contained public rooms, where the king and his court carried out the business of empire. The other, less accessible parts consisted of living quarters. The queen had a double suite with a reception room and a courtyard. There were separate quarters for the palace women. There were large suites with private bathrooms for the more important women and many smaller rooms for the less important. At the entrance were offices for the eunuch staff and a guardhouse.[111]

Royal women were wealthy and well fed compared to other women and men in the Late Assyrian period. Yet the skeletons of royal women show that they had significant health problems. Most of the royal skeletons had degenerative joint disease, and more than half showed evidence of childhood diseases. They were also weak from lack of exercise, yet they were healthier than lower-class women.[112]

In the Late Assyrian period, there was one high office in the palace held by a nonroyal woman, called the *shakintu*. She was the highest administrator in the queen's household. There is evidence of *shakintu* women in the royal palaces in all three Assyrian capital cities, Asshur, Nimrud, and Nineveh. In Nineveh, there were several royal palaces and a *shakintu* in each one. The *shakintu* at Nimrud had a scribe named Attar-palti, a deputy named Kabal-aya, and an assistant who sometimes served as a judge for cases within the women's quarters. There were *shakintu* women also in other cities and towns in Assyria. A provincial *shakintu* corresponded with the king about the behavior of the governor of the province. The *shakintu* had reported him; the king wrote to correct him; and the *shakintu* reported back to the king that the governor still had not performed the king's command. The *shakintu* wrote this letter in the first person.[113] These letters demonstrate that the position and influence of the *shakintu* extended far beyond the women's quarters.

The *shakintu* women were wealthy and owned slaves and land, yet very few of their names are known. One *shakintu* woman, Zarpi, bought the woman Bililutu from her brother. It was noted in the document of sale that the brother owned his sister. Another *shakintu* bought two women slaves, one of whom was named Banitu-teresh. Other documents record slave sales to and by unnamed *shakintu* women and land sales to *shakintu* women. They had their own eunuchs and made loans of silver, barley, and animals.[114]

The archives of the *shakintu* women were closely guarded in a secure place in the palace. One such archive has been found in the southwest palace of Sennakherib in Nineveh. It contained nineteen documents, written between 694 and 681. Two women who served as *shakintu* at this time were named Adda-ti and Akhitalli. Adda-ti made loans in silver and took land, men, and their wives and children as pledges. A contract states that the pledges would be freed as soon as the money was repaid. Adda-ti bought a slave woman for silver. In the same year, the *shakintu* made a loan of eleven ewes and their rams. Akhitalli, *shakintu* of the main palace of Nineveh, was named in five documents, which recorded slave sales and land sales. In one sale, Akhitalli bought a woman, Anat-dalati, and her infant daughter for thirty sheqels of silver. In another, she bought three slaves for four minas. Akhitalli bought an orchard and seventeen persons, including two wives, a mother, and a sister, from a village that belonged to the queen and a large estate of eighty hectares. Other documents in the *shakintu* archive recorded more slave and land sales. Three slave-sale records stated that the buyer was the *shakintu* of the central city, that is, of main palace in Nineveh. In the first of these documents, the *shakintu* bought a man and a woman named Akbara for one mina of silver. In the second, she bought twenty slaves, of whom at least three were wives and one was a daughter. The third document is fragmentary, but stated that the *shakintu* bought an unknown number of slaves for ten minas of silver. Another fragmentary document stated that the *shakintu* of Nineveh sold thirty-one persons and forty hectares of land for a price of seventeen and a half minas of silver.[115]

Another smaller *shakintu* archive was found in the fort at Nimrud. It was located in an inside room of the queen's residence. The rest of the fort was military. The archive contained records of court decisions, slave sales, and loans made by women. The witnesses to these documents were doorkeepers and lockkeepers, personnel of the women's quarters.[116]

The extant documents did not mention *shakintu* marriages or husbands, but a *shakintu* in Nimrud had a daughter, for whom she arranged a splendid wedding. She hired a goldsmith and bought wine and jewelry in Nineveh and Asshur. She provided her daughter's settlement and gave her in marriage, both acts normally performed by the father. The settlement included gold plate, objects of silver, jewelry, many clothes, chairs, other objects made of copper, and a bronze bed. The mother designed the marriage contract, which provided that if the bride did not have sons, she could provide her husband with a slave girl. If the latter produced sons, they would belong to the bride. If she liked the slave girl, she could keep her, but if not, she could sell her. If the bride came to hate her husband, she could give back her settlement. If the husband hated the bride, he had to give her twice the value of her settlement.[117] This contract was much more favorable to the bride than most marriage contracts of the time.

A few other documents in the archive recorded legal transactions made by named women. The lady Barsipitu bought four slaves, including a man, his brother, and his wife and daughter. The lady Lateggiana bought a woman named Abikhali for nine sheqels of silver. The lady Indibi made an interest-free loan of seventeen minas of silver. If it was not paid back on the due date, interest would accrue at two sheqels per month for each mina. The debtor had pledged his vineyard, his wife and two daughters, a slave and his daughter, and all the rest of his property.[118]

In two land and slave sale documents from the archive of the *shakintu*, the buyers were ladies of the palace. In the first, a lady of the palace bought land and twenty-three slaves, including six wives, three mothers, and two daughters. Only the male slaves were named. The slaves were taken in pledge until the purchase price was paid. The second recorded the sale of a house, for which the lady of the palace paid in full.[119] These documents demonstrate that women palace personnel also became quite wealthy.

Although Assyrian kings took the title of high priest for themselves, one Middle Assyrian king gave a gift of jewelry to his daughter, Muballitat, whom he called "the great high priestess." It is probable that she was a lower-level priest or held other religious office, since at this time in Assyria the office of high priest was held by the king.[120]

Palace archives contained some evidence of women priests. The king was the head of the state religion, but other members of the royal family, including sisters and daughters of kings, could participate in temple rites. Queen Naqia performed religious rites with her husband and son, both kings. The wife of a governor was a priest, who was a guest in the palace when the king died. Her husband took her out of the palace, where contact with a dead body would render her ritually unclean, and she sacrificed a goat. Another ritual stated that women removed the upper parts and intestines from the sheep killed for sacrifice. A purification ritual noted women officiants. A woman *ugbabtu* priest borrowed barley from a man. A Late Assyrian hymn mentioned *kulmashitu* women, who were singers in the temple at Arbel.[121]

Some women held administrative offices in the temple, including that of temple steward. A list of temple personnel in Nineveh reported six women stewards and six women temple scribes. A letter mentioned a temple stewardess who was involved in an investigation of a theft from the temple. A cook confessed and was beaten to death. In another document, a priest related to the king that he had seen two beautiful young girls in the temple. He knew their names and reported them to their families. The text suggested that it was both unusual and improper for girls to be in the temple.[122] There were a few women who were priests and held other religious offices in Late Assyria.

Religious rites and festivals in the ancient Near East were generally celebrated with music and song, with many women musicians. Assyrian art depicted musicians in the temples and palaces, and a Late Assyrian hymn mentioned several musical instruments, including a lyre. One Late Assyrian document described a palace singer and his daughters, who sang at the death of the king. Assyria frequently acquired foreign musicians as booty in war and as tribute paid by vassal states. In the Late Assyrian period, the palace at Nineveh had over two hundred foreign women musicians from Aram, Kush, Tyre, Kassite Babylonia, Arpad, Ashdod, and Khatti. Assyrian kings gave orders that captured musicians were not to be harmed. This was evidently not known or widely believed by conquered peoples, since in at least one captured town, the musicians ran away from the Assyrians and escaped into the countryside.[123]

Many women were dedicated as oblates, which means "offered," to the gods. Oblates could be married or unmarried. A man bought a woman named Alhapimepi to be his wife and dedicated her and their children as oblates to the goddess Ishtar of Arbel. An official of the palace at Nimrud bought a woman for ten sheqels to dedicate to the goddess. A woman oblate of Ishtar was given a large gift by her husband. Mullissu-khammat, an oblate of Ishtar, was given by her father to a husband, who gave her a large marriage settlement. Since she was an oblate of Ishtar, neither her husband nor his family had authority over her. The *shakintu* of the old palace at Nimrud bought the woman Banat-Emashmash for ten sheqels of silver and made her an oblate of the goddess Mullissu. A queen dedicated a married woman named Milkikhaya to the goddess, providing her with a document that protected her from vicarious liability for any claims or judgments against her husband.[124] Oblate women had greater legal protection and freedom from the social restrictions and obligations of other women.

State archives in the Late Assyrian period noted the importance of prophecy. Assyrian prophets claimed to transmit the speech of the gods to human recipients. There were more female prophets than male prophets. Kings consulted prophets before making important decisions. For example, the woman prophet Mullissu-kabtat told King Asshurbanipal that the goddess said not to be afraid. Prophets also transmitted oracles to queens and queen mothers. Prophets more often worked for the palace than for temples. Both women and men prophets were mentioned by name in court documents and letters. Their prophecies were generally deemed true when in favor of the king and false when against the king. Prophets were paid when their prophecies of future events came to pass. Kings also consulted male and female ecstatic prophets and dream interpreters. King Adad-nerari III wrote a detailed budget of expenses for the temple of Asshur, which included a large quantity of barley for the women prophets.[125]

During the brief civil war between the assassination of Sennakherib and the accession of Esarhaddon, Naqia, the queen mother, consulted the woman prophet Akhatabisha about the fate of her son. The prophecy was given in response to Naqia's petition, but the report was addressed to the king and stated that the kingdom and the power were his. Six prophecies addressed to the queen mother have been found in the archives of Nineveh.[126]

Although the majority of prophets served the palace, there were also many in the temples. One woman prophet, Mullissu-abu'usri, uttered a prophecy in the temple that the king's throne must be removed from the temple and then the throne would overcome the enemies of the king. A priest of the temple wrote to the king, asking his permission before allowing the removal of the throne. Another priest wrote to the king relaying the prophecy of a woman. She had spoken the words of a goddess who asked why the king had taken wood from her sacred grove and given it to the Egyptians. If the wood was returned, the prophet said that the king would again have prosperity. In a religious ritual, men and women prophets were given bread. Women prophets were named on temple personnel other lists.[127]

Records from the Late Assyrian period documented sales of women as brides. Fathers and mothers sold their daughters to prospective husbands, and many such brides were very young. Sale documents noted that the price of a young marriageable girl was ten to eighteen sheqels of silver, about half the price of a slave woman. A parent bought a girl named Mullissu-khasina as a wife for his or her son. More often, men bought wives for themselves. A military officer bought Alhapimepi for his wife. The contract stated that if they did not get along, she could pay him ten sheqels and leave. As long as he lived, his wife and their children would be oblates of Ishtar. Brothers sold their sister, Akhatabisha, and a father sold his daughter, Pushki, as brides.[128]

Payment of the bride-price was necessary even in the case of deportees from conquered lands. A letter to the king concerned a population of Arameans who had been deported to a new area and wanted wives. The writer had found prospective brides, but their fathers would not give them in marriage unless they were first paid the bride-price.[129] This was their right under Assyrian law, and so the state had to provide the money to the deportees so that they could marry.

Owners of male slaves bought wives for them. In three separate acts of sale, a royal military commander bought three girls, Salentu, Abidala, and Gularishat, as wives for three of his male slaves. Slave brides cost thirty sheqels of silver. Slaves were more expensive than free women because slaves worked for their owners.[130]

During the reigns of the last Late Assyrian kings, there were numerous records of slave sales. The sale contracts often included warranty clauses, stating that the sale could be rescinded if, within ninety or one hundred days, the girl was found to have certain named defects: demonic possession, epilepsy, or insanity. In a few slave sales, the buyers were women. Abirakhi, sister of a *shakintu*, bought three slave women: Yaqarakhe, her daughter, and Abiyakhia. The lady Urkittutashmanni bought a girl named Nabu-ramat. The lady Simqi-Issar bought the slave woman Belet-issea from the *shakintu*. A woman of Asshur bought the woman Abilikhiya.[131]

In most Late Assyrian slave sales, the buyers were men, and many of the slaves bought were women, some of whose names were recorded in the sale documents. The king's eunuch bought male and female slaves, including the women Mullissu-ummi, Marqikhita, Akhatitabat, and Arbail-sharrat. The king's treasurer bought slave women named Nanaia-da and Samsi, who had a nursing infant. The royal overseer bought Mullissu-duru'usur. A court attendant bought the woman Putushisi. Cohort commanders of the crown prince bought Khambusu with her daughter, the women Arbail-sharrat and Issar-remenni, and a young girl named Ummi. A royal charioteer bought two males slaves and women named Ununi and Uquputu. Another charioteer bought three women: Khazala, Khuda, and Akhati'imma. Another bought three named men and two unnamed girls. A royal bodyguard bought the woman Eduqidiru and her daughter, Babaya. A priest of Bel in Nineveh bought an unnamed woman slave. A scribe bought the woman Nanna-lurshi for one and a half minas of silver, a very high price. A man bought a young girl, Akhatabisha, for only two and a half sheqels. A city ruler sold the woman Rama-Ya, a Hebrew name, to a man. One man exchanged his slave woman, Abilikhia, for a male slave.[132] Most slave sale contracts included a clause prohibiting litigation.

Men bought male slaves together with their wives, daughters, and sons, thus keeping slave couples and families intact. Most Late Assyrian documents recording the sale of male slaves included their wives, and the purchase price was for two slaves. An official bought a slave man and his wife, Busuku. Another man bought a camel driver and his wife, Rimuttu. The king's charioteer bought a hatter and his wife. A fragmentary document notes the sale of a weaver and his wife.[133] Late Assyrians valued stability in slave marriages.

Even more slave sale documents recorded the sale of whole families together. A cohort commander bought two families: a man, his wife Bani, two sons, and daughter Rama; and a man, his wife Naga, his brother, and his son. The village manager of the crown prince bought a man, his wife, his mother, two brothers, and two sisters. The same man bought a man, his two wives, Mesa and Badia, two sons, and two weaned daughters. Another village manager bought a man and his wife, son, and four daughters. A royal charioteer bought two couples and two families. Another royal charioteer bought two families: a man, his wife, and an infant; and a man, his two wives, and three sons. A third royal charioteer bought from a chief singer the family of a tailor, his wife, his mother, and two sons. He also bought two other families, consisting of the men, their wives, one son, and two daughters. A court official bought a man, his wife, and four sons. A deputy governor sold several families, including men, with their wives, sons, daughters, and brothers.[134] In the sale documents, men, their sons, and their brothers generally were named, whereas their wives, daughters, sisters, and mothers often were not. Assyrian slave sale records show that most buyers were men and that a high percentage of the slaves sold were women.

Many documents recorded sales of land that included men, women, and children who were sold with the land. The queen's eunuch bought whole villages, with fields and orchards and the people who lived and worked there. Sales of land included women, some named, such as Bita and Yaqira, Mesa and Badia, and many other women not named, with their unnamed daughters and infants. A large land grant to the chief eunuch of Asshurbanipal included at least twenty-four women, twenty of them named. Some were listed with their husbands, and some also had children. An official of a governor bought land with male slaves, their wives, daughter, nursing child, and a young girl. A man bought a large estate with a house, a field, an orchard, and eighteen persons, including at least six women. Another purchased a house, an orchard, a field, and people. Records of vineyard sales included the vine tenders, and their wives and children.[135]

The slave and land purchase records attest that some Late Assyrian women were able to buy and own property. Other documents illustrate that women could receive property by gift. A father made an *inter vivos* donation to his daughter, Ba'altiyabati, of a house in Nineveh and eleven persons, including bakers, a fuller, other slave men and their wives and children.[136]

A few women borrowed and lent money and grain. A man lent barley to a woman priest. In a reversal of the more common gender roles, a *shakintu* lent money to a man and took the man's son as a pledge. Another *shakintu* lent barley to a male official.[137]

Women pledges and slaves were often objects of litigation by men. A man borrowed fifty minas and gave a woman, Takilat-Arbail, as a pledge. If she died or ran away, the debtor was responsible. When he repaid the debt, he got the woman back. A man borrowed twelve minas of silver from a royal horse trainer. His wife, Amat-Kurra, his daughter, Abirakhi, and his two sons were given in pledge for the loan. If the debt was not repaid within a certain period of time, all persons pledged became the property of the creditor. For example, a brewer borrowed money, for which he pledged the woman Lamashi. If he did not repay the money within ten days, the creditor took ownership of the woman. When the debtor repaid the loan in full, his or her pledges were redeemed and freed. A man repaid his debt to a merchant and redeemed his pledges: a man, his wife, Arbail-sharrat, and their daughter.[138]

The situation of pledges was like temporary slavery. They had to work for the creditor until the debt was paid. A man had paid one mina to redeem the woman Arbail-khammat and her son from the estate of a royal eunuch, whom they served as debt-slaves. Then he lent them money for grain, a plow, and an ox for a total of twelve and a half minas. Since they could not pay, the woman agreed that she, her son, and three other persons would serve the creditor to work off the debt.[139] The woman had come full circle and was again a debt-slave.

Court records demonstrated that very few women filed lawsuits, with the exception of the representatives of the *shakintu*. The *shakintu* women sent their representatives to bring or defend lawsuits, something other women could not do. In some cases the *shakintu* was the plaintiff, in others the defendant. In one such suit, the representative of the *shakintu* was the plaintiff. She sought damages from the surety of a slave girl named Musa'itu, who ran away. The man who was surety for the slave girl had to pay thirty sheqels of silver, half of the purchase price. If the slave girl was later found, he would get his money back and the woman owner of the slave girl would receive her purchase price of one mina plus damages from the owner of the house where the slave girl was found. In another case, a woman named Kabal-aya, the representative of the *shakintu*, sought collection of a debt. The debtor paid ten sheqels of silver and one woman; the debt was cleared and the case was concluded.[140]

Letters are a different literary genre from sale records and infuse human feeling into statistics. A few of the many letters from the Late Assyrian period found in the archives of kings and provincial governors mentioned women. A man wrote to King Sargon II, asking for the release of the daughter, Kali, and other family members of a fugitive vassal being held by the commander of a fortress. Crown prince Sennakherib wrote to his father, Sargon II, forwarding military reports and letters of the chief steward of the woman Akhatabisha. A woman wrote to the king expressing gratitude for his protection of her people against the Chaldeans. A king wrote to his agent in Harran, asking whether the latter had followed his orders concerning certain women. An official wrote to the king, requesting a doctor for Babu-gamilat, a woman servant of the king, and for Saggilramat, the wife of a guard, and for another woman, all of whom were ill. A report written to Esarhaddon by Asshurbanipal mentioned the case of an Aramean woman who was staying with the king's servants. A Late Assyrian man wrote to a governor, asking the latter to woo a woman of his court for the writer, who promised to pay for this favor in silver. Another man wrote to the governor of Nippur stating that he was sending the wife of a man held prisoner and asked the governor to release the man to her.[141] The last case demonstrates that women could travel and carry out official responsibilities and that their authority to do so was recognized by senior officials.

The people of Ur wrote to the Assyrian king affirming their faithful vassalage and complaining that they had nothing to eat but their own sons and daughters. The people of Babylon wrote to King Asshurbanipal, restating the rights of all men and all women, even foreign women, within the territories of Babylon.[142]

Most Middle and Late Assyrian kings were illiterate and depended on scribes to read and write documents for them. Thus scribes were very important. A Late Assyrian teacher in Nippur wrote a letter mentioning a number of women, Saggilu, Kulla, and Esaggilu, who were owners of slave boys. The writer asked that one or two boys belonging to the women be sent to him as apprentice scribes. He promised to pay for them and be their guarantor. If the recipient could not send a slave boy, then he wrote that it would be all right to send a woman. He mentioned the women Tirutu, and Qibidumqi as possible candidates. He ended the letter with a passionate plea: "let them come and learn to read."[143] Thus, women were trained as scribes in the Late Assyrian period. There were many women scribes in the royal palaces. Scribes had to take a test before the king before being hired as palace scribes. Attar-palti was a woman scribe in the queen's household at Nimrud. Six women scribes could write in Aramaic as well as cuneiform script. A fragmentary text from Nineveh described women scribes with their styluses and writing boards. Male scribes, however, had greater prestige than women scribes. One king apologized to a god for having used a woman scribe when requesting an oracle.[144]

The general practice in the ancient Near East was to call persons by name and patronymic, naming the person's father and sometimes even grandfather. Yet in some Late Assyrian letters, men were called by their matronymic, sons of their mothers.[145]

The status of women in Late Assyrian documents was remarkably high considering the ever more androcentric ideology of kingship and the scarcely visible status of woman in Middle Assyrian law. Late Assyrian women could buy, own, and inherit land and slaves. Many women were wealthy, and a few held positions of power in the palace and temple. Women were named in legal documents and letters, and their portraits were sculpted in art. The evidence illustrates primarily the status of royal and upper-class women. There is almost no evidence about the lives or social status of ordinary women. There is somewhat more documentation about slave women, and at least the Late Assyrian system kept slave marriages and families intact.

Women Victims

In the Middle and Late Assyrian periods, women were frequently punished for crimes they did not commit. They were punished collectively or vicariously for the crimes of their husbands or fathers, and they had no way to defend themselves against false accusations.

In a Late Assyrian case in Nineveh, a man was convicted of stealing three hundred sheep from the crown prince and killing a shepherd. The fines for the sheep were very large and he had to pay two copper talents blood money for killing the shepherd. When the man was unable to pay, he himself, his family, and his land were taken.[146] Women were innocent victims of the collective and vicarious punishment of the crimes of the male heads of their families and households.

In another case, a man committed a crime and was fined one mina. He could not pay the fine, so he gave his family and other members of his household as pledges for the amount of his fine. The pledges were used as debt-slaves, who had to work for the creditor. Their status could have been permanent if they were given for the full value of the debt. They could be abused and even killed with impunity by the creditor.[147] Women became debt-slaves through the fines incurred by their husbands or fathers as penalties for committing crimes. The monetary penalties of men became life-threatening servitude imposed vicariously on innocent women.

A Late Assyrian document contained a negotiated settlement of a murder case. When both sides agreed, the settlement was recorded. The murderer contracted to give the woman Kurra-dimri, the daughter of a scribe, to the son of the murder victim as compensation for the blood shed and to cleanse the murderer of his blood guilt. If the murderer did not fulfill his obligation, the victim's family would kill him at the grave of the victim.[148] The text did not state the relationship between Kurra-dimri and the murderer. The murderer had to choose between giving up this woman and his own death. The choice was not difficult, especially if he regarded the woman as property. Thus an innocent woman was the victim, vicariously punished for the crime of a man.

A man was required to hand over another man by a certain date. If he did not, he would have to pay "the fine of his house." This phrase indicated that the members of his family and household would be taken as part of the punishment if he failed to deliver.[149] The punishment of the man was extended collectively to include the innocent members of his family.

A Late Assyrian man stole a slave girl belonging to the queen. The penalty was a fine of half a talent, which he could not pay, so he was put in chains.[150] The queen was a victim of theft. The slave girl was actually, but not legally, a victim of a man's crime.

Women were victims of violent crimes against their persons. A fragmentary letter from the reign of King Sargon II listed crimes committed, including the murder of a man and his wife in their own home by another man and his brother. An official wrote to King Asshurbanipal that "they" were killing his women [. . .] in the king's houses. Another man wrote to an official that a girl belonging to him had been brought into a military camp as an adult woman, used for sex, and made pregnant. In this case, the guilt of the perpetrator was confirmed by witnesses and he was sent to the governor for judgment and punishment. A deputy governor wrote to King Sargon II that an official of the governor had slandered him. Then the man came with two hundred Chaldeans and entered the house of the writer. There they molested his slave girls, put them in the storerooms, killed his pigs, and looted his property.[151]

A letter written to King Esarhaddon described the rebuilding and resettlement of a town that had been destroyed. Men whose houses had been demolished were given new houses. Men whose wives had been taken away were given new women. The text did not provide any information as to who had taken the wives or for what purpose, such as putting them into the ruler's harem or making them sex slaves. Another man appealed to the king for help because someone was giving his house, land, and wife to a runaway exorcist. The wife was a victim of abuse of power, rather than of a crime as such. Her husband showed greater concern for the loss of his land than that of his wife. A provincial official wrote to King Sargon II that he had settled deportees in vacant houses and provided them with oxen, sheep, and women. The royal bodyguard took the oxen, sheep, and women, and the deportees ran away. The Late Assyrian governor of Nippur wrote to King Asshurbanipal that another official seized control of Nippur and arrested, flogged, and sold its free citizens, presumably women as well as men. When the governor rebuked the man, the latter shamed him in front of the assembly.[152]

A man wrote a petition to the king asking for help. Another man had starved his mother and brothers to death, taken his property, and was pursuing other family members. His mother had been an innocent victim, losing her life because of a quarrel between men.[153]

Wealthy women were victims of the incompetence or fraud of their servants. A *shakintu* owned a field that was tax exempt. She put it up as pledge. Her messenger disappeared and caused the field to be forfeited. The creditor got the field, but lost the tax exemption.[154] Servants were also victims of abuse by other servants or by their masters. A scribe reported to the king that another scribe had mistreated the writer's servant woman.[155]

Women were victims of sale into slavery, even by their own families. A Middle Assyrian contract of sale stated that a husband sold his wife, Marat-Ishtar, a woman of citizen class, and received payment in full. She had been a free woman and his legal wife. The text unfortunately did not preserve the reason for the sale. A Late Assyrian father who was in debt sold his daughter, Akhatabisha, to his creditor. The sale was irrevocable. An Assyrian man sold his wife; no reason appears in the fragmentary text. A woman named Daliyah sold her young daughter, Anadalati, as a slave for thirty sheqels of silver.[156]

Although religious prostitution was a custom rather than a crime, women may have been victimized by the practice. According to ancient Greek historians, Mesopotamian women were required to perform sacred prostitution before consummation of marriage. Women had to sit in a temple of the goddess Ishtar and wait until a man chose them. The man threw money in the woman's lap and then had intercourse with her outside the temple. The woman was then free to leave. Ugly women had to wait much longer than beautiful women. The value the Assyrians placed on virginity before marriage makes it unlikely that this rite occurred at the time of marriage. There is evidence that there were women prostitutes in some temples, but not on the nature or time span of their prostitution. Temple prostitution inevitably resulted in the birth of children. An official sold a boy conceived by his daughter during her time of temple prostitution to a man who promised to make the boy his eldest son and heir. The brothers of Naramtu took the son their sister had conceived in her time of prostitution, raised him, and then dedicated him to the temple of Ninurta in Nimrud.[157] In both cases, the immediate families did not want children born of temple prostitution.

Women Offenders

Witchcraft was a capital offense more often attributed to women than to men. Witches were believed to cause physical harm to the victim's body, such as fever, pain, abnormal flux of bodily fluids, afflictions of the mouth and skin, leprosy, and death. A witch was believed to sever the victim's relationship with the gods by false accusation and by oozing sores, which were thought to make even the gods turn away. A focal point was the mouth. The witch caused maladies to the mouth of the victim and stopped it up, making it impossible for the victim to eat, drink, or speak. The witch used her mouth in the offense, through speech and spittle, which was believed to infect all it touched.[158]

Anti-witchcraft rituals were styled as trials. Witches made false accusations against their victims and then stopped up their mouths so that they could not defend themselves. In one ritual-trial, the victim had to prove his or her innocence before the court in order to break the power of the witch, turning the witch's false and evil words back into her own mouth. Then the court could rule in favor of the victim and declare the witchcraft null. At this point the parties were reversed. The victim became the prosecutor and the witch the defendant. The fact that the witch had performed evil witchcraft had already been proven and no other evidence was required for conviction. The penalty was death by fire. In another ritual, the witch was tried before several gods, who purified the victim in the process. In this trial, no evidence of witchcraft was presented. It was presumed that the gods knew that the witch was guilty. The accuser asked the court to impose the penalty of death by fire. If the witch was not present, a statue of her could be thrown into the fire.[159]

Many acts of witchcraft involved the use of water by the witch and affected the body fluids of the victim. Abnormal flux of body fluids was considered to be a source of pollution and rendered the victim unclean. Such pollution was also perceived as a threat to the state. The punishment of the witch had to remove the impurity and pollution from the persons affected and from the state. This was effected by the penalty of death by fire or water.[160]

Treason was a capital crime. Several letters named women involved in a conspiracy to overthrow King Sennakherib. A slave woman from Harran was accused of speaking in favor of the chief conspirator and of the assassination of the king. A daughter of a high official was mentioned, but the gaps in the text make it impossible to know what her role had been. The official who wrote the letters urged the king to put the conspirators to death and obliterate their seed, which implied collective punishment of the offender and his or her innocent children. A faithful vassal official wrote to King Esarhaddon and Queen Mother Naqia that the sister of a notorious rebel leader had entered the state with an Elamite army, whereby her brother terminated the state's status as vassal to Assyria. The unnamed woman and her brother committed treason against the Assyrian king.[161]

Some late Assyrian men and women conspired and together committed crimes. A report was made to King Esarhaddon about a provincial rebellion. It involved scribes, a priest, officials of the governor, the chief scribe, his wife,

Zaza, and their sons. The scribe and his wife were accused of taking the servants of the queen and crown prince and slandering the messengers of the king. The writer of the report urged the king to put Zaza and her sons to death, but did not ask for the death of her husband. This was not vicarious punishment of the innocent, since the sons had taken part in the conspiracy. The report also accused Zaza and the wife of the priest of causing cosmic disorder.[162]

A man wrote to King Asshurbanipal complaining that a royal magistrate and a lower-class woman from Babylon had arrested his family and taken his property, despite a prior court ruling exculpating his family. The letter did not name or specify the role of the woman, but acting contrary to the order of a court was a capital offense.[163]

A person wrote a letter to the king, complaining that he or she was dying because of an unspecified act of a woman. The writer demanded justice from the king and requested a sealed order and a person of authority to enforce it.[164] An official with responsibility for the palace women wrote to King Esarhaddon. The letter is fragmentary, but suggested that the women had gone out of the palace or even left the city, and committed other offenses. The writer asked the king to interrogate the women and not to be deterred by their weeping.[165]

The crimes of theft and fraud were committed by men and women, and by men using women. In the provinces, a man sold his daughters for money, then sent them a bag of salt, with the message to run away and come home, thereby defrauding the buyers.[166]

Women committed unspecified offenses that were punished by fines. A Late Assyrian document from Nineveh reports that a large fine of forty minas of copper had been imposed on the *shakintu*, the woman administrator of the palace. A fragmentary Late Assyrian court decision imposed a fine of thirty sheqels on a woman. A Late Assyrian document from Asshur recorded that a man paid the fine of a woman, which was twenty minas of copper. A Late Assyrian document from Nineveh ordered a man to produce his slave woman, named Shulmu'itu, by the first of the month and to pay the fine of ten sheqels she had incurred. Few women, free or slave, were able to pay their own fines.[167]

There were fewer records of women offenders in Assyria than in other ancient Near Eastern civilizations. The primary reason was that Assyrian men kept tight control over Assyrian women, restricting them to the house, one effect of which was that the ways in which women could commit crimes were limited.

Punishment

In Old Assyria II, crimes such as homicide were resolved by the family of the victim, whose representative summarily executed the offender. The records of murder cases from the Late Assyrian period demonstrate that by then homicide was under the jurisdiction of the state and required trial before a court, with testimony and interrogation of witnesses. Payment of compensation to the victim's representative was an alternative to the death penalty. The state mediated negotiation of the amount of compensation and kept written records in the state archives. When the murderer could not pay the compensation, he or she was put to death.

One Late Assyrian document contained a protocol for the resolution of a murder case. A stranger was killed in the village. The killer, a villager, was known. The family of the victim was not known. Ten men of the village and the offender took responsibility for the resolution of the case. The eleven agreed to pay the blood money when a representative, such as the wife, brother, or son of the victim came to claim it. It is noteworthy that a woman could represent her family in the role of the "avenger of blood," seeking compensation for the murder of her husband. The eleven affixed their seals to the top of the document. Seven witnesses signed at the bottom.[168] By the Late Assyrian period, private jurisdiction and summary execution had disappeared. The Late Assyrian empire had procedures for the administration of criminal justice from the king to provincial and local courts.

The crime of witchcraft was punished by death by fire. Many texts on witchcraft focused on the mouth and the tongue, the organs that received and caused harm. The witch was alleged to use wool and flour mash, among other things, to stop up her victim's mouth so that the victim could not testify against her. The witch was also alleged to prop open the victim's mouth so that he or she could not speak and so that the tongue could more easily be torn out. When the witch was convicted, the acts that the witch had done to the victim were done to the witch. These texts come from a different literary genre, anti-witchcraft rituals, and it is not certain that these penalties were actually carried out on women convicted of witchcraft.[169] Death by fire was the usual penalty for witchcraft, but it was not mentioned in the ritual. Fire was necessary to purify the victim and the state.

Several Late Assyrian letters mention the penalty of corporal mutilation by pulling out or cutting out the offender's tongue for lying to the king. A stone relief from the reign of Asshurbanipal depicted Assyrian men carrying out this penalty.[170]

Many other crimes reported in documents from the Middle and Late Assyrian periods were penalized by fines. Yet capital and corporal punishment show up in unexpected places, such as royal decrees and contracts. Contracts are generally not part of criminal law; however, some Late Assyrian contracts for sales of houses, land, and slaves prescribed harsh and cruel penalties for anyone who breached them or brought litigation against them. The principle behind certain penalties was that the offender had breached the contract or litigated by speech, using his or her mouth. One penalty involved using the tongue to pick up seeds thrown onto the ground. The offender had to gather up eight liters of seeds, which were scattered over a very large area. This penalty shredded and wore out the tongue, so that the offender could not commit another offense involving speech. The more common punishment involved stopping up the mouth by eating and drinking. For example, the convicted offender was forced to eat a mina of wool just sheared from a sheep and to drink a bucket full of tanner's paste. When the wool and the paste entered the stomach, the mixture swelled up, causing great pain, and sometimes death.[171]

Some contracts went beyond law and humanity in the penalties for breach. In contracts for the sale of four slaves and for the sale of a house and land, the antilitigation clauses required child sacrifice for breach: burning the offender's firstborn son to death before the god Sin and burning his eldest daughter to death before the goddess Belet-seri. A fragmentary contract required as penalty burning the firstborn son in the temple of Adad.[172] These contracts indicate that child sacrifice was far from unthinkable and may have taken place in temples or shrines.

Some Late Assyrian treaties had similar penalties. A king made a treaty in which the penalty for breach was to eat dust mixed with asphalt and drink donkey urine. Another king similarly required a vassal who breached the vassalage treaty to eat asphalt and drink donkey urine.[173] The penalty clauses of treaties were often phrased in the genre of curses, but many of the penalties were employed in actual practice.[174]

Summary: Assyrian Documents

A comparison of Old Assyrian I with Middle and Late Assyrian documents demonstrates the radical decline of the status of women. From a high point in the early Old Assyria I period, when women merchants were literate professionals in business, who owned and inherited property and were an integral part of the life of the city-state, the Amorite dynasty diminished women into irrelevance and invisibility, which continued and increased in subsequent Assyrian history. Yet despite the restrictions men placed on women, in the Late Assyrian period a few women reemerged from obscurity, exercised visible roles with real power as queens and queen mothers, while other women worked as professional scribes and held lower level positions in the religious cult.

Documents from the Old Assyria II period permitted private jurisdiction and summary execution by the male head of the family for homicide and adultery. Later the state took jurisdiction over all crimes. Many cases were documented in the Middle and Late Assyrian periods in which women and girls were raped, tortured, mutilated, and killed. Assyrian documents reported many collective and vicarious penalties, including mutilation and death, which were imposed on innocent women for crimes committed by men. Women witches who practiced evil magic were put to death by fire. There were some attempts to make the punishment fit the crime, such as eating and drinking unpleasant or toxic substances for crimes of speech uttered through the mouth. The standard penalties used by the state were death, corporal punishment, corporal mutilation, and fines.

ROYAL ASSYRIAN CONQUEST ANNALS

The annals of Middle and Late Assyrian kings narrated accounts of wars—which the Assyrians always won—and cities and lands destroyed. The literary genre of the royal conquest annals is quite different from that of letters, other documents, and inscriptions written by the same kings. The royal conquest annals made the events of wars crueler and larger than life.[175] The reader of the annals must take care to differentiate between historical event and exaggeration.

The conquest annals were addressed to gods and future kings. Yet the address to the god Asshur, for example, can also be read as an address to the people of Assyria. The annals were actually written by professional scribes, who used the literary model of the annals of previous kings and embellished the detail, especially the cruelty to captives, to make the present king seem greater than his predecessors. Success in battle confirmed the legitimacy of a king, showing that he was doing the will of the gods and that therefore he and his country or empire were in harmony with the gods. Fame was important to Assyrian kings because it was believed to be the only means of survival after death.[176]

The titles kings chose for themselves illustrate the growing virile understanding of kingship. In the Old Assyria II period, the god Asshur was called king, and the human kings were his regents. Middle Assyrian kings took for themselves the titles of "king," "king of Assyria," and later "king of the universe," as well as titles of self-aggrandizement, such as "strong king," "unrivaled king," "warrior," "lion," "hero," "capturer of hostages," "victorious over all lands," "king of kings" and "lord of lords." The kings also used religious titles, such as "chosen by the gods," "destructive weapon of the gods," "beloved" and "favorite" of the gods. One title, used by at least two kings, was "sun god of all people," which implied that the king considered himself a god in this life.[177] Assyrian kings created a mystique of superhuman greatness about themselves, which separated them ever farther from mortal humankind, until some kings pronounced themselves gods.

Status of Women

Women were almost invisible in the royal conquest annals. There was little mention of Assyrian women, only of captive foreign women. The status of the latter was as objects of some value, taken with animals and other material objects as the booty of war. The invisibility of Assyrian women is significant.

Women Victims

The killing, rape, torture, and enslavement of non-Assyrian women and girls in war were not crimes under military law. These women were the victims of actions of Assyrian kings that would have been crimes under civilian law if committed outside the context of war and if the royal perpetrators of such offenses had not exalted themselves above the jurisdiction of human law. The kings' accounts of wars and conquests made frequent reference to captive women and girls put to death, tortured, or sent to Assyria as booty or slaves. The victims were too numerous and too depersonalized to be called by name.[178]

Middle Assyrian kings took captive and brought back to Asshur the wives, sons, and daughters of the kings they conquered and killed. If the sons swore fealty to the Assyrian king and promised to pay the annual tribute assessment, the kings sent them back to their cities to rule as his vassals.[179] The texts did not state what happened to the wives and daughters.

Late Assyrian kings also brought home the wives and daughters of conquered kings as booty. One Late Assyrian king inspected the horses, wives, sons, and daughters of a conquered king in that order. Women musicians were also taken as booty. The tribute paid to one Assyrian king by a city in Khatti included many objects of gold and bronze and two hundred adolescent girls. In some wars, Assyrian kings took the sisters and nieces of kings and the daughters of nobles for their large dowries.[180] The kings added such women to their harems.

Women Offenders

Assyrian women offenders were not mentioned in the conquest annals. Non-Assyrian women captured in war generally had not committed any offense against the conquering Assyrians.

Punishment

In war, captive peoples were not under the protection of civil law, and military penalties were extremely harsh. When Assyrian kings conquered foreign cities and states, numerous women were among their victims. Sometimes they were punished for the offenses of their husbands, fathers, or sons, who had committed the crimes of fighting against the Assyrians or failing to pay them tribute.

Middle and Late Assyrian kings seemed to grow in their cruelty to conquered peoples or at least in the cruelty about which they bragged. Each tried to outdo his predecessors. War captives, including women and girls, were reputedly decapitated, impaled, flayed alive, burned alive, mutilated, and sold into slavery. King Asshurnasirpal II wrote that he cut out tongues, gouged out eyes, cut off hands, arms, noses, ears and other extremities and had a special predilection for adolescent girls and boys, whom he burned alive.[181]

The last significant Assyrian emperor was Asshurbanipal, who defeated Elam and killed the king, whom he personally disliked. He had the king's head brought to him, slashed the face, and spat on it. When Asshurbanipal attacked Elam a second time, he looted its capital, desecrated its temples, leveled its cities, and violated its royal tombs. When an Arab vassal king rebelled, Asshurbanipal captured the king and brought him back to Nineveh, where he put a collar and leash on him and set him as a watchdog at a city gate.[182]

Summary: Royal Assyrian Conquest Annals

Middle and Late Assyrian kings themselves wrote or dictated numerous inscriptions dealing with their almost constant wars, bragging about their victories and the destruction they had wreaked. The structure of the inscriptions was based on previous royal inscriptions to which new details were added. The literary form involved rhetorical exaggeration. One purpose of the inscriptions was to state the accomplishments of the kings and to portray them as greater than those of their predecessors. The second purpose was to instill fear in their vassal states and enemies. The kings addressed their inscriptions to the gods and to future kings. The inscriptions were kept in the palace archives and read by the scribes who wrote them down and the inner circle of palace officials. The basic message reached the people, vassal states, and enemies: those who broke their oath of loyalty would be cruelly punished by the gods through the Assyrian kings and their armies.[183]

According to the annals, Assyrian kings subjected captive women and men to rape, torture, mutilation, and death. The question is how much was true and how much was exaggeration. The Middle Assyrian king Salmanu-ashared I claimed to have blinded 14,400 war captives. King Tukulti-Ninurta I asserted that he destroyed and burned 180 cities. He bragged that in one city he had burned all the inhabitants alive. King Tukulti-apil-Esharra I claimed to have cut off the heads of his enemies and stacked them in piles like hay stacks around their city. King Asshur-bel'kala blinded some male captives and decapitated and impaled others. The Late Assyrian king Asshur-Dan II sold the sons and daughters of his enemies into slavery. King Asshurnasirpal II bragged that he had mutilated, decapitated, flayed, and impaled those he conquered and had burned to death their adolescent boys and girls. King Asshurbanipal decapitated one conquered king and publicly humiliated another king.[184]

The sadistic cruelty claimed by the Middle and Late Assyrian kings and their scribes was rationalized by portraying their enemies as rebels against the Assyrian gods and the order established by these gods. Assyrian kings presumed to restore the order created by the gods by killing those who rejected the Assyrian gods. In so doing, the kings believed they became part of the divine work of creation.[185]

It is necessary to balance the exaggerated accounts of atrocities in the royal annals against contemporary art and other inscriptions, documents, and letters written by the same kings. Art provided a mixed representation. Stone reliefs in Late Assyrian royal palaces depicted Assyrian soldiers inflicting various forms of torture, including flaying and and tightening a vise around the head of a prisoner. Palace reliefs portrayed Assyrian soldiers raping a woman and beating captives while forcing them to grind up the bones of their fathers. Only one set of reliefs portrayed Assyrian soldiers killing women, but these were Arab women who had fought against them. A palace relief showed the impalement of several captives. Many reliefs documented the practice of decapitation. One depicted a prisoner with a human head hanging from his neck in front of an Assyrian soldier with his right arm raised as if to strike the prisoner. Another showed King Asshurbanipal and his wife drinking at a victory feast with the head of the defeated Elamite king hanging from a nearby tree. In other reliefs, soldiers were shown counting heads that had been put in a pile, and other soldiers depositing four heads at the foot of a royal eunuch. Yet in all these reliefs, the heads were few and the piles were small, not like the great numbers claimed in the annals. The reliefs also bore witness to the deportation of captive peoples, dressed according to their country of origin. The women deportees were depicted mourning, often with small children, and segregated from the men. Late Assyrian palace art created a visual world that coincided with some of the forms of cruelty claimed in the royal annals, but modified as to extent.[186]

Letters documented a more nuanced picture of Assyrian military conquests, revealing a more human side of the military campaigns. As commander in chief of the army, King Sargon II wrote orders to his subordinate to investigate the plight of widows and children of soldiers killed in battle, make sure they had not been sold into slavery, and bring them to the king so that he could help them. Assyrian officers wrote to their commanders that they had no food or clothing and were starving. Commanders wrote to their king begging for more soldiers. An official wrote to the king that he remained faithful and fulfilled his mission, although the enemy had taken, plundered, and sold his land, his people, his wives, sons, and daughters, and all his property. At least some of Assyria's enemies feared surrender to the Assyrian king less than the alternatives. When the king of Elam ran away from the Assyrians, his mother, wife, and sons surrendered to the Assyrian king. When another ruler chose resistance rather than submission, the Assyrian commander took personal charge of his wife and other prisoners.[187] There is no evidence that they were harmed. However, in another document stylized as a letter, the king rewarded and promoted an officer who claimed to have plundered Aramean women and their goods.[188]

The evidence is plentiful that the Assyrians used war captives for forced labor, in which case they were more valuable healthy than disabled. There is also ample evidence that the Assyrians deported captive peoples to distant corners of the empire. Since the Assyrians wanted the deportees to be content and to settle in their new location, opening up more crop land for the empire, it is unlikely that they mutilated them by blinding or amputation of limbs or other essential body parts, since that would have made it more difficult for them to build houses and earn their livelihood. The amputation of other body parts, such as an ear or a nose, left a visible mark but did not affect the victim's ability to work.

Even when balanced against other documents, the evidence depicted a world in which women were invisible, except as victims, and kings carried sadistic cruelty to the extreme. The royal conquest annals of Middle and Late Assyrian kings portrayed a patriarchal world gone mad.

CONCLUSION: WOMEN, CRIME, AND PUNISHMENT IN ANCIENT ASSYRIA

The extant laws, documents, and artifacts of ancient Assyria leave many gaps and are sometimes inconsistent in the information they provide about the status of women, women victims of crime, and criminal offenders. Yet, at the same time, they provide significant information both in what was written and in what was not written.

The administration of criminal justice in ancient Assyria began with a system of courts and established procedures in the merchant society of the early Old Assyria I period. The change of rule to an Amorite dynasty in the Old Assyria II period resulted in the disappearance of the former system and its replacement by the tribal custom of private justice, executed without trial by the father or husband of the victim or the patriarch of the victim's clan. During the Middle Assyrian period, a state system for the administration of justice developed, but many of old customs persisted. The state had jurisdiction over most crimes, but not all. Even when the state conducted trials, the husbands of women offenders often decided and carried out the sentence. In the earlier hybrid stage, the state carried out on the male offender whatever punishment the husband had chosen to impose on his wife. Later the state still permitted the husband to choose the punishment, but it executed punishment on both offenders. The state increasingly took jurisdiction over crimes, as it realized that all crimes affected the state as well as the individuals involved. In the Late Assyrian period, private jurisdiction over crimes disappeared and the state adjudicated all crimes. In Assyria this development took centuries longer than in other ancient Near Eastern civilizations. At the same time, Late Assyrian kings began claiming to be gods and put themselves above the jurisdiction of law.

Documents written in the Old Assyria I period provide a glimpse into the lives of women as wealthy business professionals, property owners, heiresses, scribes, and priests. Old Assyrian I documents demonstrate that women owned and inherited property, made contracts, and conducted business. There were women priests and other women religious officials. Women could initiate divorce and bring cases in the court; they transacted business in partnership with their husbands. Polygyny existed among merchants, but was based on the geographical fact that merchant spouses did not live in the same city. Husbands were limited to one additional wife in their city of residence. Old Assyrian law affirmed principles such as justice and protection of the weak, values that were prominent in the Sumerian and Babylonian legal systems but not in later Assyria.

The lives of women changed radically after an Amorite king took over the rule of Assyria at the end of the nineteenth century. As the might of Assyria grew and its cities became parts of an empire, the freedom and rights of women came to an abrupt end. The radical change in the status of Assyrian women was not a linear retrogression. The highest point in their status was in the Old Assyria I period. Under kings of Amorite descent, the status of women dropped to its nadir and stayed there for almost a millennium until it rose slightly in the Late Assyrian period with the appearance of a few queens, women officials, scribes, priests, and prophets. The Middle and Late Assyrian documents focused primarily on royals, high officials, and the very wealthy and rarely mentioned the lives of ordinary women.

When Amorite kings ruled Assyria, it became the most androcentric and militaristic society in the ancient Near East. Middle and Late Assyrian kings had almost complete personal dominance over the realms of politics, economics, religion, the administration of justice, and war. Most of the important political, economic, judicial, and religious roles and all military roles were closed to Assyrian women. Kings maintained control over their subjects by decreeing harsh penalties for not reporting crimes, effectively turning their people into spies. They controlled their palace women by a system of eunuch spies. Middle and Late Assyrian documents were, for the most part, written as if women did not exist. Not only were women no longer named as owners or inheritors of property, but women became property. Fathers sold their daughters as brides and as slaves. Women no longer worked in business or trade, as skilled artisans or in other professions. Women were shunned by men because of blood tabus, which rendered them impure during menstruation and after childbirth. Women were not legal persons and therefore were not protected by the law.

Assyrian men controlled women by regulating marriage and childbearing. Men bought their wives from other men, often at a very young age. Polygyny was widespread, and ordinary men and even slaves had more than one wife. Kings literally kept their palace women under lock and key in the women's quarters. Husbands kept their wives secluded inside their houses. When wives did go outside of their houses, male control accompanied them through the requirement of the veil. Men barred their women from contact with men outside their households under pain of death.

Wives had a duty to produce children for their husbands. The childbearing role of women was controlled by laws through which men could be certain that their children had been sired by them. Men could initiate divorce, but women could not. Men were not required to give anything to a divorced ex-wife. Sons were expected to support their widowed mothers in old age, but Assyrian law required the mother to "serve" her sons in return. Yet when a husband was absent on military service and had not left sufficient resources for the support of his wife and children, the city provided support, which the husband had to pay back when he returned.

Women were victims of rape, but most of the rape laws were written in favor of men, who punished women for having been raped. Rape was viewed as a sexual act of a wife which had escaped the control of the husband. Unless a rape took place before witnesses, it was treated as adultery. The husband had the legal right to remove this challenge to his authority by killing his wife and the rapist. Assyrian men did not tolerate uncertainty about the legitimacy of their children.

Assyrian women were victims of the crimes and punishments of men. Assault and battery on a pregnant woman causing miscarriage was a crime against the husband of the woman, who lost his future child, and a crime against the state, which lost a future citizen. Yet under the principle of *talion*, the male offender was not punished, but his pregnant wife, innocent of any offense, was beaten until she had a miscarriage. An early law on rape did not punish the rapist but gave his innocent wife to the father of the victim to be raped. Assyrian women were victims of *talion* and vicarious punishment.

Assyrian women were categorized as property. When men took out loans, they could pledge their wives and daughters as collateral. Women pledges taken for the full amount of a loan became the property of the creditor, who had the right to abuse, sell, or kill them. Husbands were permitted by law to abuse, beat, mutilate, or kill their wives for various offenses.

The most serious nonsexual crimes committed by women were those that threatened the power, domination, and control of men. Such crimes were punished by death or mutilation. The male god and the king were symbols of male omnipotence. A woman who blasphemed against the god or swore improperly by the king was put to death. One who cursed a member of the royal family or a royal official was flogged and mutilated. A woman found guilty of stealing her husband's property when he was sick or weak or had died was subject to the penalty of death or to amputation of her ears or nose. A woman who fought with a man, causing injury to his testicles, was punished by public flogging and amputation of her fingers or breasts. Witchcraft was a crime against men, who believed that women had mysterious powers that they used against men. Men overcame their fear and took back control by burning witches to death.

The sexual crimes of women threatened the need of Assyrian men to preserve their authority and control over women at any cost. The dominance of men began with the father's control over his children and the husband's control over his wife. Women's crimes of illicit sex with other men took control away from the man who "owned" the woman. If the woman had consented to sex with another man, her husband lost his marital authority in the household and his honor in the public realm. If there was any possibility that a child had been conceived, the husband could lose control over the legitimacy of his progeny. The husband regained his honor and control by killing his wife, which effectively destroyed any illegitimate fetus. The king exercised the same authority over his wives and harem women. If a palace woman even spoke to a man, she was put to death.

A woman who committed the crime of intentional abortion was punished by death by the most painful means, impalement, and by denial of burial. The woman had taken control of her unborn child away from her husband and the state, the child's legal owners, and killed it. In aborting her fetus, a woman shed the blood of her closest blood relation. This act endangered the family and the state because it angered the gods and caused pollution. Thus abortion was viewed as a crime against the husband, the state, and religion. The crime of abortion was adjudicated by the state. The death of the offender was considered necessary to placate the anger of the gods and to cleanse the state of pollution. Denial of burial was necessary to prevent pollution of the land. Men were thereby able to exercise control over the bodies of women even after their deaths.

Crimes committed by women against men were punished by corporal punishment and corporal mutilation. Women were sometimes punished corporally by flogging, but more often by corporal mutilation. Since women were property, like sheep, their bodies could be cut up. The amputation of external body parts was a permanent and public reminder to all of a woman's crime, a deterrent to other women and a witness to the absolute dominance of Assyrian men.

The penal laws had a double standard based on gender. Laws prescribed the collective extension of the punishment of male offenders to include their wives, children, and other household members. Innocent women who had committed no crimes could be punished both collectively and vicariously for the crimes of their husbands or fathers. Women who committed crimes were themselves punished, but their punishment was not extended to other members of their families.

The most drastic punishment, forced child killing by the parent, was prescribed for the relatively minor offense of breach of contract. The offending parent was required to burn his or her eldest son and daughter to death before statues of a god and goddess. This was not a religious act but a punishment of the parent.

The cruel and harsh nature of Assyrian treatment of war captives, as narrated by kings in their royal annals, was not matched by any other civilization in the ancient Near East. The sadistic cruelty of Assyrian kings and their savage treatment of conquered states and peoples, torturing and killing the people, desecrating the temples, burning and leveling the cities, ruining the fields with salt, cutting down trees, destroying irrigation and drainage canals— even if the kings' descriptions of such deeds were exaggerated, many of these acts did occur. In the end their enemies were left with nothing to lose. It was inevitable that Assyrian violence would be turned back upon Assyria. The Late Babylonian army destroyed the capital, Nineveh, in 612 BCE, and by 605 Assyria had ceased to exist as a political entity. The Judean prophet Nahum wrote: "City of bloodshed, utterly deceitful, full of booty, endless plunder . . . Nineveh is devastated, who will bemoan her? . . . All who hear clap their hands. For who has ever escaped its endless cruelty?"[189]

Part Four

KHATTI

T HE HITTITES WERE AN INDO-EUROPEAN PEOPLE who migrated from
the north into Asia Minor in the third millennium BCE. During the second
millennium, the Hittite kingdom, Khatti, grew powerful, conquered other
Anatolian city-states, and unified much of Asia Minor. In 2000, its capital was
Kanish, a trading center with a large colony of Assyrian merchants. The trade
brought peace and economic prosperity; the destruction of Kanish brought
economic collapse and wars. Later, the capital was rebuilt at Khattusha, one of
the few places in Asia Minor that had water all year. The Hittites ventured into
Mesopotamia and conquered Babylon in 1595. The Hittites did not annex
their conquests or impose Hittite culture on them. Geographically, Khatti was
a bridge between southwest Asia and Europe. Despite their proximity to the
Mediterranean and the contemporary Minoan and Mycenean Greek civilizations, in commerce and conquest, the Hittites were more involved with the
lands and trade routes of southwest Asia.[1]

Khatti was ruled by a king. The Hittites believed that the gods gave them a
king to be their shepherd. The ideal king would show compassion, feed the
hungry, and clothe the naked. The king was the high priest and acted as the
mediator between the gods and the people. The king was also the chief judge,
who heard capital cases, complex cases, and appeals. As high priest, the king
had to be ritually pure to offer sacrifice. As judge, he had to avoid any contact
with offenders who had committed crimes involving pollution. Kings claimed
to be representatives of the god of justice, beloved and protected by the god.
Khatti was a military society, and kings were commanders in chief of the army.
Khatti had a standing professional army, and, in addition, the king could call
up his feudal tenants and the men of his vassal states for military service. After
their deaths, Hittite kings—and sometimes their queens—were deified and
cults were established to worship them.[2]

Hittite society was feudal. It was believed that the gods owned all the land.

The king was the gods' steward, who allotted land to temples and to individuals in return for military service. Nonroyal Hittite society was military and merchant, a land where armies left Khatti to conquer other states and merchants engaged in international trade. The Hittite economy was based on agriculture and foreign trade, augmented by booty from conquests and tribute paid by vassal states. Hittite culture was less developed than those of the ancient Mesopotamian civilizations.[3]

HISTORY OF KHATTI	
Proto-Hittite	2000–1650
Old Hittite	1650–1500
Hittite Empire	1420–1200

The sources for information on women and crime in ancient Khatti are the Hittite Laws and documents, such as treaties, royal annals and decrees, official correspondence, court records, and religious texts. The Hittites used cuneiform, the common international writing system of the ancient Near East, adapting it to the Hittite language, which was Indo-European. The Hittite language lacked the feminine gender, which affected Hittite thought categories and laws. This makes the translation and understanding of the laws more difficult and creates confusion as to which precepts applied to women.[4]

In trade and conquest, the Hittites were primarily engaged with Mesopotamia and the Levant. Hittite law was influenced more by Mesopotamian laws and legal traditions than by Indo-European.[5] It was to the advantage of Khatti when its laws and those of its vassal states and trading partners were uniform.

The purpose of Hittite law was to maintain order and balance and to restore equilibrium to society when something happened to disturb that order. Hittite laws went through several revisions, which were noted in the text. The oldest Hittite criminal laws prescribed capital and corporal penalties. These were revised and replaced by penalties of monetary compensation to the victim, which was more effective in restoring the victim to the state in which he or she was before an offense occurred. The courts functioned as arbitrators and mediated compromise of disputes.[6]

THE HITTITE LAWS

Clay tablets containing a large collection of Hittite laws were found in royal archives in the Hittite capital, Khattusha. The four earliest known copies of the

Hittite Laws were from the Old Hittite period. Numerous other copies were found from the Middle and Late Hittite periods.[7]

Proto-Hittite laws were based on the ancient customs and experience of the Hittite tribes before they settled and built villages and towns in Asia Minor. Old Hittite laws retained some proto-Hittite tribal customs. There were some similarities between Hittite customs and the Amorite tribal customs of its neighbor, Assyria, but there were also many differences between the customs and laws of the two ethnic groups. The status of women was low in both traditions, and both punished crimes with capital, corporal, vicarious, and collective penalties. Old Hittite law protected honesty in trade and commerce, which was important in a merchant society. The goal of the Old Hittite system of justice was utilitarian and sought proper behavior according to Hittite customs. A crime was an action that violated custom and disturbed the equilibrium of society.[8]

The protohistoric laws and customs were collected at the beginning of the Old Hittite dynasty. A formal revision was made and promulgated by King Telepinush, the last king of the Old Hittite dynasty, who modified the penalties for crimes. Many laws noted to former, harsher penalties and prescribed new, milder penalties. For many crimes, fines were substituted for corporal and capital punishment. The edition of King Telepinush formed the basic text of the Hittite laws, to which some revisions were later added.[9]

Status of Women

The status of women, with the exception of some queens and women priests, was not very high in Hittite law and life. The primary roles of women were in marriage and family—the production of children and the administration of the household.

Hittite laws on marriage emphasized the payment of a marriage price by the suitor to the father of the bride. When a father promised his daughter in marriage to a suitor and accepted the suitor's payment of the marriage price, the couple were considered betrothed. If another man ran off with the girl, the second man had to give the betrothed suitor the equivalent of the marriage price he had paid. The girl's mother and father were not liable unless they had given their daughter to the second man. Then they had to pay back the marriage price to the betrothed suitor. If they refused, the state could separate the daughter from the second man.[10]

After a marriage contract with the prospective bride's parents was executed and the suitor had delivered the marriage price, if the girl's father or mother changed his or her mind, the parents could take back their daughter from the betrothed suitor only by paying him double the amount of the marriage price. However, if the prospective groom broke the contract by rejecting his betrothed bride before consummation of the marriage took place, he forfeited the marriage price he had paid.[11]

Although mentioned less frequently in the laws than marriage price, most brides received a dowry from their fathers. At the time of marriage, the husband brought his bride and her dowry from her father's house to his own house. If the wife died in her husband's house before having sons, her dowry went to her husband. If she died after having sons, her dowry belonged to her sons and her husband could not take any of it.[12]

There were laws regulating marriages of slaves. If a male slave paid the marriage price for a free woman and married her, her social status did not change. If a slave paid the marriage price for a free man to marry his daughter, the social status of the son-in-law did not change.[13] These laws indicate that slaves did possess money and secured by such marriges the freedom of many of their grandchildren from slavery.

When a free man married a slave woman and later they decided to separate, they had to divide the household property equally. The free spouse took all the children but one, who remained with the slave spouse as a slave of his or her owner. When a male slave married a slave woman and they later separated, the slave woman took all the children but one, and they divided their possessions equally.[14] In each case one child was kept in slavery to compensate the slave owner.

A free woman could initiate divorce. Her husband had to compensate her "for her seed," that is, for her childbearing, and her husband kept the land and the children. If a man divorced his wife, he could sell her for twelve sheqels of silver. The gaps in this text suggest that the wife may have done something wrong that justified the sale.[15]

The laws did not mention a right of women or men to own real property. Since Khatti was a feudal society, the king owned all the land. Men possessed feudal lands in return for military service. Women could not possess land, because women could not be soldiers.

Free women as well as slave women could be bought and sold. The price of a skilled artisan, potter, smith, carpenter, leather worker, fuller, weaver, or maker of clothes was ten sheqels of silver. Another law stated that the price of an unskilled woman or man was twenty sheqels of silver. Since this was twice what a skilled artisan cost in the preceding law, the discrepancy indicates that the two laws had a different time of origin.[16]

The Hittites made into law the practice of unequal pay for equal work based on gender. Laws specified the wages for free persons who performed agricultural work at harvest time. The law first described the work: to bind sheaves, load them onto wagons, put them in the barns, and clear the threshing floor. The wages for men for three months' work were 1,500 liters of barley. Without any indication that the work was in any way different for women, the wages of women for three month's work were six hundred liters of barley. Thus, insofar as the nature and duration of the work were the same, the harvest labor of women was worth only forty percent as much as the harvest labor of men. Slaves were also paid according to gender. A male slave was paid twelve sheqels of silver, a slave woman, six sheqels.[17]

Hittite women had the authority to disinherit their sons. All the mother had to do was cast off his garment. If she changed her mind, she could easily reinstate him.[18] This isolated law shows that women owned personal property that they could bequeath to their chosen heirs. Widows had authority over their children, and the law provided an added tool to make their sons obey them.

Women Victims

The Hittite Laws began with laws on homicide. Women were more often victims than offenders. In the homicide laws, the death penalty was strikingly absent. The punishment for killing a man or woman in a quarrel was compensation, the amount of which depended on the gender and social class of the victim. If the victim was a free man or woman, the penalty was payment of burial costs and four persons, men for a male victim, women for a female victim. If the victim was a slave, then the penalty was payment of burial costs and two persons, male for a slave man, female for a slave woman.[19]

In cases of intentional striking resulting in unintended death, the penalties were the payment of burial expenses and two persons if the victim had been free, one person if the victim had been a slave. The later revision of the law converted the entire penalty into a fine. The fine was eighty sheqels for a female victim whether she was a free woman or a slave.[20]

The laws presented two specific cases of homicide. In one, two persons were crossing a river, one on an ox. The other person pushed the first person off the ox and into the river, where he or she drowned. The intent could have been to kill the person on the ox or simply to cross the river without drowning. The offender himself was given to the victim's family to punish. In the other case, one person caused another person to fall into a fire, where he or she burned to death. The offender could have intended to push the victim into the fire or it could have been an accident. In this case, the offender was not directly punished but had to give one person, his wife or his child, to the victim's family. The wife or child, though innocent, was vicariously punished for the offense of her or its husband or father. The laws appear to construe intent to kill in both cases.[21] The laws did not mention trial, conviction, or sentence.

According to Old Hittite law, when a free man or woman was killed in another city, the victim's heirs were compensated by a small section of the property on which the victim had been killed. In the Late Hittite revision of this law, the penalty was much greater. When a free man was found dead on the property of another, the entire property, house, and sixty sheqels of silver were given to the victim's family as compensation. But if the victim was a woman, the compensation was reduced to a fine of one hundred twenty sheqels of silver.[22] This law demonstrates the disparity in the value of men and women.

Women were frequent victims of assault and battery. Monetary compensation was the penalty for battery, even when it resulted in mutilation or permanent disability. When someone blinded a free person or knocked out his or her tooth, the old penalty was forty silver sheqels, which was reduced in the Old Hittite revision to twenty sheqels. If the victim was a male or female slave, the fine was only ten sheqels. In the Late Hittite revision the penalty for blinding a free person during a quarrel was forty sheqels if intentional, or twenty if accidental. The penalty for blinding a slave in a quarrel was twenty sheqels if intentional or ten if accidental. If the offender knocked out one or more teeth, the penalty was twelve sheqels if the victim was a free person or six if the victim was a slave. The former fine for causing a head injury was six sheqels, three for the king and three for the victim. In the Old Hittite revision, the king waived his share and the penalty became three sheqels paid to the victim.[23]

When a person injured another causing temporary disability, the compensation included payment of medical bills, provision of a substitute to do the victim's work, and a fine of six sheqels. The Late Hittite revision raised the fine to ten sheqels for a free victim, or two sheqels for a slave. A person who broke the arm or leg of another was fined twenty sheqels when the victim was a free person, ten if the victim was a slave. The Late Hittite revision distinguished between permanent disability from the injury, for which the fine was twenty sheqels if the victim was free, ten if a slave, and temporary disability, for which the fine was ten sheqels for a free victim, five for a slave.[24]

A person who bit off the nose of a free person was fined forty sheqels, or three sheqels if the victim was a slave. The Late Hittite revision changed the fine to thirty sheqels for a free victim, fifteen for a slave. The revision decreased the amount for a free victim and increased the amount for a slave victim. The penalty for tearing off someone's ear was twelve sheqels for a free victim, three for a male or female slave. The Late Hittite revision did not change the penalty for a free victim, but increased the fine for a slave victim to six sheqels.[25] These laws indicate an increase in the value of slaves. The penalties varied on the basis of slave status, not on the basis of gender.

The Hittite laws dealt with assault and battery on a pregnant woman that caused miscarriage. The old version based the penalty on the stage of the pregnancy. When the pregnancy of a woman was full term, the fine was ten sheqels of silver for a free woman, five for a slave woman. When a free woman was in her fifth month, the fine was five sheqels. The Late Hittite revision dispensed with the distinction and increased the fines to twenty sheqels for a free woman and ten sheqels for a slave woman.[26] These revisions reflect the increased value of human infants, both free and slave. Miscarriage was understood as a loss of property, for which the property owner had to be compensated.

Kidnapping was a serious offense. The penalties were based on the nationality of the kidnapper and the victim, and whether the kidnapper took the victim to or away from Khatti. When a foreigner kidnapped a free Hittite woman or man, taking her or him back to his land as a slave, and someone recognized the victim, the kidnapper forfeited his entire household, which included his wife, children, and servants. When a Hittite kidnapped a foreigner, the penalty was six persons from his household, reduced from twelve persons in the Old Hittite revision. Innocent women and children were vicariously punished for a crime committed by a man.[27]

When a herder or an overseer, both lower-class men, eloped with a free woman without paying the marriage price, the offense was analogous to kidnapping. The act and omission by the man caused the free woman to lose her social status and become a slave for three years. A man committed the offense, but a woman suffered the penalty.[28]

If a man seized and raped a woman in the mountains, the presumption was that if the woman had cried out, no one could have heard her. Therefore the rapist was declared at fault and was punished by death. But if a man seized and raped a woman in her house, the law assumed that if she had cried out for help, someone would have heard her cries. If no one had heard her cry out, her complicity was presumed and the woman was executed. If her husband had caught them in the act, he could summarily kill them both with impunity.[29] This law began as a rape law, but mutated into an adultery law. The woman in the house may have been an innocent victim of rape. She could have cried out and no one in the house heard her cries, or the rapist could have prevented her from crying out. No matter that there was a total lack of evidence that she had not cried out or resisted, the presumption stood: if a woman was raped in her own house and no one heard her cry out, she was guilty of the capital crime of adultery. Women victims of rape were victims of the misogynistic assumption embedded in the laws that women would have sex with any man given the opportunity. The judicial system declined to investigate, ignored the facts and evidence, and executed women who were victims of rape.

Incest was strongly prohibited. Since it involved pollution, it was a matter of state concern. If a man had sexual relations with his mother, daughter, or son, all closely related to him by blood, it was condemned as an "abomination," a capital crime which offended the gods.[30] Sexual relations between a free man and his stepdaughter or with the mother or sister of his wife, in which the parties were related by marriage, were also called abominations. If a man had sexual relations with a free woman and with her daughters, it was an abomination if the man had knowledge of the relationship. If the woman and her daughters were slaves, however, it was not an offense. Sexual relations between a stepson and his stepmother were an abomination if the stepson's father was still alive. Similarly, sexual relations with the wife of one's brother were an abomination if the brother was alive. In these cases, if the father or brother was alive, the illicit relationships consisted of both adultery and incest.[31] Every form of incest that was labeled an "abomination" was a capital offense.

Incest was both a religious and a state crime. The act of incest rendered both parties polluted, which made them a threat to the state. Although men had the power to coerce the act, the laws did not state explicitly whether only the man was condemned to death, or whether the woman was also. When incest offenses were committed by slaves, both received the same penalty: deportation, but to different cities.[32] This suggests that the incest penalties for free persons also applied to both parties. The state had to be freed from the presence of polluted offenders, either by their departure or by their death. The state itself was purified by the blood of sacrificed sheep.

Women Offenders

Adultery was a capital crime for both the woman and the man. If the sexual act took place inside the woman's house, even if it was rape, the woman was presumed guilty and condemned to death. If the husband of the woman caught the couple in the act of adultery and killed them, he was immune from punishment. No judicial procedures were deemed necessary since the adulterers had been caught in the act. This law allowed the crime of adultery to be punished in private, as in tribal custom. In another law, a husband whose wife committed adultery brought her to the palace gate for trial. Either the husband or the king determined the penalty—death or life—but the penalty had to be the same for both.[33] The second law was hybrid.

Witchcraft was another capital crime that was committed by women. There were many different acts that could constitute witchcraft, but only those that caused harm to other persons were deemed criminal. Some were negligent or accidental. For example, if a person performed a purification rite and did not dispose of the remnants in the proper way but took them to another person's house, it was considered sorcery. Under the old law, the offender was sent to the king's court and tried for a capital offense. Under the revision, if anything bad happened in the house, the offender had to purify the house and pay for the loss. Other acts were *de facto* witchcraft. If a person made a clay image for the purpose of sorcery, it was a capital offense and the offender was sent to the court of the king. When a free person killed a snake while speaking the name of a person, it was considered witchcraft, and the penalty was forty sheqels of silver. If a slave did the same thing, the penalty was death. According to an edict of King Telepinush, even members of the royal family had to appear before the king's court on charges of sorcery.[34] This was unique in ancient Near Eastern law.

Any person caught harboring a runaway slave in his or her house, had to pay the owner of the slave one month's wages: twelve sheqels of silver for a male slave, six sheqels for a female slave. The Late Hittite revision increased the penalty to a year's wages: one hundred sheqels for a male slave, fifty for a female slave.[35] Although the penalty increased, the value of the work of a slave woman remained half the value of the work of a slave man.

The crime of theft was committed by men and women. The penalty for theft was usually single or multifold restitution or a fine.[36] In only one theft case was the death penalty imposed: for the theft of a bronze spear from the gate of the palace. Since theft of a wooden tool from the same location incurred only a fine, the severity of the penalty for the theft of the bronze spear indicates that the object was a symbol of royal power and the thief was thereby challenging the authority of the king.[37]

In a section regulating agricultural practices, there is an obscure capital law against sowing seed in a field that had already been sown by another. Since women did agricultural work, this law might have applied to them. The Old Hittite penalty for this offense was death. After the second sower was executed, the field and its crop were returned to the original sower. The revision of the law modified the penalty to the sacrifice of sheep, instead of the offender, plus thirty loaves of bread and three jugs of beer.[38]

Punishment

Jurisdiction over penalties in Hittite law was initially private, then hybrid, and finally was taken over by the state. Several Hittite laws left punishment for a crime to the family of the victim or the father or husband of a woman offender. This was the way crimes were dealt with in the tribal period, when there were no judicial or governmental structures and the authority of the patriarch was absolute. The older Hittite laws provided private punishment for the two crimes for which it was most often used in primitive times: homicide and adultery. In both laws, the identity and guilt of the offender were not in question. When the male head of the victim's family or clan killed an offender caught in the act of committing a capital crime, he could not be punished for homicide. In the case of adultery, the husband had the right to put his wife and the male adulterer to death with impunity when he caught them in the act. In later Hittite law, jurisdiction over sentencing became hybrid. The husband brought both parties to the king's court at the palace gate, where the case was tried and guilt determined. The husband retained some, but not all, authority to prescribe punishment. If he asked the court to spare his wife, the male adulterer could not be put to death. If the husband requested the death penalty for both offenders, the king had the final word. He could veto the husband's decision and grant clemency.[39]

Hittite laws extended the death penalty collectively to an offender's whole family, including his wife, children, and other household members, all of whom were themselves innocent of any crime. The collective death penalty was prescribed for offenses that challenged authority, whether it was the authority of the king or a judge. Official court judgments were enforced by the death penalty. The punishment for any person who disobeyed the judgment of the king was the collective execution of the offender and his or her family and household. Decapitation was prescribed for anyone who refused to obey the judgment of a magistrate.[40] The crime of adultery threatened the control of men over women in marriage. Husbands were permitted to kill their wives if they caught them committing adultery. Kings, judges, and magistrates were all men. The Hittite laws upheld male patriarchal authority by use of collective capital punishment. The simplest way to eliminate challenges to authority was to kill the challengers.

When a slave challenged the authority of his or her master, the offense was treated differently. The death of a slave, especially the collective deaths of a slave and his or her whole family, constituted an economic loss for the slave owner. Thus, a slave who rebelled against his or her owner was condemned to be put into a clay pot, which could be a situation of painful discomfort or could result in death if the pot was sealed or buried.[41]

Death was the penalty for crimes that caused pollution, such as incest and witchcraft. Blood was believed necessary to purify the state from pollution. In the earliest laws this was accomplished by the death of the offender. Later revisions substituted the blood sacrifice of animals. Witchcraft involved magical powers that men could not understand or control.[42] Putting witches to death was an effective means for men to eradicate their fear and reestablish their authority over women.

One Old Hittite customary law combined a cruel form of corporal mutilation and death. The crime was sowing seed in a field that had already been sown by another. The double sowing was believed to pollute the land, which then had to be purified by blood. The second sower was tied to the plow while two teams of oxen pulled the offender's body in opposite directions, tearing it apart. After the offender was dead, the oxen also were put to death. The severity of the form of the death penalty indicates that the offense had religious overtones: the seed symbolized the fertility of the gods, and the mixing of the seed was a form of divine incest. The blood of the offender and of the oxen shed in the field served to cleanse the field from pollution. Later revision of the law substituted the sacrifice of one sheep for the offender and two sheep for the oxen, so that purification was still effected, but by the blood of animals.[43] If the second sower was left alive, he or she could pay compensation to the victim and make offerings to placate the gods.

Some early penalties were privately implemented and were tailored to fit the crime. The Old Hittite penalty for theft of a plow was to place the neck of the offender on the plow and have the oxen pull him apart until he was dead. The offender had been caught with the evidence, so there was no question of identity or guilt. The victim was permitted to inflict summary execution. This harsh form of the death penalty was related to the fact that a plow was the basic tool with which a farmer made a living. The revision reduced the penalty to a small fine. The Old Hittite penalty for theft of bees was to subject the offender to bee stings. This penalty also was reduced to a fine of six sheqels, or three if there were no bees in the hive.[44]

When homicide was intentional, the law mandated that the offender be given to the family of the victim, but it did not state whether he or she would be killed or enslaved. Other crimes of violence against persons, including other types of homicide, assault, battery, and kidnapping, were punished by compensation with persons. Homicide in a quarrel was punished by giving four persons; accidental homicide, two persons. In each case the amount was half when the victim was a slave. Causing someone to fall into a fire and perish was punished by giving a son to the heir of the victim.[45]

The property offenses of theft, burglary, and arson were punished in most cases by compensation. One law prescribed small fines for theft of small amounts of wood. When the amount of the theft was exceptionally large, the offender was taken before the king's court, indicating that it may have become a capital offense.[46]

A change in the amounts of monetary penalties in the revision of laws often reflected a change in social circumstances. The fines for many crimes were reduced in the revisions, but in several laws they were increased. These laws indicate the increased value of persons and slaves in Hittite society.[47]

The gender and social class of the victim affected the amount of the penalty. Fines and compensation were generally reduced to half or even less when the victim was a woman or a slave. For example, when a woman was killed outside of Khatti, the compensation was only 120 sheqels of silver, whereas when a man was similarly killed, the penalty included the entire property, land, and household of the owner of the land where the male victim was found, plus forty sheqels of silver. When a slave ran away, the penalty for harboring an escaped slave man was twice as much as for a slave woman.[48] These laws illustrate the underlying Hittite belief that a man was at least twice as valuable as a woman.

When the offender was a slave, monetary penalties were less practical, since the slave had little, if any, money and the death of a slave punished the slave owner by the loss of the slave. Corporal mutilation was the most practical form of punishment. When a slave committed burglary or arson, the penalty was mutilation of his or her nose and ears. A slave who committed sorcery was dangerous and was therefore put to death.[49]

As Hittite society grew more complex, two new penalties were introduced. When an offender caused serious injury to a victim, the offender had to pay for a substitute to do the victim's work while the victim was incapacitated and pay the victim's medical bills.[50]

Summary: Hittite Laws

The Hittite Laws were collected at the end of the protohistoric period and were revised at the end of the Old Hittite period. There were continuing revisions of the same laws into the Late Hittite period. The status of women was low, because Khatti was a military and feudal society. Women were excluded from military service and feudal land tenure.

The marriage laws required the groom's family to pay the marriage price. Most brides received a dowry from their families. Women could initiate divorce and were compensated for bearing children. The husband kept the children and the land. If the husband wanted to divorce, he could sell his wife. The law established wages for different types of work. Women were, by law, paid less than men for the same or similar work.

The rape laws were governed by the presupposition that a woman would cry out if she did not consent. When a woman was raped in the countryside, her cries could not be heard and the rapist was executed. If a woman was raped in her house and no cries were heard, the crime was treated as adultery. A husband who caught them in the act had private jurisdiction to execute his wife without trial or he could bring his wife to court to stand trial for adultery. In this case the laws exemplified the transition from earlier private to later state jurisdiction over crimes.

Crimes causing pollution, such as incest and witchcraft, threatened the well-being of the state and were therefore under the jurisdiction of the state. Such crimes were punished by death because blood was considered necessary to cleanse the state from pollution. In later laws, the sacrifice of animals was substituted for that of humans.

The stated purpose of the Hittite Laws was to maintain equilibrium in the state. This balance was lost when people committed crimes that challenged legally sanctioned authority, whether that of the king, a judge, a husband, or a slave owner—all men. Male authority was reinforced and equilibrium was restored by the death of the offender.

The later Hittite Laws had a practical bent, especially in personal injury cases. The offender had to pay burial expenses or medical expenses and provide a substitute to do the work of the injured person until he or she recovered. Such penalties helped restore the equilibrium of the victim or the victim's family.

Hittite Documents and Inscriptions

The extant sources from ancient Khatti include royal edicts, royal annals, royal instructions, treaties, cultic rituals, court records, transcripts of witness testimony, official correspondence, estate records, inscriptions, dedications, letters, and artifacts. More than twenty-five thousand tablets have been found in the royal archives in Khattusha. Except for some letters and religious texts, very few documents have been found that contain information about the lives of ordinary men and women.[51]

The highest court was the court of the king, located in the capital. The king's court tried capital cases and cases too difficult for magistrates and heard appeals from lower court decisions and for relief from taxes and forced labor. Courts in cities outside the capital consisted of royal magistrates sent by the king and an assembly of the upper-class elders of the city. The king, the magistrates, and the elders were all men. The courts had cases investigated and heard mitigating testimony under oath from relatives, co-workers, and friends of alleged offenders. In trials, defendants could be forced to take exculpatory oaths, asking the gods to destroy them if they did not tell the truth.[52]

An Old Hittite king warned his officials in the provinces not to take bribes or gifts from the rich, but to listen to the complaints of the poor. The district governors visited the towns and villages of their provinces. The king instructed them to call the people together and hear all complaints, even those of slaves and widows. They should judge the complaints and make the plaintiffs' grievances right. Cases that were too difficult for the district governor should be sent to the king. Royal magistrates were forbidden to give judgments in favor of their superiors, family members, or friends, but instead were to listen to the complaints of widows, women dependents, single women, and slaves and treat them the same as male plaintiffs, rendering judgments that were true and just.[53]

Another Hittite king instructed district governors, royal magistrates, and elders of towns to judge cases and assign penalties according to local law and custom. For example, towns that employed the death penalty for certain crimes should continue to do so, and towns that imposed exile should continue to do that. A treaty between Khatti and another state explained the differences in their laws on incest. What was punished by death in Khatti was permitted in the other state, namely, sexual relations with the sister and other relatives of a man's wife. The ruler of the other state was put on notice never to commit such acts in Khatti under pain of death.[54]

Status of Women

Hittite kings held the offices of ruler, chief judge, high priest, and commander in chief of the military. Women were completely excluded from the judicial system and the army. Most women were excluded from political and religious roles. But there were a few exceptions.

In Khatti, queens had power and authority and played a role in government. Queens were official wives of the first rank and had the responsibility to bear royal heirs. Queens had important political, economic, and religious roles. Hittite queens had far more official powers and duties than queens of other ancient Near Eastern civilizations. Some queens co-signed treaties with their husbands. Queens chose wives for vassal kings and cult personnel. They sent war captives to help Hittite widows with children. In the Hittite empire, queens had their own seals with the title "Great Queen," which meant above all other queens. They issued edicts and conducted official business in their own right, independently of the king. Queens derived power from their wealth, much of which came from temple endowments.[55] Queens were responsible for administering the royal household, with its large bureaucracy of palace officials.

Queens were given the title and office of "Tawananna," with the duty to preside over the state religion. This high and powerful office was held only by women. Only one queen at a time could hold this office, and the title and office were held for life. If the king died, the queen continued to hold the office as queen mother. The next queen had to wait until the old Tawananna died before she received the office, with its powers and privileges. The Tawananna was the highest priest of Khatti, the head of the Hittite religion. She presided over the important rites and ceremonies of Khatti, sometimes with the king, other times alone. The Tawananna also had influence over affairs of state. She had the authority to collect tribute and taxes. The Tawananna held a position of great power and influence. When there was a question about the right of a man to succeed to the throne, it was resolved by his relationship to the Tawananna.[56]

Many Hittite kings practiced political marriage. They took foreign wives and married off their daughters to foreign rulers to cement political alliances. A Middle Hittite king gained influence over Babylon by marrying a Kassite/Babylonian princess. The same king sent his son to the widowed queen of Egypt in response to her request for a husband. A Hittite king married a Hurrian woman named Nikalmati. Another Hittite king stated that the god commanded him to marry Pudukhepa, the daughter of a Hurrian high priest. The pharaoh of Egypt wrote requesting marriage with a Hittite princess; he sent many gifts and promised to send the marriage price on receipt of the report of his messengers. Hittite kings arranged marriages for their sisters, daughters, and nieces to vassal kings to strengthen their loyalty.[57]

Some Hittite queens are known by name. The Middle Hittite queen Pudukhepa corresponded extensively with the pharaoh of Egypt. She wrote to the pharaoh that she was unable to send slaves as part of the dowry of the Hittite princess whom she gave in marriage to the pharaoh. She wrote about political matters and about raising the royal princesses, including those of other mothers. When the pharaoh wrote to her husband, he sent copies of his letters to her. The king and queen both affixed their seals to peace treaties with Egypt and the Canaanite city-state of Ugarit. Pudukhepa, a priest of Ishtar before her marriage, became Tawananna immediately, because the former one had died. She wrote long prayers for her husband and promised the goddess that she would organize her festivals, perform her purification rites, worship her, and obey her ordinances. In another prayer she asked the gods to intercede for her, recalling reparations she had made. Pudukhepa and her royal husband were pictured pouring libations before the altar of the goddess. Pudukhepa had a special role in the administration of the cult of a lesser goddess named Liliwani. She wrote a document in which she vowed to make annual gifts to the goddess. She made lists of the families who were members of the cult, which she updated when members moved away or died. After the death of her husband, she and her son, the new king, jointly sealed royal documents and took depositions of palace officials who were accused of stealing from the royal stores. In her old age she exchanged letters with the king of Ugarit.[58]

Queens who did not have the title of Tawananna still accompanied their royal husbands in the performance of religious rituals. The ritual for the festival of the war god was performed by the king and queen together. The king and queen entered the forecourt of the temple and washed their hands. Then they entered the temple and prostrated themselves before the statue of the god. The king then went to his throne, while the queen entered the inner temple. Sacrifices were performed and a sacrificial meal was served to the royal couple. The king and queen performed a drinking rite before the statues of various gods. Music and dance were performed during the ceremonies.[59] The differences in the roles of the royal couple were that the queen entered the inner temple, thus approaching the god more closely, while the king was given a gold lance, symbolizing maleness and war.

The Middle Hittite queen Ashmu-Nikkal and her husband, the king, prayed about the plunder of temples by enemy tribes, who had taken temple slave men and women for their own use. The king and queen promised to restore the slaves to the temples and reinstate the sacrificial cults. Another prayer of Queen Ashmu-Nikkal and her husband mentioned the orders of temple personnel three times: priests, the "mothers-of-the-god," and the holy priests. "Mothers-of-the-god" were mentioned with priests in official documents of instruction for temple officials. There were special festivals for the "mothers-of-the-god," as for priests and other cultic officials. Since the "mothers-of-the-god" were named with other orders of priests, they must have been priests or other religious officiants who performed cultic functions. They also served as witnesses in court.[60]

There were also *katra/i* women, who held an important religious office during the Middle and Late Hittite periods. They sang, danced, and played musical instruments, led processions, made libations, and were named on the official lists of temple personnel. They were prominent in the cult of Ishtar.[61]

There is evidence that Hittite women functioned as priests. The defining act of priesthood in the ancient Near East was the offering of sacrifice, generally the blood sacrifice of animals upon an altar. In one example, a woman priest called the "Old Woman," presided over a purification ritual. She set up a wooden altar, on which she put sacrificial loaves of bread. Next she consecrated a goat, cut it up, cooked the pieces and offered the special parts, such as the liver, heart, head, and womb, upon the altar. Then she poured out libations. Next she consecrated a buck, which she killed and let its blood run into a bronze cup. All of these acts were characteristic functions of priesthood. In Khatti, both women and men presided over rituals of blood sacrifice. All the male and female religious personnel and the royal family were permitted to eat and drink at the sacrificial meal.[62]

A number of rituals written by women and performed by women priests have been preserved. A ritual to counteract impotence was written and performed by the woman Pissuwattis. She gave the petitioner a mirror and a distaff, symbols of women. After he walked through a gate, she took these away and gave him a bow and arrows, symbols of men. Then she prepared an altar and made the man sleep beside it for three nights. During this time, he reported his dreams to her and she analyzed them. She broke sacrificial loaves at dawn, noon, and nightfall. She consecrated a sheep which was then sacrificed. Arzakiti, a *katra/i* woman, was coauthor of a purification ritual that filled eight tablets. Other literate women—Anniwiyani, mother of an augur, and Ayatarsha, a slave—also composed rituals.[63]

A ritual for reconciliation of family members after quarrels was composed by the woman Mashtigga. First the woman priest called the "Old Woman" took wool and wax tongues and threw them into the fire for the angry words and curses that had been spoken. Then she made hands and tongues of dough, broke and burned them. She sprinkled the two persons who had quarreled with water to cleanse their mouths and tongues. A white sheep was brought in and she had them spit the curses into its mouth, after which the sheep was killed and buried. This was repeated with a black sheep, which was then burned. Next the woman priest purified the petitioners with water and additional sacrifices.[64] The family quarrels for which this ritual was used were between father and son, husband and wife, and brother and sister.

A ritual against witchcraft was performed by the woman priest called the "Old Woman." First she took clay, then mud, and tied them to the petitioner to absorb the evil magic. Then she threw them into a pit. She took dregs of wine and a broken loaf of bread, symbols of the words and acts of sorcery, and threw them into a fire, where they were destroyed. Then she put out the fire with water and declared the sorcery overcome, as she heaped curses upon the witch.[65]

When a king and queen had spoken blasphemy in the presence of the god, there was a ritual of purification, using statues of the god and representatives of the king and queen. The woman priest first used cleansing herbs on both. Then she burned a soda plant and made it into soap, symbolizing that the pollution was cleansed by fire and made into soap. Next she gave the petitioners an onion to peel off layer by layer, just as the layers of blasphemy would be peeled off the statue representing the god. Then she took a little boat, filled it with tokens of curses and blasphemy made of silver and gold, and sent the boat down the river, where it disappeared. At the end of the rite, animals were presented for sacrifice as substitutes for the king and queen. The woman priest prayed that the final traces of pollution would enter the animals and be consumed by fire.[66]

Since the king was a priest, he had to avoid contact with anyone or anything, including his palace women, that might make him ritually impure, thereby preventing him from offering sacrifice. A defeated army was considered polluted and had to be purified before entering the city. Blood shed by violence contaminated the entire city, which then required a major purification rite.[67]

Hittite prayers demonstrated fixed gender expectations. They asked the gods to give a man virility and potency, and a woman femininity and motherhood. Another document mentioned that women covered their heads, a symbol of submission and inferiority to men. The work of men was tilling the soil; the work of women was milling flour. In funerals, the bones of a man were placed on a chair; those of a woman, on a stool.[68]

The Hittite army was a misogynistic milieu. The induction ceremony, in which all soldiers had to take part, involved an oath, actions, and props. The officers brought in women's clothes; a spindle and distaff, symbols of women; and an arrow, the symbol of men. The officers broke the arrow and said to the soldiers that if any soldier broke his oath, the gods would turn him into a woman. He would be dressed as a woman, his head covered by a veil, and his weapons would be broken, taken away, and replaced by the spindle and distaff.[69]

Two women performed rituals in an unlikely context, the Hittite army. A Hurrian woman doctor, Azzari, recited words over oil, with which she anointed the general and his horse, chariot, and weapons. Another woman, Nikkaluzzi, made two statues, one of clay with the name of the king, and the other of wood with the name of the enemy. Both were put into a fire, where the clay statue was baked and the wooden statue destroyed.[70]

Hittite misogynism was expressed in a story in which a husband said to his wife: "You are a woman and of a womanly nature: you know nothing at all." For Hittite men in general, the term "woman," was negative and had connotations of ignorance, magic, and danger.[71]

Male temple officials had to eat, drink, and sleep inside the temple to retain their ritual purity. Cult officials were permitted to have sex with temple women inside the temple if they were ritually pure when they went to the woman and bathed at dawn the next morning. Contact with a woman rendered male priests impure, and they could not offer sacrifice until they had been ritually cleansed. If a priest did not bathe at dawn and approached the sacrifice while he was impure, it was a capital offense both for the priest and for anyone who failed to report him. If a temple official left the temple and went home and slept with his wife, it was also a capital offense. Sexual relations with a temple woman caused less impurity to a priest than sex with his own wife, which could cost him his life. Temple officials were instructed not to let their wives, children, or slaves enter the doors of the temple, because they would introduce impurity into the sacred space. For a male priest to give food or drink from the sacrifice to his wife or child was considered a sacrilege.[72]

There were rites to restore purity. One ritual of Tunnawi, the Old Woman, was called the Ritual of the River. She went to the river at night, sacrificed bread, poured libations, and made clay figures. The next day, those who were unclean came to the river. She put wool over them and recited formulae transferring their impurity to the clay figures. The Old Woman washed her hands and removed the wool, and the petitioners bathed in the river.[73]

Most Hittite women were married. A prospective groom or his family negotiated the marriage price with the bride's family. Some mothers had a voice in the arrangement of the marriages of their daughters. When the groom delivered the agreed marriage price, the couple were considered betrothed. Most brides received a dowry from their families. Marriage was celebrated with elaborate ceremony by the wealthy. The bride was veiled until she and the groom were alone and then he removed the veil. The Hittite religious cult had special women's rites for pregnancy, childbirth, and purification after childbirth. A mother had to wait three months if her infant was a boy, or four months if it was a girl, before she could be purified and reenter the community.[74]

What is known about the lives of nonroyal women is found mostly in art and commercial documents such as estate lists. The lives of ordinary women were mostly confined within their households as daughters, wives, mothers, and widows. A Hittite family generally consisted of a father and mother, one or two children, and many animals. One estate list enumerated a man, his wife Azzia, his son, two daughters, Anitti and Khantawiya, eight oxen, twenty-two sheep, eighteen ewes, four lambs, eighteen goats, five kids, thirty-six cattle, forty apple tress, and forty-two pomegranate trees. Hittite women were not, however, as secluded as women in Assyria, nor were they considered the property of men. The extent of a woman's involvement with other activities depended more on economic than social factors. Wealthy women had slaves to do the work of the household. Poor women had to work outside their homes to earn enough money to feed and clothe their families. Women worked as millers, bakers, cooks, and cellar keepers. Men were paid twice as much as women for the same work. The millstone, used to grind grain into flour, was a symbol of the work of women. Women millers in the temple made the sacrificial loaves for the gods. Women worked as weavers and fullers, making cloth and clothing. Women held cultic office, serving as priests and other temple functionaries. Women were servants, scribes, musicians, singers, and dancers in the palace and the temple. Women were tavern keepers, midwives, and physicians. Men believed that women had an intuitive knowledge of magic, which made them more accepting of women in medicine.[75] The Hittites were the only people in the ancient Mediterranean and western Asia who used the millstone as the primary symbol for the work of women. Every other society used the spindle and distaff, because the most important work of women was thought to be spinning and weaving. The Hittites also used these symbols, but they were secondary to the millstone.

When Hittite men were in debt, they sent their wives or children to the creditor as debt-slaves to work off the debt. A royal decree urged all officials to proclaim a jubilee period when all debt-slaves would be released. War captives who had been enslaved would also be released. The Old Hittite king Khattushilish I wrote that he personally took the hands of women captives from the millstone and the hands of male captives from the sickle and freed them from forced labor.[76]

The silent power of women sometimes made a political difference. On one occasion, when a Hittite king was about to attack a city, the ruler ran away, but told his mother and other elderly women to fall at the feet of the Hittite king. The king was so moved that he agreed not to attack the city. An early Hittite king bragged that when he conquered a city he did no harm to its people but treated them as his own mothers and brothers.[77]

Hittite men feared the powers of women. In the Old Hittite period, the Tawananna held great power independently of men. King Khattushilish I wrote that he feared his wife's "magic" and called her a "snake," which carried the innuendo of witchcraft. The Tawananna, women priests, and witches were beyond the control of men, who believed and feared their supernatural powers.[78]

Women Victims

The order for the succession of kings was not established by law in the Old Hittite period. A king could designate a favorite son or an adopted husband of his daughter, as crown prince, but often kings did not designate any successor. The nondecision of the king caused enmity within the royal household. Queens and their sons were killed by factions trying to eliminate rival claimants to the throne. At the end of the Old Hittite period, King Telepinush issued an edict describing past royal murders and how his own life and that of his wife, Ishtapariya, had been threatened. He then prescribed clear principles for succession.[79] Early Hittite women were victims of royal power struggles.

The crime of intentional homicide was addressed in a royal edict. The choice of penalty, death or compensation, was left to the heir of the victim.[80] If the heir chose revenge and the murderer was put to death, it did not help the members of the victim's household, especially the women. If the victim's heir chose compensation, the money could help the family of the victim recover and provide dowries for daughters. When a murderer was executed, his wife and daughters were left destitute and became economic victims of his crime.

Many innocent women were victims of the Hittite practice of collective punishment, the extension of the punishment of an offender to his wife and children. The offense could be as small as angering one's master. The rationale for collective punishment was that the offense angered the gods and only the blood of many persons could assuage that anger. In the Old Hittite period, persons, even members of the royal family, convicted of witchcraft or failure to report sorcery incurred the death penalty upon themselves and their entire households.

There are many examples of collective punishment imposed by Hittite kings on palace personnel. When one Hittite king became angry with the palace kitchen staff, he sent them all to undergo the river ordeal. Anyone proven guilty was put to death with his wife and children. No offense was mentioned to justify such punishment. If a royal shoemaker or leatherworker used leather not from the palace without informing the king and was caught, the penalty was death for the offender and his wife and children. A man convicted of using magic against the crown prince, who became King Khattushilish III, was sentenced to give his wife, children, and property to his intended victim.[81]

One Hittite ceremony for induction into the army included the presentation of a blind woman and a deaf man. The officers exhorted the soldiers if they ever did harm to the king or queen, they would be made blind and deaf and then would be executed with their wives and children.[82]

There were strict laws for temple employees that prescribed corporal mutilation or collective capital punishment. When a temple slave made his or her master angry, the penalty was either mutilation of the nose, eyes, or ears, or death for the offender, his wife, children, brothers, sisters, in-laws, and other relatives. A herder who took a young or fattened animal for himself, his superiors, or his family and substituted an inferior animal for the god was put to death with his wife and children. A person accused of taking the best piece of sacrificial meat for himself and giving the god an inferior piece had to swear an exculpatory oath denying the accusation, asking the god to punish him and his wife and children if he was not telling the truth.[83] The Hittites took oaths sworn to the gods very seriously. Children were the most important asset to Hittite men and women. The penalty for perjury was a formidable curse that the offender might never have children.[84]

The wives and daughters of temple personnel were excluded from the temple because they were considered unclean and threatened the required ritual purity of the male priests. The same wives and daughters, innocent of any crime, could be executed if their husband or father visited them in their home outside the temple or brought a small piece of meat from the sacrifice for his family. The lives of such women were rather insecure.

Women Offenders

In Khatti the royal family was not above the law. A royal princess, Ziplantawi, spoke evil of her brother, the king, and his family. She was accused of witchcraft. The daughter of a king caused the people of the capital to rebel against her father, which resulted in a civil war. After she was caught, she was sentenced to loss of her possessions and exile. The king still loved her and would not have her executed. He wrote that she had done wrong, but he would not do wrong to her in return. A man related to the royal family, his wife, and his son plotted against a king's brother, making false accusations against him to the king. The man was not punished because of his advanced age. His wife and son were sent into exile.[85]

The office of Tawananna was sometimes abused, for example, when the Tawananna and her children became involved in palace plots or worked against the king. One king claimed that the Tawananna had killed his wife. He sought an oracle that called for her death. The king declined to kill her but took away her priesthood. A Middle Hittite king accused the Tawananna of cursing his family. Another Tawananna was convicted of trying to kill the wife of the king by use of witchcraft. She was removed from her office and exiled from the capital. An Old Hittite king so hated a Tawananna that he prescribed death for any person who spoke her name. A Middle Hittite king deposed his Babylonian stepmother from the office of Tawananna on charges of "introducing inappropriate custom" and wasting the temple assets she was administering. He exiled her from the capital.[86]

Hittite men were afraid of the secret powers of women and consequently tried to control them. Pregnancy was the greatest power and mystery of women. Abortion was viewed as a serious crime against family and the state. Penalties varied according to whether the act was intended or accidental, the social status of the woman, whether her husband had other children, and whether the woman had a history of miscarriages and premature births.[87] Abortion performed by a wife destroyed the husband's control over his wife, her body, and their unborn child.

Women who held the temple office of *katra/i* complained that they had not been paid the accustomed valuables and food rations. Their complaint reached the palace, and an official was sent to investigate. Then other temple officials accused the *katra/i* women of blasphemy.[88]

Women worked in temples and were subject to the same penalties as men if they committed a crime. Temple officials were instructed not to allow anyone to take gold, silver, garments, or bronze implements for their own use, because these belonged to the god. A person who took and sold anything that belonged to the god was put to death, as was the person who bought the object from the thief. After the food from sacrifice was given to the god, anyone who took some for himself or herself from the god's portion was put to death.[89]

Punishment

Old Hittite law treated intentional homicide and adultery as private crimes for which the next of kin of the murder victim or the husband of the adulteress could choose the sentence: death or compensation. This practice still utilized tribal custom, taking two important crimes out of the jurisdiction of the state.

Collective capital punishment was another practice in Old Hittite law that stemmed from tribal custom. It was justified by reference to angry gods who would take their revenge against an offender and his or her entire household. Collective capital punishment of an offender and his innocent family was prescribed for many crimes in ancient Khatti, some major crimes, such as homicide, sorcery, and sacrilege, and many minor offenses, such as using the wrong material in making shoes or garments for the king or simply angering the king. Such crimes were punished by the death of the offender, his wife, children, other relatives, and slaves.[90]

Some criminal penalties combined corporal mutilation and collective capital punishment or used them as alternatives. A soldier who harmed the king or queen was made blind and deaf and then executed with his wife and children. A temple slave who angered his or her master was punished by mutilation of the nose, eyes, or ears, or by death with his wife, children, siblings, in-laws, all other relatives, and male and female slaves. King Telepinush used decapitation of capital offenders instead of collective punishment, so that no one else in the offender's family or household was punished. A Middle Hittite king decreed that a slave who committed theft could be blinded. Upper-class war captives were blinded and then ransomed by their people. Other war captives were blinded and made to work in milling, which did not require sight and was humiliating because it was considered women's work. An Old Hittite king claimed to have humiliated a conquered king by harnassing him to pull a wagon like a mule.[91]

The punishment for witchcraft depended on the social status of the offender and of the victim. In the Old Hittite period, those who practiced sorcery in the capital, even members of the royal family, were tried by the king and, if convicted, sentenced to death with their households. A queen was banished into exile. A free person convicted of using witchcraft against a member of the royal family was turned over, with his wife and property, to the victim.[92]

Sacrilege took many forms, all punished by death. Theft from a temple was not ordinary theft because the object stolen belonged to a god. This made the offense a sacrilege, which resulted in pollution of the temple. A temple could be cleansed only by blood, preferably the blood of the offender who was responsible for the impurity. The introduction of impurity or pollution into the temple was always a capital offense.

Hittite documents, inscriptions, and artifacts underscore the extensive use of collective, capital, and corporal punishment in the Old Hittite period, a time when the Hittites were still close to their tribal roots. The customs of collectively and vicariously penalizing the innocent family members of offenders treated women as objects of property. The last Old Hittite king abolished collective punishment. The custom was revived in the empire, although many capital and corporal penalties were replaced by fines.

Summary: Hittite Documents

Hittite queens had important political and religious roles. The Tawananna had great power as head of the religious cult. Other women were priests, held other religious offices, and wrote long and elaborate religious rituals.

Hittite men defined the roles of women on the basis of their misogynistic gender expectations. Men considered women impure and a threat to the purity of men, especially men who worked in temples. Many Hittite men feared the mysteries of women, which they could not completely understand or control.

According to Hittite documents, royal women and children were murdered in palace succession struggles. The employment of collective capital punishment for even the slightest offense of palace and temple workers resulted in the deaths of many innocent wives and children.

Criminal penalties were often dependent on the gender and social status of victims and offenders. Crimes against women were punished less severely than crimes against men. Women who committed crimes were punished more harshly than men who committed the same crimes.

Conclusion: Women, Crime, and Punishment in Ancient Khatti

The situation of women, crime, and punishment in Khatti was different from that in Mesopotamia and is more difficult to document. The sources are fewer and reveal less about women and crime. The historical period of the Hittite kingdom and empire was much shorter; the nuances of the language are less well known; and the scarce art and artifacts seldom depicted women.

Hittite law was influenced by its own tribal customs and to a lesser extent by the laws of its Mesopotamian vassal states and trading partners, especially Assyria. Hittite laws were different from other ancient Near Eastern laws in that there was only one basic collection of laws, which was periodically revised, the revisions were included with the original text. This produced greater continuity of law than in civilizations that had several different law collections, often separated by many centuries.

Khatti had a well-organized system for the administration of justice. The king was the highest court of appeal and presided over capital and complex cases. Royal magistrates presided over local courts with councils of elders. Kings kept a check on court personnel to eliminate bribery and favoritism. All the officials in the judicial system were men.

Hittite society was organized in a feudal system. As in Assyria, the land belonged to the king, who granted possession and use of land in exchange for military service. Since women could not be soldiers, they could not possess feudal land, which was a primary source of wealth. Without wealth, women were excluded from power and influence in society. Under Hittite law, women were owned by men and could be bought and sold. The monetary value of the labor of a free woman was less than half the value of the labor performed by a man. The value of the work of a slave woman was half that of a slave man. Men further controlled women by requiring them to be veiled.

In Hittite society, those few women who were queens and priests avoided classification as property. Queens had real power and authority; they administered the palace and performed important roles in the religion. Queens issued edicts and had formal correspondence with foreign heads of state and district governors. They cosigned international treaties with their husbands. They were not part of the feudal system and thus could own real property and make legal transactions. Some were called "Great Queen," as their husbands were called "Great King," meaning above all other queens and kings in the empire.

In Hittite religion, literate women composed the texts of many rituals. Women and men priests presided over sacrifices and other rites. Women sang, played musical instruments, and danced in religious rites. On the other hand, women were considered unclean and a source of pollution for men. Women who did not work in a temple were forbidden to enter the temple or partake of the sacrifice, lest they contaminate the male priests and thereby disrupt the cult.

The majority of Hittite women were wives and mothers. Marriage in Khatti was generally monogamous. Kings usually had one queen but also had harems. Hittite marriage law required that the marriage price be paid by the prospective groom, and most brides received a dowry from their families. Married couples set up a new household, instead of residing with the groom's family. Husbands could divorce, but had to give compensation to their ex-wives. Women of poor families had to work in the marketplace to earn money to feed and clothe their families. Women were millers, bakers, cooks, weavers, fullers, clothes makers, tavern keepers, midwives, and physicians.

Although many women stayed inside their homes, palaces, or temples, where they were protected from crime, this was not always possible. Hittite princesses and other royal women were murdered in internecine palace struggles over succession. Other Hittite women were victims of homicide, rape, and false accusation. Many women were victims of the collective and vicarious punishment of crimes committed by their husbands or fathers. Women and men were subject to death or corporal mutilation for offenses as insignificant as angering the king or their master or mistress.

Hittite women committed crimes, including members of the royal family. Queens who killed or attempted to kill other persons in succession struggles were punished by exile or death. Other men and women who committed major crimes, such as homicide, rape, adultery, and theft from the palace or temple, were punished by death.

The Hittites believed that certain crimes, such as sacrilege, witchcraft, and incest, angered the gods and caused pollution, thereby endangering the state.

The temple, palace, land, or person polluted had to be purified by blood. In early times, this was effected by human sacrifice, but animal sacrifice was later substituted for this rite of purification.

Early Hittite law utilized some unique forms of corporal and capital punishment. Persons who stole bee hives were subjected to bee stings. Slave offenders were put into clay pots. Persons who stole a plow were executed by being tied onto the plow and pulled apart by teams of oxen pulling in opposite directions. Those who rejected the judgment of a magistrate were decapitated.

Some penalties depended on the gender of the victim or offender. Men received light punishments for most crimes against women. When women were killed unintentionally, assaulted, battered, kidnapped or robbed, the male perpetrator was merely fined. When the victim of a crime was a woman or a slave, the fine was half of the amount required for a male victim. When a man committed a serious crime, his wife and daughters could share his punishment or be punished in his stead. There was no collective or vicarious punishment for men when their wives or mothers committed crimes.

Hittite criminal law underwent several major revisions. Private jurisdiction disappeared as the state took jurisdiction over all crimes. Collective and vicarious punishments were abolished. There were initially many capital and corporal penalties. In the revisions these were generally reduced to restitution and monetary compensation or fines. The amounts of many fines were decreased in the revisions except when the value of a slave, a fetus, or a free woman had increased in Hittite society. Distinctions were added in the revisions, such as the intent, social class, gender, and nationality of the victim or offender, whether an injury caused permanent or temporary disability, the place and time that the crime occurred, and the nature and value of a stolen object.

The treatment of crime and punishment in the Old Hittite period revealed the influence of tribal customary law. The use of penalties of death, corporal mutilation, collective and vicarious punishment, and private summary procedures indicate a society not very far from its tribal past. Such practices were built on principles of patriarchy, the unquestioned authority of men and inferiority of women. The forms of punishment used by the Hittites were often different from those of the Amorites in Mesopotamia. Both peoples were influenced by their tribal past, but their tribal histories and customs were quite different.

In theory the Hittites used law to restore and maintain right order within society. When a crime was committed, it disrupted the equilibrium of society. Punishment was structured to restore the balance by returning the victim to his or her state before the crime occurred. In later Hittite law, monetary compensation and payment of expenses incurred restored the economic status of victims of property crimes. But for crimes of violence against persons, such a system required a belief that the value of a human life could be quantified in monetary terms. The victim of murder or rape could not be restored to wholeness by the payment of money.

Hittite sources present a different view of women, crime, and punishment in the ancient Near East. The empire of Khatti, although small and short-lived, was at one point the equal of Egypt. Hittite queens exercised political and diplomatic authority on a par with the powerful queens of Egypt. Yet this did not greatly affect the lives of the majority of Hittite women, who led restricted and generally uneventful lives as wives and mothers. The information gleaned from Hittite sources provides a unique glimpse from the north about women, crime, and punishment in the second millennium.

Conclusion: Women, Crime, and Punishment in the Ancient Near East

C♉

T HE ANCIENT NEAR EAST included many different cultures and empires. The Sumerian, Babylonian, Assyrian, and Hittite civilizations all left evidence about women, crime, and punishment. In most cases the evidence was fragmentary. Several substantial collections of laws, but no systematic, comprehensive law codes, have been found from these early civilizations. Many other ancient inscriptions, royal chronicles, royal annals, court records, contracts, deeds of sale, ration lists, letters, art, and architecture shed light on the subjects of women, crime, and punishment. The extant texts and artifacts provide sufficient information to build a picture of the lives of women and their encounters with crime in each civilization.

There were two vastly different forces at work in the ancient Near East in the third and early second millennia BCE: tribalism and urbanism. Whether a people was tribal or urban was the factor that most influenced the development of customs, laws, and societies. Sumer was an urban society, with no documented memory of a tribal past. Babylonia and to a greater extent Assyria were very much in touch with their Amorite tribal past. Khatti remembered its own different and more distant tribal past.

In urban societies, people lived and worked together, created cities, and produced literature, art and architecture, music and dance. The status and lives of women were not very different from those of men. Women had freedom to learn and work professionally in administration, religion, medicine, and the arts. Cities had structures of government and systems of judges and courts for the administration of justice. The state had jurisdiction over crimes. In urban societies, creativity, invention, and innovation blossomed.

The three greatest differences between urban and tribal societies were the status of women, jurisdiction over crimes, and punishment of crimes. In urban Sumer, women were almost equal to men. They acquired wealth and independence and worked in professions of their choice. In the urban merchant society of Old Assyria I, there were thousands of literate, competent professional businesswomen and men working in partnership to develop a prosperous, politically and economically important middle class. Tribal societies were patriarchal, and the position of women was controlled by and subordinated to the authority of men. Women had no voice in political decision making or religion, no professional positions or training, and they were kept secluded within the tents or houses of men, silent and invisible. Tribal customary law upheld the dominance of men over women and, in support of this, introduced concepts of women as sources of pollution and impurity. Some tribal law put women totally under the control of men, reducing their status to property owned by men. By the first millennium, many vestiges of tribalism had been forgotten or assimilated into the laws of empires. Women slowly began to regain the rights they had lost a thousand years earlier.

The second difference between urban and tribal societies was jurisdiction over crimes. In the urban civilization of Sumer, the state had jurisdiction over all criminal cases. Before settlement in cities, tribes did not have systems for the administration of justice, courts, or judges. Crimes were dealt with privately without trial by the male head of the tribe, clan, or family, who was both judge and executioner. The Amorite regimes in Babylonia and Assyria, and Anatolian Khatti as well, retained the tribal custom of private jurisdiction by the male head of the family or clan at least over the crimes of murder and adultery. The widespread use of private administration of justice increased the power of husbands and patriarchs, diminished that of women, and decreased the authority of the state judicial system. By the first millennium, private jurisdiction had been abolished and most states had taken jurisdiction over all crimes.

The third significant difference between urban and tribal societies was the form of punishment of crimes. In urban Sumer, the death penalty was rarely used and most crimes were punished by fines. The Sumerians punished only the offender, not his or her spouse or children. In tribal societies, capital and corporal penalties were initially used to punish crimes for practical reasons, because they required no apparatus and could be executed immediately. Even after the people had settled in cities, capital punishment was frequently imposed, and harsh forms of execution were developed, including impalement, death by fire, drowning, being thrown off a tower, and being torn apart by oxen. Tribal societies used corporal punishments such as flogging and mutilation, amputating parts of the offender's body. Collective punishment was extended beyond a male offender to his innocent wife and children. Under the Amorite tribal principle of *talion,* innocent persons such as wives and daughters were vicariously punished for the crimes of male offenders, who were not punished at all. Collective and vicarious punishments were not used at all when the offender was a woman. As tribal societies became urban, such penalties disappeared. Collective and vicarious punishment had dropped out of use by the end of the second millennium in Late Babylonia and Khatti. Only Late Assyria continued to use both in the first millennium.

War and peace were significant factors in the development of ancient civilizations. Societies such as Sumer and Babylonia, which enjoyed longer periods of peace, had more time to think and learn, read and write, and build great edifices. Societies such as Assyria and Khatti which were constantly at war, depleted their resources and energy conquering and killing in distant lands.

Before the advent of cities, laws grew out of the orally transmitted customs of tribes. In all ancient Near Eastern civilizations, kings were the primary sources, collectors, and promulgators of written law. Many kings claimed a divine commission to produce laws, giving their laws greater authority and commanding obedience on the part of their subjects.

Sumerian kings articulated their ideal of justice for all their people without distinction of class. Justice meant eliminating crime, correcting abuses, and protecting widows, orphans, the poor, and the weak. Sumerian and Old Babylonian kings sought justice by preventing the strong from oppressing the weak and teaching the people the way of justice through written laws. Sumerian and Old Babylonian kings stayed in close contact with their people. Assyrian kings sought power, not justice, and placed themselves far above their people and the peoples they conquered. Hittite kings called themselves representatives of the god of justice, and their concept of justice was proper order in society.

All four civilizations were monarchies, but kings had varied ideologies of kingship and degrees of autocracy. Sumerian kings, aided by their competent wives and high priest daughters, had small empires, which they governed in peace, focusing on justice. Babylonian and Assyrian kings ruled extensive empires. Babylonian kings concentrated more on building than on war, while Assyrian kings focused on military conquests. By the first millennium, Late Babylonian kings had great economic power and Late Assyrian kings had great military might. A few kings of both empires employed the resources of intelligent and competent queens. Hittite kings, with the help of queens and queen mothers, pursued conquest and commerce.

Most kings in the civilizations of the ancient Near East had sexual relationships with more than one woman. Yet there is a great difference between Sumerian and Babylonian kings, who often had more than one wife and one or more consorts, all of whom were formally "married" to the king and were given official titles, positions, and duties, and Assyrian and Hittite kings, who had large, impersonal harems, in which the women were not named but were collected for their beauty and kept available for the king's sexual pleasure.

In all four civilizations, kings used their daughters for political advantage. Young princesses were sent to far-away lands to marry unknown kings, usually much older, to form alliances or to seal treaties made by their royal fathers. These young women lost their homes, families, friends, language, religion— virtually everything that was familiar to them. If they were clever, they learned the languages, adopted the customs, and obtained and exercised power in their new lands. This custom created an international network of interrelated royal families. Daughters corresponded with their fathers, provided them with important information and mediated disputes between the states. When daughters lived in smaller states which were attacked, their fathers sent armies to defend them. Kings of Sumer, Akkad, and Babylonia made their daughters high priests of the ancient city of Ur for their own political advantage. Royal women high priests were intelligent and powerful and, to varying degrees, they helped their fathers rule their empires.

In these ancient societies, men feared women not only for their wealth, status, or influence but because they possessed powers that men could not understand or control. All women had mysterious flows of blood and the ability to have children grow inside their wombs. Men feared blood and the unknowable and uncontrollable. There were three types of women who were especially feared by men: celibate women priests, cult prostitutes, and witches. These women did not marry and were thus not under the domestic authority of men. They were believed to have magical or supernatural powers that were beyond the understanding and control of men. In Late Assyria and Late Babylonia, where educated and productive women priests were a lost memory, men put women priests in the same category as witches and prostitutes. In the ancient Near East, such men overcame their fears by killing women whom they could not control.

SUMER

In the third millennium, a unique urban civilization existed in southern Mesopotamia. It consisted of many city-states and several small empires. From the beginning, people worked together to build and maintain canals for irrigation and trade and drainage systems to protect their crops from flooding. The civilization of Sumer was sophisticated and cosmopolitan. In its city-states there was high literacy and great creativity, invention, and innovation. The city-states were generally ruled by kings, who articulated their ideal of justice for all people without distinction of wealth or class.

There is evidence of one ruling queen and many wealthy and influential wives of kings. Sumerian queens administered large temple economies, supervising thousands of workers. Akkadian and later Sumerian kings made their daughters high priests of the most important cities of their realm. Other royal daughters were married to kings of other states to forge political alliances. Queens, women high priests, and women priests were wealthy and powerful. Some of the later kings had more than one wife, but polygyny was not widespread. Sumerian marriage required both marriage gifts and a dowry. Wives managed the household economy, and husbands had to pay compensation if they divorced their wives. Women owned property and inherited from their fathers if they had no brothers. Women were priests and wrote hymns and other religious works, signed and sealed contracts, ran businesses, and were skilled artisans. Women worked in textile and pottery manufacturing, grain milling, oil pressing, and beer brewing, and as midwives, physicians, and tavern keepers. Sumerian law protected women when they were weak and vulnerable, as in times of sickness, divorce, and widowhood.

Sumerian women were victims of crimes of violence, including murder, rape, assault, and battery. Women who owned property were victims of theft. In the earliest legal texts of Sumer, theft of produce and fruit from the gardens and trees of poor widows and single mothers was forbidden by law. Women falsely accused of crimes were subjected to the river ordeal, which could result in death despite their innocence.

In historical Sumer, women committed the capital crimes of homicide and adultery. False accusation was punished by the penalty of the case. Property crimes were punished by restitution, and the penalties for assault and battery and most other crimes were fines.

In ancient Sumer, women were legal persons, and their lives were minimally restricted. Women were victims of the crimes of men, but the men were punished for committing the crimes. When women committed crimes, they were tried by a court and punished if convicted. The Sumerians punished only offenders, not their wives or families. A Sumerian hymn proposed rehabilitation of offenders by compassion, nurturence, and training in truth.

The civilization of Sumer in the third millennium BCE was more advanced than those that followed in its treatment of women, crime, and punishment, as well as in its creativity, art, and invention.

TRANSITION

In the early second millennium, the city-states of Sumer were taken over by Amorite kings. The transition between Sumer and the Amorite empires of

Babylonia and Assyria began during the dynasties of Isin and Larsa. The status of women was lower, although kings still appointed their daughters high priests of Ur and other cities. Women still had sufficient wealth to make dedications to temples, but records of women buying or selling real property or conducting other business transactions become increasingly rare. Fewer women worked outside the household.

Women in the Isin/Larsa period were victims of murder, rape, assault, and battery. A man who raped a virgin was punished by forced marriage to his victim. In addition, women given as pledges for the debts of their husbands or fathers could be abused or even killed by the creditor with impunity. Laws protected the authority of fathers, husbands, and property owners.

During the Isin/Larsa period, women committed crimes, but their punishments were not always equitable. A wife who repudiated her husband was thrown into the river to drown, although a husband who disowned his wife incurred only a small fine. Women accused of committing adultery and murder were convicted with minimal evidence and sentenced to death.

BABYLONIA

In the first half of the second millennium, the Old Babylonian empire ruled southern Mesopotamia. Its laws were influenced by both Sumerian law and Amorite customary law. The lives of women were more restricted in Babylonia than in Sumer, but less restricted than in Assyria. Old Babylonian kings embraced the Sumerian ideal of making justice a reality by protecting the weak, including widows and orphans. Polygyny was restricted. Marriage laws required marriage gifts, a dowry, and a written contract. Women could avoid responsibility for their husbands' debts by written prenuptial agreements. Husbands gave their wives *inter vivos* donations attested by sealed documents. Husbands were not allowed to abandon wives who became ill or disabled. Husbands could divorce, but had to provide compensation. It was very risky for a woman to initiate divorce. She had to prove herself without fault and her husband at fault before a court. If she won, she was granted a divorce, but received no property. If the woman lost, she was put to death. Widows inherited the usufruct of their deceased husband's estate for life. When away for military service, husbands had the duty to provide support for their wives and children during their absence. Women owned nonfeudal real property. Women were legal persons and could file lawsuits to enforce their rights. There were many women priests and many other women religious officiants; some lived in cloistered celibate communities and others married, although they were not permitted to have children. Some women were literate and worked as scribes.

Other women worked as weavers, fullers, millers, tavern keepers, and wet nurses.

There is evidence of the influence of Amorite customs, which upheld the dominance of men over women and the concepts of pollution, ritual purity, and the blood tabu. Restrictions on the lives of women outside their homes began to appear. It was no longer proper for a woman to go outside the city to visit a shrine or to go up on the roof of her house, where she might be seen by men. Fewer women owned property or held state or religious offices.

In Old Babylonia, women were victims of crimes of violence, including murder, kidnapping, rape, incest, and battery causing miscarriage and death. Women were victims of robbery, but if the robber was not caught the state paid them restitution. When women were falsely accused of adultery, they were subjected to the river ordeal to restore their husbands' tarnished honor. Men handed over their wives or daughters as pledges for their debts, but for the first time abuse of pledges was made a crime.

Old Babylonian women committed crimes that endangered the state or religion, and all such crimes came under the jurisdiction of the state. The crimes of incest between mother and son, entry into a tavern by a women priest, and witchcraft caused pollution, which was believed to be very dangerous to the state and religion. Other crimes committed by women directly affected the state. Women tavern keepers who failed to report criminal conspiracies discussed in their taverns endangered state security, and those who gave false measure jeopardized commerce. Other crimes threatened the authority of property owners and the economic institution of slavery. Helping a runaway slave was a serious crime because it undermined the authority of slave owners. Slave women who challenged the authority of their master or mistress were branded, confined to slave quarters, or sold. The worst crime of all, in male Babylonian eyes, was when a wife involved in an adulterous relationship caused the death of her husband. This was the ultimate challenge to the authority of the husband. Married women committed crimes when they went out of their houses, were extravagant, wasted money, neglected their domestic duties, or disparaged the honor of their husbands. A woman whose husband was away for several years but had left her well supplied, committed a crime if she entered the house of another man. A woman who left her husband's house and took anything with her committed the crime of theft.

Under Amorite influence, private jurisdiction and the death penalty were common in Old Babylonia and were used to uphold the authority of men over women. Private jurisdiction by patriarchs of clans and husbands increased the power and dominance of men in tribal society and marital relationships. Such men had the right to kill alleged offenders, often their own wives, summarily without trial if the offender was caught in the act of murder or adultery.

The state had jurisdiction over other crimes. When a wife committed adultery and caused the death of her husband, the penalty was death by impalement. The crime of incest between mother and son was punished by death by fire to purify the state from the pollution that incest engendered. Other forms of incest, adultery, infidelity of a wife whose husband was a prisoner of war, and tavern keepers who gave false measure, were punished by drowning the woman offender. Death was also the penalty for assault and battery, theft from the palace or temple, and false accusation and perjury in capital cases. Penalties for some crimes were based on the social status of the victim and offender. The rape of a betrothed virgin of the free citizen class was punished by death, but rape of a virgin slave woman was punished by a fine paid to her owner for his monetary loss. The death of a free woman was homicide, a crime against a person, and was punished by death; the death of a slave woman was an economic loss compensated by money paid to her owner. Since slave women were property, not legal persons, property, crimes committed against them were penalized by fines paid to their owners.

Corporal punishment and corporal mutilation were introduced into Old Babylonia from Amorite customary law. In some cases the body part involved in the offense was removed, such as the hand of a surgeon who caused his patient's death or the breast of a wet nurse in whose care an infant died. In cases of children who rebelled against parental authority, a hand could be cut off for striking, a tongue taken out for malicious speech, and an eye removed for running away. The tribal principle of *talion* was also used, especially in cases of personal injury: an eye for an eye, a broken bone for a broken bone. When it was applied to a person, as, for example, a husband or father who committed a crime of violence against the wife or daughter of another, the man was punished by the same violence being done not to himself but to his wife or daughter: a raped daughter or murdered wife for a raped daughter or murdered wife. The result was the vicarious punishment of innocent women for the crimes of others. Old Babylonian criminal law utilized many forms of punishment characteristic of tribal customary law, such as frequent use of the death penalty, corporal punishment, corporal mutilation, the principle of *talion* and vicarious punishment. In Babylonia, however, such penalties were never as prevalent or as cruel as in Assyria.

Middle Babylonia was under foreign occupation, and little is known except that at least one king revived the tradition of appointing royal daughters as high priests of Ur. On the other hand, fathers sold their daughters as brides.

Late Babylonia had moved beyond its tribal past in most areas. The status of many women improved. At least one queen mother had extensive influence. Marriage required marriage gifts, a dowry, and a written contract. The gifts and dowry were given not to the fathers but directly to the couple, who established a new household. Divorce was discouraged by requiring large sums as compensation. Widows inherited the amount of the marriage gifts and the usufruct of the late husband's house and property. Women owned, bought, and sold real property. They derived income from shares of temple benefices. They were legal persons who litigated in the courts. There were a few women priests and prophets and at least one royal woman high priest. Women who held religious offices and widows were more independent than other women. Yet there was also a focus on the biological aspects of women. Virginity before marriage was highly valued. The purity of all who worked in the temple was considered very important and the authorities even checked the purity of such persons' wives and mothers. Babylonian women had more restrictions and fewer rights against those who harmed them than Sumerian women, and innocent women were punished for the crimes of men. Late Babylonian women committed crimes of adultery and witchcraft, which were still punished by death; however, most of the earlier Amorite tribal forms of capital punishment and corporal mutilation had dropped out of use in favor of restitution, compensation, and fines.

ASSYRIA

During the earliest period of Old Assyrian history, there was a unique and strong merchant middle class in which women were literate professionals who ran international trading companies. The rights of women were almost as extensive as in Sumer, but when an Amorite king seized the throne at end of the nineteenth century, women lost all rights and influence. Assyria was far distant from Sumer and did not have a well-established urban culture or legal tradition; its cities were taken over quickly by Amorites still very much in touch with their tribal customs.

Middle Assyrian laws reflected a still primitive society closer to its tribal origins than Babylonia or Old Assyria I. Kings practiced polygyny and had extensive harems. Marriage required a marriage price and a contract; a dowry was common but not a legal requirement. Fathers sold their daughters to prospective husbands at a very young age. Husbands were permitted to beat and otherwise punish their wives for offenses and husbands could divorce their wives without compensation. Women did not own or inherit property, but were liable for their husbands' debts. Women had to be represented by men in the courts. Respectable married women had to be veiled when out of doors. As women lost their public political roles, religious offices, and wealth, they lost their status and power. As the dominance and power of men over women increased, women were more and more confined to their homes. As women lost their legal personhood, they were no longer protected by law and became the property of men.

In ancient Mesopotamian civilizations, children supported their mothers in old age. Only in Assyria, however, was the mother required to serve the son who took care of her. In general, Assyrian women did not have wealth or power, or significant roles in religion or politics. There were exceptions, however. Two professional women, a midwife and a religious officiant, served the women locked up in the king's harem. In Late Assyria, three queens had influential roles, and there were also women prophets.

Assyrian men were concerned about ritual purity. Men, especially priests, had to avoid any contact with menstruating women lest they be contaminated. Blood rendered a woman and anyone with whom she came in contact unclean. Thus, women were secluded during menstruation and after childbirth. The blood tabu derived from ancient tribal custom.

In Middle and Late Assyria, women were victims of murder, rape, sexual assault, and battery causing miscarriage and death. Women were falsely accused of serious crimes. Women in the king's harem endured life imprisonment without contact with the world or people outside, and women in debt servitude were sold into slavery. Betrothed women were liable for the criminal penalties of their betrothed and husbands, even while still living in their fathers' house. Assyrian husbands had the legal right to beat, mutilate, and kill their wives. When men committed certain crimes, the penalties were carried out vicariously on their wives or daughters. Under the principle of *talion*, the innocent pregnant wife of an offender who had beaten the pregnant wife of another causing her to miscarry could be beaten until she had a miscarriage.

A man who sexually assaulted a woman was punished by amputation of his finger or lower lip. When a man raped a virgin, the penalty was vicarious punishment by multiple rape of the rapist's wife, who was herself innocent of any crime, and the marriage of the rapist to the victim, now diminished in value. When a man who had no property committed murder, his daughter or son was given as compensation to the family of the victim to kill or enslave. The vicarious punishment of the crimes of men resulted in the deaths, injuries, and enslavement of innocent wives and daughters.

Assyrian women, despite their seclusion, committed many crimes. The worst offense a woman could commit under Assyrian law was abortion, which offended the gods, the state, and the husband. Women committed other capital crimes against religion, including sacrilege, theft from a temple, blasphemy, and witchcraft. In the palace harem, women who blasphemed, stole, fought with other women, stood too close to a man, or conversed with a man faced the death penalty. Married women committed crimes by traveling with or visiting the house of a man not their husband. Assyrian women who challenged the authority of men were severely punished. Women who cursed the king or other royal persons and women who physically assaulted men were fined, flogged, and mutilated—punishments usually reserved for men. Women who stole from a sick husband took advantage of his weakness and thus challenged his authority.

In Assyria the primary forms of punishment were capital and corporal. The harshest form of the death penalty, impalement, was prescribed for women who committed abortion. Women of the royal harem who blasphemed or cursed a god were executed by having their throats cut. Death was the penalty for murder, rape, adultery, procurement for sex, assault and battery causing miscarriage and death of the woman or death of a male fetus, and theft from the palace or temple.

Some crimes of violence were punished by multiple penalties, including public flogging, mutilation, terms of penal servitude, and fines. Among the offenses punished in this way were nonfatal assault and battery and false accusation of women. When a prostitute was struck causing miscarriage, the offender was given the same number of blows and had to pay for the life of the fetus.

Men controlled women by the imposition of the requirement of the veil. Respectable married women had to wear a veil whenever they went outside. A prostitute who wore a veil in public was flogged and hot pitch was poured over her head, disfiguring her face. A man who saw a prostitute veiled and did not report it was punished by flogging, corporal mutilation, and a term of penal servitude. The veil was a public sign of sexual unavailability and male ownership. Women who disobeyed the laws on veiling challenged the authority of men.

Assyrian kings bragged in their annals about their harsh treatment of war captives. They claimed to have inflicted cruel forms of execution and corporal mutilation. The literary genre used by scribes in writing these annals suggests that many of the claims may be exaggerated. Some documents mitigated the conduct of the conquerors, but other documents and art confirmed the cruelty.

The Assyrians seemed to be adept at devising cruel forms of punishment. Perhaps the worst of all appeared not in annals of war and conquest but in ordinary contracts. In the Late Assyrian period, a penalty for breaching the nonlitigation clause of contracts was to burn to death the person's firstborn son and daughter before a god or goddess. This was not a religious sacrifice, but a legal penalty for breach of contract.

Assyrian men put women ever more completely under their control until women were reduced to the status of property owned by men. With the exceptions of Old Assyrian merchant women and several queens in the Late Assyrian period, women had no power or place in Assyrian society. Women received little protection from Assyrian law and were victimized by laws that prescribed vicarious punishment. The facts that women physically attacked men and crushed their testicles often enough that laws were promulgated against this indicates that Assyrian women were not passively content with their position and treatment. No other ancient Near Eastern civilization either controlled the lives of women so completely or mentioned women physically attacking men.

KHATTI

The kingdom of Khatti was a tribal, feudal, and military society. In the Hittite Laws, with the exception of queens, the status of women was low, although not as low as that of Assyrian women. Queens had administrative duties, held the highest priesthood, were wealthy and powerful, and even issued edicts. There were several other ranks of priesthood and religious office held by women. Some women were literate and wrote rituals. Marriage required a marriage price and a dowry. When a man divorced his wife, he did not have to give her compensation and he was entitled to the property and the children. When a wife died, her husband kept her dowry and personal possessions. Men controlled their women by keeping them veiled. Women did not own property, but were property owned by men. A husband could sell his wife for twenty sheqels of silver. The value of a woman slave was half the value of a male slave. The work of a woman was valued at about half of the worth of the same work performed by a man. Women were able to work outside the house as millers, weavers, fullers, clothes makers, and bakers, and as musicians, singers, and dancers in the religious cult.

Hittite women were victims of the violent crimes of murder, rape, forced incest, assault, battery, kidnapping, and robbery. When a woman was raped inside her house, she was punished by death on the assumption that she did not call out or resist. In the Old Hittite period, women were victims of the widespread use of collective and vicarious punishment. When men were convicted of capital crimes, even such minor offenses as angering the king, the death penalty was extended to their wives and children, and sometimes even to their siblings and slaves, resulting in the execution of many innocent women and children.

In ancient Khatti, most crimes were under the jurisdiction of the state, which determined guilt and punishment. In Old Hittite law, intentional homicide and adultery were still under private jurisdiction. The male representative of a murder victim or the husband of a wife caught in adultery chose and carried out the punishment, usually death. In the later revision of the laws, the state took jurisdiction over all crimes. Hittite women also committed the capital crimes of witchcraft, theft of a sacred object from the palace, incest, and disobedience to the judgment of the king or a magistrate. Women committed some property crimes, such as theft and helping a runaway slave.

Hittite women, including members of the royal family, were duly punished when they committed crimes. Hittite tribal customs and penalties were much less harsh and cruel than those of Assyria and the Amorite tribes in Mesopotamia. The oldest laws specified penalties of death and corporal mutilation. Later laws prescribed monetary penalties. The death penalty was prescribed for intentional homicide, rape, adultery, incest, and bestiality. Fines were the punishment for unintentional homicide, kidnapping, assault and battery, robbery, burglary, and helping an escaped slave. The Hittites had several unique penalties; for example, one who stole a plow was bound on the plow and torn apart by a team of oxen, and one who stole bees was punished by bee stings.

In early Hittite law, the crime of witchcraft was punished by death. In the later revision, the penalty was determined by the social status of the offender. When witchcraft was committed by a queen, the penalty was exile; by a free citizen, the collective death of the offender and her or his family; by a slave, the loss of nose, ears, or eyes, or death with all family members. Compensatory penalties were likewise assessed according to the social status and gender of the victim or offender. When the victim was a woman or slave, the penalty was half. If a woman helped a runaway slave, the fine was doubled if the slave was male. If the offender was a slave, who had no money, the penalty was capital or corporal. Collective punishment was extensive. It was abolished at the end of the Old Hittite period but revived during the empire.

Crimes that caused pollution, such as incest, witchcraft, and sowing a field that had already been sown, were punished by death. The Hittites believed that the people and the land were purified from pollution not by fire and water but by blood. Initially this was the blood of the human offender. Later the blood of sacrificial animals was deemed sufficient.

CONCLUSION

The documents and artifacts of the ancient Near East are three to five thousand years old. Yet despite their antiquity, the ancient texts reveal ideas about women, crime, and punishment that are relevant for all time. The earliest lawgivers passionately stated that the purpose and goal of law was to do justice and eliminate oppression.

The extant ancient Near Eastern texts show a negative development, albeit nonlinear, of the status and rights of women. Women had almost the same rights as men in the oldest civilizations of Sumer in the south and Old Assyria I in the north. Women in these societies were trusted, literate, competent administrators of large businesses. In the subsequent empires of tribal societies, women had few, if any, legal rights and lost their legal personhood. They were denied education, wealth, and important positions in society or religion.

Most women were married and lived their lives under the authority of men. Polygyny further enhanced the authority of husbands and diminished the position of wives. There is also a correlation between the increased use of capital and corporal punishment and the diminution of the status of women. Capital and corporal punishments were associated with patriarchal authority and protection of men's rights of power and dominance over women.

Women who committed crimes that challenged the authority of men were perceived to be very threatening to the political, economic, and religious systems. The most efficient way to limit challenges to male authority was to eliminate the challengers. An unfaithful wife who had her husband killed, a woman who squandered her husband's assets or disparaged his reputation, and a wife who aborted her husband's unborn child were all put to death.

The ancient Near Eastern civilizations had different attitudes toward the punishment of crime. In the oldest society of all, Sumer, a poet eloquently wrote that the purpose of punishment for crimes was to rehabilitate offenders to become good and righteous citizens, as a mother lovingly teaches her children. The subsequent Amorite tribal-based societies viewed criminal penalties as means of revenge and retribution. When tribal societies were in the nomadic stage, the forms of punishment, capital and corporal, were determined by the lack of structures and courts. Yet even after settlement and the creation of kingdoms and empires, the kings of at least one such society, Assyria, created ever more cruel forms of punishment. The tribal-based societies believed that certain crimes engendered pollution, which was dangerous for the people and the state. The means of purification of pollution were fire and water in the Amorite tribal-based societies of Babylonia and Assyria, whereas in the Anatolian tribal-based society of Khatti purification was effected by blood. Only Assyria prescribed the penalty of killing one's own children.

The ancient texts were for the most part silent about disenfranchised women who owned no property, and who lived as the property of men. However, the existence of criminal laws in these same societies dealing with women who physically assaulted men and crushed their testicles indicates that at least some women were not content to be silent, acquiescent nonpersons, but expressed in a very graphic way their rage at the patriarchal domination of men over every aspect of their lives.

Each ancient Near Eastern civilization was different and existed in a different physical, political, and economic environment. The extant literary and legal texts of each civilization are fragmentary and incomplete; yet these texts, enhanced by the visual expressions of art and artifact, provide a rich and varied background for understanding the lives, crimes, and punishments of women in the ancient Near East. Each civilization has contributed many varied pieces, which can be put together—not as one picture for all, but one for each civilization. It has been possible to construct four mosaic scenes, which can be admired but never captured. For knowledge and understanding of women, crime, and punishment in ancient Near Eastern law and society are continually evolving as each new seeker delves into the mystery.

Chronology and Names

EARLY DYNASTIC LAGASH (LAGASH I)			
Kings	*Dates*	*Spouses*	*Daughters*
Enkhegal	c. 2710		
Ur-Nanshe	c. 2540	Menbara'abzu	Ninusu
			Abda
Eannatum			
Enannatum I		Ashume'eren	
Entemena	c. 2450	Ninkhilisug	
Enannatum II			
Enetarzi		Dimtur	Geme-Bau
Lugalanda	2384-2378	Baranamtara	Geme-Nanshe
			Mishaqa
Uru-inimgina	2378-2371	Shagshag	Geme-Bau
			Gemetarsirsir

EARLY DYNASTIC UR	
Kings	*Queens*
Meskalamdug	
	Puabi (queen)
Akalamdug	Ashusikidilgir
Mesannepada	Nin-banda (queen, wife)
	Nin-Tur
A'annepadad	
Meskiagnuna	Gansamannu
Annane	
Meskiag-Nanna	
Elulu	
Balulu	

AKKADIAN DYNASTY			
Kings	*Dates*	*Spouses*	*Daughters*
Sargon	2371-2316	Tashlultum	En-kheduanna (HP, Ur)
Rimush	2315-2307		
Manishtusu	2306-2292		
Naram-Sin	2291-2255		En-menanna (HP, Ur)
			Tutanapshum (HP, Nippur)
			Shumshoni (HP, Sippar)
			Me'ulmash
Sharkalisharri	2254-2230	Tutasharlibish	
HP=high priest			

SECOND DYNASTY OF LAGASH (LAGASH II)				
Kings	*Relationship to Ur-Bau*	*Dates*	*Spouses*	*Daughters*
Ur-Ningirsu I				
Lugalushumgal				
Puzur-Mama				
Ur-Bau		2158-2150	Nin-khedu	En-annepadda (HP)
Gudea	son-in-law	2145-2135	Nin-alla	
Ur-Ningirsu II	son		Nin-niginesi	
Ugme	son			
Ur-Gar	son-in-law		Nin-kagina	
Nammakhani	son-in-law		Nin-khedu	

UR III DYNASTY			
Kings	*Consort*	*Title*	*Daughters*
Ur-Nammu	SI.A.tum/Watartum	wife	En-nirgalanna (HP, Ur)
Shulgi	Shulgi-simtī	queen, consort	En-nirzianna (HP, Ur)
	Ea-nisha	consort	Shat-Sin
	Geme-Ninlila	consort	Simat-Enlil
	Taddin-Eshtar	consort	Liwirmitashu (Q, Markhashi)
	Ninkalla	consort	Simat-Ishtar
	ME-Ea (or Simat-Ea)	consort	Baqartum
	Geme-Sin	wife	Simat-Shulgi
	Sur-gur-[ ]	consort	Shat-Shulgi
	Taram-Uram		Taram-Shulgi (Q, Anshan)
			Queenturturmu
			Tulid-Shamshi (P)
Amar-Sin	Abi-simti	queen	En-makhgalanna (HP, Ur)
	Kubatum	consort	Geme-eanna
	Puzurusha	consort	Queenkhedu
	Uda'adzéna'ad	consort	Queenlil-leman
	Zaga'ANbi(?)	consort	Queenlil-tukulti
	[x]-natum	consort	Paki-Nanna
			Simat-Ishtar
			Shatmami
			Sheluputum
			Tadin-Ishtar
			Tesinmama
Shu-Sin	Kubatum	queen, consort	Geme-Enlila
	Tiamat-bashti	consort	Shaterra
	Ishdumkin	consort	Taburkhattum
			Kunshimatum
Ibbi-Sin	Geme-Enlila	queen	Shulgi-simti
			Mametum
			Tukinhattamigrisha
			Taddin-Ishtar

HP=high priest
Q=queen

FIRST DYNASTY OF ISIN (ISIN I)			
Kings	*Dates*	*Wives*	*High Priest Daughters*
Ishbi-Erra	2017-1985		
Shu-ilishu	1984-1975		
Iddin-Dagan	1974-1954		
Ishme-Dagan	1953-1935		En-anatuma (HP, Ur)
Lipit-Ishtar	1934-1924	Lamassatum	En-ninsunzi (HP)
Ur-Ninurta	1923-1896		
Bur-Sin	1895-1875		
Lipit-Enlil	1874-1870		
Erra-imitti	1869-1862		
Ennlil-bani	1861-1838		
Zambia	1837-1835		
Iter-pisha	1834-1831		
Ur-dukuga	1830-1828		
Sin-magir	1827-1817	Natuptum	
Damiq-ilishu	1816-1794		

LARSA DYNASTY			
Kings	*Dates*	*Wives*	*HP Daughter or Sister*
Naplanum	2025-2005		
Emisum	2004-1977		
Samium	1976-1942		
Zabaia	1941-1933		
Gungunum	1932-1906		
Abisare	1905-1895		
Sumuel	1894-1866		En-shakiag-Nanna (Ur)
Nur-Adad	1865-1850		
Sin-iddinam	1849-1843		
Sin-eribam	1842-1841		
Sin-iqisham	1840-1836		
Silli-Adad	1835		
Warad-Sin	1834-1823		
			En-anedu (Ur)
Rim-Sin	1822-1763	Simat-Ishtar	
		Beltani	
		Rim-Sin-Shalabashtashu	

Note: En-anedu was the sister of kings Warad-Sin and Rim-Sin

ESHNUNNA		
Kings	*Dates*	*Daughters*
Bilalama	c. 1990	Mekubi (Q, Elam)
Dadusha	c. 1820	Inibshina

OLD BABYLONIA	
Kings	*Dates*
Sumuabum	1894-1881
Sumulael	1880-1845
Sabium	1844-1831
Apil-Sin	1830-1813
Sin-muballit	1812-1793
Hammurabi	1792-1750
Samsuiluna	1749-1712
Abi-esuh	1711-1684
Ammiditana	1683-1647
Ammisaduqa	1646-1626
Samsuditana	1625-1595

MARI			
Kings	*Dates*	*Spouses*	*Daughters*
Yaggid-Lim	1820		
Yakhdum-Lim	1810		18+
			Inibshina (P)
			Yamama
			Nagiha
			Ishtar-tappi
(Assyrian Occupation)			
Zimri-Lim	1780-1760	Shibtu	20+
		Damhurasi	Erishti-Aya (P)
			Inibsharri
		Yatar-Aya	Kiru
		Umumtabat	Shimatum
			Tizpatum
			Ibbatum
			Naramtum
			Dukhsatum
			Kikhil
			Akhatum
			Khazala

Note: the numbers 18+ and 20+ mean those kings had 18/20 or more daughters. Only some of their names are known.

KARANA		
King	*Queen*	*Daughters*
		Iltani (Q)
		Amat-Shamash (P)
		Lamassani
Aqbahammu	Iltani	

LATE BABYLONIA (LB)			
Kings	Dates	Spouses	Daughters
Nabu-apil'usur	625-605		
Nabu-kudurri'usur II	604-562	Mede	Kasshaya
Amel-Marduk	561-560		
Nergal-sharru'usur	559-556	Kasshaya	
Labashti-Marduk	555		
Nabu-naid	555-539		Erishti-Sin (HP, Ur)
Bel-sharru'usur (regent)			

MEANING OF NAMES OF LATE BABYLONIAN KINGS		
Babylonian Name	Hebrew or Common Spelling	Meaning of Name
Nabu-apil'usur	Nabopolassar	Nabu protect the heir
Nabu-kudurri'usur	Nebukhadn/rezzar	Nabu protect my heir
Amel-Marduk	Evil-Merodach	Man of Marduk
Nergal-sharru'usur	Neriglissar	Nergal protect the king
Labashi-Marduk		
Nabu-naid	Nabonidus	Nabu is praised
Bel-sharru'usur (regent)	Belshazzar	Bel protect the king

OLD ASSYRIA I (OA I)	
Kings	*Dates*
Kikkia	
Akkia	
Puzur-Asshur I	
Shalim-ahhe	
Ilushuma	
Erishtum I	1906-1867
Ikunum	
Puzur-Asshur II	
Naram-Sin	
Erishum	

OLD ASSYRIA II (OA II)	
Kings	*Dates*
Shamsi-Adad I	1813-1781
Ishme-Dagan	1780-1741

KINGS OF MIDDLE ASSYRIA		
Reign	*King*	*Meaning of Name*
1392-1366	Eriba-Adad I	Adad has replaced
1365-1330	Asshur-uballit I	Asshur has kept alive
1329-1320	Enlil-nerari	Enlil is my help
1319-1308	Arikdenili	Judgment of god is long-lasting
1307-1275	Adad-nerari I	Adad is my help
1274-1245	Salmanu-ashared II	Salmanu is foremost
1244-1208	Tukulti-Ninurta I	My trust is Ninurta
1207-1204	Asshur-nadin'apli	Asshur is the giver of the heir
1203-1198	Asshur-nerari III	Asshur is my help
1197-1193	Enlil-kudurri'user	Enlil protect the eldest son
1192-1180	Ninurta-apil-Ekur	Ninurta is the heir of Ekur
1179-1134	Asshur-dan I	Asshur is strong
1132-1115	Asshur-resha'isshi I	Asshur has lifted my head
1114-1076	Tukulti'apil-Esharra I	My trust is the heir of Esharra
1075-1074	Ashared'apil-Ekur	Heir of Ekur is foremost
1073-1056	Asshur-bel'kala	Asshur is the lord of all
1055-1054	Eriba-Adad II	Adad has replaced
1053-1050	Shamshi-Adad IV	Adad is my sun
1049-1031	Asshur-nasir'apli I	Asshur is the protector of the heir
1030-1019	Salmanu-ashared II	Salmanu is foremost
1018-1013	Asshur-nerari IV	Asshur is my help
1012-972	Asshur-rabi II	Asshur is great
971-967	Asshur-reshi'isshi II	Asshur has lifted my head
966-935	Tukulti'apil-Esharra II	My trust is the heir of Esharra

KINGS OF LATE ASSYRIA			
Kings	*Dates*	*Wives*	*Daughters*
Asshur-dan II	934-912		
Adad-nirari II	911-891		
Tukulti-Ninurta II	890-884		
Asshur-nasir'apli II	883-859	Mullissu-mukannishat-Ninua	
Salmannu-ashared III	858-824		
Shamshi-Adad V	823-811	Sammu-ramat	
Adad-nirari III	810-783		
Salmannu-ashared IV	782-773		
Asshur-dan III	772-755		
Asshur-nirari V	754-745		
Tukulti-apil-Esharra II	1744-727	Yaba	
Salmannu-ashared V	726-722	Banitu	
Sharrukin II	721-705	Atalia	Akhatabisha
Sin-akhe'eriba	704-681	Naqia/Zakutu (Q)	Shadditu
		Tashmetumsharrat	
Asshur-akhu'iddina	681-669	Esharra-khammat	Sherua'eterat
Asshur-bani'apli	669-630	Libbalisharrat	
Asshur-etel-ilani	630-627		
Sin-sharrishkun	627-612		
Asshur-uballit II	611-609		

MEANING OF NAMES OF LATE ASSYRIAN KINGS			
Reign	*King*	*Hebrew or Common Form*	*Meaning*
934-912	Asshur-dan II		Asshur is strong
911-891	Adad-nerari II		Adad is my help
890-884	Tukulti-Ninurta II		My trust is Ninurta
883-859	Asshur-nasir-apli II	Asshurnasirpal II	Asshur is the protector of the heir
858-824	Salmanu-ashared III	Shalmaneser III	Salmanu is foremost
823-811	Shamshi-Adad V		Adad is my sun
810-783	Adad-nerari III		Adad is my help
782-773	Salmanu-ashared IV	Shalmaneser IV	Salmanu is foremost
772-755	Asshur-dan III		Asshur is strong
754-745	Asshur-nerari V		Asshur is my help
744-727	Tukulti-apil-Esharra	Tiglathpileser III	My trust is the offspring of Esharra
726-722	Salmanu-ashared V	Shalmaneser V	Salmanu is foremost
721-705	Sharru-kin II	Sargon II	The king is legitimate/ established
704-681	Sin-akhe-eriba	Sennakherib	Sin has replaced the brothers
680-669	Asshur-akhu-iddina	Esarhaddon	Asshur has given a brother
668-631	Asshur-bani-apli	Asshurbanipal	Asshur is the creator of the heir
630-627	Asshur-etel-ilani		Asshur is the prince of the gods
626-612	Sin-sharru-ishkun		Sin has established the king
611-609	Asshur-uballit II		Asshur has kept alive

MEANINGS OF NAMES OF LATE ASSYRIAN WOMEN			
Spelling Used	Assyrian	Meaning	Language
Abidala	Abi-dala	father has saved	WSem
Abidimri	Abi-dimri	father is my protection	WSem
Abikhali	Abi-kha'ili	father is my strength	WSem
Abiyakhya	Abi-iakhia	father revives	Aram
Abilikhia/Abilikha	Abi-likhia	may the father live	WSem
Abirakhi	Abi-rakhi	father is pleased	Aram
Abirakhimu	Abi-rakhimu	father is compassionate	WSem
Abiramu	Abi-ramu	father is exalted	WSem
Aburisha	Abu-risha	father rejoice	Akk
Adda-ti	Adda-ati	Adda is my deliverance	Aram
Akha	Akha	brother	WSem
Akhassunu	Akhassunu	their sister	Akk
Akhata	Akhata	sister	WSem
Akhatabisha	Akhat-abisha	her father's sister	Akk
Akhatabu	Akhat-abu	his father's sister	WSem
Akhati'imma	Akhati-imma	her mother's sister	WSem
Akhatitabat	Akhati-tabat	my sister is good	Akk
Akhi'ile	Akhi-ile	the brother is his god	WSem
Akhitalli	Akhi-talli	brother is my protection	Aram
Akhu'a	Akhu'a	my brother	Akk
Alhapimepi	Al-hapi-mepi	Apis bull brought to Memphis	Egyptian
Amat-Kurra	Amat-Kurra	servant of Kurra	WSem
Anatdalati	Anat-dalati	Anat has saved/delivered	WSem
Arbail-khammat	Arbail-khammat	[Ishtar of] Arbel is mistress	Akk
Arbailitu	Arbailitu	the one from Arbel	Akk
Arbailitubeltuni	Arbailitu-beltuni	the one from Arbel is our lady	Akk
Arbail-lamur	Arbail-lamur	may I see [Ishtar of] Arbel	Akk
Arbail-sharrat	Arbail-sharrat	[Ishtar of] Arbel is queen	Akk
Attar-palti	Attar-palti	Attar is my escape	WSem
Ba'altiyabata	Ba'alti-iabata	my Lady has given	Aram
Babu-gamilat	Babu-gamilat	Babu spares	Akk
Banat-Emashmash	Banat-Emashmash	Emashmash has created	Akk
Banitu	Banitu	creator	Akk
Banitu-ayali	Banitu-aiali	Banitu is my help	Akk
Banitu-atkal	Banitu-atkal	Banitu I have trusted	Akk
Banitu-belusri	Banitu-belu-usri	Banitu protect the lord	Akk
Banitu-dannat	Banitu-dannat	Banitu is strong	Akk
Banitu-duri	Banitu-duri	Banitu is my protective wall	Akk
Banitu-sharrat	Banitu-sharrat	Banitu is queen	Akk
Banitu-tashmanni	Banitu-tashmanni	Banitu has heard me	Akk
Banitu-teresh	Banitu-teresh	Banitu has desired	Akk

	MEANINGS OF NAMES OF LATE ASSYRIAN WOMEN (*cont.*)		
Spelling Used	*Assyrian*	*Meaning*	*Language*
Banitu-ummi	Banitu-ummi	Banitu is my mother	Akk
Barsipitu	Barsipitu	woman from Borsippa	Akk
Belet-issea	Belet-issea	the Lady is with me	Akk
Damqaia	Damqaia	good	Akk
Esharra-khammat	Esharra-khammat	[Mullissu of] Esharra is my mistress	Akk
Gula-rishat	Gula-rishat	Gula exalts	Akk
Kharra	Kharra	free or scorched	Aram, Heb, Arabic
Khazala	Khazala	gazelle	Arabic
Issar-remanni	Issar-remanni	Ishtar have mercy	Akk
Kabal-aya	Kabal-aia	bound to Aya	WSem
Lasakhittu	La-sakhittu	unwanted	Akk
Lateggiana	La-teggi-ana-[...]	do not be negligent to [a god]	Akk
Libbalisharrat	Libbali-sharrat	the Inner City is queen	Akk
Marqikhita	Marqikhita	perfumer	Aram
Milkikhaia	Milki-khaia	the king is my life	WSem
Muballitat	Muballit[...]	the one who revives is [...]	Akk
Mullissu-abu'usri	Mullissu-abu-usri	Mullissu protect the father	Akk
Mullissu-beltu'usri	Mullissu-beltu-usri	Mullissu protect the mistress	Akk
Mullissu-duri	Mullissu-duri	Mullissu is my protective wall	Akk
Mullissu-duru'usri	Mullissu-duru-usri	Mullissu protect the city wall	Akk
Mullissu-khammat	Mullissu-khammat	Mullissu is mistress of the family	Akk
Mullissu-khasina	Mullissu-khasinat	Mullissu is the one who protects	Akk
Mullissu-ibni	Mullissu-ibni	Mullissu has created	Akk
Mullissu-iddina	Mullissu-iddina	Mullissu has given	Akk
Mullissu-ila'i	Mullissu-ila'i	Mullissu is my god	Akk
Mullissu-kabtat	Mullissu-kabtat	Mullissu is honored	Akk
Mullissu-mukanishat-Ninua		Mullissu gathers Nineveh	Akk
Mullissu-sharrat	Mullissu-sharrat	Mullissu is queen	Akk
Mullissu-ummi	Mullissu-ummi	Mullissu is my mother	Akk
Mussa'itu	Mussa'itu	relaxed	Akk
Nabu-ramat	Nabu-ramat	Nabu is beloved/exalted	Akk
Nanaia-da	Nanaia-da	Nanaia has saved/delivered	Akk
Nanaia-dammiqi	Nanaia-dammiqi	Nanaia show favor	Akk
Nanaia-dannat	Nanaia-dannat	Nanaia is mighty	Akk
Nanaia-lurshi	Nanaia-lurshi	Nanaia be my guardian	Akk
Nanaia-sharrat	Nanaia-sharrat	Nanaia is queen	Akk
Naqia	Naqi'a	pure	Aram
Naramtu	Naramtu	beloved	Akk
Rama-Ya	Rama-Ia	Yahweh has thrown	Heb

MEANINGS OF NAMES OF LATE ASSYRIAN WOMEN *(cont.)*			
Spelling Used	*Assyrian*	*Meaning*	*Language*
Rama-Ya	Rama-Ia	Yahweh has thrown	Heb
Sammu-ramat	Sammu-ramat	Sammu is exalted/beloved	WSem/Akk
Sams	Samsi	my sun	Arabic
Sukkitu	Sukkitu	woman of the shrine	Akk

Notes:

Names of unknown derivation and meaning have not been included.

The source for the meaning of most of the names is Karen Radner and Heather Baker, eds., The Prosopography of the Neo-Assyrian Empire. *Vols. 1/1-3/1. Helsinki: The Neo-Assyrian Text Corpus Project, 1998–2003. The volumes published to date include names beginning A–S.*

PROTO-HITTITE KINGS	
Anitta	c. 1790
Labarnash	c. 1690

OLD HITTITE KINGDOM (OH)

Kings	Dates	Wives
Khattushilish I	1655-1625	
Murshilish I	1625-1590	
Khantilish I	1590-1555	
Zidantash I	1555-1550	
Ammunash	1550-1545	
Khuzziyash I	1530-1525	
Telepinush	1525-1500	Ishtapariya

HITTITE EMPIRE (HE)

Kings	Dates	Wives
Tudkhaliyash I	1420-1400	Nikal-mati
Khattushilish II	1400-1380	
Tudkhaliyash II	1380-1360	
Arnuwandash I	1390-1380	Ashmu-Nikal
Tudkhaliyash III	1380-1370	
Shuppiluliumash I	1360-1340	Kassite woman
Arnuwandash II	1340-1330	
Murshilish II	1330-1320	Gasshulawiya (Q)
Muwatallish II	1320-1290	
Urkhi-Teshub	1290-1286	
Khattushilish III	1286-1265	Pudukhepa (Q, P)
Tudkhaliyash IV	1250-1225	Sharruma
Arnuwandash III	1225-1220	
Shupiluliumash II	1220-1200	
Suppiliuma II	1210-1200	

Notes

ᔕ

The following abbreviations of collections of laws and chronological periods are used in the notes:

Laws		*Chronological Periods*		
EA	Edict of King Ammisaduqa	Sumer	ED	Early Dynastic
HtL	Hittite Laws			Lagash II
LBL	Late Babylonian Laws			Ur III
LE	Laws of Eshnunna			Isin I
LH	Laws of Hammurabi	Babylonia	OB	Old Babylonia
LL	Laws of Lipit-Ishtar		NB	New Babylonia
LU	Laws of Ur-Nammu		Isin II	
LX	Laws of X		LB	Late Babylonia
MAL	Middle Assyrian Laws	Assyria	OA	Old Assyria
MAPD	Middle Assyrian Palace Decrees		MA	Middle Assyria
SLEx	Sumerian Laws Exercise Tablet		LA	Late Assyria
SLHF	Sumerian Laws Handbook of Forms	Khatti	OH	Old Hittite
			HE	Hittite Empire

INTRODUCTION TO ANCIENT NEAR EASTERN LAW AND SOCIETY

1. The term *ancient Near East,* which could more accurately be called "ancient southwest Asia," is used in this work to refer to the continent of Asia and does not include the ancient civilization of Egypt in North Africa. The geographical area also includes Arabia and Persia/Iran. This work focuses on Mesopotamia and Asia Minor.

2. The first settlements, which were isolated and produced only food, appeared from 9000 to 6000 BCE, and the movement into towns, which produced nonfood commodities, including pottery, took place from 6000 to 3200. Much of this period was a time of peace and stability. Hans J. Nissen, *The Early History of the Ancient Near East: 9000–2000 B.C.,* 40, 43. Amélie Kuhrt, *The Ancient Near East: C. 3000–330 B.C.,* 1:6–7, 12–14, 19–21, 23–26. Christopher Eyre, "The Agricultural Cycle, Farming and Water Management," in *Civilizations of the Ancient Near East,* ed. Sasson, 1:175, 177, 180–86. Karl Butzer, "Environmental Change in the Near East and Human Impact on the Land," in ibid., 1:136–37, 142–45. Jerrold S. Cooper, *Presargonic Inscriptions,* 24–29, nos. 1.6, 1.9, 1.17, 1.20 (Ur-Nanshe); 33–39, 42–43, nos. 3.1, 3.6 (Eannatum); 66–67, no. 5.26 (Enmetena also built a reservoir). All three were kings of Lagash I. Marc Van De Mieroop notes that the two distinct ecological zones also became distinct cultural zones (*The Ancient Mesopotamian City,* 8).

3. Jerrold S. Cooper, "Third Millennium Mesopotamia," in *Women's Earliest Records,* ed. Lesko, 47–51. Denise Schmandt-Besserat, "An Ancient Token System: The Precursor to Numbers

and Writing," *Arch* 39 (1986): 32–39. Tokens in the shapes of animals, tools, and other com-modities were pressed into clay balls (*bullae*), and numbers were inscribed on clay tablets. Such objects have been found with Sumerian pottery dated in the mid-fourth millennium. P. Kyle McCarter, *Ancient Inscriptions: Voices from the Biblical World*, 4–6. H. W. F. Saggs, *Babylonians*, 26, 27, fig. 5: numbers; 46, fig. 23: clay tokens; 45–47, figs. 22, 24–27: pictographs and numbers; Susan Pollock, *Ancient Mesopotamia: The Eden That Never Was*, 156, fig. 6-3: clay tokens from Uruk. J. N. Postgate, *Early Mesopotamia: Society and Economy at the Dawn of History*, 52–54, figs. 3.1: tokens from Uruk; 3.2: bulla and tokens from Susa; 3.3: numbers from Jebel Aruda in Syria (about 3200). Stone documents recording real estate transactions from about 2900 were found at Ur. These have been called the oldest legal documents. Postgate, *Early Mesopotamia*, 67, fig. 3.14.

4. William W. Hallo and William K. Simpson (*The Ancient Near East: A History*, 27, 151–52) and Kuhrt (*Ancient Near East*, 1:23) place the development of historical writing in the Sumerian city-state of Uruk, between 3200 and 2900 BCE.

5. J. Black and W. Tait, "Archives and Libraries in the Ancient Near East," in *Civilizations in the Ancient Near East*, ed. Sasson, 4:2198, 2202–3, 2206–7. The empires of Ur III, Isin I, and Larsa kept extensive business records. There was an isolated attempt to collect judicial decisions in Girsu/Lagash in the Ur III period. The early eighteenth-century kings Shamshi-Adad I of Asshur and Zimri-Lim of Mari had royal archives. In the second millennium, the Hittites had a library at Khattusha. The Middle and Late Assyrian kings had a library at Asshur, and in the first mil-lennium, the Late Assyrian kings had libraries at Nineveh, Nimrud, and Khorsabad. There was a Late Babylonian library at Sippar. Kings in all four civilizations had archives.

Field archaeology in Iraq has been extremely difficult since the Iran–Iraq war in the 1980s. Some archaeological sites were damaged by American bombing in 1991 and 2003. Many sites were looted during the twelve years of economic sanctions against Iraq. After the American inva-sion in 2003, many of the artifacts and documents in the National Archaeological Museum and Library in Baghdad were stolen, damaged, or destroyed, and some major archaeological sites, such as Isin, have been stripped by looters and destroyed.

6. The excavation of temples skewed the evidence, and historians must be careful not to make erroneous conclusions on the basis of temple texts alone. Kuhrt, *Ancient Near East*, 1:7–8, 10–11; Van De Mieroop, *Ancient Mesopotamian City*, 9, 12. One such find led to the false conclusion that early Sumerian cities were "temple states" for which the economy was controlled by the temple. This was based on a single archive of the Bau temple at Lagash from the twenty-sixth to twenty-fifth centuries. It took years and the excavation of palaces and whole cities to disprove the "tem-ple-state" theory with evidence of royal and private economies existing at the same time. According to Marc Van De Mieroop, the theory of linear evolution from temple to palace econ-omy to private enterprise, based on the decrease in temple and palace documents and the find-ing of archives of merchant families in the Old Babylonian period, is likewise incorrect (*Society and Enterprise in Old Babylonian Ur*, 3). T. Johannes Renger, "Interaction of Temple, Palace, and 'Private Enterprise' in the Old Babylonian Economy," in *State and Temple Economy in the Ancient Near East*, ed. Lipinski, 1:249–56.

PART ONE: SUMER

1. The Sumerian cities of Shuruppak and Ur and the Semitic city of Kish existed before 5000 BCE. Cuneiform writing began in the Sumerian city of Uruk in the late fourth millennium. Writ-ten history began in the early third millennium. Godfrey R. Driver and John C. Miles, *The Baby-*

lonian Laws, 1:1 n. 5. Dates are from *Cambridge Ancient History,* 1/2:998–1000. Since nouns in Sumerian did not have gender, it is often difficult for the translator to know whether nouns and names refer to masculine or feminine subjects. D. O. Edzard, "The Sumerian Language," in *Civilizations of the Ancient Near East,* ed. Sasson, 4:211.

2. Each cuneiform sign designated a word or a syllable. Most Sumerian words were only one or two syllables in length. D. O. Edzard, "Sumerian Language," 2108.The cuneiform writing system was sufficiently flexible that it was used by the Akkadians, Babylonians, and Assyrians, who spoke Semitic languages; by the Hittites, who spoke an Indo-European language; and by Sumerians and Hurrians, whose languages are unrelated to each other or to any known language group. Cuneiform was the standard writing system used in the ancient Near East from the third through the mid-first millennium BCE. Piotr Michalowski, *Letters from Early Mesopotamia,* 1. Marc Van De Mieroop, *Cuneiform Texts and the Writing of History.* McCarter, *Ancient Inscriptions,* 5: chart on development of cuneiform writing. Postgate, *Early Mesopotamia,* 55: chart on development of cuneiform; 57, fig. 3.5: early cuneiform tablets from Jemdet Nasr (3000) and Abu Salabikh (2450). Russ VerSteeg, *Early Mesopotamian Law,* xxiii: archaic cuneiform tablet from Ur (about 3000), xxii: later cuneiform clay tablet with envelope, xxiv: cuneiform contract on clay tablet with envelope. Cuneiform was also carved into stone.

3. The word *civilization* derives from the Latin word *civitas,* meaning "city." The first cities were religious, trade, and political centers. Empires were founded by the rulers of the Mesopotamian city-states of Akkad, Ur, Babylon, and Asshur (Assyria). The office of *en,* high priest, emerged from the temple context in the late fourth millennium. The office of king, *lugal,* was first documented at Kish about 2700 in the context of military and political leadership. Both derived power from control over temple and palace estates. Large households formed around multigenerational families. The size and wealth of households led to social stratification. Households were classified as public (temple and palace) and private (families). Hallo and Simpson, *Ancient Near East,* 33–34. Postgate, *Early Mesopotamia,* 73–76. Elizabeth Stone, "The Development of Cities in Ancient Mesopotamia," in *Civilizations of the Ancient Near East,* ed. Sasson, 1:235–39. Charles K. Maisels, *The Emergence of Civilization,* 154–56, 170–71.

4. Villages had become cities by the late fourth millennium. Van De Mieroop, *Society and Enterprise in Old Babylonian Ur,* 1. City-states were surrounded by agricultural villages. In the third millennium, the city-states were fortified with walls. *Art of the First Cities,* ed. Aruz, 5–6. Pollock, *Ancient Mesopotamia,* 2, 6. Samuel Greengus, "Legal and Social Institutions of Ancient Mesopotamia," in *Civilizations of the Ancient Near East,* ed. Sasson, 1:469–70. Thorkild Jacobsen, "Primitive Democracy in Ancient Mesopotamia," *JNES* 11 (1943): 159–72. Uruk was called *Erech* in the Hebrew Bible and *Warka* in Arabic.

5. Samuel N. Kramer, "Poets and Psalmists: Goddesses and Theologians," in *Legacy of Sumer,* ed. Schmandt-Besserat, 13–16. The goddess Inanna, "queen of heaven," survived and later merged into the goddess Ishtar. In some cases, the revision of myths occurred because male priests wanted their temples to have greater wealth and status. G. Leick, *The Babylonians,* 103–4. Piotr Michalowski postulates other factors, such as the conquest of cities with goddess cults and the popularity of one goddess cult absorbing other goddess cults ("Round about Nidaba: On the Early Goddesses of Sumer," in *Sex and Gender in the Ancient Near East,* ed. Parpola and Whiting, 422).

6. William W. Hallo, "Women of Sumer," in *Legacy of Sumer,* ed. Schmandt-Besserat, 28. Julia M. Asher-Greve, *Frauen in altsumerischer Zeit,* 168–69. Marc Van De Mieroop, "Women in the Economy of Sumer," in *Women's Earliest Records,* ed. Lesko, 54. In the Sumerian King List, Ku-Bau was called a king and was said to have ruled Kish for one hundred years during the Early Dynastic period. In the *Cambridge Ancient History* (1/2:998), her reign is dated between 2450 and 2370. William W. Hallo, *Early Mesopotamian Royal Titles: A Philologic and Historical Analysis,* 13. Douglas Frayne, *Sargonic and Gutian Periods (2334–2113 BC),* 198–99, nos. 2001–2:

Tutasharlibish. Frayne, *Ur III Period (2112–2004)*, 172, no. 69: Shulgi-simti. The Sumerian word for queen was *nin*. The title was sometimes given to wives of kings, but it did not denote a ruling queen, especially in the reign of a powerful and polygynous king like Shulgi.

7. The social classes of women and men were the same. Asher-Greve, *Frauen in altsumerischer Zeit*, 169–70. King Uru-inimgina of Lagash canceled debts, thereby freeing debt slaves. Cooper, *Presargonic Inscriptions*, 1:73. Male captives of war were killed or enslaved, whereas most women captives were enslaved. A few slaves were born into slavery.

8. Sargon became king in 2371 and had conquered his empire of Sumer and Akkad by 2350. In contrast to the other city-states of Sumer, Kish ruled a much larger area, which was inhabited by Semitic peoples from at least the mid-fourth millennium BCE. The people of Kish and Akkad spoke and wrote in the east Semitic language called Akkadian and used the cuneiform writing system. The Sumerian King List recorded kings with Semitic names in the first dynasty of Kish, from the twenty-eighth century. Driver and Miles, *Babylonian Laws*, 1:1 n. 5. Van De Mieroop, *Cuneiform Texts and the Writing of History*, 66–72. Postgate, *Early Mesopotamia*, 40. The infancy narrative of Sargon's birth was elaborated in the first millennium. According to literary sources, the mother of Sargon was a high priest, which meant that she was probably royal or noble, and his father was unknown, which was understood to imply that he might have been a god. His name in Akkadian was Sharrukin, meaning "king is legitimate." The dynasty lost its empire by the mid-twenty-third century, although the dynasty continued to rule the city-state of Akkad until 2193. Michael Roaf, *Cultural Atlas of Mesopotamia and the Ancient Near East*, 96–99. VerSteeg, *Early Mesopotamian Law*, xx: bronze head, possibly of Sargon. Julian Reade, *Mesopotamia*, 14: bronze mask, possibly of Sargon.

9. The Amorites were desert and mountain nomadic tribes. In Akkadian, they were called *Amurru*, meaning "from the west." They entered Mesopotamia from Syria in the west and spoke a West Semitic language related to Aramaic and Hebrew. Amorite was not a literary language, although Amorite names and speech forms are found in Old Babylonian and Mari texts. Sabatino Moscati et al., *An Introduction to the Comparative Grammar of the Semitic Languages*, 8–9. Amorites were mentioned from the Akkadian period on. Piotr Steinkeller, *Third Millennium Legal and Administrative Texts from the Iraq Museum, Baghdad*, 86–87, 108–9, nos. 48, 73. Hallo and Simpson, *Ancient Near East*, 71–77. H. W. F. Saggs, *The Greatness That Was Babylon*, 64–65. Jean Bottéro, *Mesopotamia*, 288. Frayne, *Ur III Period*, 328, no. 17. The wall of King Shu-Sin was 170 miles (270 kilometers) long. A. Haldar, *Who Were the Amorites?* Robert M. Whiting, "Amorite Tribes and Nations of Second-Millennium Western Asia," in *Civilizations of the Ancient Near East*, ed. Sasson, 2:1231–42. Some tribes had more affinity for Old Babylonia tradition, others for Old Assyria II. Amorite tribes made various political and military alliances with each other.

10. Martha Roth, *Law Collections from Mesopotamia and Asia Minor*, 13. Saggs, *Babylonians*, 51. Saggs, *Greatness That Was Babylon*, figs. 13A–B (indoor plumbing: stone toilet and drainage conduit).

11. King Uru-inimgina was the last ruler of the first dynasty of Lagash. The name Uru-inimgina was also transliterated Uru-KA-gina. The KA represents the name of the cuneiform sign, not its sound. VerSteeg, *Early Mesopotamian Law*, 18–19. Samuel N. Kramer, *History Begins at Sumer*, 45–50, 102. Asher-Greve, *Frauen in altsumerischer Zeit*, 163. Many of his inscriptions were found on cones and an oval plaque (OP). Cooper, *Presargonic Inscriptions*, 1:70–83. George R. Barton, ed. and trans., *The Royal Inscriptions of Sumer and Akkad*, 1:85. Saggs states that the reforms of Uru-inimgina showed a "concern for social justice" (*Greatness That Was Babylon*, 44, 322).

12. Barton, *Royal Inscriptions*, 1:80–83: Cone B 9.26–10.37. 1:84–87: Oval Plaque (OP) 2.16–22. Samuel N. Kramer found this an attempt at equal pay ("Poets and Psalmists," in *Legacy of Sumer*, ed. Schmandt-Besserat, 13). Wages were paid in rations of food, clothes, and other

commodities. Uru-inimgina also lowered the rations of male burial officials. The term used here for woman priest was *ugbabtu* (*nin-dingir*). The Sumerian title comprised two words: *nin*, "queen" or "lady," and *dingir*, "goddess." Jean Bottéro, *Religion in Ancient Mesopotamia*, 122. Samuel N. Kramer, *The Sumerians: Their History, Culture, and Character*, 321.

13. Barton, *Royal Inscriptions*, 1:78–81: Cone B 3.18–4.21, 7.12–28 (abuses), 7.8–11, 9.7–13 (houses and fields of women). Kramer, *Sumerians*, 321. I. M. Diakonoff, "Some Remarks on the 'Reforms'of Urukagina," *Revue d'assyriologie et d'archéologie orientale* 52 (1958): 10, 12.

14. Barton, *Royal Inscriptions*, 1:76–79, 82–85: Cone A 5.1–5. Cone B 5.22–6.3, 11.17–19. OP 2.11–14, 3.6–9. Cooper, *Presargonic Inscriptions*, 1:72, 75–76.

15. Kramer, *Sumerians*, 322: OP. Kramer, "Poets and Psalmists," in *Legacy of Sumer*, ed. Schmandt-Besserat, 12. Polyandry denotes marriage between one woman and more than one man. Polygyny means marriage between one man and many women. Polygamy means many marriages.

16. Barton, *Royal Inscriptions*, 1:86–87: OP 3.14–24, 8. In later Mesopotamian laws, adultery was punished by death.

17. Steinkeller, *Third Millennium Legal and Administrative Texts*, 21–23, no. 2: contract for sale of real property from Lagash during the reign of Uru-inimgina. Cooper, *Presargonic Inscriptions*, 76–77, no. 9.3, does not include penalties for either offense. Kramer notes the penalty for polyandry and theft was death by stoning (*Sumerians*, 322, citing OP). Stoning was simple and required no apparatus other than stones. The guilt of the offender was inscribed on the stones used. Kuhrt views this as a royal affirmation of male domination (*Ancient Near East*, 1:39).

18. The government of the Ur III empire was more centralized than that of Akkad. Kings appointed governors of other cities, and royal messengers traveled back and forth to keep the king informed. Saggs, *Greatness That Was Babylon*, 208. After the Akkadian empire, Sumerian kings called themselves "king of Sumer and Akkad." Hallo and Simpson, *Ancient Near East*, 70, fig. 13: bronze statue of Ur-Nammu with basket on his head, going to participate personally in temple building or restoration. Saggs, *Babylonians*, 84–85, fig. 50: fragments of a stone stela from Ur depicting Ur-Nammu before the goddess, carrying tools for rebuilding her temple; 86, fig. 53: copper figurine of Ur-Nammu carrying a basket on his head for the work on a temple.

19. In Sumerian, the names of high priests were prefixed by the nongendered title *en*. The Akkadian language distinguished between genders. *Entu* was the title of women high priests. The office of *en* was the highest priesthood, and those who held it were of the highest rank in society. Hallo and Simpson, *Ancient Near East*, 58–59; Frayne, *Ur III Period*, 86–87, nos. 52, 53: Taramu-ram, daughter-in-law of Ur-Nammu, had at least one farmer in her employ; 88, no. 54: En-nir-galana, daughter of Ur-Nammu, *en* of Ur.

20. Many scholars now attribute the laws to King Shulgi. Jacob Klein, "Shulgi of Ur," in *Civilizations of the Ancient Near East*, ed. Sasson, 2:854. We retain the name of Ur-Nammu in the title of the laws but concur that Shulgi was probably the final redactor of the laws. Shulgi probably built the laws on an earlier collection begun by Ur-Nammu. Klein, "Shulgi of Ur," 851, 855. Bottéro, *Religion in Ancient Mesopotamia*, 154–56. Saggs, *Babylonians*, 85–90. William W. Hallo, "Nippur Originals," in *DUMU-E2-DUB-BA-A: Studies in Honor of Ake Sjöberg*, ed. Behrens et al., 237. King Shulgi was an extraordinary man—general in the army, professionally trained scribe, mathematician, conservationist, runner, musician, and linguist. He created the administration of government for the empire; revised the calendar; standardized weights and measures; built factories, gardens, systems of irrigation, roads, and a chain of hostels along the trade routes. He had a passion for justice and defended the poor and weak. For Shulgi, doing justice was the duty of the king. It involved destroying evil and letting no one debase another person. Shulgi was involved in the copying of texts. He founded the scribal school at Nippur, and its curriculum became normative for other scribal schools in Ur III Sumer and in OB. Shulgi changed the pur-

pose of scribes from making one copy of a text to making many and taking the responsibility for the transmission of the text for future generations. Jacob Klein, "From Gudea to Shulgi: Continuity and Change in Sumerian Literary Tradition," in *DUMU,* 301.

21. The Laws of Ur-Nammu (LU) were written in Sumerian. Text A was found in Nippur; Text B in Ur; Text C in Sippar. Text A is the most complete, containing the prologue and laws 4–20. Text B contains laws 7–37. Text C, which was found in 1981, contains the prologue and laws 1–10. Roth, *Law Collections from Mesopotamia and Asia Minor,* 14. Because Text C was discovered after the publication of *Ancient Near Eastern Texts Relating to the Old Testament,* ed. Pritchard, the text and numbering of the Roth edition are used here. The extant texts on clay tablets are fragmentary because clay was easily broken. VerSteeg, *Early Mesopotamian Law,* xxi: fragments of a stela of Ur-Nammu.

22. Roth, *Law Collections,* 15–17: Prologue A iii 104–113, iv 162–168, 170, C ii 30–39, 46–51; *Ancient Near Eastern Texts,* ed. Pritchard, 523–24.

23. LU 15. Roth, *Law Collections,* 18–19.

24. LU 9–11. Roth, *Law Collections,* 18. The sheqel and the mina were measures of weight. One sheqel equaled eight grams. Sixty sheqels equaled one mina. The metal weighed was silver, gold, lead, or copper, depending on availability and affecting the value. Silver was generally used in Sumer. One silver sheqel was equal to approximately two or three days' wages.

25. LU 4–5. Roth, *Law Collections,* 17. Raymond Westbrook, "The Female Slave," in *Gender and Law in the Hebrew Bible and the Ancient Near East,* ed. Matthews et al., 223–24. The latter part of the text of LU 4 is fragmentary. LU 5 did not say that the woman became a slave by marrying a slave.

26. LU 24. Roth, *Law Collections,* 20. The fine was ten sheqels of silver.

27. LU 6, 8 (slave). Roth, *Law Collections,* 17–18, translated the first "virgin wife." Since there were several stages in the legal contracting of marriage in ancient Sumer, it is more accurate to say that the virgin was betrothed, since her being still a virgin meant that the marriage had not been consummated. Jerrold S. Cooper points out that there were no words in Sumerian or Akkadian for virgin or virginity, which were instead called by negative terms: "undeflowered" or "not having known a man" ("Virginity in Ancient Mesopotamia," in *Sex and Gender in the Ancient Near East,* ed. Parpola and Whitney, 91–93). The concept also connoted young in age.

28. LU 13, 14. Roth, *Law Collections,* 18. *Ancient Near Eastern Texts,* ed. Pritchard, 524 (LU 10–11). VerSteeg, *Early Mesopotamian Law,* 140. According to LU 28 (Roth, *Law Collections,* 20), the penalty for perjury by a witness, a crime similar to false accusation, was fifteen silver sheqels.

29. LU 18–22. Roth, *Law Collections,* 19. *Ancient Near Eastern Texts,* ed. Pritchard, 524–25 (LU 15–19). The fine for cutting off a foot was ten sheqels; for shattering a bone, one mina (sixty sheqels); for cutting off a nose, forty sheqels; and for knocking out a tooth, two sheqels. The law does not state whether the fines were paid to the state or to the victim. The leniency of the fines stands in stark contrast to the corporal penalties of equivalent mutilation or death in later ancient Near Eastern legal systems.

30. LU 3. Roth, *Law Collections,* 17. VerSteeg suggests that it might also be viewed as kidnapping (*Early Mesopotamian Law,* 125). The evidence does not support this. Prisons were rarely found in the ancient world and rarely mentioned in Sumerian texts. At most they had a small jail, but nothing comparable to a modern prison facility.

31. LU 1. Roth, *Law Collections,* 17. LU 2 also prescribed the death penalty, but the offense is unclear.

32. LU 7. Roth, *Law Collections,* 17–18. The translation in *Ancient Near Eastern Texts,* ed. Pritchard, 524 (LU 4), is that the wife by "employing her charms followed after another man and he slept with her." This law portrayed the woman as the principal actor in initiating the offense. When it came to sex, the man was usually mentioned first, since sex was the domain of the man. In LU 6, a man initiated and carried out the crime of rape, and he alone was sentenced to death.

In LU 7 the normal order was reversed. Thus, the woman alone was deemed guilty of the crime and she was sentenced to death.

33. LU 28, 29. Roth, *Law Collections*, 20. The operative principle in the refusal to take the oath was that the Sumerians were afraid of punishment by the gods if they swore an oath falsely. In LU 29, the fine was the amount in litigation. This prefigures the use of the "penalty of the case" in later ancient Near Eastern legal systems.

34. LU 25–26. Roth, *Law Collections*, 20. O. R. Gurney and Samuel N. Kramer translate the phrase: "presuming herself to be the equal of her mistress," which strengthens the challenge to authority ("Two Fragments of Sumerian Laws," in *Studies in Honor of Benno Landsberger on His Seventy-Fifth Birthday,* ed. Güterbock and Jacobsen, 16). Roth translates it: "someone acting with the authority of her mistress." In *Ancient Near Eastern Texts* a Sumerian proverb is cited which stated that a rebellious slave was made to eat salt (p. 525 n. 24). Roth suggests that the "strike" might be a slap on the cheek, which was an offense against the honor of the victim, rather than physical injury ("Mesopotamian Legal Traditions and the Laws of Hammurabi," *Chicago-Kent Law Review* 71 [1995]: 30). See the Laws of Hammurabi below.

35. LU 17. Roth, *Law Collections*, 19. No penalty was prescribed for the slave in the extant text of the law. The slave owner could punish the slave once he got her back.

36. Laws of Lipit-Ishtar (abbreviated LL) Prol. i.20–ii.15, Epil. xxi.5–17. Roth, *Law Collections*, 24–25, 33–35. Barton, *Royal Inscriptions,* 1:306–7: similar inscriptions on clay cones. *Ancient Near Eastern Texts,* 159. Driver and Miles, *Babylonian Laws,* 1:12. The laws were written in Sumerian, although the language spoken in the time of Lipit-Ishtar was Akkadian. The first Isin dynasty was the last non-Amorite dynasty in ancient Sumer. The time was called the Isin/Larsa period. More than half the laws on the extant tablets cannot be deciphered or restored, and the legible laws treat more civil than criminal subjects. Many fragmentary clay tablets have been found that contain copies of various parts of the laws of Lipit-Ishtar made in later centuries by students in the scribal schools of Nippur; these are helpful in restoring the text of the laws. In the epilogue, Lipit-Ishtar stated that he had erected a stone stela containing the laws. Two small fragments from a stela have been found that might be from the original.

37. LL 22–23. Bottéro, *Religion in Ancient Mesopotamia,* 121. In Sumerian art, however, there are more male priests than female.

38. LL 29. Roth, *Law Collections*, 32. Compare LU 15, which had only the penalty of double restitution. Roth, *Law Collections*, 18–19. LL 29 added the prohibition against a marriage between the bride and the second man.

39. LL 21, 23. Roth, *Law Collections*, 30–31.

40. LL 24 (polygyny), 28 (sick wife). Roth, *Law Collections*, 31–32, and 35 n. 8. The translation "lost her sight" is that of Miguel Civil, "New Sumerian Law Fragments," in *Studies in Honor of Benno Landsberger on His Seventy-Fifth Birthday,* ed. Güterbock and Jacobsen, 2, based on new fragments of text. Roth has "loses her attractiveness." The more likely point was that she could not perform her work. See the Laws of Hammurabi 148 below.

41. LL 21, 23, 24. Roth, *Law Collections*, 30. *Ancient Near Eastern Texts,* 160.

42. LL fragments b and c showed that daughters inherited in order of birth. LL 22. Roth, *Law Collections*, 26, 30. Bottéro, *Religion in Ancient Mesopotamia,* 121. There were several types of women priests and religious officials in Sumer and later Mesopotamian civilizations. The titles are also given in Akkadian because the Sumerian titles were limited to Sumer, whereas the Akkadian titles were used in other ancient Near Eastern civilizations. The Sumerian titles are added in parentheses. The religious offices named in this law were *ugbabtu* (*nin-dingir*), *naditu* (*lukur*), and *qadishtu* (*nu-gig*).

43. LL 25–26. Roth, *Law Collections*, 30. *Ancient Near Eastern Texts,* 160. Francis R. Steele, "The Code of Lipit-Ishtar," *American Journal of Archaeology* 52 (1948): 441.

44. LL 27, 30. Roth, *Law Collections*, 31–32. *Ancient Near Eastern Texts,* 160. The first law

made barren wives more secure in their position. The second law discouraged men from jeopardizing their marriages by affairs with prostitutes.

45. LL Prol. ii.16–24. LL 20b, c. Roth, *Law Collections*, 25, 30. *Ancient Near Eastern Texts*, 160. Other ancient Near Eastern laws stated that children must support both their mothers and fathers.

46. LL 18. Roth, *Law Collections*, 29.

47. LL fragments d, e, and f. Roth, *Law Collections*, 26–27. Civil, "New Sumerian Law Fragments," 5. The price of the life of the fetus was thirty sheqels of silver, which was about ten to fifteen days' wages. In Sumerian law, feticide was considered a property crime, not a form of homicide. A wife could bear more children if she had not been too seriously injured. The next section of the law is missing and may have dealt with the death of the slave woman.

48. LL 33. Roth, *Law Collections*, 33. Sumerian law considered sexual misconduct of a wife or betrothed to be the crime of adultery. Illicit sex committed by an unmarried and unbetrothed daughter was a lesser crime, and in that case false accusation was punished merely by a fine. Loss of virginity by a betrothed woman was a serious offense against her betrothed, including loss of honor and property loss. If the girl was not betrothed, it was only an economic offense against a father. The proof of virginity was by oath. Cooper, "Virginity in Ancient Mesopotamia," 93–95.

49. LL 11. Roth, *Law Collections*, 28. In modern law, this concept is called negligence.

50. LL 12. Roth, *Law Collections*, 28. *Ancient Near Eastern Texts*, 160.

51. LL 17 prescribed the penalty of the case for false accusation in general. The penalty of the case was the penalty the defendant would incur if guilty. When the accusations were false, the false accuser would incur that penalty. LL 33 prescribed a fine of ten sheqels for false accusation of loss of virginity by a daughter. LL e (death); d, f, 9, 10, 13, 33 (fines); 4, 5, 11, 12 (restitution). Roth, *Law Collections,* 26–33.

52. LL Epilogue xxi.49–xxii.52. Roth, *Law Collections*, 34. Prologues and epilogues were written in a different literary genre from that of laws. The tradition of cursing anyone who altered or destroyed an important inscription began with the late Early Dynastic kings En-metena of Lagash, who threatened death by the gods, and Lugalzagisi of Uruk and Umma, who threatened any king who moved his boundary stone with death by snakebite. Cooper, *Presargonic Inscriptions*, 54–56, 95–96. These are not examples of collective punishment. A curse text of King Sargon of Akkad was the first known to threaten loss of progeny. Frayne, *Sargonic and Gutian Periods [2334–2113 BC]*, 27–29, no. 11.38–48: destruction of name and progeny. The Isin curse text in the Laws of Lipit-Ishtar extended the punishment to the offender's heirs, born or not yet born. These curse texts may provide a literary basis for later development of collective punishment.

53. Sumerian Laws Exercise Tablet (abbreviated SLEx) 1, 2. Roth, *Law Collections*, 42–43. The date of composition and the provenance of these laws are not known; the extant copies were made by students at a scribal school. Roth (*Law Collections*) and *Ancient Near Eastern Texts* (p. 525) date the tablet about 1800 BCE. The first dynasty of Isin was the latest date for the composition of the laws. There is no evidence of Amorite influence in the SLEx.

54. SLEx 1, 2. Roth, *Law Collections*, 42–43. *Ancient Near Eastern Texts*, 525.

55. SLEx 7–8. Roth, *Law Collections*, 44. The first translation is by Roth; the second is that of J. J.Finkelstein in *Ancient Near Eastern Texts*, 526.

56. SLEx 5–6. Roth, *Law Collections*, 44. *Ancient Near Eastern Texts*, 525–26. Roth added parenthetically that the child was adopted, but this reading is uncertain.

57. SLEx 1–2, 7–8. Roth, *Law Collections*, 44. *Ancient Near Eastern Texts*, 525–26. The end of law 8 is missing.

58. Ur-Nanshe was an early king of the first dynasty of Lagash (twenty-sixth century). Cooper, *Presargonic Inscriptions*, 1:24–25. Dietz Otto Edzard, *Gudea and His Dynasty*, 36, 98. LL Epilogue xxi.36–40. Douglas Frayne, *Old Babylonian Period (2003–1595)*, 47–58, nos.1–6.

59. Asher-Greve, *Frauen in altsumerischer Zeit*, 146–47. Menbara'abzu was wife of Ur-Nanshe; Ashume'eren, wife of Enannatum II; Nin-khilisu, wife of Entemena—all kings of Lagash I. Inscriptions naming Early Dynastic queens Puabi and Nintur were found in the royal Sumerian tombs at Ur, but there is no available evidence that they ruled, although one cylinder seal found at Ur was inscribed "Puabi the queen." Cooper, *Presargonic Inscriptions*, 1:97. The name of Early Dynastic queen Shu'am is know from her cylinder seal, but the name of her husband is not on the Sumerian King List. Hallo, *Early Mesopotamian Royal Titles*, 13.

60. *Cambridge Ancient History* (1/2: 998) dates the reign of Ku-Bau in the Early Dynastic period, between 2450 and 2370. Hallo, "Women of Sumer," in *Legacy of Sumer*, ed. Schmandt-Besserat, 27–28. Rivkah Harris, *Gender and Aging in Mesopotamia*, 112. According to legend, Ku-Bau began as a tavern keeper and ruled Kish for a hundred years. Harris, *Gender*, 140–41. The name is also transliterated Kubawa and Kubaba. Two problems with the Sumerian King List are that it gave mythic dimensions to the regnal years of antediluvian kings and it made all dynasties consecutive, although many were in fact concurrent or overlapping. The List was set in its final form during the Isin dynasty. Jean-Jacques Glassner, "Women, Hospitality and the Honor of the Family," in *Women's Earliest Records*, ed. Lesko, 89.

61. Pollock, *Ancient Mesopotamia*, 120, 123, 147. Zainab Bahrani, *Women of Babylon: Gender and Representation in Mesopotamia*, 105–8. Van De Mieroop, *Cuneiform Texts and the Writing of History*, 155–57. The archive of the E-Bau at Girsu/Lagash contained 1,600 tablets, most of which dated from the last three kings of the first dynasty of Lagash. The institution was first called *E-Mi*, the household of the queen. Uru-inimgina changed the title to *E-Bau* (household of the goddess Bau) for political reasons, but this did not change the institution. Dimtur was the wife of King Enentarzi and had a daughter named Geme-Bau. Baranamtara was the wife of King Lugalanda and had two daughters, Geme-Nanshe and Mishaga. Shagshag was the wife of King Uru-inimgina and had two daughters, Geme-Bau and Gemetarsirsir. Cooper, *Presargonic Inscriptions*, 1:71–72, 75, nos. 9.1, 9.2. Van De Mieroop, "Women in the Economy of Sumer," in *Women's Earliest Records*, ed. Lesko, 54–56. Asher-Greve, *Frauen in altsumerischer Zeit*, 146–47. Documents from a minor town in the Lagash area listed 4,000 adult and 1,800 child weavers. According to Richard A. Henshaw, wives of the kings of Lagash administered temples from 2500 to 2370 BCE. (*Female and Male: The Cultic Personnel*, 18).

62. Frayne, *Sargonic and Gutian Periods (2334–2113 BC)*, 36–37, no. 2001, Tashlultum, 198–200, nos. 2001–3, Tutasharlibish. She was the wife of Sharkalisharri, the great-grandson of Sargon and the last significant king of Akkad. Her name meant "she has found the king of her heart." Foster, in *La Femme dans le Proche-Orient Antique*, ed. Durand, 53.

63. Michalowski, *Letters from Early Mesopotamia*, 79, letter 127.

64. The animals were collected and distributed at Puzrish-Dagan for temples in Nippur and elsewhere, and the majority of the donors of animals for sacrifice were women. The royal wives were assisted by women officials. A woman named Apillatum assisted Shulgi-simti. Women who worked under the queen were royal daughters and wives of palace officials and of governors. Van De Mieroop, *Cuneiform Texts and the Writing of History*, 157–58. Van De Mieroop, "Women in the Economy of Sumer," 57–58.

65. Van De Mieroop, "Women in the Economy of Sumer," 58, 62–63. Over 100,000 tablets from the reigns of Ur-Nammu and Shulgi have been found in Ur, Girsu, Umma, Nippur, and Puzrish-Dagan, which document the economic power and administrative roles of queens and wives of governors. Douglas Frayne, *Ur III Period (2112–2004 BC)*, 355–56, nos. 2013–14, Ninkhilia.

66. Hallo, "Women of Sumer," 28, 30–33. Cooper, *Presargonic Inscriptions*, 190, 199, 207. Asher-Greve, *Frauen in altsumerischer Zeit*, 147.

67. Frayne, *Ur III Period*, 287–89. Kuhrt, *Ancient Near East*, 1:40–41: exchange of gifts.

68. Wives were called *dam* (wife) and *nin* (queen); consorts were called *lukur*. Frayne, *Ur III Period*, 167–70: Shulgi had two or three wives, six consorts, and thirteen daughters—most, but not all, of their names are known; 171–72, nos. 67–68: Amat-Sin (*dam*); 172–74, nos. 69–71: Shulgi-simti (*lukur* and *nin*); 174–80, nos. 72–81: Eanisha (*lukur*); 180, no. 82: Geme-Ninlila; 181, nos. 83–84: Ninkala, citizen of Nippur; 182, no. 85: Shuqurtum (*lukur*). According to Piotr Michalowski, Shulgi-Simti, Geme-Ninlila, and Eanisha were all legal wives of King Shulgi ("Royal Women of the Ur III Period: Geme-Ninlila," *Journal of Cuneiform Studies* 31[1979]: 171–76). Van De Mieroop has a detailed list of titles and citations ("Women in the Economy of Sumer," 58–60).

69. Frayne, *Ur III Period*, 267–68: Amar-Sin had Abi-simti as wife, five consorts, and fifteen daughters; 336–38, nos. 28–29: Shu-Sin had Kubatum as wife, three consorts, and four daughters; 375: Ibbi-Sin had one wife, Geme-Enlila, and five daughters. Hallo, "Women of Sumer," 27–32. Harris, *Gender and Aging in Mesopotamia*, 113. Van de Mieroop, "Women in the Economy of Sumer," 58–60. Kubatum may have been a consort of King Amar-Sin and may have had children by him. Hallo named Abi-Simti as wife of both kings Amar-Sin and Shu-Sin, and as queen mother in the reign of King Ibbi-Sin; her title was *nin*, "queen" (*Early Mesopotamian Royal Titles*, 33). Jean Bottéro has a long love poem addressed to Shu-Sin, possibly by Kubatum (*Everyday Life in Ancient Mesopotamia*, 110–11).

70. Frayne, *Old Babylonian Period*, 98–99, 293–96, 303, nos. 1, 2, 16–17, 22–23: the Amorite king Rim-Sin of Larsa had at least three official wives, called *dam*. One wife, Simat-Ishtar, was queen (*nin*).

71. Henshaw, *Female and Male*, 240: Nubanda. Her husband, who ruled about 2600–2550, called himself the "spouse of the *nu-gig*." She was a religious officiant but not a priest. Van De Mieroop, "Women in the Economy of Sumer," 54. Glassner, "Women, Hospitality and the Honor of the Family," 81, 89. According to Glassner, there were 177 women mourners and 92 men "lamenters" at the funeral. According to Asher-Greve, there were 617 people, including 164 singers and 118 women mourners (*Frauen in altsumerischer Zeit*, 147–51). All three queens held the religious office of *qadishtu* (*nu-gig*). The *qadishtu* women were not priests as such. Shulgi-Simti was a *naditu* (*lukur*) priest and was also called a "priest of the journey." Henshaw, 193. Asher-Greve, 157–58.

72. Edzard, *Gudea and His Dynasty*, 10, no. 1.4 (Nin-niginesi), 174, 179–80, nos. 7.90, 98, 99 (Nin-alla), 197–98, no. 5 (Nin-khedu), 189, 198–202 nos. 1, 6–10 (Nin-inimgina). Hallo suggests that Ninmetabare might have gone to Ur to marry the king or his son, or, less likely, that she served as a priest in Ur ("Women of Sumer," 28). Frayne, *Ur III Period*, 86, no. 52: Taramuram, 87–88, no. 54: En-nirgalana, 170–71, no. 66: Siatum, 174–75, no. 69: Shulgi-simti, 180–81, no. 83: Ninkala, 182, no. 85: Shuqurtum, 184, no. 88: Ninturturmu, 185, no. 89: Simat-Enlil, 203–4, no. 2012: Khalalamma (reign of Shulgi), 284, no. 2009: Khala-Baba (reign of Amar-Sin), 382–83, no. 2004: Amanili (reign of Ibbi-Sin). Marc Van De Mieroop, "Gifts and Tithes to the Temples in Ur," in *DUMU-E2-DUB-BA-A: Studies in Honor of Ake Sjöberg*, ed. Behrens et al., 401. The temples in Ur had an accounting center that listed donations until the mid-nineteenth century. Many wives of kings had names beginning with *nin*, meaning "queen." When *nin* was thus used as a title, it is followed by a hyphen.

73. Barton, *Royal Inscriptions*, 1:70–73: donations of Baranamtara; Michalowski, "Royal Women of the Ur III Period: Geme-Ninlila," *Journal of Cuneiform Studies* 31 (1979): 174–75. Bahrani, *Women of Babylon*, 98, 109, 111–12.

74. Laurie Pearce, "The Scribes and Scholars of Ancient Mesopotamia," in *Civilizations of the Ancient Near East*, ed. Sasson, 4:2266. Hallo, "Women of Sumer," 28–30. Pollock, *Ancient Mesopotamia*, 169. Her literary style suggests that she had a Sumerian mother. There is an example of one of her hymns in Postgate, *Early Mesopotamia*, 26. Joan Goodnick Westenholz states that after her ordination, En-kheduanna spent the rest of her life in the residence (*gipar*) of the

temple, where she collected and redacted hymns from all over Sumer and Akkad ("Enheduanna, En-Priestess, Hen of Nanna, Spouse of Nanna," in *DUMU-E2-DUB-BA-A: Studies in Honor of Ake Sjöberg,* ed. Behrens et al., 540, 545–47, 550–56). Sabina Francke, "Kings of Akkad: Sargon and Naram-Sin," in *Civilizations of the Ancient Near East,* ed. Sasson, 2:835–36. Hallo and Simpson, *Ancient Near East,* 58–59. Bahrani, *Women of Babylon,* 113–15, states that overseeing a libation was an important act in itself, and disagrees with Winter that the other figures on the disc were men, citing seals portraying women pouring libations, and that women priests were limited in function and subordinate to male priests. Winter, in *La Femme dans le Proche-Orient antique,* 190–201, emphasizes the continuity between women high priests in the Early Dynastic period and En-kheduanna. The headdress of women priests had a rolled brim. Saggs, *Babylonians,* 72, fig. 42. Seal inscriptions from Ur mentioned her estate overseer, scribe, and coiffeur. Frayne, *Sargonic and Gutian Periods (2334–2113 BC),* 35–36, 38–39, no. 16: inscription on disc; nos. 2003–5: seals and seal impression.

75. Frayne, *Sargonic and Gutian Periods,* 122–23. En-menana, high priest of Ur, was attested on a clay tablet, door socket, and stone plaque, as well as on the seals of her scribe and doorkeeper (ibid., 145–46, nos. 33–34); 176–77, nos. 2018–20; Tutanapshum: 122–23, nos. 18–20; 175, no. 2017; Shumshani: 157, no. 51; Lipushia'um: 159–60, no. 54. Inscriptions of royal women high priests were used to document divisions of history just as inscriptions of kings were.

76. Frayne, *Ur III Period,* 88, no. 54: En-nirgalana, 183, no. 87: En-nirziana, 269, no. 19: En-makhgalana.

77. Frayne, *Old Babylonian Period,* 30–31, 44–45, nos. 1.4.3, 4, 13, 14: En-anatuma (reign of Ishme-Dagan of Isin), 58, no. 16: En-ninsunzi (reign of Lipit-Ishtar), 257, no. 2.13.32: En-anedu (reign of Warad-Sin of Larsa), 290–91, 300–301, nos. 14, 20: En-anedu (reign of Rim-Sin). En-anatuma had a son. Two seal impressions named A'abba, son of En-anatuma (45, no. 14). There is no evidence whether the son was born before she took office or whether *entu* high priests could marry. A seal from the reign of Shulgi named the wife, Inannaka, of the *en* priest at Nippur, showing that a male *en* high priest could marry. Frayne, *Ur III Period,* 212, no. 2025. There is no evidence of child-rearing in the temple residence (*gipar*). En-anedu was said to have been predestined from the womb to the *en* priesthood, to have brought well-being to the city of Ur, and to have helped restore the residence of the high priestess. Michalowski, *Letters from Early Mesopotamia,* 120, letter 243. Van De Mieroop names En-shakiag-Nanna, daughter of King Sumuel of Larsa, *entu* high priest of Ur before Larsa conquered Isin ("Gifts and Tithes to the Temples in Ur," 401; idem, *Society and Enterprise in Old Babylonian Ur,* 57). Joan Oates, *Babylon,* 61–62. Frayne, *Old Babylonian Period,* 40, no. 1.4.9: Shima'iltum was an *egisitum,* a celibate religious officiant, and Tarampalanigrisha was an *amalutum,* a cultic officiant and temple administrator (reign of Ishme-Dagan of Isin). Henshaw, *Female and Male,* 206, 214–15, nos. 14.10.1, 14.13.

78. Edzard, *Gudea and His Dynasty,* 24–25, nos. 12–13: En-annepadda. Harris, *Gender and Aging in Mesopotamia,* 103–4. Hallo, "Women of Sumer," 28–34, 138, fig. 18: text of letter. Van De Mieroop, *Society and Enterprise in Old Babylonian Ur,* 63, 76: En-anedu. Pearce, "Scribes and Scholars of Ancient Mesopotamia," 2266. William Hallo, "Sumerian Historiography," in *History, Historiography and Interpretation: Studies in Biblical and Cuneiform Literature,* ed. Tadmor and Weinfeld, 13–17. Ninshatapada was the daughter of Sin-kashid, ruler of Uruk and governor of Durum under the first Isin dynasty. The letter, written about 1800, used phrases and the style of King Rim-Sin of Larsa, who had conquered Durum in the previous year.

79. Van De Mieroop, "Gifts and Tithes to the Temples of Ur," 401; idem, *Society and Enterprise in Old Babylonian Ur,* 63, 96, 99–100, 115–17, 176. En-anedu was quite wealthy and also made loans. Two seal impressions named A'abba, son of En-anatuma. Frayne, *Old Babylonian Period,* 44–45, no. 14.

80. The *en* was the highest-ranking priest and could be either female or male. In those cities

where a goddess was served by male priests, the men who held political power often took both the office of high priest and that of ruler. Conversely, in cities where a god was served by women priests, religious leadership remained separate from political leadership and the authority of the high priestess was subordinated to that of the king. Hallo and Simpson, *Ancient Near East*, 175. The practice of kings appointing their daughters as high priestess began with the Akkadian dynasty of Sargon and continued through the Isin and Larsa dynasties. It reappeared in Middle and Late Babylonia. Years were named for women high priests as well as for kings.

81. Barton, *Royal Inscriptions*, 80–81. Claus Wilcke, "Care of the Elderly in Mesopotamia in the Third Millennium B.C." in *The Care of the Elderly in the Ancient Near East*, ed. Stol and Vleeming, 31–32. In the Akkadian period, an *ugbabtu* priest was witness to a slave sale contract, and the wife of a temple administrator (*sanga*) testified that a slave was free from claims and could be sold. Steinkeller, *Third Millennium Legal and Administrative Texts*, 91–92, 100–101, nos. 52, 61. Frayne, *Ur III Period*, 186–87, nos. 92–93: Tulid-Shamshi. Ration lists for the estate of the Ur III *ugbabtu* priest Geme-Lama show that she had a male supervisor of the women weavers and an elderly male janitor; her other employees were women. Henshaw found women *ugbabtu* (*nin-dingir*) priests in ten cities, women *naditu* (*lukur*) priests in four cities, and men and women *en* high priests in five cities (*Female and Male*, 18). The *qadishtu* (*nu-gig*) were named on the ration lists for upper-class women. The *ugbabtu* and *naditu* priests were attested on ration lists for temple officials. The *naditu* were the most numerous women priests. Henshaw, *Female and Male*, 7, 45, 47, 207. See LL 22. Asher-Greve found the most active women named between 3100 and 2400 BCE were women priests and religious functionaries (*Frauen in altsumerischer Zeit*, 157–58). There were also women dream interpreters. Asher-Greve, in *La Femme dans le Proche-Orient Antique*, 29–32.

82. King Gudea of Lagash described celibate women priests who offered the sacrifice as "eunuch priests." Barton, *Royal Inscriptions*, 202–3: inscription on statue dedicated by Gudea; 238–39: inscription on cylinder by Gudea. Translation of the "Lamentation Over the Destruction of Ur," Henshaw, *Female and Male*, 207. The temple archives of Lagash named 180 women musicians (*nartu*) and 62 male and female musicians (*kalu*) in seven temples. A special dialect of Sumerian, called *emesal*, which was attributed to goddesses but not gods, was used by women in rites, prayers, hymns and other literature. It was not a spoken language. Gordon Whittaker, "Linguistic Anthropology and the Study of Emesal as (a) Women's Language," in *Sex and Gender in the Ancient Near East*, ed. Parpola and Whiting, 634–36, 641. Saggs, *Babylonians*, 78. There were women basket bearers in ancient Greek religion.

83. The woman priest who represented the goddess in the sacred marriage rite was generally a *naditu* (*lukur*), not an *en* high priestess. There are extant love songs, written for the sacred marriage rite from the perspective of the woman priest. Bottéro cites one written for the Ur III king Shu-Sin (*Religion in Ancient Mesopotamia*, 155–56). Kings of Ur III and king Iddin-Dagan of Isin were reported to have taken part in the ritual of sacred marriage. Henshaw, *Female and Male*, 240 (Shulgi). Samuel N. Kramer states that the practice ended with the Sumerians (*The Sacred Marriage Rite*, 57). G. Leick, *The Babylonians*, 103.

84. Klein suggests that the story of the birth of Shulgi from a sacred marriage rite between his father and an en-priestess of Nippur may be understood as a solution to a theological problem. The god of Nippur had promised Ur-Nammu a long reign, but he was killed and his reign cut short. The divine conception of Shulgi at Nippur provided a way out: the promised long reign was manifested through that of the god-given son. Klein, in *La Femme dans le Proche-Orient Antique*, 106. Van De Mieroop, *Society and Enterprise in Old Babylonian Ur*, 109–10. Enanatuma, daughter of king Ishme-Dagan of Isin and high priest of Ur, had a son, A'abba, who later became governor of Ur. The women high priests of Ur did not leave their residence. It is possible that the son was conceived in a sacred marriage rite, but generally the priestess in that rite was a *naditu*, not an *entu*. Moreover, a daughter, even if she was a high priest, could not have

sex with her father because that was the worst form of incest and was punished by the death of both—unless the identification of the priestess with the goddess was so rationalized that it ignored incest.

85. Henshaw, *Female and Male,* 240. Both queens held the religious office of *qadishtu* (*nu-gig*), which was sometimes associated with cultic prostitution. It was prestigious for a woman to play the role of the goddess. It was also a form of prostitution, although one must be careful not to impose on the ancient texts modern mores about prostitution. Ur-Nammu was declared a god after his death. Shulgi proclaimed himself a god during his lifetime.

86. Enmerkar was named in the Sumerian King List as ruling for 420 years after the flood. Kramer, *Sumerians,* 329. *Ancient Near Eastern Texts,* 266. The sorcerer, a male witch, was called *mashmash,* which later became the title for an official in charge of healing and purification rituals. The woman was called *umma,* a wise woman. Frederick Cryer and Marie-Louise Thomsen, *Witchcraft and Magic in Europe: Biblical and Pagan Societies,* 23–25. In the ancient Near East, there was both good magic, which was associated with healing, and evil magic. In Mesopotamian law, evil magic, sorcery, and witchcraft were capital crimes.

87. Glasser, "Women, Hospitality and the Honor of the Family," 75–76, 86–89, based on Akkadian tablets and property records. The names of women have not been found in Akkadian property records. Bottéro, *Everyday Life in Ancient Mesopotamia,* 114–15. Kramer, in *La Femme dans le Proche-Orient Antique,* 108, citing "The Curse of Agade," suggests that Akkadian girls went out to "dancing places."

88. Van De Mieroop, *Society and Enterprise in Old Babylonian Ur,* 218 (Ur, Larsa period).

89. Harris, *Gender and Aging in Mesopotamia,* 24, 98, 143. Glassner, "Women, Hospitality and the Honor of the Family," 75, 78, 83–86, 88–89, based on the Gilgamesh Epic and property records from Lagash and Girsu. The work of men and women reflected the division in ancient legend whereby men worked outside the house and women worked inside.

90. Kramer, in *La Femme dans le Proche-Orient Antique,* 109–11.

91. Julia Asher-Greve, "Decisive Sex, Essential Gender," in *Sex and Gender in the Ancient Near East,* ed. Parpola and Whiting, 13, 15. Kramer, in *La Femme dans le Proche-Orient Antique,* 107–9.

92. Sumerian Laws Handbook of Forms (abbreviated SLHF), 4.12–14, 17–18. Roth, *Law Collections,* 46, 50. Roth dates this text, written on a prism, about 1700. It contained model clauses for contracts. *Ancient Near Eastern Texts,* 217 (Ur III, Shulgi).

93. Piotr Steinkeller, *Sale Documents of the Ur III Period,* 201, 238, 276, nos. 29, 62, 88.

94. Asher-Greve, *Frauen in altsumerischer Zeit,* 108–9: sale of land. The transaction was pictured on a stone relief. Both women priests were dressed the same. The sale of a house was inscribed on a clay cone. Barton, *Royal Inscriptions,* 68–71, no. 10. The sale took place in the Lagash I dynasty. Before coinage, prices were paid in kind.

95. Steinkeller, *Sale Documents,* 183, 295, 316, 334, nos. 14, 102, 117, S3 (women sold slaves), 316, no.177 (woman bought slave). Steinkeller, *Third Millennium Legal and Administrative Texts,* 95–96, 100–101, no. 57: two men and Bibi, wife of a singer, sold a slave; no. 61: a man and his wife, Geme-e, sold a man, and their hands were filled with silver.

96. Steinkeller, *Sale Documents,* 191, 301, 327, nos. 20, 108, 127: women sold themselves into slavery; 327, 334, nos. 127, S3: woman guarantors of slave sales.

97. Steinkeller, *Sale Documents,* 217, 221, 222, 226, 268, 312, 327, nos. 42, 45, 46, 49, 81, 115, 117 (women sold by family members, Ur III).

98. Barton, *Royal Inscriptions,* 124–25: inscription of king Rimush of Akkad noted 9,624 captives from Elam alone.

99. Steinkeller, *Sale Documents,* 217, 227, 228, 295, nos. 42, 50, 51, 102 (seals); 227, 266–67, 280, 283, 318, nos. 51, 79, 91, 94, 119 (witnesses) (Ur III). Quoted text translated by Steinkeller, *Sale Documents,* 295, no. 102. Steinkeller, *Third Millennium Legal and Administrative Texts,* 97, no. 58. rev. 12 (witness to slave sale).

100. Steinkeller, *Third Millennium Legal and Administrative Texts*, 100–101, no. 61, 18: unnamed woman witness at trial. Michalowski, *Letters from Early Mesopotamia*, 49–50, letter 68: witness list for trial: two men and one woman, wife of a priest, all citizens of Nippur.

101. Claus Wilcke, "Care of the Elderly in Mesopotamia in the Third Millennium B.C.," in *The Care of the Elderly in the Ancient Near East,* ed. Stol and Vleeming, 49–51. The trial was held before a three-judge panel during the reign of Shu-Sin. This case illustrates the early use of the legal principle of *res judicata*, which means that a matter once decided by a court cannot be relitigated.

102. Van De Mieroop, "Women in the Economy of Sumer," 63–64. Harris, *Gender and Aging in Mesopotamia*, 21, 106–7, 149, 154. Ur III tablets from Girsu and Umma document thousands of women working in the textile industry, in other skilled trades, and in agriculture. Alexander Uchitel, "Women at Work: Weavers of Lagash and Spinners of San Luis Gonzaga," in *Sex and Gender in the Ancient Near East,* ed. Parpola and Whiting, 622, 625–27. Most women weavers were paid thirty to forty liters of barley. Pollock asserts that by the third millennium, women almost completely dominated textile manufacture (*Ancient Mesopotamia,* 102–4). Women worked for temples in textile manufacturing and agriculture. A letter from Adab attests a slave girl named Amalal, who worked in a leather shop but ran away. Michalowski, *Letters from Early Mesopotamia*, 29, letter 23. A law regulated the sale of beer on credit by women tavern keepers. Laws of X (LX) j, l. Roth, *Law Collections*, 38. Michalowski, *Letters from Early Mesopotamia*, 102, letter 196: wet nurse (Ur III). Piotr Michalowski and C. B. F. Walker, "A New Sumerian 'Law Code," in *DUMU-E2-DUB-BA-A: Studies in Honor of Ake Sjöberg,* ed. Behrens et al., 389, col. 2.14–16: tavern keepers, beer on credit. SLHF 7.34–36. Roth, *Law Collections*, 53.

103. Van De Mieroop, "Women in the Economy of Sumer," 63–67. Steinkeller, *Third Millennium Legal and Administrative Texts*, 77–78, no.42: grain rations for men were 60 liters, for women 30, for boys 10–30, for girls 10–20 (Akkadian period). With the exception of weaving, women and men did the same work. Ration lists record their pay, which was in rations of grain (barley), oil, and wool. Men generally received twice as much grain as women, the same amount of oil, and slightly more wool. Harris, *Gender and Aging in Mesopotamia*, 90, 106–7, 149. Payment in rations gave workers less independence than wages paid in silver. I. J. Gelb, "The Ancient Mesopotamian Ration System," *Journal of Near Eastern Studies* 24 (1965): 230–43.

104. Wilcke, "Care of the Elderly," 26–32, 35. Ration lists from the Lagash region, reign of Shulgi. Uchitel, "Women at Work," 625–27. Dependent children were taken into account in the allotment of rations, but the elderly had none.

105. Wilcke, "Care of the Elderly," 46–49. Widows owned real property via dowry or *inter vivos* donations by husbands (Early Dynastic). A judgment gave a house to a son after his widowed mother married a stranger (Ur III).

106. Wilcke, "Care of the Elderly," 42–45. An early document records the sale of a house to a son for his father and his mother. The price included silver, wool, garments, and barley; the surveyor was paid copper, bread, and soup.

107. Harris, *Gender and Aging in Mesopotamia*, 98, 100, 148. Compassion was considered a female trait; the Sumerian and Akkadian languages used the same word for "womb" and "compassion." Miguel Civil, "On Mesopotamian Jails and Their Lady Warden," in *The Tablet and the Scroll,* ed. Cohen et al., 78.

108. The first Isin dynasty was founded by Ishbi-irra of Mari, who had previously worked for the last king of Ur III. Ishbi-irra later ruled Ur and Nippur, which legitimized his political and religious claim to the title of King of Sumer. Hallo and Simpson, *Ancient Near East*, 86–88. King Ishme-Dagan of Isin appointed his daughter, En-anatumma, high priest of Ur. Van De Mieroop, "Gifts and Tithes to the Temples in Ur," in *DUMU-E2-DUB-BA-A: Studies in Honor of Ake Sjöberg,* ed. Behrens et al., 401. Van De Mieroop, *Society and Enterprise in Old Babylonian Ur*, 155, 216.

109. W. F. Leemans, *Legal and Economic Records from the Kingdom of Larsa*, 9, no. 2: deed for house lot, which sold for six and two-thirds sheqels of silver; 34–37, no. 2: the division of an estate, listing nine slave girls, each by name, among the assets of the deceased; 46, no. 31: book-keeping for rations. Unnamed commodities were distributed to named women, including Nidit-tum, Iltani, Belissunu and Nana-ummi, on several ration lists. There were distributions of food and wool for clothing to unnamed girls, and food was distributed to slave girls. One line indicates that barley was distributed to a disabled woman. Leemans, 46, no. 31: disabled woman; 47–49, 71–77, 84, 87–88, nos. 32, 34, 47–50, 57, 61: distributions to named women; 53–55, 87–88, nos. 38, 61: distributions to girls; 50–51, no. 35: distribution to slave girl; 87–88, no. 61: distribution of money. These documents were written during the reigns of Kings Warad-Sin and Rim-Sin of Larsa. Van De Mieroop, *Society and Enterprise in Old Babylonian Ur*, 216.

110. The name Amorite, *Amurru*, means people from the west. The Amorites learned to speak the languages of the places where they settled: Sumerian, Akkadian, Babylonian, and Assyrian. Robert M. Whiting, "Amorite Tribes and Nations of Second-Millennium Western Asia," in *Civilizations of the Ancient Near East*, ed. Sasson, 2:1234. Although Amorite customs varied from tribe to tribe, all relegated women to low status and punished crimes harshly.

111. Martha T. Roth, "The Slave and the Scoundrel: A Sumerian Morality Tale," *Journal of the American Oriental Society* 103 (1983): 282. The judgment left open the possibility that it was lawful to rape a virgin slave girl if her owner gave consent. Kramer, in *La Femme dans le Proche-Orient Antique*, 108–9, citing the "Instructions of Shuruppak," line 67. He notes that in mythic literature, the young male god who raped a young girl goddess was punished by exile to the underworld.

112. Barton, *Royal Inscriptions*, 132–33. Inscription by Manishtusu, son of Sargon. He gave back her house "forever." The land that he restored to her would produce sufficient income for her support. Michalowski, *Letters from Early Mesopotamia*, 78, 80, letters 125 (money), 131 (field) (Ur III).

113. Roth, *Law Collections*, 53. SLHF 8.3–10. Michalowski, *Letters from Early Mesopotamia*, 79, letter 128: a letter directed a man to give the wife, named Aya-kala, of another man as a pledge. If a slave woman was pledged for a man's debt in silver, he got his slave woman back when he paid off his debt in silver. The abuse of pledges was made a crime in the Babylonian laws of Hammurabi. LH 116. There were written work quotas for women and men. A late Sumerian document states that the work quota of women was twenty sheqels of wool. The work quota was the amount the worker was expected to produce in a specific place or time, not the work quota for all Sumerian women in all times and places.

114. Michalowski, *Letters from Early Mesopotamia*, 79–80, nos. 126, 130, 132 (wives), no. 129 (married slave girl), no. 127 (petition to queen). Van De Mieroop, *Society and Enterprise in Old Babylonian Ur*, 159–60.

115. Roth, "The Slave and the Scoundrel: A Sumerian Morality Tale," *Journal of the American Oriental Society* 103 (1983): 275–79.

116. Kramer, in *La Femme dans le Proche-Orient Antique*, 109–11, citing the hymn "Exaltation of Inanna," written by En-kheduanna.

117. Steinkeller, *Third Millennium Legal and Administrative Texts*, 21–23, no. 2: contract for sale of real property (Lagash, reign of Uru-inimgina).

118. O. R. Gurney and S. N. Kramer, "Two Fragments of Sumerian Laws," in *Studies in Honor of Benno Landsberger on his Seventy-Fifth Birthday*, ed. Güterbock and Jacobsen, 13, 19. This fragment is similar to LU 7.

119. *Ana ittishu* VII.A.5–6 (bilingual Sumerian and Akkadian text). Driver and Miles, *Babylonian Laws*, 1:25–26, 2:308–11. The late date of this text and the insertion of the death penalty to punish an offense of words by a wife challenging the authority of her husband indicate Amorite influence. Van De Mieroop, *Society and Enterprise in Old Babylonian Ur*, 218: adultery.

120. Edzard, *Gudea and His Dynasty,* 77, Cylinder A, 12.25b–13.9. Barton, *Royal Inscriptions,* 216–19.

121. Civil, "On Mesopotamian Jails and Their Lady Warden," in *The Tablet and the Scroll,* ed. Cohen et al., 72–74, 76. The hymn was written by a scribe. In it, Nungal declared that she built the walls of the prison, which she compared to a womb, with tears and compassion and used the image of washing as purification. Sumer. The prison was an annex of the palace. Many copies and fragments of this text were found in the scribal school at Nippur from the Isin/Larsa period. Civil cites a text of king Gudea, who imprisoned some convicted of capital offenses. Frayne, *Ur III Period,* 283, no. 2008: stone tablet found in Susa, dedication for life of king Amar-Sin: "For the goddess Nungal, lady of the prison, lady who causes people to live."

122. Driver and Miles, *Babylonian Laws,* 2:308–11. *Ana ittishu* VII.A.1–6. This series of laws on repudiation of a parent or spouse used the penalties of forfeiture of possessions and sale of the offender for money. The insertion of the death penalty for the wife in paragraph 5 interrupts the parallelism and indicates Amorite influence.

123. Van De Mieroop, *Society and Enterprise in Old Babylonian Ur,* 218: impalement, based on a fragmentary text from Ur.

124. LX Epilogue. Roth, *Law Collections,* 39, written in the Isin/Larsa period. Compare this to the curse in a temple building inscription of Ur III king Amar-Sin that if anyone erased his inscriptions, the snake of the god would kill him and his progeny. Frayne, *Ur III Period,* 254–55, no. 9. Michalowski and Walker first published LX and suggested a date in the reign of king Ishme-Dagan of Isin, a predecessor of Lipit-Ishtar. "A New Sumerian 'Law Code,'" in *DUMU-E2-DUB-BA-A: Studies in Honor of Ake Sjöberg,* ed. Behrens et al., 383, 389, 395. The curse in LX went beyond its predecessors by extending the punishment to all the innocent young women and men of the city. Later Assyrian law would put this into practice.

125. Martha Roth, "Gender and Law: A Case Study from Ancient Mesopotamia," in *Gender and Law in the Hebrew Bible and the Ancient Near East,* ed. Matthews et al., 175. Three texts recorded this trial, only one of which has been published. Thorkild Jacobsen, "An Ancient Mesopotamian Trial for Homicide," in *Studia Biblica et Orientalia,* vol. 3, *Oriens Antiquus,* 130–50. Roth had access to casts of the other two. She dates the extant tablets in the early second millennium.

126. The victim was a *neshakku* priest, a high-level temple office that was usually held by members of the upper class. Henshaw, *Female and Male,* 28–30, 35, 141. Roth called him an official of the cult of Enlil in Nippur ("Gender and Law," 176). Postgate called him "the priest" (*Early Mesopotamia,* 278). *Ancient Near Eastern Texts* (p. 542) and Kramer (*History Begins at Sumer,* 57) called the victim the son of the *neshakku* priest. Roth, "Gender and Law," 176 n. 10: the chair represented the office of the victim. Westbrook (*Studies in Biblical and Cuneiform Law,* 48) and Thorkild Jacobsen ("An Ancient Mediterranean Trial for Homicide," in *Toward the Image of Tammuz,* 209) suggest that the chair represented the presence of the victim, who needed the act of blood revenge to quiet his soul.

127. Roth, "Gender and Law," 178–80. The speaker for the assembly used the Akkadian verbs "to know" and "to learn," which also meant sexual knowledge (as does a similar verb used in the Hebrew Bible). A different verb, "to tell," which had no sexual connotations, was used in the section relating the facts. Tikva Frymer-Kensky sees two stereotypes at work: that women are "weak and easily intimidated" and that "women are inherently dangerous and wives are suspect" ("Gender and Law," in *Gender and Law,* ed. Mtthews et al., 19–20). The first was used by the defense and the second by the assembly. A century later, in the Old Babylonian Laws of Hammurabi, failure to report a crime (LH 109) and murder of a husband by a wife who was in an adulterous relationship (LH 153) were both capital offenses.

128. Roth ("Gender and Law," 175–80) concurs with the translations of Jacobsen ("An

Ancient Mesopotamian Trial for Homicide," in *Studia Biblica et Orientalia*, vol. 3, *Oriens Antiquus*, 130–50). J. J. Finkelstein in *Ancient Near Eastern Texts*, 542; Postgate, *Early Mesopotamia*, 278, text 15.3; and Van de Mieroop, *Ancient Mesopotamian City*, 122. All relied on the text of Jacobsen, which found all four guilty. On the other hand, Kramer suggests that the assembly believed that the husband had not supported his wife, which was his legal duty, and thus she had no reason not to remain silent after his murder, even if she knew his enemies had been involved (*History Begins at Sumer*, 3rd ed., 56–58). In Kramer's version, the assembly found that the wife had not participated in the murder and thus she was not sentenced to death. Kramer's *History Begins at Sumer* was originally published in 1956. In the most recent edition (1981), under *Corrigenda* (p. 352), Kramer reaffirms his position and argues that the majority position is based on restorations made to the text by Jacobsen with which he disagrees.

129. Samuel Greengus places the text in the Isin/Larsa period and notes similarities to other cases, including the preceding case, decided at about the same time by the assembly of Nippur ("A Textbook Case of Adultery in Ancient Mesopotamia," *Hebrew Union College Annual* 40–41 [1969–70]: 33–44). The tablet containing this case was found at Nippur, and the archaeological evidence confirms the date; both the name (*puhrum*) and role of the assembly were the same. The trial took place in a royal court, and the decision was attributed to the king. In the majority of later laws, the penalty for adultery was death. LE 28. LH 129. Greengus suggests that the shaving penalty in this case could indicate slavery. Roth, "Slave and the Scoundrel," 282. Roth, "Gender and Law," 180–81. Previously in Sumerian law there were only three examples of corporal penalties—two in the law of Uru-inimgina and one in LU 25. The corporal penalties in this case were common in Amorite penal law.

130. The name of the eponymous official for the year of the trial contained the name Ishme-Dagan, which was also the name of a king of Isin. Greengus, "Textbook Case of Adultery in Ancient Mesopotamia," 35.

131. Asher-Greve, Catalogue: 207–12; Plates: XXX, 593, 598, 624, 627, 628, 629; XXXI, 631, 632, 648, 652, 664, 667 (Early Dynastic period). Cooper, *Presargonic Inscriptions*, 69: Baranamtara), 97 (Puabi), 98 (Ashusikil-dingir), 98–99 (Nin-banda). Shu'am, wife of an Early Dynastic king, was also named on a seal. See also Frayne, *Sargonic and Gutian Periods (2334–2113 BC)*, 198–200, nos. 2001–3 (Tutasharlibish); R. Mayr, "The Depiction of Ordinary Men and Women on the Seals of the Ur III Kingdom," in *Sex and Gender in the Ancient Near East*, ed. Parpola and Whiting, 360, 363–65, figs. 1c, 6–9. Seals have been found at every site in ancient Mesopotamia.

132. Michalowski, *Letters from Early Mesopotamia*, 84, letter 141: seal of scribe of the high priestess Geme-Lama. Frayne, *Ur III Period*, 337–38, no. 28: Kubatum, no. 29: Tiamat-bashti. Both were called "beloved consort (*lukur*) of Shu-Sin"; 338–39, no. 30: Shabi, daughter of a king, was called chief consort (*lukur*) of Shu-Sin. Henshaw, *Female and Male*, 192: Tiamat-bashti and Kubatum, 204: Hekunsig, who was an *ugbabtu* (*nin-dingir*) priest in Early Dynastic 3, 207: Ninkinda was the "chief" or "great" *qadishtu* (*nu-gig*) of Ur. *Ancient Near East in Pictures*, ed. Pritchard, 221–22, 332, 334, figs. 693: women at shrine of god, 698: woman priest making libation, other women carrying kid and other cult objects (Akkadian dynasty), 700, 701: seals showing women priests leading men to the enthroned god (Ur III). *Art of the First Cities*, ed. Aruz, 122, fig. 37: marble cylinder seal depicting a woman and a man approaching a male king or god, seated on throne (Early Dynastic 3). Mayr, "Depiction of Ordinary Men and Women," 361, fig. 2: seals of Geme-Ashar and Nurusheli). The introducers in the presentation scenes were goddesses or women priests.

133. Cooper, *Presargonic Inscriptions*, 1:22–23: Abda, 52–53: Ashume'eren, 68: Geme-Bau, 90–91: Pakalam and Akalam, 93–94: Bara'irnun, 100: Khesamanu, 103: Nin-banda, 104: Megirimta, making a dedication for her life. Barton, *Royal Inscriptions*, 116–17: dedication for wife of Sargon. Frayne, *Sargonic and Gutian Periods*, 36–37, no. 2001: Tashlultum. Edzard, *Gudea and*

His Dynasty, 10: Nin-niginesi, 174, 179–80: Nin-alla, 197–98, 207: Nin-khedu, 198–202: Nin-inimgina. Frayne, *Old Babylonian Period*, 59, 1.5.7: Lamassatum, 302–3, 2.14.23: Rim-Sin-shalabashtashu for daughter, Lirishgamlum.

134. Asher-Greve, *Frauen in altsumerischer Zeit*, 138–45, 184. The graves were from the Early Dynastic 2 period (2700–2500). *Art of the First Cities*, ed. Aruz, 108–32: drawings of Puabi's tomb and death scene, gold artifacts and jewelry. Julian Reade, *Mesopotamia*, 53, figs. 52, 54: jewelry of Puabi, 58, fig. 59: headdress and earrings of Puabi. Hallo, "Women of Sumer," 26–27. Saggs suggests human sacrifice or mass suicide (*Greatness That Was Babylon*, 323). The evidence of the burials alone is insufficient to ascertain a custom of human sacrifice. George Roux, "The Great Enigma of the Cemetary at Ur," in Bottéro, *Everyday Life in Mesopotamia*, 31–35. Roux notes that the name Puabi was Akkadian, meaning "word of my father." She was explicitly called queen (*nin*). Seals and pottery named other queens, including Ninbanda, and a woman priest named Khekunzig, the queen (*nin*) of a god. None of the kings mentioned on artifacts in the tombs is listed on the Sumerian King List. Henshaw assigns the harp to Puabi and suggests that she sang, probably in the cult (*Female and Male*, 18). An inscription above one royal tomb named queen Nin-tur, wife of an early king of Ur. Pollock, *Ancient Mesopotamia*, 210–11.

135. Henshaw, *Female and Male*, 84–86: musical instruments, 87–97, 101–3: singers, 114–16: dancers. *Ancient Near East in Pictures*, ed. Pritchard, 62, 356, fig. 192: soundbox of lyre with four tiers of animal figures, inlaid with shells, with seated donkey playing the lyre, from Ur (Early Dynastic 3), fig. 193: reconstructed lyre with gold head of bull and bands of mosaic and gold, from Ur (Early Dynastic 3), fig. 195: terra-cotta; woman playing double pipes (Nippur), fig. 196: two women playing harp and percussion before three male gods with weapons (Akkad), fig. 198: silver pipes with finger holes (Ur, grave, Early Dynastic 3), 356, fig. 847: stone votive plaque from temple of Inanna, banquet, women musicians, eight-stringed harp, seated woman holding cup and plant (Nippur, Early Dynastic 3). Reade, *Mesopotamia*, 51, fig. 48: lyre from Ur (Early Dynastic 3). Ilse Seibert, *Women in the Ancient Near East*, plate 5: detail of "Ur Standard," male lyre player and woman singer, royal tombs of Ur (Early Dynastic 3), plate 10: two women dancing on pinhead in bronze (Lagash, Early Dynastic 3). Part of a shell inlay of a woman musician was found in the palace of Kish. *Art of the First Cities*, ed. Aruz, 91, no. 50: Kish (Early Dynastic 2); *Ancient Near East in Pictures*, 61, fig. 191: relief, procession, women playing pipes and eleven string lyre, from Girsu (early twenty-first century).

136. *Art of the First Cities*, ed. Aruz, 74–75, no. 33: limestone relief of woman high priest, libation poured by man (*gipar* of Ur, Early Dynastic 3), 200, no. 128: alabaster disc relief of En-kheduanna (*gipar* of Ur, Akkadian). The dress of the women high priests is illustrated on the disc of En-kheduanna and on seals. Seibert, *Women in the Ancient Near East*, plate 21: disc of En-kheduanna. Harriet Crawford, *Sumer and the Sumerians*, 154, no. 8.4 (drawing).

137. Frances Pinnock, "The Iconography of the Entu-Priestesses in the Period of the Ur III Dynasty," in *Intellectual Life of the Ancient Near East*, ed. Prosecky, 339–43.

138. Seibert, *Women in the Ancient Near East*, plate 23: relief on votive tablet of woman seated on throne (Lagash, twenty-second to twenty-first century), plate 12: queen or woman high priest seated on throne, found in temple at Mari (mid-third millennium). *Art of the First Cities*, ed. Aruz, 73, no. 32: Sin temple at Khafajah, Early Dynastic 3). The plaque may have been a dedication to the temple (banquet). See Seibert, *Women*, plate 6: woman priest receiving offerings from the people, alabaster vase from Uruk (early third millennium), plate 7: white marble head of woman priest from Uruk (early third millennium), plate 14: silver vase relief of woman priest named Kurinahiti making drink offerings and bowing before goddess (Elam, twenty-third century). Bahrani, *Women of Babylon*, 99, plate 21: headless stone statue of woman praying (Girsu, about 2100), 102, plates 22 and 23: stone votive statues from Kish. *Women's Earliest Records*, ed. Lesko, 52, fig. 18: standing woman from temple of Inanna (Early Dynastic 3). *Art of the First*

Cities, ed. Aruz, 66–67, no. 28: full statue of woman standing (Early Dynastic 3, Inanna temple in Nippur), plate 16: alabaster statue of woman praying (2500).

136. *Ancient Near East in Pictures,* ed. Pritchard, 173, 309, fig. 507: Bau seated on geese throne (Ur, Ur III), fig. 508: woman or goddess seated on throne (Ur, reign of Ishme-Dagan of Isin). *Art of the First Cities,* ed. Aruz, 153–55, no. 92: seated woman (Early Dynastic 3, Mari). Harris, *Gender and Aging in Mesopotamia,* 53, fig. 3. Hallo, "Women of Sumer," 30–34, fig. 16: statue of Enanatuma, high priest daughter of the king of Isin, seated.

140. *Ancient Near East in Pictures,* ed. Pritchard, 8, fig. 22: woman (Early Dynastic 2). *Art of the First Cities,* ed. Aruz, 66–67, no. 28: full statue of woman standing (Early Dynastic 3, Inanna temple in Nippur), 70, no. 29: limestone statue of standing woman (Early Dynastic 3, Girsu), 153–55, 162, fig. 42: greenstone statue of standing woman (Early Dynastic 3, Nippur). Seibert, *Women in the Ancient Near East,* plate 13a: small sculpture of woman's head, Diyala (about 2500), plate 16: alabaster statue of woman praying (2500), plate 17: head of young woman, Asshur (about 2350), plate 20: diorite statue of beautiful woman, Lagash (twenty-first century), plate 22: terra-cotta head of woman or goddess (twenty-second to twenty-first century), plate 25: head and upper torso of woman, Umma (about 2000).

141. Pollock, *Ancient Mesopotamia,* 102–4. Women worked in textiles and pottery. *Ancient Near East in Pictures,* ed. Pritchard, 43, 266, fig. 144: upper-class woman spinning, fanned by servant (Susa). Seibert, *Women in the Ancient Near East,* plate 9: mosaic of three women working, two weaving, one spinning (Mari, Early Dynastic). Crawford, *Sumer and the Sumerians,* 125, no. 7.1: standing woman spinning (Mari). Archaeologists have found spindle whorls and loom weights, confirming this work of women beyond any doubt. Seibert, *Women,* plate 19: women harvesting dates (about 2350). Crawford, *Sumer,* 116, no. 6.5: dress of ordinary woman (Early Dynastic).

142. Seibert, *Women in the Ancient Near East,* plate 8: standing couple (Nippur; about 2500), plate 24: terra-cotta relief of couple embracing (Nippur, about 2000), plate 27: three couples in sexual embraces, plate 28: terra-cotta relief of couple standing, facing each other, with arms intertwined (Lagash, early second millennium). Harris, *Gender and Aging in Mesopotamia,* 144, fig. 2: seated couple. *Women's Earliest Records,* ed. Lesko, 70, fig. 21: standing couple embracing (Girsu, reign of Ur Ningirsu).

143. Naked male priests: *Ancient Near East in Pictures,* 197–98, 321–22, figs. 597 (Girsu), 600 (Akkad), 603, 605 (Ur, about 2500).

144. The most common characteristics of Amorite customary law were a low and restricted status of women and widespread use of capital, corporal, collective, and vicarious punishment. There is no evidence of collective or vicarious punishment in Sumer. The two formal Sumerian law collections, Laws of Ur-Nammu and Laws of Lipit-Ishtar, together had thirty-one criminal laws, twenty-three of which were punishable by fines or restitution. Five laws prescribed capital punishment, and only one had a mild physical punishment. There were no other corporal penalties. In contrast, the early Amorite city-state of Eshnunna had thirty-one criminal laws, of which eighteen were punishable by fines and seven by death. Babylonian and Assyrian law used many more capital and corporal punishments, as well as collective and vicarious penalties, and increased restrictions on women.

PART TWO: BABYLONIA

1. The Old Babylonian (OB) period lasted until 1595, when Babylonia was conquered by the Hittites. During the Middle Babylonian (MB) period, Babylonia was ruled by Kassites, the

second dynasty of Isin and Assyria. The Late Babylonian (LB) period, also called the Chaldean period, lasted until 539, when the Persians conquered Mesopotamia. The LB period began almost one thousand years after the end of the OB period, raising problems concerning continuity in law and ethnicity. Jack Sasson, "King Hammurabi of Babylon," in *Civilizations of the Ancient Near East*, ed. Sasson, 2:901. From the beginning of the OB period, the languages of Mesopotamia were Semitic: the East Semitic languages of Akkadian, Babylonian, and Assyrian, and the West Semitic languages of Amorite and Aramean.

2. Eshnunna had existed from at least the mid-third millennium. It was prominent from 2000 until its conquest by Hammurabi in 1762. At its greatest expanse, it ruled north and northwest Mesopotamia, including the city-states of Asshur and Mari. William W. Hallo and William K. Simpson, *The Ancient Near East: A History*, 87, 97–99. Robert M. Whiting, "Amorite Tribes and Nations of Second-Millennium Western Asia," in *Civilizations of the Ancient Near East*, ed. Sasson, 2:1235. Douglas Frayne, *Old Babylonian Period (2003–1595)*, 494, 499. The site of ancient Eshnunna is called Tell Asmar.

3. Martha Roth (*Law Collections from Mesopotamia and Asia Minor*, 57) and Hallo and Simpson (*Ancient Near East*, 99) date the Laws of Eshnunna (LE) late in the reign of King Dadusha (1819–1785), who was named in the superscription, although the left side of the text is missing. The LE were written in the Old Akkadian language, the oldest Semitic language in Mesopotamia and the basis of the later dialects of Babylonian and Assyrian. Godfrey R. Driver and John C. Miles, *The Babylonian Laws*, 1: 6–7. Roth, *Law Collections*, 58. *Ancient Near Eastern Texts Relating to the Old Testament*, ed. James B. Pritchard, 162. Russ VerSteeg, *Early Mesopotamian Law*, 30.

4. LE 27–28. Roth, *Law Collections*, 63, 69 n. 11. Reuven Yaron, *The Laws of Eshnunna*, 58–59. *Ancient Near Eastern Texts*, 162. The text stated "consent of her father and *mother*" (italics added). There is no mention of a requirement of a dowry.

5. LE 25. Roth, *Law Collections*, 62–63. Yaron, *Laws of Eshnunna*, 58–59. *Ancient Near Eastern Texts*, 162.

6. LE 17. This law treats death after betrothal. The subjects are unclear in this and the following laws. Roth (*Law Collections*, 61) and Yaron (*Laws of Eshnunna*, 55) understand this law to mean that if either the bride or the groom died, the marriage gifts would revert to the legal owner. LE 18. This law treats death soon after marriage. LE often mentioned where the bride or the couple resided to indicate whether the marriage was complete.

7. LE 29–30. Roth, *Law Collections*, 63. Yaron, *Laws of Eshnunna*, 60–61. *Ancient Near Eastern Texts*, 162.

8. LE 59. Roth, *Law Collections*, 68, 70 n. 32. Yaron, *Laws of Eshnunna*, 78–79. *Ancient Near Eastern Texts*, 163. Roth has the husband go away. Yaron thinks that the antecedent of "he" is unclear (pp. 221–22). The law does not state who kept the children. There was a movement to restrict polygyny at this time. The Laws of Hammurabi upheld monogamy except for three special cases: LH 141, 144–45, 148.

9. LE 41. Roth, *Law Collections*, 65. Yaron, *Laws of Eshnunna*, 68–69.

10. LE 51 and 52. Roth, *Law Collections*, 67. Yaron, *Laws of Eshnunna*, 74–77. A marked slave could not leave the city without permission of his or her owner. Diplomats were warned to mark their slaves at least with temporary markings and to keep them close to them.

11. LE 26, 31. Roth, *Law Collections*, 63–64. Yaron, *Laws of Eshnunna*, 58–59, 62–63. *Ancient Near Eastern Texts*, 162. The rape of a free virgin inevitably caused a significant property loss to her father. The girl became damaged merchandise, a liability to marry off, who would bring her father much less in marriage gifts.

12. LE 42–47. Roth, *Law Collections*, 65–66. Yaron, *Laws of Eshnunna*, 68–71. In LE 44–45, Yaron reads a broken arm or leg, whereas Roth has a broken hand or foot.

13. LE 24. Roth, *Law Collections*, 62. Yaron, *Laws of Eshnunna*, 56–57. There were two classes

of free persons in Eshnunna and Babylonia: upper-class citizen (*awilu*) and commoner (*mushkenu*).

14. LE 22–23. Roth, *Law Collections*, 62. Yaron, *Laws of Eshnunna*, 56–57. *Ancient Near Eastern Texts*, 162. VerSteeg aptly calls those distrained "debt-hostages" (*Early Mesopotamian Law*, 110).

15. LE 40, 49–50. Roth, *Law Collections*, 66–67, 70 n. 26. Yaron, *Laws of Eshnunna*, 72–75. *Ancient Near Eastern Texts*, 163.

16. LE 28. Roth, *Law Collections*, 63. Yaron, *Laws of Eshnunna*, 58–59. *Ancient Near Eastern Texts*, 162. VerSteeg, *Early Mesopotamian Law*, 119. Yaron suggests that the male adulterer was the one who was put to death (pp. 284–85). Roth disagrees and affirms her translation on the basis of context, law, and language. The husband would not have had jurisdiction over the male accomplice.

17. LE 15. Roth, *Law Collections*, 61. Yaron, *Laws of Eshnunna*, 52–53. This law is in command form and does not contain a penalty clause.

18. LE 12–13. Roth, *Law Collections*, 60–61. Yaron, *Laws of Eshnunna*, 50–51. Neither of these laws explicitly mentioned theft or breaking into a house or field. Yaron translates field as "crop," with the implication that it was ripe to steal. The day/night distinction is characteristic of the law of burglary. Trespass at night was a capital crime because it could jeopardize the lives of persons.

19. LE 58, 60. Roth, *Law Collections*, 68. Yaron, *Laws of Eshnunna*, 78–80. The text of LE 60 is quite fragmentary. Most scholars concur that it prescribed the death penalty for a guard who was negligent in guarding a house, allowing a burglary to occur.

20. LE 53–57. Roth, *Law Collections*, 67–68. Yaron, *Laws of Eshnunna*, 76–79.

21. LE 33–34. Roth, *Law Collections*, 64. *Ancient Near Eastern Texts*, 162. Yaron questions whether in LE 35 someone who adopted the child of a palace slave woman had the alternative of providing a slave of equal value to the palace or an obligation to return the child (pp. 62–65). Yaron prefers the obligation to return the child. Nothing was said in the law about whether the mother might have further contact with her child if it was returned to the palace slave quarters.

22. Four major Amorite dynasties and empires were roughly contemporary: Larsa, from 2025 to 1763; Eshnunna, from 2030 to 1762; Old Assyria, from 2010 to 1781; and Old Babylonia, from 1894 to 1595. At the beginning of the OB period, the Sumerian language was still used in writings, as was the Semitic language Old Akkadian, of which Old Babylonian was a dialect. All the written languages of the time used the cuneiform writing system. Old Babylonian was the dominant spoken language in southern Mesopotamia during the OB period. Hallo and Simpson, *Ancient Near East*, 98–99. Amélie Kuhrt, *The Ancient Near East: C. 3000–330 B.C.*, 1:108–9. Benjamin Foster, "Western Asia in the First Millennium," in *Women's Earliest Records*, ed. Lesko, 141).

23. The list of cities conquered is in the prologue of the Laws. It began with the religious center of Nippur and ended with the imperial triad of Babylon, Sumer, and Akkad. Roth, *Law Collections*, 77–80, Prol. 1.50–5.13. Hammurabi called himself "King of All the Amorite Land." Frayne, *Old Babylonian Period*, 344–46, no. 10. The first Amorite dynasty of Old Babylonia lasted for three hundred years. The OB dynasty and the OB period of history were chronologically coextensive. Sasson, "King Hammurabi of Babylon," in *Civilizations of the Ancient Near East*, ed. Sasson, 2:902. Julian Reade, *Mesopotamia*, 85, fig. 95: stone relief of Hammurabi.

24. Roth, *Law Collections*, 73. Driver and Miles, *Babylonian Laws*, 1:28–30, 36. *Ancient Near Eastern Texts*, 163–64. Roth and Driver and Miles date the promulgation of the Laws near the end of Hammurabi's reign. The relief pictures Hammurabi and Shamash, god of the sun and of justice. The stela, which is 7½ feet or 2.25 meters high, is presently in the Louvre. It has forty-five columns of writing. A stela is a much more substantial source than clay tablets, which could hold only part of a text, were easily broken, and thus often fragmentary. The Hammurabi stela was

discovered in the acropolis of Susa, the ancient capital of Elam, on the eastern frontier of Mesopotamia. It was most likely brought there by the Elamite king Shutruk Nahhunte I as a trophy of war in the mid-twelfth century B.C.E. Part of the text was chiseled off, but some of the erased parts have been preserved in other copies. There were duplicate stelae in Babylon, Sippar, and Nippur. The text of the Susa stela is supplemented by fragments of other stelae and numerous copies on clay tablets. Samuel Greengus, "Legal and Social Institutions of Ancient Mesopotamia," in *Civilizations of the Ancient Near East*, ed. Sasson, 1:471. Martha Roth, "Mesopotamian Legal Traditions and the Laws of Hammurabi," *Chicago-Kent Law Review* 71 (1995): 19–22.

25. Roth, *Law Collections*, 76–81. *Ancient Near Eastern Texts*, 164–65, Prol 1.27–50, translated by Roth, 76. The image of holding someone safe in one's lap could apply to a shepherd or a mother. The prologue and epilogue were written in an archaic poetic literary style, whereas the laws were in straightforward legal prose. The images of "king of justice" (*shar misharim*) and "shepherd (*re'um*) of the people" were used in both the prologue and the epilogue. Hammurabi also noted his wisdom, piety, kindness, and care for the welfare of his people.

26. Roth, *Law Collections*, 133–36. *Ancient Near Eastern Texts*, 177–80. The epilogue began with the words "the just decisions of Hammurabi" (*dinat misharim*). Epil. 47.1–8. Roth, "Mesopotamian Legal Traditions and the Laws of Hammurabi," *Chicago-Kent Law Review* 71 (1995): 20. Jean Bottéro translates it "verdicts of justice" (*Mesopotamia*, 179). H. W. F. Saggs, "specimen decisions" (*The Greatness That Was Babylon*, 189). Some Babylonian citizens were literate, but the majority of the people were not. In the epilogue (48.3–19), a wronged citizen was urged to have the laws read to him in order to understand his case and his rights. However, only men were citizens.

27. A bilingual, Sumerian and Old Babylonian, inscription in Sippar listed Hammurabi's tangible accomplishments, such as building fortifications and canals, and his greatest accomplishment in regard to Sippar, which was making Sippar and Babylon live together in peace. L. W. King, *The Letters and Inscriptions of Hammurabi, King of Babylon*, 3:177–79. Bottéro, *Mesopotamia*, 182–83. The concept of justice derived from two Babylonian words: *kittu* meaning "firmly established," and *misharu*, meaning "to go straight, in the right way; to be in order." Versteeg, *Early Mesopotamian Law*, 48–50. At the end of the prologue (5.16–20), both words were used together: *kittam u misharam*, which Roth translates "truth and justice" (*Law Collections*, 81). *Ancient Near Eastern Texts* has "law and justice" (p. 165).

28. Driver and Miles called the Laws of Hammurabi "a series of amendments to the common law of Babylon" (*Babylonian Laws* 1:41, 45–48). The incomplete nature of the LH is demonstrated by the subjects that were left out: for example, the LH treated assaults but not murder, looting of a burning house but not arson, and so on. Hammurabi himself did not intend to make a codification of existing law or a collection of all the laws of Babylonia. A law code articulates the principles of right and wrong, which can then be applied to cases. Common or case law starts from concrete cases and how these were dealt with by previous judges in order to find principles that fit the case at bar. The LH, as a collection of exemplary situations rather than specific cases, was neither a code nor a compendium of case law, but somewhere between the two. On occasion Hammurabi alluded to details from cases to derive a principle. The older abbreviation for the Laws was CH, for "Code of Hammurabi"; most scholars today agree that it is not a code and use the title "Laws of Hammurabi" (LH).

29. Saggs, *Greatness That Was Babylon*, 188–89. Jurisprudence is the science and art of judging. The compilation of law for the empire was a complex undertaking because the empire included subjects of many nationalities and legal traditions. Bottéro, *Mesopotamia*, 184.

30. The list of conquered cities in the prologue indicates that Hammurabi promulgated the laws for the empire, not just for the city of Babylon. The lengthy curse in the epilogue on anyone who tried to change his laws indicates that Hammurabi intended his laws to set precedents for

future jurisprudence. Curses included loss of kingship after a reign of disorder, suffering, famine, death, destruction of his city, dispersion of his people, supplanting of his dynasty, and the obliteration of his name and memory. Epil. 49.18–51.91. Roth, *Law Collections*, 136–40. *Ancient Near Eastern Texts*, 178–80 (Rev xxvi 18–xxviii 90). These curses were far more extensive then those of previous kings, and most of the suffering fell upon the offender's innocent people. Roth notes that the intended audience for the laws was first the gods and then victims of injustice and the vassal states of the empire ("Mesopotamian Legal Traditions and the Laws of Hammurabi," *Chicago-Kent Law Review* 71 [1995]: 17–24).

31. LH 5. Roth, *Law Collections*, 82. According to LH 5, judges sat with the assembly and could be deposed by the assembly. The king could remand cases back to the local courts. Driver and Miles, *Babylonian Laws*, 1:76–77. Greengus, "Legal and Social Institutions of Ancient Mesopotamia," in *Civilizations of the Ancient Near East*, ed. Sasson, 1:469, 472–73.

32. Joan Oates suggests that free citizens (*awilu*) were landowners and that commoners (*mushkenu*) were feudal tenants or vassals of the king (*Babylon*, 68-69). Insofar as slaves were property, not persons, they were not a social class. Some penalties for crimes and prices for services were based on the social class of the victim or recipient. LH 198–208 (assaults), 215–17, 221–23 (doctors' fees). Roth, *Law Collections*, 121–22, 124.

33. LH 128 (written contract), 159–61 (marriage gifts), 162, 167 (dowry), 171–72. Roth, *Law Collections*, 105, 111–15. The groom also provided food and drink for the betrothal or marriage feast, after which these were not mentioned again.

34. LH 159–61. Roth, *Law Collections*, 111–12. *Ancient Near Eastern Texts*, 173.

35. LH 151–52. Roth, *Law Collections*, 110. *Ancient Near Eastern Texts*, 172. The community property of the marriage included both assets and liabilities.

36. LH 141, 144–45, 148–49. The exceptions permitted polygyny, not polyandry.

37. LH 148–49. Roth, *Law Collections*, 109. *Ancient Near Eastern Texts*, 172. Driver and Miles, *Babylonian Laws*, 2:59. The husband could build separate quarters to house his sick wife. The disease of the first wife was a "*la'bum* disease," which could be a fever, a skin disease, or leprosy. I.Tzvi Abusch, *Babylonian Witchcraft Literature*, 68–69, 73. Compare LL 28.

38. LH 144–45. Roth, *Law Collections*, 108–9. Driver and Miles, *Babylonian Laws*, 2:57. *Ancient Near Eastern Texts*, 172. The terms used in both laws were *naditu* and *shugitu;* the second was a lower religious office.

39. LH 186, 190–91. Roth, *Law Collections*, 119–20.

40. LH 141. Roth, *Law Collections*, 107–8.

41. LH 150. Roth, *Law Collections*, 109–10. *Ancient Near Eastern Texts*, 172. This law describes an *inter vivos* donation. The word for son, *maru*, could have a generic meaning when used in the plural (as here): children. The word for daughter was *martu*. M. E. J. Richardson, *Hammurabi's Laws*, 217–18.

42. LH 177. Roth, *Law Collections*, 116. *Ancient Near Eastern Texts*, 174.

43. LH 172–74. Roth, *Law Collections*, 114–15. *Ancient Near Eastern Texts*, 173–74. The widow had the *usufruct* of the property. *Usufruct* is a legal term that means the "use" of a house and the "fruit" or income of the land for the remainder of the person's life. It denotes possession, but not ownership. Her children had ownership, but not possession, until she died.

44. LH 167. Roth, *Law Collections*, 113. *Ancient Near Eastern Texts*, 173. This law uses the word *maru* (singular), meaning "son," once, and the plural, *mari*, twice. Roth and *Ancient Near Eastern Texts* translate it "children"; Richardson, as "sons" (*Hammurabi's Laws*, 218).

45. LH 162–64. Roth, *Law Collections*, 112. *Ancient Near Eastern Texts*, 173.

46. LH 178–84 named two kinds of women priests, *ugbabtu* and *naditu*, and four types of religious functionaries: *sekretu, qadishtu, kulmashitu,* and *shugitu.* The *qadishtu* has been called a sacred prostitute in the cult of Ishtar. The *shugitu* was of lower status and is sometimes translated "lay priestess," although she did not perform priestly functions. Rivkah Harris, "Indepen-

dent Women in Ancient Mesopotamia?" in *Women's Earliest Records*, ed. Lesko, 151. Richard A. Henshaw, *Female and Male: The Cultic Personnel*, 236–40.

47. LH 183–84. Roth, *Law Collections*, 118. The religious office in both laws was *shugitu*. *Ancient Near Eastern Texts*, 174. Driver and Miles, *Babylonian Laws*, 1:336.

48. LH 180–82. Roth, *Law Collections*, 118. The terms are *naditu* and *sekretu* in LH 180, and *naditu*, *qadishtu*, and *kulmashitu* in LH 181. *Ancient Near Eastern Texts*, 174. Driver and Miles, *Babylonian Laws*, 1:336–37. A *naditu* priest of Shamash could not marry and often lived in a cloister. A *naditu* priest of Marduk could marry, but could not have children. If a *naditu* inherited land with feudal obligations, she was exempt from their performance.

49. LH 138–40. Roth, *Law Collections*, 107. *Ancient Near Eastern Texts*, 172. When a husband had not paid any marriage gifts, he had to give his ex-wife sixty sheqels of silver as the divorce settlement. If he was a commoner, he had to give his ex-wife only twenty sheqels of silver. The law did not state whether the wife of the commoner was of the same class.

50. LH 137. Roth, *Law Collections*, 107. *Ancient Near Eastern Texts*, 172. The terms are *naditu* and *shugitu*. The *naditu* provided children; the *shugitu* bore children. The divorce settlement, giving the wife half of all the property, suggests an early concept of community property, the combined acquisitions and gains accumulated during the course of a marriage in which each spouse owns an undivided half interest. Louisiana Civil Code arts. 2326, 2336.

51. LH 142–43. Roth, *Law Collections*, 108. Roth translates one phrase as the husband denying sexual relations to the wife. *Ancient Near Eastern Texts*, 172, has the wife refuse the husband.

52. LH 35–38. Roth, *Law Collections*, 88. *Ancient Near Eastern Texts*, 167–68. Driver and Miles, *Babylonian Laws*, 1:111–13. If someone attempted to buy any of these, the sale was illegal, the money paid was forfeit, and the property was returned to its legal owner, the king.

53. LH 39–40. Roth, *Law Collections*, 88. The term used for woman priest was *naditu*. *Ancient Near Eastern Texts*, 168. The buyer or lessee had to perform the service obligation that went with the land. Nonfeudal property could also be used to satisfy a debt.

54. LH 117–19. Roth, *Law Collections*, 103–4. *Ancient Near Eastern Texts*, 171.

55. LH 175–76. Roth, *Law Collections*, 115–16. *Ancient Near Eastern Texts*, 174. Driver and Miles, *Babylonian Laws*, 1:336. The daughter of a citizen received no dowry if she married a slave of the temple.

56. LH 170–71. Roth, *Law Collections*, 113–14. *Ancient Near Eastern Texts*, 173.

57. LH 278–79. Roth, *Law Collections*, 132. These laws provided an early form of consumer protection.

58. LH 28–29. Roth, *Law Collections*, 86. *Ancient Near Eastern Texts*, 167.

59. LH 133–36. Roth, *Law Collections*, 106–7.

60. LH 130. Roth, *Law Collections*, 106. *Ancient Near Eastern Texts*, 171. Driver and Miles, *Babylonian Laws*, 2:53. The victim was called "virgin wife," indicating that she was betrothed but that the marriage had not yet been consummated. The previous law, LH 129, on adultery, allowed hybrid jurisdiction: either state punishment of both parties, or the husband could decide on a lesser penalty for his wife, in which case the state could not execute the adulterer.

61. LH 154, 157. Roth, *Law Collections*, 110–11. *Ancient Near Eastern Texts*, 172. Driver and Miles, *Babylonian Laws*, 1:320. See Leviticus 18:17; 20:14; 21:9. In this law, the father had died; otherwise the crime would have included both incest and adultery.

62. LH 155, 156. Roth, *Law Collections*, 110–11. *Ancient Near Eastern Texts*, 172. Water, like fire, was a symbol of purification. Both took away the pollution by burning or washing. Fire was more thorough because it destroyed the polluted object or person. Bottéro, *Mesopotamia*, 229.

63. LH 158. Roth, *Law Collections*, 111. *Ancient Near Eastern Texts*, 172–73. If the woman was not related by blood or marriage, the religious tabu was not broken, the offense did not require ritual purification, and the penalty was only a fine.

64. LH 110. Roth, *Law Collections,* 101. The terms used here are *naditu* and *ugbabtu;* both designated women priests. *Ancient Near Eastern Texts* understands "open" in the sense of opening a door, although it could mean buying a tavern and opening it for business even if the women did not live in a temple or cloister and were no longer working as priests (p. 170). Driver and Miles, *Babylonian Laws,* 1:206–8. See LH 157 and Leviticus 21:9; Joshua 2:1; 6:25; Judges 11:1; 16:1; 1 Kings 3:16; Ezra 23:44.

65. LH 209–14. Roth, *Law Collections,* 122–23. The principle of *talion* mandated the likeness of the punishment to the offense committed: an eye for an eye, a daughter's life for a daughter's life. The word *talion* comes from Latin, meaning "of the same kind." The principle derived from Amorite West Semitic tradition. It was used in Assyrian and Hebrew law, but not in the laws of Sumer or Khatti. Oates, *Babylon,* 75. Saggs, *Greatness That Was Babylon,* 179.

66. LH 196–202, 208, 211–14. Roth, *Law Collections,* 121–23, 125. *Ancient Near Eastern Texts,* 175–76. LH 196–97, 200: penalties were based on *talion* when victims were of the same class; LH 198–99, 201, 208, 211–14: fines when victims were of a lower class; LH 202: public corporal punishment when victim was of a higher class.

67. LH 1–4. Roth, *Law Collections,* 81–82. *Ancient Near Eastern Texts,* 166. Tikva Frymer-Kensky, "Tit for Tat: The Principle of Equal Retribution in Near Eastern and Biblical Law," *Biblical Archaeologist* 43 (1980): 230–33. See Deut 19:15–19.

68. LH 127. Roth, *Law Collections,* 105. *Ancient Near Eastern Texts,* 171. The woman priest was an *ugbabtu.* The penalty of cutting off half of a person's hair could designate the "slave lock," an external mark of slave status that could not legally be removed unless the slave was freed.

69. LH 131–32. Roth, *Law Collections,* 106. Driver and Miles, *Babylonian Laws,* 1:283–84.

70. LH 22–24. Roth, *Law Collections,* 85. Cities were divided into districts or wards, each of which had its own local officials.

71. LH 115–16. Roth, *Law Collections,* 103. Driver and Miles, *Babylonian Laws,* 2:46–47. See LH 214, 230, 252. Roth, *Law Collections,* 141 n. 21. The fine was twenty sheqels of silver.

72. LH 26. Roth, *Law Collections,* 85–86. *Ancient Near Eastern Texts,* 167 n. 52. Driver and Miles, *Babylonian Laws,* 1:116–17. The land was owned by and reverted to the king.

73. LH 153. Roth, *Law Collections,* 110. *Ancient Near Eastern Texts,* 172. Driver and Miles, *Babylonian Laws,* 1:313–14. A pole was thrust upward through her body, on which she hung until she died. The law did not state the penalty of her male accomplice. The crime here resembles the crime assumed without evidence by the assembly of Nippur in the murder trial of Nindada, who was condemned to death (Isin/Larsa period).

74. LH 157. Roth, *Law Collections,* 111.

75. LH 2. Roth, *Law Collections,* 81.

76. LH 129. Roth, *Law Collections,* 105. The couple were bound and thrown into the river to drown. This was not the "river ordeal," which sought to prove guilt or innocence when the evidence was insufficient. In the river ordeal, the accused jumped into the river. Driver and Miles, *Babylonian Laws,* 1:284. Adultery did not cause pollution but did cause shame and loss of honor to the husband. Water, a symbol of purification, was also a means to restore lost honor.

77. LH 133b. Roth, *Law Collections,* 106. *Ancient Near Eastern Texts,* 171 n. 105. In LH 129, 133b, 143. The death penalty was prescribed by drowning. Here the woman had been tried and found guilty and was thrown into the river to drown as her punishment.

78. LH 143. Roth, *Law Collections,* 108.

79. LH 6 and 8. Roth, *Law Collections,* 82. Driver and Miles, *Babylonian Laws,* 1: 81.

80. LH 141–43. Roth, *Law Collections,* 107–8. Roth and Driver and Miles (*Babylonian Laws.* 1:299) understand the phrase to mean that the husband denied sexual relations to the wife. *Ancient Near Eastern Texts* has the wife refusing the husband (p. 172).

81. LH 25. Roth, *Law Collections,* 85. The penalty was death, without formal trial.

82. LH 7. Roth, *Law Collections*, 82. Driver and Miles, *Babylonian Laws*, 1:85–86. Since neither minors nor slaves could normally own property, they did not have the legal capacity to transfer it.

83. LH 9–11 (death penalty), 11,13 (penalty of the case).

84. LH 108–9. Roth, *Law Collections*, 101. Driver and Miles, *Babylonian Laws*, 1:202–5.

85. LH 15–20. Roth, *Law Collections*, 84–85. Driver and Miles, *Babylonian Laws*, 1:106–8. LH 15–16 dealt with slaves of the palace or belonging to a commoner. LH 17-20 dealt with fugitive slaves.

86. LH 146 and 147. Driver and Miles, *Babylonian Laws*, 2:56–57. The woman priest was a *naditu*. Roth, *Law Collections*, 109. Roth's translation has "place upon her the slave-hairlock" in place of branding. *Ancient Near Eastern Texts* has "mark her with the slave-mark" (p. 172). Although the woman was already a slave, she had a special status in the household by having borne children to the husband. The penalty relegated her to a lower form of slavery. LH 226–27 prescribed amputation of a hand or death for removal of a slave hairlock.

87. LH 194. Roth, *Law Collections*, 120. *Ancient Near Eastern Texts*, 175. Driver and Miles, *Babylonian Laws*, 1:405–6; 2:77. If she did it a second time, her remaining breast would be amputated. Without her breasts, the wet nurse could not repeat the offense.

88. LH 192–93. Roth, *Law Collections*, 120. *Ancient Near Eastern Texts*, 175. The adoptive mother was a *sekretu*, a form of religious office lower than priesthood.

89. In Sumer, Uru-inimgina mandated the penalty of death in three laws; LU in four; LL in one; and SLEx in none. In Babylonian law, LE had six and LH thirty-six laws that prescribed capital punishment, including one by impalement, three by fire, five by water, five by *talion*, and twenty-five generic. Corporal mutilation was found only in the earliest Sumerian law. In LH, sixteen laws imposed corporal penalties; two, corporal punishment; thirteen, corporal mutilation; and three, corporal mutilation via *talion*. The death penalty was generally not imposed on slaves because their death would cause an economic loss to their owners.

90. LH 153. Roth, *Law Collections*, 110.

91. LH 110 (women *naditu* or *ugbabtu* priests), 157 (incest). Fire also symbolized ritual sacrifice to placate the gods. Despite the blood relationship, incest between father and daughter was penalized only by exile of the father. LH 154.

92. LH 108 (wine), 155 (incest). Roth, *Law Collections*, 102, 111. The LH used different vocabulary for the river ordeal, which was used to establish guilt or innocence.

93. LH 133 (wife of prisoner of war), 143 (dishonor husband). Roth, *Law Collections*, 106, 108. In LH 21and 227, the death penalty was prescribed, and hanging was mentioned. A burglar who made an opening in a house to gain entry and a man who tricked a barber into removing the slave mark of a slave were put to death. It is uncertain whether either case involved death by hanging or whether the corpses were hung up after execution. The bodies were hung up in the places where the crimes were committed: the hole in the wall made by the burglar and the doorway of the barber's shop, presumably as a deterrent to others.

94. LH 129 (adultery), 130 (rape), 14 (kidnapping), 22 (robbery). Roth, *Law Collections*, 84–85, 105–6. LH 14 and 22 consist of a brief conditional clause, "if a person did x," followed by the penalty clause—the offender "shall be put to death."

95. LH 15–16, 19 (escaped slave), 109 (tavern keeper). Roth, *Law Collections*, 84–85, 101. Each of these laws stated that the offender "shall be killed."

96. LH 1–3 (death for false accusation of capital crimes), 4, 13 (penalty of the case in non-capital cases). Roth, *Law Collections*, 81–83. For Sumer, see LU 29, LL 17. Roth, *Law Collections*, 20, 29.

97. LH 9–10 (death for theft of lost property), 11 (death for false accusation of theft), and 253 (amputation of hand for theft of seed or fodder) were earlier laws. LH 6 (death for theft from inside temple or palace), 8 (theft from outside palace or temple, thirtyfold restitution for citizen,

or tenfold restitution for commoner, death if unable to pay restitution) and 254–55, 259–60 (multifold restitution or fines) were later. Roth, *Law Collections,* 82–84, 128–29.

98. There were few references to corporal mutilation before LH, and these were in the earliest known laws of Sumer. The practice disappeared for six hundred years between Uru-inimgina and Hammurabi. The only exception was very mild—nose piercing—in the late Isin/Larsa period, contemporaneous with the OB dynasty. This has been attributed to Amorite custom.

99. LH 218, 226 (doctor), 184 (barber), 194 (wet nurse). Roth, *Law Collections,* 120, 123–24. Roth translates 194 as "without the consent of the [dead child's] father and mother." The former couple could inform the new clients. The translation of Meek in *Ancient Near Eastern Texts* has the new clients (p. 175).

100. LH 192–93, 195. Roth, *Law Collections,* 120.

101. LH 196 (eye), 197 (bone), 200 (tooth), 209–10 (miscarriage/death), 229–30 (builder). Roth, *Law Collections,* 120–22, 125. For fines when victims were of the lower class, see LH 198–99, 201, 212, 214, 231. If the offense was the killing of a child, the penalty would be the death of the child of the murderer, while the murderer himself did not receive any punishment. LH 210, 230. Tikva Frymer-Kensky believes that *talion* first appeared in OB law, that its use in the LH was for the protection of persons of the citizen class, and that the origin of *talion* was West Semitic, that is, Amorite ("Tit for Tat," 233). *Talion* was found in Assyrian and Hebrew laws but not in the laws of Sumer or Khatti.

102. LH 202: citizen struck cheek of citizen of higher rank, 205: slave struck citizen. Roth, *Law Collections,* 121–22, 132. When both persons were of the same social class, it was a minor offense. In LH 203–4 a citizen struck the cheek of a citizen, and the fine was sixty sheqels. If both were commoners, the fine was ten sheqels. Roth, "Mesopotamian Legal Traditions and the Laws of Hammurabi," *Chicago-Kent Law Review* 71 (1995): 13–37. In LH 282, if a slave repudiated the authority of his or her owner, the owner had to prove legal ownership of the slave in court and then could cut off the slave's ear. For the same offense in the Hurrian city-state of Nuzi, the slave was blinded. Versteeg, *Early Mesopotamian Law,* 156–57.

103. EA 3. *Ancient Near Eastern Texts,* 526–68. The OB name for an edict of justice was *misharum.* Ammisaduqa, an Amorite, ruled from 1646 to 1626. Driver and Miles (*Babylonian Laws,* 2:319–23) and F. R. Kraus (*Ein Edikt des Königs Ammi-saduqa von Babylon*) had only texts A and B, so their edition of EA is very fragmentary. The translation and numbering of J. J. Finkelstein in *Ancient Near Eastern Texts* are used here, because he also had text C. As the economy worsened at the end of the OB dynasty, such edicts were issued more frequently. Dominique Charpin, "The History of Ancient Mesopotamia: An Overview," in *Civilizations of the Ancient Near East,* ed. Sasson, 2:817. These edicts resemble the seventh "jubilee" year in the Hebrew Bible, a time of rest for the land and a time for a more egalitarian redistribution of resources. Exodus 23:10–11. Leviticus 25.

104. EA 16–17. *Ancient Near Eastern Texts,* 528.

105. EA 20–21. *Ancient Near Eastern Texts,* 528.

106. EA 5–7, 22. *Ancient Near Eastern Texts,* 526–28. The edict did not deal explicitly with criminal law; however, it prescribed penalties for use of coercion in collection of taxes and for the use of fraudulent loan documents by creditors. The penalties were restitution and fines, but if these were not paid, the penalty was death.

107. EA 18. *Ancient Near Eastern Texts,* 528. This is similar to LH 109, according to which women wine sellers were sentenced to death for giving false measure.

108. L. W. King, *The Letters and Inscriptions of Hammurabi, King of Babylon,* 3:110–16: three arrest warrants signed by Hammurabi. The first summoned eight defendants, the second five, and the third eight. Many were for officials and soothsayers (a soothsayer was a seer who claimed to foretell the future). Rivkah Harris, *Ancient Sippar: A Demographic Study of an Old-Babylonian City (1894–1595 B.C.),* 39, 130–31 (king's runner).

109. Harris, *Ancient Sippar*, 39, 116–19, 127, 129. Seal inscriptions affixed to court records called royal judges "servants of the king." Harris accepts this as evidence that judges were appointed or confirmed in office by the king. LH 5.

110. King, *Letters and Inscriptions*, 3:20–22 (Hammurabi, bribery), 133–34 (Abi-eshu, slave).

111. King, *Letters and Inscriptions*, 3:38–41(Hammurabi); Marten Stol, *Letters from Yale*, 16–19, no. 25 ("ordinances"). The image of "yoke" derives from the yoke worn by a pair of oxen to keep them together. A Late Assyrian king, Sennakherib, used the expression "the yoke of my rule," which connoted obedience to legal authority. Marc Van De Mieroop, *Cuneiform Texts and the Writing of History*, 44.

112. King, *Letters and Inscriptions*, 3:135–36 (Abi-eshu). The city court was in Sippar.

113. *Chronicle of the Kings of the First Dynasty of Babylon*, in King, *Letters and Inscriptions* 3:212–53. Sasson, "King Hammurabi of Babylon," in *Civilizations of the Ancient Near East*, ed. Sasson, 2:905, 909. Frayne, *Old Babylonian Period*, 493–94, 499, nos. 3–4, 2007: Mekubi, daughter of king Bilalama of Eshnunna.

114. King, *Letters and Inscriptions*, 3:170–71. The governor had told the two men to take their petition to his wife. Frayne, *Old Babylonian Period*, 563, no. 2: Inibshina, 540, no. 2: another ruler gave a seal to his wife. The kings of Eshnunna were Bilalama and Dadusha.

115. Most of the letters begin with the formula "speak" or "say" to the recipient, "thus says" the writer. This could be a customary form of address, or it could mean that the recipient was illiterate and the letter had to be read aloud by a scribe. Stol, *Letters from Yale*, 38–39, 142–45, 148–49, 154–55. Letters 228, 240: written by women; letters 52, 230, 252: written to women. The writer of letter 52 wrote to the woman who was his superior and asked her to write back to him.

116. The question of the extent of literacy cannot be answered definitively. Laurie E. Pearce, "The Scribes and Scholars of Ancient Mesopotamia," in *Civilizations of the Ancient Near East*, ed. Sasson, 4:2266. William W. Hallo, "Nippur Originals," in *DUMU-E2-DUB-BA-A: Studies in Honor of Ake Sjöberg*, ed. Behrens et al., 237–39. The most prominent scribal school in the OB period had been founded by the Ur III king Shulgi at Nippur. It flourished until about 1720.

117. Stol, *Letters from Yale*, 36–39, 114–15, 148–49, 166–67, letters 51, 179, 240, 275. The writer of letter 275 asked that wool be sent immediately because the "girls," spinners or weavers, were idle. Stol, *Letters from Yale*, 54–55, letter 82: A wife owned a storehouse. She put a roof on it and lived there with the wife of another man. Harris, *Ancient Sippar*, 271–72, 275, 281, 285.

118. Marten Stol, "Private Life in Ancient Mesopotamia," in *Civilizations of the Ancient Near East*, ed. Sasson, 1:486. Elizabeth C. Stone, "Adoption Texts from Nippur," in *Adoption in Old Babylonian Nippur and the Archive of Mannum-mesu-lissur*, ed. Stone and Owen, 60, no. 25. Frayne, *Old Babylonian Period*, 563, no. 1: King Dadusha of Eshnunna.

119. *Ancient Near Eastern Texts*, 544. It was signed by five witnesses (reign of king Ammiditana).

120. *Ancient Near Eastern Texts*, 219 (thirteenth year of King Samsu-ilunu).

121. Marc Van De Mieroop, *Society and Enterprise in Old Babylonian Ur*, 213.

122. Marten Stol, "The Care of the Elderly in the Old Babylonian Period," in *Care of the Elderly in the Ancient Near East*, ed. Stol and Vleeming, 64, 67, 72–74, 79, 83–85. LH 178: brothers had the legal duty to support their priest sisters. After the sisters died, their property went to their brothers. Slaves not freed were returned to the donor.

123. Stol, *Letters from Yale*, 38–39, 90–91, 100–101, 106–7, 114–17, 148–49. Letters 53, 58, 144, 148, 156, 165, 177, 181, 240.

124. Roth, "Mesopotamian Legal Traditions and the Laws of Hammurabi," *Chicago-Kent Law Review* 71 (1995): 32–33. Both acts were public. The first publicly humiliated the son, and he could do nothing to restore his honor because it was his mother who slapped him. The will was from Emar.

125. *Ancient Near Eastern Texts,* 545. OB document from Mari. The shaving probably marked him as a slave. Compare the penalties of corporal mutilation in LH 192–93.

126. Stol, "Care of the Elderly in the Old Babylonian Period," 62–63, 97, 112–13. The word translated here as "respect," also meant "fear" and "honor," which expanded the meaning of respect. According to Stol, respect was more important than tangible support. Stone, "Adoption Texts from Nippur," 46–49, 70, nos. 9–13, 32 (Nippur), 74, 81–82, nos. 37, 45. Van De Mieroop, *Society and Enterprise in Old Babylonian Ur,* 217: adoption contract from OB Ur. Prebends were subdivisions of temple benefices.

127. Stone, "Adoption Texts from Nippur," 54, no. 20. Shallurtum was also the name of a daughter of OB king Sumula'el, but there is no evidence that this is the same woman.

128. Stone, "Adoption Texts from Nippur," 50–53, nos. 14, 15–17 (Nippur).

129. King, *Letters and Inscriptions,* 3:83–84. Letter 38. Stol, *Letters from Yale,* 6–7, 40–41, 94–95, 120–21, 138–39, 160–61, 166–67. Letters 9, 55, 149, 185, 223, 265, 274. Letter 55 contained the price of twelve silver sheqels for a slave girl. Hermann Ranke, *Babylonian Legal and Business Documents,* 30–31, no. 14: list of estate assets (reign of Hammurabi); *Ancient Near Eastern Texts,* 218–19, 219, nn. 37–38. Text dated in the seventh year of the reign of king Ammiditana. See LH 278.

130. Harris, *Ancient Sippar,* 5, 38–39, 60, 143. Ulla Jeyes, "The Naditu Women of Sippar," in *Images of Women in Antiquity,* ed. Cameron and Kuhrt, 260–72. The second OB king, Sumulael, took control of Sippar and rebuilt its wall. The city contained houses and shops for its people.

131. Gudrun Colbow, "Priestesses, either Married or Unmarried, and Spouses without Title: Their Seal Use and Their Seals in Sippar at the Beginning of the Second Millenium BC," in *Sex and Gender in the Ancient Near East,* ed. Parpola and Whiting, 86–88. Seals of the Ur-Utu family archive were found in the excavation of Tell ed-Der. The family claimed descent from an ancient king of Sippar.

132. Harris, *Ancient Sippar,* 39, 119, 127, 129–31. *Ancient Near Eastern Texts,* 218. Judges also served as witnesses for land sales and adoptions by *naditu* priests. The woman scribe was mentioned in the record of litigation between two women priests over ownership of real estate.

133. Harris, *Ancient Sippar,* 155, 161, 166–73, 186, 204–8. The chief male priest was the *sanga.* Sons of *sangas* became *sangas. Sangas,* their wives, and other family members received rations of food and money. One wife was named Ruttum. One list had 850 men working at the harvest; some may have been slaves hired from the *naditu* women. The temple did well with its sheep industry, because temple wool sold for less than palace wool.

134. Harris, *Ancient Sippar,* 5, 7–9. King Hammurabi built a dike to prevent flooding in the fields, dug a canal, and built a wall for the cloister. Frayne, *Old Babylonian Period,* 332–36, 348–49, nos. 1–2, 12. The word for cloister, *gagu,* meant place of hiding. There were also cloisters in Nippur, Kish, and Susa, but none as large or influential as Sippar. Most of the cloistered women were *naditu* priests. Women *ugbabtu* priests and women holding the religious office of *sekru* also lived in the cloister. Others who resided inside the cloister were women servants, cooks, and weavers. Harris, *Ancient Sippar,* 304–5.

135. Rivkah Harris, "Independent Women in Ancient Mesopotamia," in *Women's Earliest Records: From Ancient Egypt and Western Asia,* ed. Lesko, 151, 153–55.

136. Harris, *Ancient Sippar,* 5, 73, 117, 199–203, 273, 278, 281, 288, 306, 308. When women became *naditu* priests, they took a religious name often hyphenated with the name of a god or goddess. This is why there are so many women with the same name in the cloister records. *Naditu* priests were also daughters of judges and artisans. One judge had a son who was a judge and two daughters, Aya-talik and Aya-reshat, who were wealthy *naditu* priests of Shamash. Male reed-workers, goldsmiths, potters, and scribes had daughters and sisters who were *naditu* priests.

When women priests could not afford animals or other materials for sacrifice, their families often provided them. They prayed for their families and made offerings to the goddess, Aya, wife of the god Shamash. Richard A. Henshaw, *Female and Male: The Cultic Personnel,* 193–94. Jean Bottéro, *Religion in Ancient Mesopotamia,* 122.

137. Harris, *Ancient Sippar,* 310. Sales of 66 of 97 fields, 39 of 64 houses in good repair, 23 of 28 plots of land, and 9 of 13 orchards were to *naditu* priests. Sales of 13 houses and 18 of 24 empty lots were made by *naditu* priests. The *naditu* Iltani bought a house in the suburbs of Sippar for seventeen sheqels of silver. Ranke, *Babylonian Legal and Business Documents,* 20, no. 2 (reign of king Ammisaduqa).

138. Harris, *Ancient Sippar,* 20–21. The donation was the inheritance of her mother, given by her father.

139. Colbow, "Priestesses, either Married or Unmarried, and Spouses without Title: Their Seal Use and Their Seals in Sippar at the Beginning of the Second Millenium BC," in *Sex and Gender in the Ancient Near East,* ed. Parpola and Whiting, 86–87. The seals and seal use by OB women was no different from that of men. Sellers, lessees, debtors, and adoptive heirs sealed; in general, buyers, lessors, creditors, and adopting parents did not.

140. *Ancient Near Eastern Texts,* 218. Written in the seventh year of the reign of King Samsu-ilunu (1749–1712). The rent was set at one and a half sheqels of silver for one year, with an initial payment of two-thirds of a sheqel of silver. Harris, *Ancient Sippar,* 21, 28, 30–32, 50–51, 85, 114, 193, 220–25. In 19 of 28 lease contracts, and 5 of 5 leases of orchards, the lessors were women priests. There are at least 6 extant lease contracts made by the woman priest Ribatum. Ranke, *Babylonian Legal and Business Documents,* 23–24, no. 7: lease of house by Ribatum for one year for three sheqels (reign of Hammurabi), 22, no. 5: lease by Mellatum (reign of Ammiditana). Some leases were for one wing or one story of a house. The king of Larsa was Warad-Sin. Women priests also made loans of grain, which were paid back with interest at the harvest. Ranke, 25, no. 10.

141. Lambert, in *La Femme dans le Proche-Orient Antique,* 128. The male god An replaced the goddess Inanna at Uruk. Shamash became the god of Larsa and Sippar. He was given Aya as his consort. Marduk was the god of Babylon. Harris, *Ancient Sippar,* 189–90, 196, 198–99, 244–47, 304–5. Pearce, "The Scribes and Scholars of Ancient Mesopotamia," in *Civilizations of the Ancient Near East,* ed. Sasson, 4:2266.

142. Harris, *Ancient Sippar,* 313–14 (reign of Sin-muballit). There was a male steward over the women *ugbabtu* priests. Frayne, *Old Babylonian Period,* 416–17, no. 2011 (reign of Ammiditana). Women who held the lower office of *sekru* were generally upper-class women, who brought large dowries and could inherit.

143. Ranke, *Babylonian Legal and Business Documents,* 28–30, no. 13. Erishti-Aya lived in the reign of King Ammisaduqa. The purification may have been the rite performed after childbirth, since Surratum was nursing the infant. Ranke suggests that it might have been a rite for adopting foreigners or slaves.

144. Stol, "The Care of the Elderly in the Old Babylonian Period," in *Care of the Elderly in the Ancient Near East,* ed. Stol and Vleeming, 97–107. One *naditu* left her fields to one daughter of each of her three brothers. Stol thinks that the three nieces were probably also *naditu* priests. It was possible to adopt a nephew. The *kulmashitu* Beltani left her estate to her nephew, who then had to provide support by sending her rations for life. The adoption contracts confirmed the adopted person as heir. The father of an heir could support the adoptive mother and gain her inheritance. Stol uses the English word "nun" for *naditu,* but the meaning is very different. Nuns are not priests. This work uses "woman priest," adding the word *naditu* or *ugbabtu* to indicate the type of priest.

145. Harris, *Ancient Sippar,* 315–16. In a litigation text, Ruttum and Shamakhtum, sisters and *naditu* priests of Shamash, were listed before Beletum, *naditu* of Marduk.

146. Albert Kirk Grayson, *Assyrian Royal Inscriptions,* 1:317–18. *Naditu* priests of Marduk could also buy and own slaves.

147. Harris, *Ancient Sippar,* 179. The parents performed the transfer of dowry in the temple. The woman was called both *naditu* and *kulmashitu.* Ranke, *Babylonian Legal and Business Documents,* 26–27, no. 11 (reign of King Ammiditana).

148. Harris, *Ancient Sippar,* 308–9, 315, 317–21. The secondary wife was usually a *shugitu.*

149. Ibid., 324–28. Henshaw, *Female and Male,* 87, 203. *Kulmashitu* meant "set apart."

150. Harris, *Ancient Sippar,* 328–30. Henshaw, *Female and Male,* 87, 195, 207, 209. *Qadishtu* also meant "set apart" in a different sense. The triliteral root *q-d-sh* means "holy" in Hebrew and other Semitic languages. They sang hymns during rituals. At least one lived in the cloister at Sippar. Harris suggests that some may have been midwives or wet nurses.

151. Harris, *Ancient Sippar,* 321–22. Henshaw, *Female and Male,* 112, 196. The *shugitu* played a sexual role in religious ritual. A diviner foretold the future by means of the techniques of divination. Many were from lower class families.

152. Stol, *Letters from Yale,* 38–39. Letter 52. King, *Letters and Inscriptions,* 3:6–9. Letter 2. Written by Hammurabi concerning captured women of Elam. King, *Letters and Inscriptions,* 3:117–18. Letter 2.1. King Samsuiluna ordered travel arrangements for the statue of the goddess Annunitum, which was being taken to Sippar. The king ordered that "she" be transported in comfort, "as in a shrine." King adds: "with the same dignity and comfort as if she were in her own temple."

153. There were extensive alliances among Amorite tribes throughout Mesopotamia. Mari was an ally of Babylonia against Assyria. Hammurabi ultimately betrayed the alliance. After he took Mari, Hammurabi left officials and scribes who spent two years cataloging and shipping to Babylon everything they considered valuable and useful. Then they knocked down the city walls and burned what was left. Jack M. Sasson, "King Hammurabi of Babylon," in *Civilizations of the Ancient Near East,* ed. Sasson, 2:911. Frayne, *Old Babylonian Period,* 345–47, no. 11.27- 30: a third-person description of or by Hammurabi, describing the destruction of Mari.

154. Mari (Tell Hariri) existed from the early third millennium. It had been a client state of the empire of Akkad. Stephanie Dalley, *Mari and Karana,* 12–15. Mari was an important city-state because of its location on the trade routes as a transfer point between the land routes and the river routes. It was the gateway from the east to the Mediterranean, Syria, Canaan, and Egypt. Mari became wealthy by taxing the goods that passed through it. Archaeologists have found twenty-five thousand cuneiform documents, mostly letters, in the palace of Mari.Third-millennium Mari was also known through its art. *Art of the First Cities: The Third Millennium B.C. from the Mediterranean to the Indus,* ed. Aruz, 153–55, 161–62, nos. 92–93, 104. Ilse Seibert, *Women in the Ancient Near East,* plates 9, 12.

155. Abraham Malamat, *Mari and the Early Israelite Experience,* 34–37. The population of Mari was a mixture of settled and seminomadic tribes. In Mari, the settlement process was synchronic; that is, urban and seminomadic tribes lived at the same time and place, but in two very different lifestyles. Sociologists call the lifestyle of seminomadic tribes that inhabited the lands surrounding a city-state "enclosed nomadism."

156. The Mari documents were written between 1810 and 1760. Kuhrt, *Ancient Near East,* 1:95. J. N. Postgate, *Early Mesopotamia: Society and Economy at the Dawn of History,* 49. Malamat, *Mari and the Early Israelite Experience,* 6. The earlier documents date from the rule of Yasmakh-Addu, the incompetent younger son of the Assyrian king Shamshi-Adad I. Adad was the Akkadian (East Semitic) form of the god-name; Addu, the Amorite (West Semitic) form. Dalley, *Mari and Karana,* 32. Oates, *Babylon,* 56, 62–65; 62, fig. 42: wall painting in palace of investiture of Zimri-Lim; 63, fig. 43: diagram of palace of Zimri-Lim, which had 260 rooms. Seibert, *Women in the Ancient Near East,* 29: relief of woman or goddess smelling a flower (Mari, palace of Zimri-Lim).

157. Frayne, *Old Babylonian Period,* 608–10, nos. 3–6. Bernard F. Batto, *Studies on Women at Mari,* 51. Malamat, *Mari and the Early Israelite Experience,* 8, Yakhmama, daughter of King Yakhdun-Lim, sister of Zimri-Lim, 11: women's quarters in Mari palace. Some scholars avoid the Arabic word "harem" because it evokes connotations from later Islamic and Turkish customs. This work will use the word sparingly to denote both the place in a palace where the king's women resided and the king's women who lived in this place. This is very different from the practice of polygyny by Sumerian kings, where each of the king's women had a legal status as wife or consort. Each was named, had a real relationship with the king, and performed public functions. The harem, which first appeared with Amorite kings, was a collection of nameless women, kept locked up together for the sexual pleasure of the king. Women of the harem had no public role and were the chattel of the king. Many such women were war captives. Wolfgang Heimpel, *Letters to the King of Mari,* 251, letter 26.197; 256, letter 26.204; 282, letter 26.277.

158. Frayne, *Old Babylonian Period,* 617–18, no. 4. Shibtu was the king's primary wife. She was called a *kezertum.* This was a nonpriestly office associated with the cult of Ishtar and with the offices of *shugitu* and *kharimtu,* all of which had sexual roles. The title meant a woman who had her hair curled a certain way. In one text, a king sent for a pretty *kezertu.* They were often listed with musicians and associated with the lamentation over the bull god in Uruk. On ration lists in Mari, they were listed before *sekretu,* women scribes, and apprentice singers. Henshaw, *Female and Male,* 197–200.

159. Batto, *Studies on Women at Mari,* 9–11, 13–20, 26–28. The king changed his mind and chose the women for his harem himself. Zimri-Lim had been in exile in Aleppo (Yamhad) while Shamshi-Adad controlled Mari. There he met Shibtu, the daughter of the king of Aleppo. He did not marry her until after he had regained the throne of his father at Mari. Malamat, *Mari and the Early Israelite Experience,* 12. Postgate, *Early Mesopotamia,* 60, text 3.3: letter written by Shibtu on sealing the royal archives. Dalley, *Mari and Karana,* 72, 121 (Naname). Heimpel, *Letters to the King of Mari,* 246, letter 185; 257–60, letters 26.207, 208, 211, 213, 214; 267, letter 26.236.

160. Shibtu had her own seal with one exception: Zimri-Lim kept the seal to the wine storage room. He lent it to Shibtu when he needed some wine sent to him, but she had to return the seal to the king. Sasson, " King Hammurabi of Babylon," in *Civilizations of the Ancient Near East,* ed. Sasson, 2:910–11. Frayne, *Old Babylonian Period,* 627–28, no. 7: seal of Shibtu. Letters published in J.-M. Durand, *Archives épistolaires de Mari* I/1, 264–66, 368–69, 440–41, nos. 100b, 185b, 212. The king was frequently absent on military campaigns. Zimri-Lim had been an ally of Hammurabi and had dispatched his own troops to Babylon to help Hammurabi conquer Larsa in the south. Heimpel, *Letters to the King of Mari,* 246–47, letter 26.185; 259–60, letter 26.212.

161. Frayne, *Old Babylonian Period,* 628, 637, nos. 8, 2017. Both were called *geme* of Zimri-Lim.

162. Batto, *Studies on Women at Mari,* 11, 21–23. In one ration list in Mari she was named after Shibtu; in another, after the royal daughters. Another secondary wife, Yatar-Aya, was the next name on the ration list, and she received the same allotment of oil as Damkhurasi. Both received more oil than the king's daughters and sister.

163. Batto, *Studies on Women at Mari,* 50–51. Lafont, in *La Femme dans le Proche-Orient Antique,* 115, 117. Ibbatum married the ruler of Andarig. She wrote to her father defending her husband's actions.

164. Batto, *Studies on Women at Mari,* 37–42. Lafont, in *La Femme dans le Proche-Orient Antique,* 115–16. Inibsharri married the ruler of Ashlakka. Naramtum married the ruler of Eluhut. Batto, 51. Malamat, *Mari and the Early Israelite Experience,* 12. Batto, 37–42. The head covering could have been a veil designating her married status. The letter, however, used a word different from the Assyrian term for veil in the MAL.

165. Lafont, in *La Femme dans le Proche-Orient Antique,* 117–19. Kiru and Shimatum married Khaya-sumu, the ruler of Ilansura. Heimpel, *Letters to the King of Mari,* 291, letter 26.304;

298, letter 26.315; 301–3, letters 26.322, 324; 490–93, letters 10.32–34, 10.135; 498, letter 14.118. One letter announced that Kiru had borne a son. Heimpel, *Letters,* 312, letter 26.352. It is possible that the marriage to Kiru took place because Shimatum had failed to bear a son. Shimatum wrote letters about dreams and what to name girl children. D. Charpin in *Archives épistolaires de Mari I/2,* ed. Charpin et al., 44. Shimatum complained that Kiru had taken her gardener. Kiru complained that their husband had taken her slave woman and given her to Shimatum. Dalley, *Mari and Karana,* 108. W. H. Römer, *Frauenbriefe über Religion, Politik und Privatleben in Mari,* 31, 33. Shimatum also wrote to Zimri-Lim, giving him political reports. Batto spelled the name Shibatum and presented a different picture of the relationships, describing Kiru as the first wife and queen (*Studies on Women at Mari,* 13, 42–48). Charpin admits that there is no other evidence of a king giving two daughters to the same vassal king. Another daughter, Naramtum, was also in an unhappy political marriage. Batto, 51.

166. Batto, *Studies on Women at Mari,* 48–50. Lafont, in *La Femme dans le Proche-Orient Antique,* 117. Tizpatum married the ruler of Shuna.

167. Batto, *Studies on Women at Mari,* 50, notes that all three were in political marriages (*marrat sharrim*). Lafont, in *La Femme dans le Proche-Orient Antique,* 116–17. Khazala married the ruler of Shuda.

168. It is not certain whether this was the same Inibshina who was the sister of Zimri-Lim, or another woman of the same name. Kuhrt, *Ancient Near East,* 1:105–6. Römer, *Frauenbriefe über Religion, Politik und Privatleben in Mari,* 80. Batto, *Studies on Women at Mari,* 59–61. She was listed after the king's daughters in the ration lists. The position of unsealing and resealing the archives was similar to that of Shibtu, although Shibtu had greater authority. Unpublished texts from Mari name a woman Inibshina who made large business transactions in grain and who may have been the wife of a governor.

169. Batto, *Studies on Women at Mari,* 64–72. The prophets came to her with their prophecies, and even the temple administrator reported his dreams to her. The grain contributions may have been a form of income tax. Dalley, *Mari and Karana,* 101, 132. Her letters began with the same formulae as those of Shibtu. Those of Addu-duri focused more on the cult and temple furnishings. She sent her own dream and the prophecy of a woman temple ecstatic to the king, warning him not to trust the king of Eshnunna. Harris, *Gender and Aging in Mesopotamia,* 113.

170. Batto, *Studies on Women at Mari,* 72–73 (Amadugga). Dalley, *Mari and Karana,* 88–89.

171. Malamat, *Mari and the Early Israelite Experience,* 94. A dream prophet was different from a prophet as such. Batto, *Studies on Women at Mari,* 111–13. The only other information on the *qadishtu* was that she was a member of a northern tribe.

172. Batto, *Studies on Women at Mari,* 79–85. Heimpel, *Letters to the King of Mari,* 244, letters 26.178, 179; 267–68, letters 26.237, 238, 240. The governor first prepared rooms previously used by weavers and artisans. Then he decided the site was too close to the palace, took more omens, and prepared the former room of the pastry cook for the priestess. Lafont, in *La Femme dans le Proche-Orient Antique,* 120.

173. Ibid., 85–88.

174. Ibid., 93–102. Erishti-Aya lived too far from Mari for any visits with her family. Daughters of the kings of Babylon were *naditu* priests in the cloister at Sippar.

175. Ibid., 119–25. Quotation from Römer, *Frauenbrief,* 31, translated by Malamat, *Mari and the Early Israelite Experience,* 91. Karel van der Toorn, "From the Oral to the Written: The Case of Old Babylonian Prophecy," in *Writings and Speech in Israelite and Ancient Near Eastern Prophecy,* ed. Ben Zvi and Floyd, 220–32. Prophecies were transmitted with a lock of hair and a piece of the hem of her garment as proof of the identity of the prophet. There is little evidence about women prophets in the OB empire. Prophecy was oral, and there were many reasons why it was not written down, written but not preserved, preserved but later destroyed, or preserved and not found.

176. Dalley, *Mari and Karana,* 53, 72–73, 83, 93, 99, 109–10. One ration list had 35 senior, 14 junior, and 7 "very junior" women musicians.

177. Batto, *Studies on Women at Mari,* 5, 137–38. Dalley, *Mari and Karana,* 100, 104. At least one tablet attested to women owning land. W. G. Lambert, "The Language of Mari," in *La civilisation de Mari,* ed. Kupper, 30.The language of Mari was closer to Old Babylonian than to Assyrian.

178. Dalley, *Mari and Karana,* 20, 25–26, 36–44, 53, 62, 82–87, 101–5, 126, 172. The site of Karana is called Tell ar-Rimah. The people of Karana worshiped the Babylonian gods Shamash and Marduk.

179. Stol, *Letters from Yale,* 42–43, 82–83, 90–91, 94–95, 142–45, 148–49, letters 58, 144, 148, 240 (travel), 129, 230 (honor women).

180. Stol, "The Care of the Elderly in the Old Babylonian Period," in *Care of the Elderly in the Ancient Near East,* ed. Stol and Vleeming, 101. Stol, *Letters from Yale,* 80–81, 140–41, letters 127, 225.

181. Heimpel, *Letters to the King of Mari,* 275, letter 26.254.

182. Raymond Westbrook, *Studies in Biblical and Cuneiform Law,* 14.

183. Heimpel, *Letters to the King of Mari,* 265, letter 26.232.

184. Heimpel, *Letters to the King of Mari,* 422, letter 27.32.

185. Stol, *Letters from Yale,* 66–69, 134–35, 162–65, 168–69, letters 104, 215, 270, 279. The text of the last letter is quite fragmentary. It is not possible to tell whether the distrainees were men or women. The writer seems to have entrusted the silver to another man, who was supposed to deliver it but had not.

186. Heimpel, *Letters to the King of Mari,* 399, letters 26.518, 519: in another raid near Asshur, the same tribe took captive one hundred persons and fifty cattle.

187. Heimpel, *Letters to the King of Mari,* 478, letter 2.26.

188. Heimpel, *Letters to the King of Mari,* 490, letter 10.29.

189. Heimpel, *Letters to the King of Mari,* 343, letter 26.402.

190. Heimpel, *Letters to the King of Mari,* 440, letter 27.85.

191. Heimpel, *Letters to the King of Mari,* 412, letter 27.2.

192. Stol, *Letters from Yale,* 34–37, letter 49. An *ex parte* communication between a party and the judge would not be permitted in a court today.

193. *Ancient Near Eastern Texts,* 218 (reign of Sumulael). This is another example of the principle of *res judicata.*

194. *Ancient Near Eastern Texts,* 543-44, text A. The lot was about 133 square feet. The mayor was also chief judge of the city.

195. *Ancient Near Eastern Texts,* 544, text B. This time he challenged four women over the same will. Three of the women were *naditu* priests named Lamassi, Beltani, and Iltani. The fourth was the adopted daughter in the first case. Neither text defines the exact status of the daughter. She was probably a temple functionary of some type and already lived in the temple compound as the daughter of the woman priest. This case shows that the Babylonians were serious about enforcing the principle of *res judicata.*

196. Gabriela Voet and Karel Van Lerberghe, "A Long Lasting Life," in *DUMU-E2-DUB-BA-A: Studies in Honor of Ake Sjöberg,* ed. Behrens et al., 525–29.

197. Harris, *Ancient Sippar,* 25. She had twelve sheqels worth less land.

198. Ibid., 128.

199. Postgate, *Early Mesopotamia,* 279, text 15.4. The specific religious office of the plaintiff in the first case was not given. The defendant must have been a *naditu* of Marduk, since she was married.

200. Postgate, *Early Mesopotamia,* 282. Stol, *Letters from Yale,* 16–19, letter 25.

201. Harris, *Ancient Sippar*, 313 (Sippar, reign of Apil-Sin). Stol, "Care of the Elderly in the Old Babylonian Period," 101.

202. Batto, *Studies on Women at Mari*, 61–64. Dalley, *Mari and Karana*, 102–3 (Mari).

203. Driver and Miles, *Babylonian Laws*, 1:63–64. Yitschak Sefati and Jacob Klein, "The Role of Women in Mesopotamian Witchcraft," in *Sex and Gender in the Ancient Near East*, ed. Parpola and Whiting, 571–73. These authors found only five OB texts on witchcraft, and all the witches were female. Witches were believed to have superterrestrial powers and could be defeated only by the gods. M. J. Geller, "A New Piece of Witchcraft," in *DUMU-E2-DUB-BA-A: Studies in Honor of Ake Sjöberg*, ed. Behrens et al., 194–200: OB copy of incantation from Nippur.

204. Heimpel, *Letters to the King of Mari*, 297, letter 26.314.

205. Heimpel, *Letters to the King of Mari*, 419, letter 27.25. The text is fragmentary at this point.

206. Heimpel, *Letters to the King of Mari*, 274–75, letter 26.253. The procedure was irregular because the soldiers had not brought a written tablet of instructions. The writer of the letter to the king stated that next time accused persons from elsewhere were brought to him, written instructions should be provided.

207. Stanley D. Walters, "The Sorceress and her Apprentice," *Journal of Cuneiform Studies* 23 (1970): 27–38. Stol, *Letters from Yale*, 162–63, letters 268, 269. Postgate, *Early Mesopotamia*, 277. Theft of seed instead of planting it was punished by amputation of a hand or multifold restitution of grain; if the offender could not pay the penalty, he or she was dragged around the field by oxen. See LH 253, 255–56. Unfortunately no subsequent text tells the outcome of the case.

208. Kuhrt, *Ancient Near East*, 1:106, adopts the interpretation that the woman had been a prostitute before her marriage. The text merely states that she had sex with a father, whom she married, and his son. These facts are more suggestive of incest than prostitution. The translation of Heimpel, *Letters to the King of Mari*, 386, letter 26.488, makes no mention of prostitution.

209. Heimpel, *Letters to the King of Mari*, 274, letter 26.252.

210. Heimpel, *Letters to the King of Mari*, 295–96, letter 26.312.

211. *Ancient Near Eastern Texts*, 544. Harris, *Ancient Sippar*, 21. The second offense was also from a marriage contract. In such cases, contract clauses were used to modify the law. Frymer-Kensky, "Gender and Law: An Introduction," in *Gender and Law in the Hebrew Bible and the Ancient Near East*, ed. Matthews et al., 24.

212. The woman was a *shugitu*. Batto suggests that the problem with the *shugitu* might have been that Zimri-Lim kept her as a hostage to control her father, who was not trusted by Zimri-Lim (*Studies on Women at Mari*, 108–13).

213. Heimpel, *Letters to the King of Mari*, 272.

214. Samuel Greengus, "Legal and Social Institutions of Ancient Mesopotamia," in *Civilizations of the Ancient Near East*, ed. Sasson, 1:474. J.-M. Durand, *Archives épistolaires de Mari I/2*, "L'Ordalie," 509–39. Driver and Miles, *Babylonian Laws*, 1:64.

215. Harris, *Ancient Sippar*, 133. The shaving of part of the head was sometimes used as a symbol of slavery. The arms might have been stretched out on a sort of stock. The amputation of body parts was a sign of a significant offense. A man wrote a letter of complaint about a building project and the poor quality of the workers. He mentioned that ears and necks were being cut off to communicate that it had become a state of emergency. Stol, *Letters from Yale*, 160–61, letter 264.

216. The Kassite dynasty lasted from about 1590 to 1155. The name *Kassite* comes from the Akkadian *kasshu*. Kassite migrations were attested as early as 1770. The Kassite language is not related to any known language and was not a written language. The Kassites learned to speak Babylonian, and scribes wrote documents in Sumerian and Old Akkadian. Kuhrt, *Ancient Near East*, 1:332–33, 348. D. Charpin, "The History of Ancient Mesopotamia: An Overview," in *Civi-*

lizations of the Ancient Near East, ed. Sasson, 2:819. The last Kassite king was killed in battle against Elam in 1155. Walter Sommerfeld, "The Kassites of Ancient Mesopotamia: Origins, Politics, and Culture," in *Civilizations of the Ancient Near East,* ed. Sasson, 2:917, 921, 926. Boundary stones were called *kudurru.* The Kassite kings supported the collection and copying by scribes of Sumerian and OB literature. William W. Hallo, "Nippur Originals," in *DUMU-E2-DUB-BA-A: Studies in Honor of Ake Sjöberg,* ed. Behrens et al., 239. Gwendolyn Leick, *The Babylonians,* 43, 46, 49.

217. Letter from Pharaoh Amenophis III to Kassite king, inquired about his "wives." Kuhrt, *Ancient Near East,* 1:4, 342, 344. Egypt often sent gifts of gold, which they mined. Prices at this time began to be measured in gold instead of silver.

218. Kuhrt, *Ancient Near East,* 1:335–37. The girl was "one half cubit in size" (if taken literally, approximately nine inches or twenty-five cm) at the time of sale. The girl's father and mother, Agargarutu, were both named. They signed the contract with their fingernail impressions in lieu of seals, which indicates that ordinary woman and men did not have the legal authority to own and use seals. The use of fingernail impressions began in the MB period. Greengus, "Legal and Social Institutions of Ancient Mesopotamia," in *Civilizations of the Ancient Near East,* ed. Sasson, 1:475. The sale of young girls as brides was also practiced in Nuzi and in Middle and Late Assyria.

219. Kuhrt, *Ancient Near East,* 1:340.

220. Ibid., 1:347–48. The work is known as "Let Me Praise the Lord of Wisdom" and the speaker resembled Job in the Hebrew Bible.

221. *Ancient Near Eastern Texts,* 219. MB (Kassite dynasty, about 1240). The amount of bail was high: thirteen and one-half sheqels of gold. The legible parts of the text indicate that the man may have been released when he received the bail money, because his wife was present and the money was given to them both. There was no indication that the wife was in prison. The text is quite fragmentary.

222. Kuhrt, *Ancient Near East,* 1:376, 378. Nabu-kudurri'usur I ruled from 1126 to 1105. He called his daughter *entu,* high priest. The second dynasty of Isin ruled from about 1155 to 1027. From 1050 to 905 there are almost no sources. About this time, the Euphrates River changed its course and left many of the southern cities uninhabited.

223. Chaldean (Kaldu) tribes gained control of the southern Euphrates. Aramean tribes came from the northwest and settled on the middle Euphrates and southern Tigris. The Aramaic language began to be used in the Phoenician-Ugaritic alphabet, which had a letter for each consonant, and thus was more functional and easier to write. By the mid-first millennium, this alphabet became the standard writing system of the ancient Near East and of the Persian empire, and it was also used to write Hebrew. Aramaic writings were generally on papyrus or parchment, which disintegrated. For the most part, only cuneiform tablets survive from this period. Kuhrt, *Ancient Near East,* 2:582–87.

224. Grant Frame, *Rulers of Babylonia: From the Second Dynasty of Isin to the End of Assyrian Domination (1157–612 BC),* 120–21, no. 3.14–15, 44–45. The king of Babylon was Nabu-shu-ma'ishkun, of Chaldean descent, who bragged about destroying cities, burning captives alive, and deporting inhabitants, all of which were characteristic of Middle and Late Assyrian kings. He also deported citizens of Babylon and their families to the steppes and looted and then destroyed their homes (3.16–17).

225. Kuhrt, *Ancient Near East,* 2:577, 582–87, 614–15. The Assyrian kings Sin-akhe'eriba (Sennakherib) and Asshur-akhu'iddina (Esarhaddon) ruled both Assyria and Babylon. Assyrian kings practiced deportation of conquered peoples on a large scale. According to Assyrian sources, LA kings Tukulti'apil-Esharra III (Tiglathpileser), Salmanu-ashared V (Shalmaneser) and Sharru-kin II (Sargon) deported more than 500,000 people from Babylonia between 745

and 702. J. A. Brinkman, *Prelude to Empire: Babylonian Society and Polititcs, 747–626 B.C.*, 20. The Babylonian tradition of the rights and privileges of the citizens of Babylon and Nippur was so strong that the LA king Asshur-akhu'iddina (Esarhaddon) acknowledged them and wrote them down. No citizen of Babylon or Nippur could be put to death without the approval of the assembly. This made it difficult for a foreign king to execute a Babylonian.

226. The sons of Asshur-akhu'iddina (Esarhaddon) were Shamash-shumukin, who ruled Babylonia, and Asshur-bani'apli (Asshurbanipal), king of Assyria, who ruled Babylon through a puppet king after the death of his brother. Kuhrt, *Ancient Near East*, 2:576, 587–88.

227. Ibid., 2:586–87. See below on women in ancient Assyria.

228. Amélie Kuhrt, "Non-Royal Women in the Late Babylonian Period," in *Women's Earliest Records*, ed. Lesko, 216. Manfred Dietrich, *The Babylonian Correspondence of Sargon and Sennakherib*, 76, fig. 11: drawing from Assyrian palace relief of Assyrian soldiers cutting down date palms in Dilbat (reign of Sennakherib).

229. The wealth of temples was great. The temple in Uruk alone owned about 6,000 cattle and 125,000 sheep. Every Babylonian citizen paid a tithe to a temple. LB kings struggled to limit the power of the priests by placing royal governors, commissioners, overseers, accountants, and scribes in the temple administration. King Nabu-kudurri'usur II (Nebukhadrezzar) and his successors "borrowed" temple slaves for their building projects. King Nabu-naid (Nabonidus) collected a fixed amount of temple produce, rent for land, and taxes. M. A. Dandamayev, "State and Temple in Babylonia in the First Millennium B.C.," in *State and Temple Economy in the Ancient Near East*, ed. Lipinski, 589–95.

230. Nabu-apil'usur (Nabopolassar) was the first LB king. His son, Nabu-kudurri'usur II (Nebukhadrezzar) conquered the Egyptian army at Karkemish in 605, forcing Egypt out of western Asia. Nabu-kudurri'usur II twice conquered Jerusalem and brought its kings, Jehoiachin and Zedekiah, to Babylon. Zedekiah had been appointed by the Babylonians but later rebelled. He was blinded and deported and Judah became a province of the Babylonian empire. 2 Kings 24:10–12; 25:1–7. Kuhrt, *Ancient Near East*, 2:589–93. There was a separation of 970 years between the OB and LB periods (1595–626). During most of those years, Babylonia had been under foreign rule. The collection and restoration of OB texts under the Kassites enabled the Babylonians who remained in the city and the deportees who returned to retain the memory of the previous high civilization of Old Babylonia and the Laws of King Hammurabi.

231. Greengus cites a LB king, probably Nabu-kudurri'usur II, who claimed to have "written down laws and judgments, pleasing to the Lord Marduk, set down for the good of the all the people" ("Legal and Social Institutions of Ancient Mesopotamia," in *Civilizations of the Ancient Near East*, ed. Sasson, 1:471). Driver and Miles base their dating of the Late Babylonian Laws (abbreviated LBL) on legal practices in LBL 5 and 9, which were unknown before this period. Although written more than a thousand years later, the LBL show familiarity with the LH through use of the same legal principles and terminology. Roth, "Mesopotamian Legal Traditions and the Laws of Hammurabi," *Chicago-Kent Law Review* 71 (1995): 20. There was a LB library in the temple at Sippar. J. Black and W. Tait, "Archives and Libraries in the Ancient Near East," in *Civilizations in the Ancient Near East*, ed. Sasson, 4:2007. The language of the LBL was heavily Aramaized Babylonian. The numbering of the laws used here is that of Roth and Driver and Miles. Since the extant text contains so few laws, it is impossible to determine whether the original attempted any degree of completeness or contained reforms of older laws or royal legislation.

232. LBL 8a, 9. Roth, *Law Collections*, 146–47. *Ancient Near Eastern Texts*, 197. Driver and Miles, *Babylonian Laws*, 1:340–41, 2:342–43. The LBL changed the institutions and terminology of legal marriage. Martha Roth, "Marriage and Matrimonial Prestations in First Millennium B.C. Babylonia," in *Women's Earliest Records*, ed. Lesko, 225, 246–48, 252.

233. LBL 10. Roth, *Law Collections*, 147. *Ancient Near Eastern Tests*, 197. Driver and Miles, *Babylonian Laws*, 2:342–43.

234. LBL 12. Roth, *Law Collections*, 147. *Ancient Near Eastern Texts*, 197. Driver and Miles, *Babylonian Laws*, 2:342–43.

235. LBL 13. Roth, *Law Collections*, 147–48. *Ancient Near Eastern Texts*, 197. Driver and Miles, *Babylonian Laws*, 2:344–45. There is a space at the end of the last line. It is possible that the original included other property besides the settlement. The term translated "remarry" was literally "enter the house of another man." This law is very different from the OB document that required that a widow could take nothing, not even her cloak, when she left her deceased husband's house to remarry.

236. LBL 15. Roth, *Law Collections*, 148. *Ancient Near Eastern Texts*, 198. Driver and Miles, *Babylonian Laws*, 2:344–45. Roth and Driver and Miles translate *mare* as "sons." *Ancient Near Eastern Texts* translates it "children." Unmarried sisters were entitled to continue living in their father's house until marriage or death.

237. LBL 6. Roth, *Law Collections*, 145. *Ancient Near Eastern Texts*, 197. Driver and Miles, *Babylonian Laws*, 2:338–39. Roth and *Ancient Near Eastern Texts* have one slave woman; Driver and Miles translate it in the plural. The LBL did not discuss women victims of crimes.

238. LBL 7. Roth, *Law Collections*, 145–46, 149 n. 7. *Ancient Near Eastern Texts*, 197. Driver and Miles, *Babylonian Laws*, 2:326–27, 338–41. The interpretation cited above is by Roth. Another interpretation, by T. J. Meek in *Ancient Near Eastern Texts* and Driver and Miles, is that the woman took plants from a field, or wood from a boat, or an oven belonging to another. This interpretation reduces the offense to theft. The penalty was triple restitution to the owner. Driver and Miles add "shoots," immature plants on which the harvest would depend. Each type of property listed was the means for a person to earn a living: by farming, fishing, baking, or making pottery. Only Roth has the second clause about the door of the house and the death penalty. Elsewhere in ancient Near Eastern law, the death penalty was standard for crimes of magic, sorcery, and witchcraft.

239. Kuhrt, "Non-Royal Women in the Late Babylonian Period," in *Women's Earliest Records*, ed. Lesko, 219, 221–23. No comprehensive royal archives have been found. The two main business firms were those of the Egibi (690–480) and Murashu (fifth century) families. The archives of these businesses contain information about wealthy women and slave women. The Late Babylonian Chronicles have been called "among the finest examples of historical writing in . . . the ancient Near East." J. A. Brinkman, "The Babylonian Chronicle Revisited," in *Lingering Over Words: Studies in Ancient Near Eastern Literature in Honor of William L. Moran*, ed. Abusch et al., 73, 74–75. He notes that it included battles lost and mistakes made, which were not found in Assyrian annals. The Hebrew Bible documents the capture of Jerusalem and deportation of its people. 2 Kings 24–25. The Greek historian Herodotos traveled in Babylonia and wrote his *History* in the latter half of the fifth century. Daniel C. Snell, *Life in the Ancient Near East: 3100–332 B.C.E.*, 101. Berossos was a hellenized Babylonian priest who wrote in poor Greek in the early third century for the Seleukid king. George Roux, "The Great Enigma of the Cemetary at Ur," in Bottéro, *Everyday Life in Mesopotamia*, 9. Roth notes tens of thousands of cuneiform tablets not yet published, including many legal documents, such as marriage and dowry contracts, pledges, loans, sales, wills, and inheritance records ("Marriage and Matrimonial Prestations," 245–46). Out of fifty thousand named persons in the published documents, only 2 percent were women.

240. Kuhrt, *Ancient Near East*, 2:589–93. Nabu-kudurri'usur's (Nebukhadrezzar) son-in-law, general Nergal-sharru'usur (Neriglissar), an Aramaean, succeeded him as king. Paul-Alain Beaulieu, "King Nabonidus and the Neo-Babylonian Empire," in *Civilizations of the Ancient Near East*, ed. Sasson, 2:972. The title "House of Palace Women" was common in Assyrian palaces, where it designated a harem.

241. Roth, "Marriage and Matrimonial Prestations," 248–49. Roth examined ten LB marriage contracts ("'She Will Die by the Iron Dagger': Adultery and Neo-Babylonian Marriage," *Journal of the Economic and Social History of the Orient* 31[1988]: 187–88). The bride was given by her father in two contracts, by her mother in one, her brother in two, her mother and her brother in three, and by herself in one. In *Babylonian Marriage Agreements: 7th to 3d Centuries B.C.*, Roth reviewed eighteen marriage contracts from the LB period (pp. 37–73). The bride was given by herself in one, by her father in six, by her mother in five, by her brother(s) in four, by her mother and sister in one and by her mother and brother in one. In one contract, the father adopted the groom. Snell states that middle-aged men married young girls, and wives were intended to survive their husbands to take care of the property and the children (*Life in the Ancient Near East*, 102).

242. Ronald H. Sack, *Neriglissar—King of Babylon*, 151, no. 13: the priest-administrator of a major temple made a written request to King Nergal-sharru'usur to marry his daughter, Gigtum, and the king responded in writing. Karen Rhea Nemet-Nejat, "Women in Ancient Mesopotamia," in *Women's Roles in Ancient Civilizations*, ed. Vivante, 90–91. The virginity clause also required no prior marriages.

243. Kuhrt, *Ancient Near East*, 2:610. Roth, "Marriage and Matrimonial Prestations," 246–50, 252–55. LB settlements also included money, jewelry, and land. Roth found gifts given to the bride's family in only three documents (*Babylonian Marriage Agreements*, 7–11, 37–38, 50–56, 58–59, 64–68; eadem, "The Dowries of the Women of the Itti-Marduk-Balatu Family," *Journal of the American Oriental Society* 111 [1991]: 19–37). Roth documented dowry settlements for this branch of the Egibi family for three generations near the end of the LB period.

244. Roth, *Babylonian Marriage Agreements*, 41–42, no. 3 (Babylon, reign of Nabu-apil'usur). Kuhrt notes that adoption was more common than polygyny ("Non-Royal Women in the Late Babylonian Period," 225–26).

245. Kuhrt, "Non-Royal Women," 226–27.

246. Roth, "Marriage and Matrimonial Prestations," 251. There are no extant records of actual divorces, only divorce clauses in marriage contracts. Divorce was mentioned in nine of eighteen marriage contracts. The husband had to pay six minas of silver as compensation to the wife and return her settlement. Roth, *Babylonian Marriage Agreements*, 13–14, 37–40, 42–52, 64–70.

247. Roth, "Marriage and Matrimonial Prestations," 251. There were many court cases in which widows claimed their settlements from their deceased husbands' estates.

248. King Nabu-naid (Nabonidus) ruled for sixteen years, until the Persians took Babylon. Kuhrt, *Ancient Near East*, 2:597–600. Amélie Kuhrt, "Nabonidus and the Babylonian Priesthood," in *Pagan Priests*, ed. Beard and North, 130 n. 32, 138, 150. *Ancient Near Eastern Texts*, 562–63. There were numerous inscriptions of King Nabu-naid and a chronicle of his reign.

249. Kuhrt, *Ancient Near East*, 2:598–600. He used Sumerian terminology, giving his daughter an *en* name, like the Sumerian women high priests. The meaning of "priest" in the LB period was not well defined. The fact that Nabu-naid was head of the state religion and attempted to substitute a different god, Sin, for Marduk, the god of Babylon, created a religious crisis. The traditional rites of Babylon were not celebrated. In the eyes of the people, this weakened the city and the empire, and they regarded Nabu-naid as a heretic. The situation became critical and Nabu-naid went into exile at Taima, in northern Arabia, for ten years. In his absence, his son Belshar'usur (Belshazzar), ruled the empire. Beaulieu, "King Nabonidus and the Late Babylonian Empire," in *Civilizations of the Ancient Near East*, ed. Sasson, 2:973–76.

250. *Ancient Near Eastern Texts*, 560–62. Two stelae of her autobiography were found in Harran with two similar stelae of Nabu-naid. Before Adad-guppi, only kings had written autobiographies. She wrote hers in the same royal style. Lambert, in *La Femme dans le Proche-Orient Antique*, 126. The style and format were probably provided by the scribes.

251. Kuhrt, *Ancient Near East*, 2:607–8. She died in the ninth year of his reign. *Ancient Near Eastern Texts*, 561–62.

252. G. Cagirgan and W. G. Lambert, "The Late Babylonian Kislimu Ritual for Esagil," *Journal of Cuneiform Studies* 44 (1992): 94, 98. The meaning of these ritual acts is obscure.

253. The meaning and functions of this office are unclear. Henshaw notes differences among scholars as to the role of the *sagittu*, some calling her a female *sanga*, others a musician (*Female and Male*, 24). Kuhrt, "Non-Royal Women," 221. The woman was not named, and the text focused on the ownership of her slave.

254. Kuhrt, "Nabonidus and the Babylonian Priesthood," 150–51. Temples had male secular workers, including cooks, bakers, brewers, oil pressers, fishers, herders, and gatekeepers. Kuhrt, "Non-Royal Women," 237–38. An applicant for a position as temple brewer had the purity of his mother checked. The widow of a deceased priest may have been permitted to stay in her late husband's home so that their sons would be raised within the temple. G. Van Driel, "Care of the Elderly in the Neo-Babylonian Period," in *The Care of the Elderly in the Ancient Near East*, ed. Stol and Vleeming, 172. The impurity of women through menstruation and after childbirth was first documented in a Middle Assyrian palace decree by King Tukulti-Ninurta I, who ruled from 1244 to 1208. See below MAPD.

255. Kuhrt, "Non-Royal Women," 220. A woman prophet played an important role in a major ritual in Babylon in about 670. Kuhrt, "Nabonidus and the Babylonian Priesthood," 119. Martti Nissinen defines a prophet as one who receives and transmits messages from a god without using human techniques or rituals (*Prophets and Prophecy in the Ancient Near East*, 1–2, 6).

256. *Ancient Near Eastern Texts*, 547 (thirty-second year of the reign of Nabu-kudurri'usur II, 573). The goddess was Ishtar. Kuhrt suggests that Balta was a temple prostitute ("Non-Royal Women," 235–36). Van Driel, "Care of the Elderly in the Neo-Babylonian Period," 176–77.

257. Sack, *Neriglissar—King of Babylon*, 167–68, no. 29.

258. Ronald H. Sack, *Cuneiform Documents from the Chaldean and Persian Periods*, 120–21, no. 89: Banitu-banat. The amount of barley was more than twelve hundred liters. Sack, *Neriglissar*, 230–31, no. 89: Nidintumbelit.

259. Sack, *Neriglissar*, 168–69, no. 30: Nada, 175–76, no. 36: Bazitum.

260. Kuhrt, "Non-Royal Women," 221–22, 228. Sack, *Neriglissar*, 173, no. 34: Ilat, 215–16, no. 76: Busasa. Raymond P. Dougherty, *Archives from Erech*, vol. 1, *Time of Nebuchadrezzar and Nabonidus*, 21–22, no. 35: Amata (Uruk, twenty-second year of Nabu-kudurri'usur II). Amata must have had a large household to consume so many meals. Van Driel, "Care of the Elderly in the Neo-Babylonian Period," 174. Roth, "Marriage and Matrimonial Prestations," 245. R. Campbell Thompson, *Late Babylonian Letters*, 178–79, letter 229: judges acknowledged woman's plea for judgment in a case. Contra Greengus, "Legal and Social Institutions of Ancient Mesopotamia," 475, who wrote that women had to be represented by men and could not be witnesses.

261. Greenfield, in *La Femme dans le Proche-Orient Antique*, 78–79. A husband or son was often co-owner of a woman's temple shares.

262. Van Driel, "Care of the Elderly in the Neo-Babylonian Period," 168. Kuhrt, "Non-Royal Women," 229. The man's brother and son would not take care of him. Contracts for adoption/elder care were more common than wills. Greenfield, in *La Femme dans le Proche-Orient Antique*, 76–77. Both cases were dated during the reign of Nabu-naid.

263. Kuhrt, "Non-Royal Women," 229–30. This is similar to the adoption-heirships made by celibate *naditu* priests in OB Sippar.

264. Benjamin Foster notes a great expansion of slavery in the LB period ("Western Asia in the Second Millennium," in *Women's Earliest Records*, ed. Lesko, 213). Dougherty, *Archives from Erech*, 1:22-23, no. 385 (third year of Nabu-naid). The other texts are from the reign of Nergal-sharru-usur. Sack, *Neriglissar*, 139–42, no. 1: male slave, wife, and daughter sold together; no. 2:

husband and wife sold slave, his wife, and two other slave women together; 145–46, no .7: father and mother, son-in-law, and daughter; 161–62, no. 23: Belilitum; 180–81, no. 42: Belilitu; 198–99, no. 59: Nubta.

265. Kuhrt, "Non-Royal Women," 232–33.

266. Dougherty, *Archives from Erech*, vol. 2, *Neo-Babylonian and Persian Periods*, 34, no. 195: Khussa; Uruk, fortieth year of Nabu-kudurri'usur II (Nebukhadrezzar). The text ends with the enigmatic phrase "plundering does not exist," which might possibly have a sexual connotation that a woman dedicated to the goddess could not be taken sexually. Saggs, *Greatness That Was Babylon*, 230–31. Van Driel, "Care of the Elderly in the Neo-Babylonian Period," 164–65. Women temple slaves could not be sold and were not used for sex. Dougherty, *Archives from Erech*, 1:36, no. 401: receipt for rations of flour, no. 161: garment of wool, no. 361: record of dedication of person as a temple slave (seventh year of Nabu-naid).

267. Kuhrt, "Non-Royal Women," 234.

268. Ibid.

269. Nissinen, *Prophets and Prophecy in the Ancient Near East*, 199, no. 135 (women even ate their bread there), 194, no. 132: LB document concerning litigation over a house claimed by her son was signed in the presence of Nannaya-belbiti, described as daughter of x, wife of y, and mother of z. In a collection of 104 sale documents from the reign of Nergal-sharru'usur, only 23 even mention women, some of whom were slaves. Sack, *Neriglissar*, 139–241.

270. Kuhrt, "Non-Royal Women," 233. Greenfield, in *La Femme dans le Proche-Orient Antique*, 77. Reign of Nabu-naid.

271. Greenfield, in *La Femme dans le Proche-Orient Antique*, 77.

272. Kuhrt, *Ancient Near East*, 2:610. Kuhrt, "Non-Royal Women," 230–33. Prostitution in ancient Babylonia was different from contemporary prostitution, as were the experiences of women prostitutes.

273. Kuhrt, "Non-Royal Women," 231–32. The offense was not perceived as theft, since then the penalty would have involved immediate restitution. Greenfield, in *La Femme dans le Proche-Orient Antique*, 77. The temple had not sold her, but someone else had either taken her from the temple or found her outside the temple, and then sold her.

274. Sefati and Klein, "The Role of Women in Mesopotamian Witchcraft," in *Sex and Gender in the Ancient Near East*, ed. Parpola and Whiting, 576–78.

275. Kuhrt, "Non-Royal Women," 234; I. M. Diakonoff, "A Babylonian Pamphlet from about 700 BC," in *Studies in Honor of Benno Landsberger on His Seventy-Fifth Birthday*, ed. Güterbock and Jacobsen. There is no evidence of the existence of long-term incarceration.

276. Kuhrt, "Non-Royal Women," 227.

277. The adultery clause generally preceded or followed the divorce clause, and both favored the husband. Roth examined twenty-four marriage contracts written between 635 and 523. Ten of these had an adultery clause. The husband was not mentioned in the clause, but since the wife was caught in the act, he would have had the opportunity to kill her with his dagger ("'She Will Die by the Iron Dagger': Adultery and Neo-Babylonian Marriage," *Journal of the Economic and Social History of the Orient* 31 [1988]: 186–206). The insertion of the clause in the marriage contract gave the husband impunity for so doing. Roth studied eighteen marriage contracts from the LB period (*Babylonian Marriage Agreements*, 37–40, 44–49, 69–71). Five had clear adultery clauses (nos. 1, 2, 5, 6, 17), with two more fragmentary (nos. 11, 15). All of the contracts that had adultery clauses prescribed the penalty of death by the iron dagger (although no. 5 just had dagger). Six of the contracts had serious gaps or were illegible where the clause would have been.

278. Sack, *Neriglissar*, 199–201, no. 60. There many have been other penalties, but there are lacunae in the text.

279. Martha Roth notes that the state had jurisdiction, although the plaintiffs were claiming that they belonged to the temple ("A Case of Contested Status," in *DUMU-E2-DUB-BA-A:*

Studies in Honor of Ake Sjöberg, ed. Behrens et al., 481–89). The initial contract was dated in 538, the year after the Persians took Babylonia. The trial was held eight years later. The judges and scribe had Babylonian names. It is unlikely the matter would have been handled differently nine years earlier.

280. 2 Kings 25:1–7. Jeremiah 39:1–7. King Nabu-kudurri'usur II (Nebukhadrezzar) himself passed sentence. The penalty resembled the curse formulae of earlier Mesopotamian kings. LL Epil.: destruction of progeny and realm. LX Epil.: obliteration and blinding of the young men of city. LH Epil.: obliteration of ruler, his dynasty and land, no progeny, dread disease. The Middle and Late Assyrian kings claimed to have blinded war captives.

281. From 539 BCE until the twentieth century CE, Mesopotamia was conquered and ruled consecutively by Achaemenid Persians, Macedonians, Hellenistic Greeks, Parthians, Sassanian Persians, Arabians, Mongols, Ottoman Turks, and the British. After only seven decades of independence, it is presently under American and British occupation.

PART THREE: ASSYRIA

1. H. W. F. Saggs, *The Might That Was Assyria,* 21–34. Amélie Kuhrt, *The Ancient Near East: C. 3000–330 B.C.,* 1:81–89. A. Kirk Grayson, *Assyrian Rulers of the Third and Second Millennia BC,* 7, 9, 12–40. The first extant inscription, on a spear head, dates from the reign of the Akkadian king Manishtushu (about 2300). A stone plaque is dated by its reference to the reign of the Ur III king Amar-Sin (twenty-first century). Both were found in the temple of the goddess at Asshur. The first Assyrian kings who left writings ruled in the twentieth century.

2. The Assyrian colony was a district within the city of Kanish (modern Kultepe, in Turkey). It enjoyed privileges regarding taxation and military conscription. Klaas R. Veenhof, "Kanesh: An Assyrian Colony in Anatolia," in *Civilizations of the Ancient Near East,* ed. Sasson, 2:867–68. Kuhrt, *Ancient Near East,* 1:90–95. Grayson, *Assyrian Rulers of the Third and Second Millennia,* 19–21. Grayson, *Assyrian Royal Inscriptions,* 1:12.72 (judges' names). Inscription by King Erishum I, written in Asshur, copy found in Kanish. Seals and inscriptions were found in Kanish and Asshur, dating from the empire of Sargon of Akkad. Godfrey R. Driver and John C. Miles, *The Assyrian Laws,* 1–3, 376–379: three fragmentary tablets of laws from the Old Assyrian I period which deal with the assembly and the process of selecting panels of judges from the assembly to hear cases.

3. The majority of the documents have not yet been published. Rivkah Harris, "Independent Women in Ancient Mesopotamia?" in *Women's Earliest Records: From Ancient Egypt and Western Asia,* ed. Lesko, 148. Most date between 1910 and 1830. The trade involved textiles and tin from Asshur for gold and silver from Asia Minor. Marc Van De Mieroop, *Cuneiform Texts and the Writing of History,* 92–95; J. N. Postgate, *Early Mesopotamia: Society and Economy at the Dawn of History,* 69 (literacy of merchants).

4. Van De Mieroop, *Cuneiform Texts and the Writing of History,* 93–98. The sons worked in towns between Asshur and Kanish, safeguarding the shipments. There were about fifteen hundred merchant traders in Asshur, which had a population of fifteen thousand at this time.

5. Westbrook notes that the first document was styled as a contract for marriage or concubinage but used the vocabulary of slavery ("The Female Slave," in *Gender and Law in the Hebrew Bible and the Ancient Near East,* ed. Matthews et al., 231–32). The Assyrian word for legal wife was used for the primary wife in Asshur. In the second contract, *Ancient Near Eastern Texts,* ed. Pritchard, transliterates the noun *qadiltu* as *qadishtu* (p. 543). *Qadiltu* appears several times in Assyrian documents. Many scholars concur that *qadiltu* is the Assyrian form of *qadishtu.* The religious roles of the Assyrian *qadiltu* and the Babylonian *qadishtu* were similar.

6. Klaas Veenhof, "Old Assyrian and Ancient Anatolian Evidence for the Care of the Elderly," in *The Care of the Elderly in the Ancient Near East,* ed. Stol and Vleeming, 121–25, 129–34. In Babylonia, one word had both meanings. Funeral costs could be quite high and were taken out of the estate. Westbrook, "Female Slave," 231–32.

7. Veenhof, "Old Assyrian and Ancient Anatolian Evidence," 140–41. The wife received a debt-claim of one and one-half minas of silver. The annual support of the priest daughter from her brothers was six copper minas from each. In Sumerian and Babylonian law, a daughter who was an *ugbabtu* or a *qadishtu* received a share of her father's estate either as a dowry or by inheritance. See LL 22; LH 178, 179, 181.The transliteration of *qadiltu* here and in MAL A 40 as *qadishtu* supports the inference that the office of *qadishtu* existed in the OA I and MA periods.

8. Veenhof, "Old Assyrian and Ancient Anatolian Evidence," 139–40, 156–57. The father left five minas of silver, which his sons were to lend at 30 percent interest and use the income to support Shat-Adad and her mother.

9. Ibid., 126, 137–38, 140–41. The estate of Lamassatum's late husband had been divided among their four children, but the wife, Lamassatum, was not an heir. Ishtar-lamasi had been married twice, first to an Assyrian, by whom she had children, and then to an Anatolian. Her second husband paid the funeral expenses and was reimbursed out of the estate. The title, *gubabtu,* is the Assyrian reading of the Sumerogram *nin-dingir,* Babylonian *ugbabtu.* The *ugbabtu* priests were celibate. Many traders in OA I had priest daughters who also worked in the family business.

10. *Ancient Near Eastern Texts,* 217–18. This document is from the city of Kanish and was written in the twentieth century. The settlement amount, one mina of silver, was the same as that in LH 139.

11. *Ancient Near Eastern Texts,* 218. The debt originated in Kanish, but the trial took place in Asshur. The beginning of the document listed the seals of the plaintiffs, including Akhakha. The end of the document stated that she was represented by a man who was not her brother.

12. *Ancient Near Eastern Texts,* 542. This text was found in Asia Minor and was written in the nineteenth century. One of the families in this case was the same family who appeared in the previous case. The older brothers represented their sisters and minor brothers. This indicates that women and minors did not have the legal capacity to represent themselves in the law courts. In the preceding document, T. J. Meek translates the religious office of Akhakha as "nun." In the second document, J. J. Finkelstein, in *Ancient Near Eastern Texts,* translates the office as "abbess." Both English nouns represent Western notions of monasticism, not those of the ancient Near East. While there is no evidence of monasteries of women in nineteenth-century Assyria, the cloister at Sippar in the south was flourishing at this time and its women came from many other parts of Mesopotamia. Rivkah Harris, *Ancient Sippar: A Demographic Study of an Old-Babylonian City,* 3–5.

13. Grayson, *Assyrian Rulers of the Third and Second Millennia,* 46.

14. Veenhof, "Old Assyrian and Ancient Anatolian Evidence for the Care of the Elderly," 136–40, 157.

15. *Ancient Near Eastern Texts,* 218. Robert H. Pfeiffer, *State Letters of Assyria,* 145–46, no. 199. The text noted that her grandfather had been a shepherd, which indicated her class status. It was unusual to combine the death penalty with a monetary penalty.

16. Grayson, *Assyrian Rulers of the Third and Second Millennia,* 21. Grayson, *Assyrian Royal Inscriptions,* 1:13, no. 75. The king was Erishum I (OA I, early nineteenth century). The locus of the perjury was in the court at the Step Gate.

17. King Shamshi-Adad I was the first Assyrian king use the title "king of the universe." Previous OA kings had called themselves regents of the god (Grayson, *Assyrian Royal Inscriptions,* 1:18–28, 30, no. 175, 85–86, no. 544). He was an Amorite, as were other kings of his time, including King Rim-Sin of Larsa and King Hammurabi of Babylon. Many tablets have been found from his reign. Grayson, *Assyrian Rulers of the Third and Second Millennia,* 1:47, 50–60, 67, 77–78. He

maintained his capital at Ekallatum, from which he ruled Asshur. Shamshi-Adad I attempted to revise the Assyrian King List to include his Amorite ancestors and legitimize his dynasty. Saggs, *Might That Was Assyria,* 23–25, 33–37. His proximate successors rejected him as a foreigner, a non-Assyrian, who didn't even know how to dress properly. But by the MA period, the later kings revered him, and King Salmanu-ashared I bragged that he was a descendant of Shamshi-Adad I. The OA II period came to a close during the reign of his son, Ishme-Dagan, when King Hammurabi of Babylon conquered Asshur in 1762. Robert M. Whiting, "Amorite Tribes and Nations of Second-Millennium Western Asia," in *Civilizations of the Ancient Near East,* ed. Sasson, 2:1238. The city called Arbel or Arbela, is Arbail in Akkadian, Irbil in Arabic.

18. Pierre Villard, "Shamshi-Adad and Sons: The Rise and Fall of an Upper Mesopotamian Empire," in *Civilizations of the Ancient Near East,* ed. Sasson, 2:879–80. The word *beltum* meant "queen" and may not be the proper name of a bride. Qatna was in Syria. Shamshi-Adad arranged the marriage without telling his son. Yasmakh-Adad preferred spending his time with women rather than governing the city-state. Letters from Shamshi- Adad to his son continually criticize his laziness and incompetence and tell him to grow up and govern. After the change of dynasty, Kunshimatum remained in Terqa. The governor of Terqa wrote to Zimri-Lim that Kunshimatum was sick. Bernard F. Batto, *Studies on Women at Mari,* 24–25.

19. Villard, "Shamshi-Adad and Sons," 873–74, 878–79. Grayson, *Assyrian Royal Inscriptions,* 1:26. Grayson, *Assyrian Rulers of the Third and Second Millennia,* 47–82.

20. In Mari, the status of women under Shamshi-Adad and his son was much lower than under its own dynasty, reflecting the differences between the Amorite tribes of Mari and those of the region of Asshur.

21. Michael Roaf, *Cultural Atlas of Mesopotamia and the Ancient Near East,* 140: map of MA empire. H. W. F. Saggs, *The Greatness That Was Babylon,* 219–20.

22. The MAL have been compared to the LH, but there are many differences. The LH was originally one document; the MAL were many. The LH was the work of one man, who was king, judge, and legal reformer; the MAL is a collection of laws from many kings and times. The LH was intended to be normative for future kings; the MAL was not. The LH was taught in Babylonian scribal schools, but the MAL was not part of the curriculum in Assyrian scribal schools. Babylonia in the time of Hammurabi was a highly civilized and well-developed commercial center. Assyria at the time the MAL were written was far less developed and civilized. Driver and Miles, *Assyrian Laws,* 12–15. There was a royal library at Asshur, begun in the MA period, and there were temple libraries in Nimrud and Nineveh. A fragmentary LA text from the catalogue of books in the library of King Asshur-bani-apli (Asshurbanipal) reported that there was a copy of the LH in the library. It is quite probable that it was studied by Assyrian kings. J. Black and W. Tait, "Archives and Libraries in the Ancient Near East," in *Civilizations in the Ancient Near East,* ed. Sasson, 4:2206. Martha Roth, "Mesopotamian Legal Traditions and the Laws of Hammurabi," *Chicago-Kent Law Review* 71 (1995): 20–21.

23. Martha Roth (*Law Collections from Mesopotamia and Asia Minor,* 153–54) and *Ancient Near Eastern Texts* (pp. 180, 186–88), date the copies found at Asshur in the eleventh century during the reign of Tukulti-apil-Esharra I. The earliest laws date from the fourteenth century. The laws were written in the Old Akkadian language in cuneiform script. Tablet A is the only tablet that has a copy, albeit fragmentary. The extant part of tablet B dealt with land law and inheritance and made no mention of women. The other tablets are quite fragmentary. Of the published fragments, C + G, K, and O contain information about women and A, B, C + G, F, M, and N have laws dealing with crimes.

24. MAL A 29–31,42–43. The MAL required payment of a marriage "price," whereas Sumerian and Babylonian laws required marriage "gifts." Ancient historians viewed the Assyrian requirement of a marriage price paid to the father of a bride as the sale of daughters. Herodotos *History* 1.196. Strabo 16.1.20. Both Herodotos and Strabo postulated an annual auction of girls

of marriageable age, in which rich men bid for the most beautiful, while poor men got the ugly and crippled. Herodotus noted that this custom was no longer practiced. No evidence of it has been found in Assyrian sources.

25. MAL A 42–43. Roth, *Law Collections,* 169–70. *Ancient Near Eastern Texts,* 183–84. Driver and Miles, *Assyrian Laws,* 410–11. The statement that the prospective groom already had children indicates that he had been previously married. Any part of the marriage price that was edible did not have to be returned.

26. MAL A 30. Roth, *Law Collections,* 164, 193 n. 22. *Ancient Near Eastern Texts,* 182. Driver and Miles, *Assyrian Laws,* 174–79, 399–401. The right of a father to marry the widow of his son to another of his sons was similar to the practice of levirate marriage in the Hebrew Bible, although in Assyria it was not mandatory. Judges 15:2.

27. MAL A 31. Roth, *Law Collections,* 164–65. *Ancient Near Eastern Texts,* 182. Driver and Miles, *Assyrian Laws,* 400–401.

28. MAL A 25, 26. Roth, *Law Collections,* 162–63. *Ancient Near Eastern Texts,* 182. Driver and Miles, *Assyrian Laws,* 396–99. There is a contradiction between A 25, which stated that, if the wife had no sons, the husband's brothers took the personal gifts that the deceased had given to his wife, and A 26b, which stated that the widow could keep such gifts if her deceased husband had no sons. The two laws probably came from different sources and time periods.

29. MAL B 1, K 2, O 3. Roth, *Law Collections,* 176–82, 188, 191. *Ancient Near Eastern Texts,* 185–86. Driver and Miles, *Assyrian Laws,* 426–41.

30. MAL A 46. Roth, *Law Collections,* 171–72. *Ancient Near Eastern Texts* (p. 184) and Driver and Miles (*Assyrian Laws,* 414–15) have "she shall do their work." Roth (p. 172) has "she shall do service for them."

31. MAL A 33, 46b. Roth, *Law Collections,* 165, 172. *Ancient Near Eastern Texts,* 182, 184. Driver and Miles, *Assyrian Laws,* 400–403, 414–15.

32. MAL A 28. Roth, *Law Collections,* 163. *Ancient Near Eastern Texts,* 183. Driver and Miles, *Assyrian Laws,* 398–99.

33. MAL A 34, 35. Roth, *Law Collections,* 165. *Ancient Near Eastern Texts,* 183. Driver and Miles, *Assyrian Laws,* 220–22, 402–3. Driver and Miles state that the situation in the first part of the law was marriage, indicated by the technical phrase that the widow entered the man's house (p. 221). Whatever the woman possessed became the property of the man after marriage. In the second part, the man entered the widow's house to have sex. What the man brought with him can be construed as payment for sex.

34. MAL A 36. Roth, *Law Collections,* 165–66. *Ancient Near Eastern Texts,* 183. Driver and Miles, *Assyrian Laws,* 402–5.

35. MAL A 45. Roth, *Law Collections,* 170–71. *Ancient Near Eastern Texts,* 184. Driver and Miles, *Assyrian Laws,* 412–15. Both laws, A 36 and 45, show concern that husbands should support their wives even when they were absent. The two laws are inconsistent as to the waiting period (five years or two years). It is probable that the two laws came from different sources or times and the compiler chose not to conflate them. The second law was probably later, since it laid an obligation on the state to support destitute wives. It also distinguished between feudal and nonfeudal property. If the absent husband's land was feudal, the king could give it to someone else and the husband would lose it. If the house and field were not feudal property, the wife could give them to the city as collateral for her support. Her husband could get them back by paying the full amount the city had paid for his wife's support.

36. MAL A 37, 38. Roth, *Law Collections,* 166–67. *Ancient Near Eastern Texts,* 183. Driver and Miles, *Assyrian Laws,* 405. The conditions were the same whether the wife lived in the house of her father or her husband.

37. MAL A 48. Roth, *Law Collections,* 173. *Ancient Near Eastern Texts,* 184. Driver and Miles, *Assyrian Laws,* 416–19.

38. MAL A 39. Roth, *Law Collections,* 167. *Ancient Near Eastern Texts,* 183. Driver and Miles, *Assyrian Laws,* 404–7. The full value of the girl was not necessarily the same as the marriage price, which could be higher.

39. MAL A 40. Roth, *Law Collections,* 167–69. *Ancient Near Eastern Texts,* 183. Driver and Miles, *Assyrian Laws,* 406–9. The veil was a type of scarf that covered the hair but not the face. Roth has "a married *qadiltu* woman." *Qadiltu* was the only religious office of women mentioned in the MAL. This indicates that a few women had some role in the religion, though far less than in Sumer, Old Babylonia, or Old Assyria I. Most scholars agree that *qadiltu* is a variant of the Babylonian religious office of *qadishtu,* which sometimes was linked with religious prostitution. The title is also found in Middle Assyrian Palace Decrees 1, paired with the midwife, both women professionals who lived and worked in the quarters of the king's women.

40. MAL A 41. Roth, *Law Collections,* 169. *Ancient Near Eastern Texts,* 183. Driver and Miles, *Assyrian Laws,* 408–11. If the husband died and his first wife had no sons, the sons of a veiled concubine could inherit shares of their father's estate.

41. MAL A 10. Roth, *Law Collections,* 157. *Ancient Near Eastern Texts,* 181. In ancient tribal society, the head of the household had the role of blood avenger for his family. This law provided an option for compromise, payment of blood money, so as to prevent a blood feud between the two families. Driver and Miles suggest that this is similar to the figure of the "avenger of blood" in Hebrew law (*Assyrian Laws,* 33–36). Numbers 35:19, 21. Deuteronomy 19:12. The role developed to prevent endless blood feuds between tribes. In MAL B 2, the crime of murder was resolved between the household of the murderer and that of the victim. The victim's next of kin had the option of deciding the penalty: death or compensation consisting of the murderer's entire inheritance. This law did not mention vicarious punishment of the murderer's son or daughter. If the murderer had a wife or child, they would in any case be victims of the loss of his life or estate. Roth, *Law Collections,* 176. *Ancient Near Eastern Texts,* 185.

42. MAL A 12. Roth, *Law Collections,* 157–58. *Ancient Near Eastern Texts,* 181. Driver and Miles, *Assyrian Laws,* 386–87. When the text states "they" would execute punishment, "they" generally referred to officials of the state. The numerous elements that had to be proved made it very difficult to convict a rapist who had not been caught in the act or seen by eyewitnesses.

43. MAL A 14, 15. Roth, *Law Collections,* 158. These laws are older than A 12, which did not confuse rape and adultery and handled the offense under state jurisdiction.

44. MAL A 55, 56. Roth, *Law Collections,* 174–75. *Ancient Near Eastern Texts,* 185. Driver and Miles, *Assyrian Laws,* 54–59, 422–23. The penalty of rape of the rapist's wife was vicarious punishment, not *talion,* which would have required the rape of his virgin daughter.

45. MAL A 9. Translation of Roth, *Law Collections,* 157. *Ancient Near Eastern Texts,* 181. Driver and Miles, *Assyrian Laws,* 384–85. In the translations of Roth and *Ancient Near Eastern Texts,* "they," the state, administered both penalties. Driver and Miles make the verb passive, without a subject.

46. MAL A 17. Roth, *Law Collections,* 159. *Ancient Near Eastern Texts,* 181. Driver and Miles, *Assyrian Laws,* 99–103, 390–91. All three translate "they" in the plural, implying that the state had jurisdiction. Since there was no evidence, there was no formal trial and the parties had to undergo the river ordeal.

47. MAL A 18. Roth, *Law Collections,* 159–60. *Ancient Near Eastern Texts,* 181. Driver and Miles, *Assyrian Laws,* 390–91. The penalties here are very different from the "penalty of the case," used elsewhere in cases of false accusation. Under that principle the penalty for false accusation of adultery would have been death. Roth translated what was cut off as "hair" or "beard" (pp. 159, 193 n. 16). *Ancient Near Eastern Texts* understands the "cutting off" as castration (p. 181). Driver and Miles take "cutting" to mean cutting off from the community (pp. 70–71, 391). The cutting of hair could also give the offender a slave hairlock, a public mark of slave status. The laws and penalties for false accusation of sodomy were similar. In MAL A 19, if a man falsely spread

rumors or stated in public that another man was being sodomized by many, and falsely stated that he could prove it but could not, the penalties were fifty blows with rods, one month of penal servitude, the cutting off of his hair, and a fine of one talent of lead. In MAL A 20, the penalties for committing sodomy were forcible sodomy by more than one man and castration.

48. MAL A 21, 50. Roth, *Law Collections,* 160, 173–74. *Ancient Near Eastern Texts,* 181, 184. Driver and Miles, *Assyrian Laws,* 106–14, 392–93, 418–19. In A 21, the woman was called *marat,* meaning daughter of a citizen; in A 50, *asshat,* wife of a citizen. Driver and Miles translate the first as a "lady by birth," designating social class, whereas the second refers to marital status. It may be presumed that the first woman was married, since there was no comment about her pregnancy being illegitimate.

49. MAL A 51. Roth, *Law Collections,* 174. *Ancient Near Eastern Texts,* 184. Driver and Miles, *Assyrian Laws,* 420–21.

50. MAL A 52. Roth, *Law Collections,* 174. *Ancient Near Eastern Texts,* 185. Driver and Miles, *Assyrian Laws,* 115, 420–21. Roth has "make full payment for a life," which leaves open the possibility of paying compensation instead of taking a life. *Ancient Near Eastern Texts* has "compensate with a life." Driver and Miles note that compensation was paid to the legal victim, and they know of no reference to a fine being paid to the state in this period (pp. 349–51).

51. MAL 39, C + G 2–3a-b. Roth, *Law Collections,* 167, 182–83. *Ancient Near Eastern Texts,* 186–87. Driver and Miles, *Assyrian Laws,* 323–28, 404–7. Roth has "the full value of a life" (p. 183). *Ancient Near Eastern Texts* has "compensate with a life" (p. 187). In C + G 3, the term of penal servitude was doubled, from twenty to forty days, if the pledge was sold to foreigners. The numbers of blows with rods is missing from both laws. It may also have been doubled. Driver and Miles, *Assyrian Laws,* 279–84. *Ancient Near Eastern Texts* adds "when she deserved it" (p. 184).

52. MAL A 44, C + G 3c. Roth, *Law Collections,* 170, 182–83. *Ancient Near Eastern Texts,* 186–87. Driver and Miles, *Assyrian Laws,* 284–87, 323–28, 412–13, 440–43. In A 44 and C + G 3, the pledge had been taken in full value of the debt, making the creditor the owner of the pledge. The meaning of the word "Assyrian" here is unclear. Driver and Miles suggest that it may denote a social class lower than free citizen, but higher than slave. *Assyrian Laws,* 284–88.

53. MAL A 32. Roth, *Law Collections,* 165. *Ancient Near Eastern Texts,* 182. Driver and Miles, *Assyrian Laws,* 189–90, 201–5, 400–401.The property transferred by the husband to his wife at marriage was called a settlement. The wife incurred liability once the settlement was transferred. It was irrelevant whether she had moved to the house of her father-in-law.

54. MAL A 1. Roth, *Law Collections,* 155. *Ancient Near Eastern Texts,* 180. Driver and Miles, *Assyrian Laws,* 17–19, 380–81. See LH 9 and MAL A 47. Driver and Miles, *Assyrian Laws,* 17–20. In MAL N, 1–2, a man who blasphemed and stole from the temple was punished by flogging and a month of penal servitude. The differences were the place—the woman stole from sanctuary of temple, the man just from temple—and value of what was taken, which was implied in the verbs: the woman "stole," the man "pilfered." In so doing, the woman offended the god. The existence of temple prostitution has not been definitively proven, although it was described by ancient historians as an Assyrian and Late Babylonian practice. Herodotus *History* 1.199. Strabo *Geography* 16.1.20.

55. MAL A 2. Roth, *Law Collections,* 155. *Ancient Near Eastern Texts,* 180. Driver and Miles, *Assyrian Laws,* 20, 380–81. There are two offenses in this law. All three translations agree that the first is blasphemy. As to the second offense, Roth has "something disgraceful," and *Ancient Near Eastern Texts* has "loose talk." Driver and Miles have "sedition." The exact meaning of the word is unclear.

56. MAL A 7. Roth, *Law Collections,* 156. *Ancient Near Eastern Texts,* 181, 185. Driver and Miles, *Assyrian Laws,* 30, 384–85.

57. MAL A 8. Roth notes that two possible restorations of the missing word are "eyes" and

"breasts" (*Law Collections*, 192 n. 10). *Ancient Near Eastern Texts* has "eyes" (p. 181). Driver and Miles suggest "nipples" (*Assyrian Laws*, 30–31, 384–85). In Hebrew law, Deuteronomy 25:11–12 stated that in a fight between two men, if the wife of one tried to help her husband by grabbing the other man's testicles, the penalty was to cut off the woman's hand.

58. MAL A 13. Roth, *Law Collections*, 158. *Ancient Near Eastern Texts*, 181. Driver and Miles, *Assyrian Laws*, 36–38, 42, 386–387. Assyrian law presumed that when a woman entered a man's house, sex between the woman and the male head of that household took place, whether as fornication, marriage, or adultery.

59. MAL A 14. Roth, *Law Collections*, 158. *Ancient Near Eastern Texts*, 181. Driver and Miles, *Assyrian Laws*, 388–89.

60. MAL A 15. Roth, *Law Collections*, 158. *Ancient Near Eastern Texts*, 181. Driver and Miles suggest, on the basis of law C 8, that trial before the king could involve both a civil (monetary) penalty and a criminal penalty, but trial before the judges only a criminal penalty (*Assyrian Laws*, 45–48, 388–89). The penalty of castration for the male adulterer fit the crime. The nose of the wife was a phallic symbol in some ancient cultures. Some have suggested that after a wife's nose had been cut off, she was no longer acceptable as a wife and could be relegated to the harem or made a slave.

61. MAL A 16. Roth, *Law Collections*, 158–59. *Ancient Near Eastern Texts*, 181. Driver and Miles, *Assyrian Laws*, 37, 50.

62. MAL A 56. Roth, *Law Collections*, 175. *Ancient Near Eastern Texts*, 185. Driver and Miles, *Assyrian Laws*, 422–25. See A 55.

63. MAL A 22. Roth, *Law Collections*, 160. *Ancient Near Eastern Texts*, 181. Driver and Miles, *Assyrian Laws*, 71–75, 392–93.

64. MAL A 23. Roth, *Law Collections*, 160–61. *Ancient Near Eastern Texts*, 182. Driver and Miles, *Assyrian Laws*, 75–79, 392–95.

65. MAL A 24. Parts of the text of this law are unclear. Roth translates the penalty "[mutilate] his wife and [not] take her back" (*Law Collections*, 161–62). *Ancient Near Eastern Texts* has "cut off the [ears] of his wife but take her back" (p. 182). Driver and Miles have "[mutilate his wife and] take her (back)" (p. 395). The ransom was three talents and thirty minas of lead. If the amount represents the "value" of the woman, it was very high. The fine has been variously translated as three times or one-third of the ransom or a standard fine. There was no allegation of adultery. Driver and Miles, *Assyrian Laws*, 78–85, 104–6, 394–97.

66. MAL A 40. Roth, *Law Collections*, 167–69. *Ancient Near Eastern Texts*, 183. Driver and Miles, *Assyrian Laws*, 406–9. Driver and Miles translate "pitch" as "asphalt," and suggest that this gave the woman a "black veil."

67. MAL A 47. Roth has "practicing witchcraft" (*Law Collections*, 172). *Ancient Near Eastern Texts* (184) and Driver and Miles (*Assyrian Laws*, 414–17) have making "magical preparations." Driver and Miles use the terms "sorcery" and "witchcraft" (*Assyrian Laws*, 118–26, 414–17, 488–89). A hearsay witness was one who heard about the crime from an eyewitness. If an eyewitness denied what a hearsay witness declared he had said, the hearsay witness could swear an oath before the god and be acquitted of perjury. An exorcist would be summoned to make the eyewitness talk and would remind the person of his oath of fidelity to the king. It is unclear whether women took an oath of fidelity to the king. If women were not legal persons, they could not take binding oaths. If they were not soldiers or feudal subjects, there was probably no need to take such oaths. The god named in A 47 was the bull, the son of the sun god. The bull has been described as two embryonic figures joined together, individually called "Truth" and "Justice." Sue Rollin, "Women and Witchcraft in Ancient Assyria," in *Images of Women in Antiquity*, ed. Cameron and Kuhrt, 37–38, 42–43. Driver and Miles, *Assyrian Laws*, 121.

68. MAL A 53. Roth, *Law Collections*, 174. *Ancient Near Eastern Texts*, 185. Driver and Miles, *Assyrian Laws*, 115–17, 420–21. The law applied to all women, not only married women. The

mandate of state jurisdiction implied that the crime of abortion caused pollution, which endangered the state. The belief in the special relationship between mother and child here is similar to that in the OB laws on incest. In LH 157, the worst form of incest was between mother and son and the penalty was death by fire.

69. MAL A 3. Roth, *Law Collections*, 155. *Ancient Near Eastern Texts*, 180. Driver and Miles, *Assyrian Laws*, 22–23, 380–83.

70. MAL A 5. Roth, *Law Collections*, 156. *Ancient Near Eastern Texts*, 180. Driver and Miles, *Assyrian Laws*, 23, 382–83. The value of the property was defined as more than five minas of lead. The phrase "take her" could have had sexual implications.

71. MAL A 4, 6. Roth, *Law Collections*, 156, 185. *Ancient Near Eastern Texts*, 180. Driver and Miles, *Assyrian Laws*, 22–29, 382–85. The omission of "nose" for the wife may be due to a gap in the text, since generally the third-party offender received exactly the same punishment as the wife. Law 6 did not state the penalty for the wife. MAL C 9 placed the duty to report on the man who was head of the household in which the property had been deposited. If he did not report to the owner of the property, then he was prosecuted for theft.

72. MAL A 2, 32. Roth, *Law Collections*, 155, 165. *Ancient Near Eastern Texts*, 180–82. Driver and Miles, *Assyrian Laws*, 380–81, 400–401. It was common in the tribal stage of some ancient peoples to punish an entire family or clan for the crime of one member. In MAL A 32, a wife was held responsible for the crimes of her husband. Early Hebrew law used collective capital punishment (Joshua 7:22–26) and vicarious capital punishment (2 Samuel 21:1–9). Later Hebrew law forbade vicarious punishment for the crimes of a family member. Deuteronomy 24:16. Herodotus *History* 3.119.

73. MAL A 59. Roth, *Law Collections*, 174–77. *Ancient Near Eastern Texts*, 185. Driver and Miles, *Assyrian Laws*, 190–91, 424–25. Driver and Miles read law A 59 in the context of laws A 57 and 58 and other laws such as A 3, 16 ,23, which left the choice of punishment to the husband. In this view, law A 59 defined acceptable penalties and set limits to the husband's ability to impose more drastic punishments on his wife. This law did not authorize husbands to kill their wives or mutilate any part except their ears. The right did not go as far as the right of the patriarch in Roman law of *patria potestas vitae necisque*, whereby a man could kill his wife and children with impunity. MAL A 59 did not permit a man to kill his wife.

74. Roth, *Law Collections*, 195. The decrees were collected and put together during the reign of Tukulti-apil-Esharra I, who was the author of the last four decrees. The earlier decrees were fewer and more fragmentary than the later ones. The tablets of the Middle Assyrian Palace Decrees were found at Asshur. In the MAPD, as in the MAL, most of the laws are conditional: if a person committed offense x, then y would be the penalty. But the MAPD also contain several commands: "you shall not do x." The penalty is generally not stated in a command, but it was understood that it was serious. MAPD 1, 6, and 7 are commands. Commentators on Hebrew law call the command form "apodictic" law. An example is the second half of the Ten Commandments. Exodus 21:13–17. Deuteronomy 5:17–21.

75. MAPD 1. Roth, *Law Collections*, 196–97. Decree of Asshur-uballit I. One late decree, of King Tukulti-apil-Esharra I, mentioned the king's wife in the singular. Kings had a primary wife, who may or may not have resided in the women's quarters. MAPD 22. Roth, *Law Collections*, 207. A resident midwife was necessary to deliver the many royal babies. The role of the *qadiltu* woman was religious, and she may have performed rituals for childbirth and purification after childbirth. There is a lacuna between the titles midwife and *qadiltu* or *qadishtu* and the final phrase "shall not go in or go out." Most take this phrase to apply to the midwife and the *qadiltu*, meaning that they had to be available to the palace women at all times. It might also mean that they knew too much about the machinations of the palace women and the king did not want such things to be known outside the women's quarters.

76. MAPD 2. Roth, *Law Collections*, 197–98, 209 n. 3. Decree of Enlil-nerari. Grayson, *Assyr-*

ian Royal Inscriptions, 1:52–53, nos. 336–41. If the official bypassed the palace overseer and told the people of the palace directly of the death, he would be tried, convicted, and punished by the amputation of his nose and ears. The text has "double hour," two hours, about the time it would take to travel six miles.

77. MAPD 8. King Tukulti-Ninurta I. Roth, *Law Collections,* 200–201. Grayson, *Assyrian Royal Inscriptions,* 1:132, nos. 858–59. The word used literally means "checked." Roth translates it "castrated," which is logical from the context but not certain. Van De Mieroop, *Cuneiform Texts and the Writing of History,* 149. It was a crime for an official to fail to report this. MAPD 20. Roth, *Law Collections,* 205–6. Tukulti-apil-Esharra I wrote a similar decree.

78. MAPD 9. King Ninurta-apil-Ekur. Roth, *Law Collections,* 201–2. Grayson, *Assyrian Royal Inscriptions,* 1:140, no. 910. The penalty was not specified. MAPD 21 d-e. Tukulti-apil-Esharra I. Roth, *Law Collections,* 206–7.

79. MAPD 21a–c. Roth, *Law Collections,* 206. King Tukulti-apil-Esharra I. Roth adds: the woman "bared her shoulders." The text is too fragmentary to translate with any certainty. Van De Mieroop, *Cuneiform Texts and the Writing of History,* 149.

80. MAPD 7. Roth, *Law Collections,* 200. Decree of King Tukulti-Ninurta I. Grayson, *Assyrian Royal Inscriptions,* 1:131, nos. 855–56. The menstruation tabu was rare in ancient Near Eastern law, but prominent in Hebrew law. See Leviticus 15:19–30; 18:19. Jean Bottéro cites an omen text, in which a man passed a menstruating prostitute on the road. The man touched her breast and the milk was thought to overcome the danger of the blood (*Religion in Ancient Mesopotamia,* 194). This text showed consciousness of menstruation and its potential danger, but did not make it a tabu.

81. MAPD 3. Roth, *Law Collections,* 198. King Adad-nerari I. This text is quite fragmentary.

82. MAPD 10, 11, 14, 17. Roth, *Law Collections,* 201–3. Grayson, *Assyrian Royal Inscriptions,* 1:139–40, no. 912. King Ninurta-apil-Ekur.

83. MAPD 19, 21b. Roth, *Law Collections,* 205–7. King Asshur-resha-ishi I. Presumably this meant a form of the death penalty. Grayson paraphrased this law, finding it too fragmentary to translate (*Assyrian Royal Inscriptions,* 1:152, no. 989). A letter of the earlier Amorite king Rim-Sin of Larsa pronounced a similar sentence: "Because he cast a boy into the oven, you throw the slave into the kiln." Marten Stol, *Letters from Yale,* 126–27, letter 197. See Daniel 3:19–23, where the Chaldean king of Babylon was said to punish offenders by throwing them into a fiery furnace.

84. MAPD 18. Roth, *Law Collections,* 204. King Asshur-dan I. The last punishment was not specified.

85. MAPD 6. Roth, *Law Collections,* 199–200. King Tukulti-Ninurta I. Grayson, *Assyrian Royal Inscriptions,* 1:131, nos. 852–53. Women could not even send for their clothes, girdle, veil, cloak, or shoes without permission. Grayson has "of the king *and* officer of the palace." Roth has "of the king *or* of the palace commander" (italics added).

86. MAPD 5. Roth, *Law Collections,* 199. King Salmanu-ashared I. Grayson, *Assyrian Royal Inscriptions* 1:100, nos. 682–83. The words "hot oil" are a conjecture where the text is unclear. The mutilation may have applied to a craftsperson who received the stolen property from the slave. People were presumed to know that slaves did not own property, so that if they were seen with expensive objects, it was obvious that the property was stolen.

87. MAPD 8, 21a–c.

88. The Euphrates River had changed its course, and most of the southern cities were uninhabited until about 750, when there was again sufficient water for irrigation. By that time the Chaldeans controlled the Euphrates south of Borsippa, and the Arameans controlled the middle Euphrates and southern Tigris. After the domestication of the camel, many Arabs migrated into southern Mesopotamia, settled there, and built fortified cities. Stephen W. Cole, *Nippur in Late Assyrian Times: C. 755–612 BC,* 13, 16–19, 23–44.

89. King Salmanu-ashared V (Hebrew Shalmaneser) besieged Israel (Samaria), until it surrendered in 721. His successor, King Sharrukin II (Sargon in Hebrew), deported the nation of Israel—27,290 people, according to Assyrian records—to Gozan and Media, on the far northern and eastern frontiers of the empire. 2 Kings 17:1–6. Between 745 and 705, Assyrian kings deported as many as 500,000 people from Babylonia. J. A. Brinkman, *Prelude to Empire: Babylonian Society and Politics, 747–626 B.C.,* 19–20. Roaf, *Cultural Atlas of Mesopotamia and the Ancient Near East,* 164, 179, 191: maps. William W. Hallo and William K. Simpson, *The Ancient Near East: A History,* 134–35: map of Assyrian empire from 1362 to 627).

90. Saggs, *Might That Was Assyria,* 98–121. Sin-akhe-eriba (Sennakherib) conquered Babylon in 689 and moved his capital north to Nineveh. He was succeeded by his son Asshur-akhu-iddina (Esarhaddon) and grandson, Asshur-bani'-apli (Asshur-banipal). King Nabu-apil-usur (Nabopolassar) founded the Late Babylonian dynasty, which freed Babylonia from Assyrian rule. Hallo and Simpson, *Ancient Near East,* 135, 144–49. The LA period ended with the fall of Asshur in 614, Nineveh in 612, and the final defeat by the second LB king, Nabu-kudurri'usur II (Nebukhadrezzar), of the remnant of Assyrians who had escaped from Nineveh at Karkemish in 605. See Jeremiah 46:2–12. Julian Reade, *Assyrian Sculpture,* 69, fig. 77: relief of Sin-akhe'eriba; 86, fig. 102: Asshur-bani'apli (about 645).

91. William W. Hallo, "Nippur Originals," in *DUMU-E2-DUB-BA-A: Studies in Honor of Ake Sjöberg,* 239–40. The MA king Tukulti-Ninurta I took the contents of the royal archives of Babylonia as war booty and kidnapped their scholars. The last MA king, Tukulti-apil-Esharra I, built a library in Asshur. In Babylonia there were libraries in Nippur and Sippar. The LA king Asshur-bani'apli (Asshurbanipal) raided the libraries and private collections in Babylonia and built a great library at Nineveh. J. Black and W. Tait, "Archives and Libraries in the Ancient Near East," in *Civilizations in the Ancient Near East,* ed. Sasson, 4:2006–7. Saggs, *Might That Was Assyria,* 116. John Van Seters, *In Search of History,* 93.

92. Albert Kirk Grayson, *Assyrian Rulers of the Early First Millennium I (1114–859 BC),* 2, 82, 103, 104, 239, 264. Grayson, *Assyrian Royal Inscriptions,* 1:14, 88, 92, 133, 136, 197–99, 201, 218, 220, 243–44, 250–51, 266. Asshur-nasir-apali II (Hebrew Asshurnasirpal) also called himself "trampler of criminals." Grayson, *Assyrian Rulers of the Early First Millennium,* 308. He rebuilt the city of Nimrud and moved the capital there. Joan Oates and David Oates, *Nimrud: An Assyrian Imperial City revealed, passim.* Roaf, *Cultural Atlas of Mesopotamia and the Ancient Near East,* 140, 179, 191. J. E. Curtis and J. E. Reade, eds., *Art and Empire: Treasures from Assyria in the British Museum,* 43, fig.1: statue of Asshurnasirpal II (Nimrud, 875–860). Albenda, in *La Femme dans le Proche-Orient Antique,* 20. Reade, in *La Femme dans le Proche-Orient Antique,* 140. The relief of Asshurbanipal included his wife, women servants, and an orchestra of women.

93. Villard, "Shamshi-Adad and Sons: The Rise and Fall of an Upper Mesopotamian Empire," in *Civilizations of the Ancient Near East,* ed. Sasson, 2:879–80. D. Charpin, "The History of Ancient Mesopotamia: An Overview," in ibid., 2:816. Shamshi-Adad I was from the OA II period, Tukulti-apil-Esharra I from the MA period, and Sharrukin (Sargon) II and Asshur-akhu-iddina (Esarhaddon) from the LA period. Esarhaddon had divinations performed before agreeing to the marriage. Starr, *Queries to the Sungod,* 24–26, no. 20.

94. Oates and Oates, *Nimrud,* 82–86, and plates 4–8. The oldest tomb had been looted. The Hebrew form of the name Tukulti-apil-Esharra III is Tiglathpileser. See 2 Kings 15:29.

95. "Lady" implied authority, in the same sense as "lord," and is understood to mean principal wife. In Assyrian, a "lady of the palace" was *sinnishat ekalli,* whereas a "palace woman" of the harem was *sinniltu ekalli.* A letter to a LA king contains a list of tribute money, garments, and undergarments that were for the "lady of the palace." Robert H. Pfeiffer lists tribute for the palace, for the "lady of the palace," and for other officials (*State Letters of Assyria,* 81–83, no. 99). Naqia was called the "lady" of Sin-akhe'eriba (Sennakherib).

96. Saggs, *Might That Was Assyria*, 78–79. Sammu-ramat was given the title "Lady of the Palace" on a monument. Jeffrey Kah-Jin Kuan, *Neo-Assyrian Historical Inscriptions and Syria-Palestine: Israelite/Judean-Tyrian-Damascene Political and Commercial Relations in the Ninth-Eighth Centuries B.C.E.*, 90–91 (boundary stone). Sammu-ramat was identified by ancient writers, including Herodotos and Diodoros, with the legendary prehistoric queen Semiramis. Deborah Gera, *Warrior Women: The Anonymous Tractatus de Mulieribus*, 68–69. Georges Roux bases his theory that Sammu-ramat was regent on the writing of Berosos ("Semiramis: The Builder of Babylon," in Jean Bottéro, *Everyday Life in Ancient Mesopotamia*, 152–53). Reade, *Assyrian Sculpture*, 45, fig. 46: stele of Shamshi-Adad V from Nimrud.

97. Naqia was a West Semitic name; on occasion she used the Akkadian equivalent, Zakutu. Little is known about her background, except that she had a sister, Abirami (also a West Semitic name) who purchased land. Naqia married crown prince Sin-akhe'eriba about 714, and he became king in 704. She gave birth to Asshur-akhu-iddina (Esarhaddon) about 712. After designating Asshur-akhu-iddina (Esarhaddon) as crown prince, the king transferred tax-exempt land to Naqia by written document with the royal seal, in which he called Naqia the "mother of the crown prince." L. Kataja and R. Whiting, *Grants, Decrees and Gifts of the Neo-Assyrian Period*, 22–23, nos. 21–23: transfer of tax-exempt town of Shabbu to Naqia. Sarah C. Melville, *The Role of Naqia/Zakutu in Sargonid Politics*, 2, 5–11, 13, 15, 18, 20–23, 28. The written sources about Naqia date mostly from the reign of her son. The administrator of Sin-akhe'eriba (Sennakherib) distributed tribute and audience gifts, consisting of silver, clothing, and food, to the king, queen, crown prince, and other palace officials. The king received very large audience gifts. The queen received both tribute and smaller audience gifts. The crown prince received only tribute, the same amount as the queen. In a second list, the queen and crown prince both received only tribute, but the crown prince received twice the amount of silver. Simo Parpola, *The Correspondence of Sargon II*, 35–36, no. 34.8-17, r. 2-11. Naqia dedicated an inscribed bead for the lives of Sin-akhe'eriba (Sennakherib), Asshur-akhu-iddina (Esarhaddon), and herself. Marc Van De Mieroop, "An Inscribed Bead of Queen Zakutu," in *Tablet and the Scroll*, ed. Cohen et al., 259–60. One other wife of Sin-akhe'eriba (Sennakherib) is known by name, Tashmetum-sharrat. She was called the "queen, my beloved wife" in an inscription on a doorway in the royal palace at Nineveh. See Reade, in *La Femme dans le Proche-Orient Antique*, 141–42.

98. Simo Parpola and Kazuko Watanabe, *Neo-Assyrian Treaties and Loyalty Oaths*, 28–58, no. 6. Asshur-akhu-iddina (Esarhaddon) wrote down his intentions in great detail in the "Succession Treaty of 672." The plan for his succession divided the empire, giving Assyria to his younger son and Babylonia to the elder. The treaty contained a long section of curses(2:45–58, nos. 37-106).

99. Naqia made the dedication for her reign. The use of "reign" (*palu*) in the inscription suggests a co-reign with her son.

100. A scribe wrote to the queen mother concerning the statues on which he inscribed her name. Stephen Cole and Peter Machinist, *Letters From Priests to the Kings Esarhaddon and Assurbanipal*, 159–60, n. 188. Pfeiffer, *State Letters of Assyria*, 164–65, nos. 229, 230, 192, no. 274: she provided lambs for sacrifice; 189, no. 269: letter to king asking him to decide which rites to perform for his mother. The bronze relief is in the Louvre. The name of Naqia is in the inscription, but the name of the king is missing. Two seals found in the palace of Sin-akhe'eriba (Sennakherib) depicted a queen standing behind a king in worship. Melville, *Role of Naqia/Zakutu*, 15, 26, fig. 1, 32, 36–49, 52, 72, 91–92. Tallay Ornan, "The Queen in Public: Royal Women in Neo-Assyrian Art" in *Sex and Gender in the Ancient Near East*, ed. Parpola and Whiting, 462, fig. 1; Mikko Luukko and Greta Van Buylaere, eds., *The Political Correspondence of Esarhaddon*, 2, fig. 1.

101. Luukko and Van Buylaere, *Political Correspondence of Esarhaddon*, 4–5, no. 2; 85, no. 94; Melville, *Role of Naqia/Zakatu*, 62–67, 70–75 (about 675). This letter continued: "what you bless is blessed; what you curse is cursed."

102. Naqia's illness in June 670 was treated by three exorcists and one physician. They used

incantations against witchcraft and curses. The document containing the loyalty oath was called the "Zakutu Treaty," using the Akkadian form of the name Naqia (Parpola and Watanabe, *Neo-Assyrian Treaties*, 62–64, no. 8). Five clauses required reporting conspiracies. The sixth, killing the traitors and bringing the corpses, is missing the last two lines, which presumably contained the name of Asshur-bani'apli (Asshurbanipal). Melville, *Role of Naqia/Zakutu*, 79–90. Divinations were made as to whether Naqia would survive her illness. Starr. *Queries to the Sungod*, 192–95, nos. 190, 191.

103. Brinkman, *Prelude to Empire*, 82, n. 400. Esarhaddon Chronicle, line 23. Babylonian Chronicle 4.22. Grayson, *Assyrian Royal Inscriptions*, 1:37, 41, 44–45. Erle Leichty, "Esarhaddon, King of Assyria," in *Civilizations of the Ancient Near East*, ed. Sasson, 2:955, 957. It is possible that the daughter was Sherua'eterat and the daughter-in-law was Libbalisharrat. Kataja and Whiting, *Grants, Decrees and Gifts of the Neo-Assyrian Period*, 89, no. 81. r. 5. Ribs from the sacrifice were taken to the tomb of Esharra-khammat.

104. Luukko and Van Buylaere, *Political Correspondence of Esarhaddon*, 23, no. 28. The editors suggest that Sherua'eterat was expressing jealous rivalry of her sister-in-law and did not want her to be called "sister," with the implication of equality. Liballisharrat made a dedication for her reign, but there is no evidence that she ever actually ruled. 22, fig. 6: drawing of Libbalisharrat from relief at Nineveh. Melville, *Role of Naqia/Zakutu*, 51, fig. 5, Reade, *Assyrian Sculpture*, 88–89, figs. 106–7, Curtis and Reade, *Art and Empire*, 122: stone relief of Asshur-bani'-apli (Asshurbanipal) and his wife drinking in a garden, with the head of one of his enemies hanging from a nearby tree (Nineveh, about 645). Ornan, "Queen in Public," in *Sex and Gender in the Ancient Near East*, ed. Parpola and Whiting, 462–63, figs. 2–4: same relief with drawing of detail.

105. Kuan, *Neo-Assyrian Historical Inscriptions*, 154–57, 172–77, 186. There were many Arabs who had migrated from the Arabian peninsula into southern Mesopotamia more than twelve hundred years before the advent of Islam. In the eighth century, the city of Nippur paid tribute to the Chaldeans and to Nadbata, queen of the Arabs. Assyrian royal inscriptions attest the conquests of the Arabs. In 738, the Arab queen Zabibe paid tribute to Assyria. In 733, King Tukulti-apil Esharra (Tiglathpileser) III conquered the Arabs, who were led in battle by Queen Samsi. The Assyrians took more than a thousand prisoners, tens of thousands of animals, gold, silver, and spices. In 716, Sharrukin (Sargon) II resettled Arabs in Samaria. The Arab queen Samsi sent him tribute. A fragmentary record from a military officer in the house notes that he had returned deserters and stray camels to Queen Samsi. Frederick Fales and J. N. Postgate, *Imperial Administrative Records, Part II*, 101, no. 162. By the end of the eighth century, other Arabs had built their own walled cities in southern Mesopotamia. Cole, *Nippur in Late Assyrian Times*, 18, 34–39. Giovanni Lanfranchi and Simo Parpola, *The Correspondence of Sargon II, Part II*, 85–86, no. 108.18–25. Urartia is also known as Ararat.

106. Grayson, *Assyrian Royal Inscriptions*, 1:2 (OA), 46, 52, 73, 76, 98, 100, 131, 132, 140 (MA). One king called himself "exalted sage," a wisdom figure that became an important image in Hebrew literature. The two MA kings who used the term "just scepter" were Tukulti-Ninurta I and Asshur-nadiniapli (*Assyrian Royal Inscriptions*, 118, 135). Asshur-bani'apli (Asshurbanipal) called himself "king of righteousness, lover of justice." Kataja and Whiting, *Grants, Decrees and Gifts from the Neo-Assyrian Period*, 32, no. 29.4–10. The word "justice" was relatively rare in Assyrian usage.

107. The OA II king Shamshi-Adad I stated "I sacrificed" in cities he had captured. Grayson, *Assyrian Royal Inscriptions*, 1:26. Other kings wrote of performing religious functions and offering sacrifices. Grayson, *Assyrian Royal Inscriptions*, 1:80; Grayson, *Assyrian Rulers of the Early First Millennium I*, 30, 45, 218, 219, 298. Later kings called themselves "priests." Grayson, *Assyrian Royal Inscriptions*, 1:80, 106, 118, 147, 148. Grayson, *Assyrian Rulers of the Early First Millennium I*, 29, 45, 89, 90, 103 (MA), 135, 168, 194–96, 226, 229, 239, 264, 281, 284, 287, 297, 298, 318 (LA). Some MA and LA kings also used the title "purification priest." Grayson, *Assyrian Royal*

Inscriptions, 1:118, 124. Grayson, *Assyrian Rulers of the Early First Millennium I,* 195, 239, 263, 281. Fales and Postgate, *Imperial Administrative Records, Part II,* 32–35, no. 36. Distribution of tribute lists of palace personnel named numerous offices of men. The word "queen" in 32.2.28–29 is at the end of a column and probably referred to an official of the queen, as in 3.3, near the top of the next column.

108. Cole and Machinist, *Letters from Priests,* 77, no. 89; 83, no. 101; 86, no. 108. The last letter also referred to horses sent by the treasurer of the queen. Pfeiffer, *State Letters of Assyria,* 132, no. 178. Leichty, "Esarhaddon, King of Assyria," in *Civilizations of the Ancient Near East,* ed. Sasson, 2:949. Fales and Postgate, *Imperial Administrative Records, Part I,* 8–9, no. 5.1.35 (treasurer), 5.1.32, 46, 5.2.16, 5.r.1.46 (eunuchs), 5.1.42, 5.2.32, 5.r6.1.42 (bodyguards), 5.2.30 (cohort commander), 5.r.1.7, r.2.5, 10, 11, no.6.1.8. Theodore Kwasman and Simo Parpola, *Legal Transactions of the Royal Court of Nineveh, Part I,* 202–4, no. 253, 255, 256, 263, no. 325.2 (sealed by scribe of the queen mother), 126, no. 143 (money), 56, no. 48.1–2 (fragmentary). Ben-Barak, in *La Femme dans le Proche-Orient Antique,* 39.

109. Kwasman and Parpola, *Legal Transactions,* 138–39, nos. 164.r.3, 165.r.6 (cohort commanders), 164.r.11, 271, no. 332.r.5 (chariot drivers), 90, no. 70 (jewelry, fragmentary). Stephanie Dalley and J. N. Postgate, *The Tablets from Fort Shalmaneser,* 92–95, nos. 39, 40 (woman scribe). Fales and Postgate *Imperial Administrative Records, Part II,* 33, no. 36.r.3.3. Fales and Postgate, *Imperial Administrative Records, Part I,* 141, no. 132 (fruit and wine), 160, no. 153.r.1.6 (meat), 176–77, no. 175 (animals for sacrifice).

110. Kwasman and Parpola, *Legal Transactions,* 199–201, nos. 251.2, 4–7, 252.6-11. Fales and Postgate, *Imperial Administrative Records, Part II,* 148, no. 221.

111. Oates and Oates, *Nimrud,* 60–65 (Northwest Palace), 190 (Fort), 213. The fort was named for King Salmanu-ashared III (Shalmaneser). According to the wine ration lists at Nimrud, the royal household at times contained six thousand people. The women's quarters were called *bitanu.*

112. Oates and Oates, *Nimrud,* 87.

113. Remko Jas, *Neo-Assyrian Judicial Procedures,* 5. Karen Radner, *Die Neuassyrischen Privatrechtsurkunden als Quelle für Mensch und Umwelt,* 165–66. Raija Mattila translates *shakintu* as "harem manageress" (*Legal Transactions of the Royal Court of Nineveh, II,* 12–13, 15–17, nos. 8–9, 12–14). Kwasman and Parpola translate *shakintu* as "harem governess" (*Legal Transactions,* 72–82, nos. 81–95, 198–200, nos. 247, 250). There is insufficient evidence to conclude that her main role was management of the palace women. It may have included this, but extended well beyond it. Fales and Postgate list twenty-three *shakintu* women in three palaces in Nineveh and in eight other towns (*Imperial Administrative Records, Part I,* 32, no. 23; 142, no. 134: fragment listed the *shakintu* of a town in Harran with other royal officials contributing oxen and sheep to a temple for sacrifice). Luukko and Van Buylaere, *Political Correspondence of Esarhaddon,* 151–52, no. 183: correspondence between the king and a *shakintu* in a province whose governor did not obey the king, probably Asshur-akhu-iddina. Dalley and Postgate, *Tablets from Fort Shalmaneser,* 80–81, no. 30 (deputy), 92–95, nos. 39, 40 (scribe). The assistant who served as judge was called *shanitu.*

114. Slave sales: Mattila, *Legal Transactions of the Royal Court of Nineveh, II,* 12–13, 15–17, nos. 8 (Zarpi, Bililutu), 9 (man), 12 (Banitu-teresh), 13 (man), 14 (Abilikhiya). Dalley and Postgate, *Tablets from Fort Shalmaneser,* 85–89, nos. 34 (daughter of an Egyptian), 35 (son), 36 (employee of *shakintu* bought girl for "upbringing"). Land sales: Mattila, *Legal Transactions,* 146, no. 175. Loans: Mattila, *Legal Transactions,* 132, no. 159 (she took the borrower's son as pledge), 302–3, no. 471. The title *shakintu* was used in Mattila, *Legal Transactions,* 12–15, 132, 146–47, 302–3, nos. 8.5; 9.5; 11.3; 12.6, 7; 159.2, 7, r.1, r.4; 175.3, 4; 176.5; 177.5, 6; 471.2; the Sumerogram MI-GAR-KUR was used in 13.5, 18 and 14.6, 16. A *shakintu* of Kilizi was named in a doc-

ument about a mule which she owned and had lent out. Kwasman and Parpola, *Legal Transactions of the Royal Court of Nineveh, Part 1*, 198, no. 247.3-5; 130, no. 152.r.2.

115. Kwasman and Parpola, *Legal Transactions of the Royal Court of Nineveh, Part 1*, 72–78, 80–82, nos. 81.1–11, 82.1–3, 84.1–3 (Adda-ti), 88.3–8, 89.3–8, r.1, 90.1, 5–14, r.4, 93. r.1–5 (Akhitalli), 85.4–9, 86.1–8, 87.1–2, 9, 94, 95, and possibly 88.5–6 (unnamed *shakintu* women). The title "*shakintu* of the central city" was held by Akhitalli and it is possible, but not certain, that she was the *shakintu* in question.

116. Dalley and Postgate, *Tablets from Fort Shalmaneser*, 9–12, 78–102, nos. 28–45.

117. Oates and Oates, *Nimrud*, 186–87, 189, 201–2, 213. This *shakintu* was very wealthy; she made loans of silver and grain. Heltzer, in *La Femme dans le Proche-Orient Antique*, 88, documents a *shakintu* of the New Palace of Nimrud named Amat-Ashtarte, who gave a large dowry to her daughter. Heltzer notes that the names of the *shakintu* and her son-in-law were both Phoenician.

118. Kwasman and Parpola, *Legal Transactions of the Royal Court of Nineveh, Part 1*, 82–86, nos. 96, 97, 98.3–7. In the last, the price was too low for a slave woman, who generally cost one-half mina (thirty sheqels). These women were upper class or even royal, but were not *shakintu*.

119. Kwasman and Parpola, *Legal Transactions of the Royal Court of Nineveh, Part 1*, 79, 86–87, nos. 91.11, 99.5–12 (names broken off). Both texts used the Sumerograms MI.ERIM-E..GAL for the woman purchaser. This can be translated into Assyrian either as *sinnishat*, meaning lady of the palace, or *sinniltu*, meaning a woman of the harem. The context makes the first more probable. Pfeiffer, *State Letters of Assyria*, 81–83, no. 99, translates *sinnishat* as lady of the palace in a let of women recipients of tribute money and goods.

120. Grayson, *Assyrian Royal Inscriptions*, 1:140, no. 914: one brief fragmentary inscription of the MA king Ninurta-apil-Ekur, who ruled from 1191 to 1179, recorded a gift of jewelry he made to his daughter, Muballita[t], whom he called high priestess. This author knows of no other MA or LA text calling a woman "high priest." Perhaps the king meant that his daughter was a "great priest," denoting excellence, instead of high priest, a very restricted office. Assyria did not have the tradition, so common in Sumer and revived in Late Babylonia, of kings making their daughters high priests.

121. The evidence is sparse, except in the case of Queen Naqia, that royal women served in important roles in religion in the Middle and Late Assyrian periods. Luukko and Van Buylaere, *Political Correspondence of Esarhaddon*, 88, no. 95. Livingstone, *Court Poetry and Literary Miscellanea*, 22, no. 8.15 (*kulmashitu*); 3:97, no. 38.46–49 (intestines). Mattila, *Legal Transactions of the Royal Court of Nineveh, II*, 71, no. 68 (barley loan to a *nin-dingir/ugbabtu* priest).

122. Fales and Postgate, *Imperial Administrative Records, Part I*, 34–35, no. 24.r.1-2 (women stewards and scribes), no. 26 (women treasurers, cupbearers, bakers, and singers). Fales and Postgate, *Imperial Administrative Records, Part II*, 95, no. 152 (temple stewardesses, number broken off). Both texts used the same word for woman steward. Cole and Machinist, *Letters from Priests*, 57–58, no. 65; 127–28, no. 157.

123. Luukko and Van Buylaere, *Political Correspondence of Esarhaddon*, 88, no. 95. Grayson, *Assyrian Rulers of the Early First Millennium I*, 218: tribute list of Asshur-nasir-apli (Asshur-naširpal) II included ten women singers, 343: fragment of another list contained women musicians. Fales and Postgate, *Imperial Administrative Records, Part I*, 32–34, nos. 24: women singers were Aramean and from Kush, Tyre, and Kassite Babylonia, 25.7: ten women singers, 147, no. 140: wine rations for women singers. Fales and Postgate, *Imperial Administrative Records, Part II*, 95, no. 152. Pfeiffer, *State Letters of Assyria*, 74–75, no. 88. Livingstone, *Court Poetry and Literary Miscellanea*, 22, no. 8.12–14. Saggs, *Might That Was Assyria*, 212. A *pyxis* (a small decorated box) contained pictures of women musicians.

124. Radner, *Die Neuassyrischen Privatrechtsurkunden*, 209–10. The oblate was called a *shelutu*

of a goddess. Two married women oblates were given large settlements by their husbands. Oblates were different from persons given to temples as slave workers. Kajata and Whiting, *Grants, Decrees and Gifts,* 108–9, no. 87 (Sin-akhe'eriba [Sennakherib] gave forty-one men, women, and children to a temple as slaves. The men were named in this text, but their wives and daughters were not); 120, no. 95 (a man gave the two sons of his sister, Lasakhittu, whom he had raised, as slaves to the temple of Nabu in Nimrud); 121, no. 96 (a man gave two young male slaves and a field to the same temple for the lives of the king and queen).

125. Martti Nissinen, *References to Prophecy in Neo-Assyrian Sources,* 167, 169–70, 172. In the beginning, prophecies were delivered orally. Asshur-akhu'iddina (Esarhaddon) and Asshur-bani'apli (Asshurbanipal) were the first kings to have prophecies written down and kept in their archives in Nineveh. Martti Nissinen, *Prophets and Prophecy in the Ancient Near East,* 103–9, 112–16, 126–32, nos. 69–72, 74, 75, 79, 81, 82, 92, 94, 95 (prophecies of women prophets, most of which originated in Arbel). Assyrian women prophets were called *raggintu.* Martti Nissinen, "Spoken, Written, Quoted, and Invented: Orality and Writtenness in Ancient Near Eastern Prophecy," in *Writings and Speech in Israelite and Ancient Near Eastern Prophecy,* ed. Ben Zvi and Floyd, 242–51, 258–60. Amélie Kuhrt, "Non-Royal Women in the Late Babylonian Period," in *Women's Earliest Records,* ed. Lesko, 220. There were both men and women dream interpreters (*sha'iltu*). Mario Liverani translates it "dream priestess" ("The Deeds of Ancient Mesopotamian Kings," in *Civilizations of the Ancient Near East,* ed. Sasson, 4:2364). Kataja and Whiting, *Grants, Decrees and Gifts,* 74, no. 69.28–31. Instead of making bread, the barley of the women prophets was delivered to the brewers, who used it to make beer.

126. Nissinen, *Prophets and Prophecy,* 109–11, 117, 125, nos. 74, 75, 78, 111, 117, 125.

127. Melville, *Role of Naqia/Zakutu,* 28. Cole and Machinist, *Letters from Priests,* 38–39, no. 37, 116–17, no. 145. Nissinen, *Prophets and Prophecy,* 166–69, nos. 110, 111, 113: women who prophesied in temples; 175–77, no. 118: ritual of Ishtar and Dumuzi; 185–87, nos. 123–25: MA and LA lists included women prophets.

128. Mattila, *Legal Transactions of the Royal Court of Nineveh, II,* 133–34, no. 161(Mullissu-khasina), 173, no. 218, 282, no.443 (Alhapimepi, an Egyptian name). Radner, *Die Neuassyrischen Privatrechtsurkunden,* 165–66. Dalley and Postgate, *Tablets from Fort Shalmaneser,* 103–5, 109–10, nos. 47, 51.

129. Saggs, *Greatness That Was Babylon,* 219–20.

130. Mattila, *Legal Transactions of the Royal Court of Nineveh, II,* 38–39, no. 34 (Salentu), 42, no. 37 (Abidala), 42–43, no. 38 (Gula-rishat). Frederick M. Fales, *Aramaic Epigraphs on Clay Tablets of the Neo-Assyrian Period,* 202–3 (Gula-rishat). Fales notes that she was sold by her brothers and her sons. Her father was dead, and she was a widow, since she had sons. Radner, *Die Neuassyrischen Privatrechtsurkunden,* 166–70, 173–80. Most of these documents date from the seventh century.

131. Kwasman and Parpola, *Legal Transactions of the Royal Court of Nineveh, Part 1,* 199, no. 250.3–8: Abirakhi, Yaqarakhe, Abiyakhia. Mattila, *Legal Transactions of the Royal Court of Nineveh, II,* 14–17, nos. 10, 11, 14, 146, no. 174 (names broken off). Kataja and Whiting, *Grants, Decrees and Gifts,* 28–30, no. 27. Named women were Bakisha, Akhu'a, Abirakhi, Issar-remanni, Kharra, Mullissu-duru, Bazitu, Banna, Sukkitu, Khanzaba, Asa, Kharra, Khitubarra, Banitu-ayali, Damqaya, Deru.., Bi'a, Ramti, Adad-talli, and ... rukhi-Mullissu. Other named and unnamed persons may also have been women.

132. Mattila, *Legal Transactions of the Royal Court of Nineveh, II,* 20–21, no. 16 (Akhatitabat), 23–24, no. 20 (Mullissu-ummi), 28–29, no. 24 (Khambusu, also written Khabbush), 31, no. 28 (Arbail-sharrat), 43–44, no. 39 (exchange), 55, 57, nos. 48, 50 (Issar-remenni and Ummii), 99, no. 115 (...dibeshalibbi), 128–29, no. 154 (Akhatabisha), 134–35, no. 162 (Nannya-da), 136–37, no. 165 (Samsi), 277, no. 435 (Putushisi), 303, no. 472 (priest). Kwasman and Parpola, *Legal Transactions of the Royal Court of Nineveh, Part 1,* 38, no. 34 (Ununi), 46–47, no. 45 (Uquputu),

107–8, no. 116 (Eduqidiru, Babaya), 157, no. 197 (Nana-lurshi), 182, no. 228 (Mullissu-duru'usur), 190, no. 239 (Khazala, Khuda, Akhati'imma), 228, no. 284 (Marqikhita), 230, no. 286 (Rama-Ya). Fales, *Aramaic Epigraphs on Clay Tablets,* 163 (Marqikhita), 188 (Akhatitabat), 175–76 (Khambusu), 196–97 (Arbail-sharrat). These were references to some of the same women or names in Aramaic epigraphs on Assyrian texts.

133. Mattila, *Legal Transactions of the Royal Court of Nineveh, II,* 159, no. 196 (Busuku). Kwasman and Parpola, *Legal Transactions of the Royal Court of Nineveh, Part 1,* 122, no. 138 (Rimuttu), 154, no. 193.3–4 (two couples), 237, no. 294 (weaver), 280, no. 342 (hatter).

134. Mattila, *Legal Transactions of the Royal Court of Nineveh, II,* 266–67, no. 424 (Bani, Rama, and Naga). See fragments 188–89, no. 247 (man, wife, two sons, daughter), 305–6, no. 475 (man, wife, sons, and two daughters). Kwasman and Parpola, *Legal Transactions of the Royal Court of Nineveh, Part 1,* 7, no. 6; 51, no. 52; 55, no. 57; 100–102, nos. 110, 111 (Mesa and Badia); 117–18, no. 130 (fourth family illegible); 145, no. 177; 155, no. 195; 182–83, no. 229; 252–53, nos. 312–13 (tailor); 258, no. 319 (Gabia); 280–83, nos. 342, 343–44 (fragmentary); 345.

135. Mattila, *Legal Transactions of the Royal Court of Nineveh, II,* 4–6, 8, nos. 1, 2, 3, 6; 139, no. 168 (Bita and Yaqira); 161, 252, 253, nos. 198, 399, 401; 191, 231–32, nos. 254, 345 (vineyards). Kwasman and Parpola, *Legal Transactions of the Royal Court of Nineveh, Part 1,* 40, no. 37 (two vineyards and two families).

136. Mattila, *Legal Transactions of the Royal Court of Nineveh,* 2:129–30, no. 155. The property was to be tax-free.

137. Mattila, *Legal Transactions of the Royal Court of Nineveh, II,* 71, no. 68: the woman priest was an *ugbabtu,* 129–30, no. 155, 132, no. 159, 302–3, no. 471.

138. Mattila, *Legal Transactions of the Royal Court of Nineveh, II,* 89–90, no. 101 (Takilat-Arbail), 151–52, no. 181; 167, no. 209. Kwasman and Parpola, *Legal Transactions of the Royal Court of Nineveh, Part 1,* 218, no. 272 (Lamashi). Dalley and Postgate, *Tablets from Fort Shalmaneser,* 110–11, no. 52 (release of pledge named Kakkua), 119–20, no. 59 (man pledged daughter and slave woman). Loan records, even for small amounts were written down, witnessed, signed, sealed, and preserved in the state archives.

139. Jas, *Neo-Assyrian Judicial Procedures,* 44–46, no. 28.

140. Ibid., 33–35, 42–43, nos. 17, 25. Both documents were found in the *shakintu* archive at Nimrud. Dalley and Postgate, *Tablets from Fort Shalmaneser,* 78–81, nos. 29–30.

141. Pfeiffer, *State Letters of Assyria,* 4–5, no. 2; 10–11, no. 11; 66–67, no. 76. The woman must have been wealthy to have a chief steward and important enough to be mentioned in an official letter to the king. The name of the last woman is only partially legible in the text: "Esi...." Luukko and Van Buylaere, *Political Correspondence of Esarhaddon,* 6, 13, 20–23, nos. 5, 17, 26, 27. Cole, *Nippur in Late Assyrian Times,* 100, no. 59; and 106, no. 101. Reade, *Assyrian Sculpture,* 60, fig. 63: relief of captive Chaldeans in the palace of Sin-akhe'eriba (Sennakherib) at Nineveh. Shar-rukin (Sargon) II had a daughter named Akhatabisha, whom he had married to the ruler of Tabal in Asia Minor and who corresponded with him.

142. Pfeiffer, *State Letters of Assyria,* 18, no. 19; 55–56, no. 62. Luukko and Van Buylaere, *Political Correspondence of Esarhaddon,* 131, no. 153. Upper-class women of Borsippa wrote to the king, but only the address survived.

143. King Asshur-akhu-iddina (Esarhaddon) was an exception; he was literate. Cole, *Nippur in Late Assyrian Times,* 103–4, no. 83. The status of the last two women was unclear, whether they were free or slaves, and why the writer deemed them apt for scribal training. The teacher seemed willing to pay any price, but wanted the students immediately.

144. Ilse Seibert, *Women in the Ancient Near East,* 52. Asshur-bani'apli (Asshurbanipal) wrote: "Forgive that a woman has written this and submitted it to you." Radner, *Die Neuassyri-schen Privatrechtsurkunden,* 83, no. 432; 86, nos. 457–58, 466. The LA list of palace scribes had more than 150 names. The queen and the queen-mother each had a scribe. Livingstone, *Court*

Poetry and Literary Miscellanea, 119, no. 49. A woman scribe from Borsippa worked in the temple at Arbel. Aramaic was a West Semitic language, written in alphabetic block letters, which were much easier to write than cuneiform. After the mid-sixth century, Aramaic became the standard language of Mesopotamia and the Persian empire.

145. Pfeiffer, *State Letters of Assyria,* 14, no. 14: son of Alshete, 20, no. 21: son of their sister, 24, no. 26: son of B's sister, 26, no. 30. Kwasman and Parpola, *Legal Transactions of the Royal Court of Nineveh, Part 1,* 113–14, no. 124.r.5: son of the woman.

146. Jas, *Neo-Assyrian Judicial Procedures,* 8–11, no. 1. The text did not state what was done with the family, servitude or death. Kwasman and Parpola, *Legal Transactions of the Royal Court of Nineveh, Part 1,* 212, no. 264. Any person who paid the penalties of three hundred sheep and two talents of copper blood money could procure the release of the shepherd and his family.

147. Jas, *Neo-Assyrian Judicial Procedures,* 54–55, no. 33. In LH 116, abuse causing the death of the pledge was a serious offense.

148. Mattila, *Legal Transactions of the Royal Court of Nineveh, II,* 105, no. 125. Jas, *Neo-Assyrian Judicial Procedures,* 65–66, no. 42. Martha Roth, "Homicide in the Neo-Assyrian Period," in *Language, Literature, and History,* ed. Rochberg-Halton, 351–63. According to Roth, the document served as the basis for negotiation between the two parties. Once it was accepted by both parties, it became a contract and both parties were bound to keep the agreement under penalty of a fine of ten minas of silver. Roth understands the woman to be the daughter of the murderer. Mattila and Jas call the woman the daughter of a scribe. Westbrook calls her a slave woman. *Studies in Biblical and Cuneiform Law,* 50–51. Roth cites another document that recorded the payment of blood money in the presence of officials, with records kept in the palace archives in Nineveh. She concludes that payment of blood money, called composition, was a viable option in LA homicide cases.

149. Jas, *Neo-Assyrian Judicial Procedures,* 77–78, no. 49. The text did not mention the offense.

150. Jas, *Neo-Assyrian Judicial Procedures,* 69–71, no. 45.

151. Reynolds, *Babylonian Correspondence of Esarhaddon,* 132–33, no. 160, 153, no. 186. Fuchs and Parpola, *Correspondence of Sargon II,* 3:48–49, no. 73; 115, no. 168.

152. Reynolds, *Babylonian Correspondence of Esarhaddon,* 46–47, no. 61, 91–92, no. 114, 168, 170, no. 202. Fuchs and Parpola, *Correspondence of Sargon II,* 3:36–37, no. 54.

153. Reynolds, *Babylonian Correspondence of Esarhaddon,* 45–46, no. 60.

154. Kwasman and Parpola, *Legal Transactions of the Royal Court of Nineveh, Part 1,* 92, no. 95.

155. Luukko and Van Buylaere, *Political Correspondence of Esarhaddon,* 39–40, no. 45.

156. Seibert, *Women in the Ancient Near East,* 14. The document named her father. It stated that the husband had to pay for his wife's "extradiction." Since her new owner had already taken custody of the woman, the husband may have had a right of redemption. Mattila, *Legal Transactions of the Royal Court of Nineveh, II,* 80–81, no. 85 (Akhatabisha). Kwasman and Parpola, *Legal Transactions of the Royal Court of Nineveh, Part 1,* 76, no. 88 (Daliya sold Anadalati), 130, no. 151.1–2 (husband sold wife). Under Babylonian law, a husband could not sell his wife.

157. The practice of sacred prostitution was attested by Herodotos (*History* 1.199) and Strabo (*Geography* 16.1.20). Driver and Miles, *Assyrian Laws,* 18–19. Such a practice would seem inconsistent with the monetary value the Assyrians placed on virginity before marriage. It is not attested in Mesopotamian sources. Daniel C. Snell, *Life in the Ancient Near East: 3100–332 B.C.E.,* 101. Mattila, *Legal Transactions of the Royal Court of Nineveh, II,* 281–82, no. 442. Kataja and Whiting, *Grants, Decrees and Gifts,* 116–17, no. 92.7–12.

158. I. Tzvi Abusch, *Babylonian Witchcraft Literature,* x–xii, 68–69, 73, 99–100, 105–6, 110–11, 116–17, 122–23, 126–30. Good magic was permitted and used in medicine for the purpose of healing. Evil magic, *kishpu,* was criminal (pp. 134–35, 137). *Maqlu* 1.1-121. *Maqlu,* which

means "burning" was a LA collection of anti-witchcraft incantations. The majority of witches in *Maqlu* were women. The symptoms of being bewitched were generally physical: fever, pain, confusion, flux of saliva, semen, or vaginal fluid, afflictions of the mouth and skin, leprosy, weakness or abnormality of infants, and death. One man blamed all his maladies on a witch. Livingstone, *Court Poetry and Literary Miscellanea*, 30, 32, no. 12. Frederick Cryer and Marie-Louise Thomsen, *Witchcraft and Magic in Europe: Biblical and Pagan Societies*, 30–36, 43–46. Yitschak Sefati and Jacob Klein, "The Role of Women in Mesopotamian Witchcraft," in *Sex and Gender in the Ancient Near East*, ed. Parpola and Whiting, 574–76, 580–86.

159. Abusch, *Babylonian Witchcraft Literature*, 138–39, 144–45. *Maqlu* 1.1–36, 71–121. Both witchcraft and anti-witchcraft rituals used figurines representing the victim, similar to the dolls used in voodoo. In anti-witchcraft rituals, figurines representing the witch were destroyed by fire and water, the two elements used for purification. Cryer and Thomsen, *Witchcraft and Magic in Europe*, 46–50; see 13–14, 18–23, 32, 38–41, 50–51. Abusch, *Babylonian Witchcraft Literature*, x–xii, 68–69, 72–73, 86–87, 99–100, 105, 110–17, 122–39, 144. Walter Farber, "Witchcraft, Magic, and Divination in Ancient Mesopotamia," in *Civilizations of the Ancient Near East*, ed. Sasson, 3:1898, citing *Maqlu* 5. Witchcraft was thought to defile the victims' relationship with the gods. Witches were tried before three gods, who also purified the victim. Sefati and Klein found that there were male witches in the LA period, but the majority were women ("Role of Women in Mesopotamian Witchcraft," 580–86).

160. Livingstone, *Court Poetry and Literary Miscellanea*, 30–32, no. 12.18, r.18.

161. Luukko and Van Buylaere, *Political Correspondence of Esarhaddon*, 52–56, nos. 59–60. Reynolds, *Babylonian Correspondence of Esarhaddon*, 83–84, no. 102. The writer also accused male members of the traitor's family of theft of money from the temple.

162. Ibid., 58, 60–62, no. 63. A priest was accused of encouraging a conspirator, and his wife Zaza of "bringing down the moon from the sky." Nissinen, *Prophets and Prophecy*, 170–75, nos. 115–17.

163. Pfeiffer, *State Letters of Assyria*, 145–46, no. 199. The text noted that her grandfather had been a shepherd, which indicated her lower-class status.

164. Luukko and Van Buylaere, *Political Correspondence of Esarhaddon*, 35–36, no. 39. The text left many questions unanswered, including the gender of the writer, the type of offense, and the nature of the order requested.

165. Reynolds, *Babylonian Correspondence of Esarhaddon*, 92–93, n. 116.

166. Fuchs and Parpola, *Correspondence of Sargon II*, 3:49, no. 74.

167. Jas, *Neo-Assyrian Judicial Procedures*, 56–57, no. 35; 58–60, no. 37; 90, no. 59 (*shakintu*). Mattila, *Legal Transactions of the Royal Court of Nineveh, II*, 185, no. 239: court decision.

168. Jas, *Neo-Assyrian Judicial Procedures*, 63–64, no. 41. Roth, "Homicide in the Neo-Assyrian Period," in *Language, Literature, and History*, ed. Rochberg-Halton, 351–63. The tablet is dated in 656. The document was signed, sealed, and sent to the capital at Nineveh, where it was preserved to use if a claim was made. Roth understands the wife, brother, or son to be the relatives of the victim, who might come to make a claim. She uses the LA debt-note formula in her analysis and cites other LA homicide cases that were resolved by payment of blood money. Offenders in a theft case pled guilty in the local court and paid restitution and a fine of three times the value of the property taken to avoid being sent to the royal court of Nineveh for trial. Kwasman and Parpola, *Legal Transactions of the Royal Court of Nineveh, Part 1*, 119–20, no. 133.

169. Abusch, *Babylonian Witchcraft Literature*, 112–17, 122–25. *Maqlu* 1.9–11.

170. Parpola, *Correspondence of Sargon II*, 160–61, no. 205.6–10 (letter written to LA king). Kataja and Whiting, *Grants, Decrees and Gifts*, 92, no. 82. r.3–5 (did not specify offense); 93, fig. 16.

171. Jas, *Neo-Assyrian Judicial Procedures*, 98. Written records were made of cases involving ongoing payments of money and debt, whereas executions and corporal punishments were com-

pleted immediately, without need for written documentation. Radner cites fifteen LA real estate contracts (*Die Neuassyrischen Privatrechtsurkunden,* 189–90). The formula used in such "contract security clauses" used the verbs "eat" and "drink." In the first penalty (ibid., 193–94), the seeds could be strewn between two city gates or over a seventy-kilometer trail. This is the distance between Nimrud and Asshur. In the second, the objects that were ingested varied. The imagery in this penalty was taken from the leather industry. It was customary to soak the skin of a sheep in the mealy paste before the wool was scraped off. Mattila, *Legal Transactions of the Royal Court of Nineveh, II,* 83–84, 147, 234, nos. 90, 176, 350, have the second penalty, while 137–38, no. 166 combines both. These contracts also prescribed additional penalties such as tenfold restitution and large fines. Many texts from Asshur, Nimrud, and Nineveh from the eighth and seventh centuries used such penalties. Kwasman and Parpola, *Legal Transactions of the Royal Court of Nineveh, Part 1,* 22, no. 20.1–5; 82–83, no. 96.

172. Kwasman and Parpola, *Legal Transactions of the Royal Court of Nineveh, Part 1,* 90–93, nos. 101.r.3–7, 102.r.3–8. No. 100 required a twelvefold fine. Nos. 101 and 102 required the eating penalties, child sacrifice, and the twelvefold fine. The context in nos. 100–101 was a slave sale contract for a man, his wife, and two sons; in 102, it was real estate contract. In the last fragmentary contract of sale, the object of the sale is missing. The legible penalty was to burn the firstborn son in the temple of Adad (229–30, no. 285. r.1–2).

173. Radner, *Die Neuassyrischen Privatrechtsurkunden,* 190. The first treaty was made by king Adad-nerari V (753–746) with the ruler of Arpad. It contained a clause adding the wearing of papyrus reeds as clothing. The second treaty was made by king Asshur-akhu-iddina with an unnamed vassal king.

174. Parpola and Watanabe, *Neo-Assyrian Treaties and Loyalty Oaths,* 46–58, no. 4. Succession Treaty of Asshur-akhu-iddina (Esarhaddon). Examples of the curses: that the enemy rape the wives before the eyes of anyone who broke the treaty (4.42); that the gods give the offender(s) venereal diseases and dripping urine (4.55); that dogs and pigs drag the breasts of the offender's young women and penises of his young men around the public squares in Asshur and then eat them; that his food be tar and pitch and drink be donkey urine (4.56); that he eat the flesh of his sons and daughters (4.69); that the blood of his wives, sons, and daughters taste sweet and that worms eat his flesh and that of his wives, sons, and daughters while they were still alive (4.75–76); that his women, sons, and daughters be captured by his enemy and their flesh be pierced with holes and burned until black (4.81, 84); that the offender, his women, sons, and daughters be killed by strangulation; that they be slaughtered like lambs; and that they be clamped into a bronze bird trap with no escape until they die (4.88, 96a, 101); that their bones never be reunited (4.97); and that the gods make the offender a woman in front of his enemies (4:91).

175. Beginning with the MA king Adad-nerari I about 1300 BCE, Assyrian kings left detailed annals of their military campaigns in chronological order inscribed on stone stelae kept in the archives of the palaces of Asshur and Nineveh. Van De Mieroop, *Cuneiform Texts and the Writing of History,* 41. The literary genre had closer affinity to Khatti and Egypt than to Sumer or Babylonia. Van Seters, *In Search of History,* 61. Kings exhorted their followers to clean and anoint their documents, to offer sacrifices, and to put them back in their places. Dire curses were invoked on those who neglected to do this or tried to make changes in the inscriptions. One such curse, after the usual clause on the destruction of the offender and his descendants, asked the goddess Ishtar to "change him from a man to a woman, may she cause his manhood to dwindle away." Grayson, *Assyrian Royal Inscriptions,* 1:21, nos. 129–30; 104–5, no. 698 (Tukulti-Ninurta I).

176. Liverani, "Deeds of Ancient Mesopotamian Kings," in *Civilizations of the Ancient Near East,* ed. Sasson, 4:2353–55, 2358–59, 2365. The annals of Assyrian kings were often rewritten and updated to include additional conquests and refocus previous statements in the light of subsequent events. The scribes were among the only literate persons in the MA and LA periods. The content of the inscriptions was indirectly addressed to the enemies of Assyria. Only the general

message of the inscriptions filtered down to ordinary women and men. Van Seters, *In Search of History*, 62.

177. OA II: vice-regent. Grayson, *Assyrian Royal Inscriptions,* 1:5–17, 22, 23, 24, 30, 32, 33, 35, 36, 38, 41. Grayson, *Assyrian Rulers of the Early First Millennium I,* 28. MA: king. Grayson, *Royal Inscriptions,* 1:42, 44, 45, 51, 56, 57, 67, 68, 70, 74, 75, 80, 85–87, 97, 99, 100, 105, 115, 123, 135, 147–51. MA: king of Assyria and king of the universe. Grayson, *Royal Inscriptions,* 1:48, 53–55, 60, 64, 72–77, 97–99, 105–15, 118, 122, 123, 128–30, 132, 135, 137–39, 141, 150, 151. MA and LA: regent of Asshur for predecessors, and king of Assyria and king of the universe for themselves. Grayson, *Royal Inscriptions,* 1:51, 53, 102, 105, 135, 149. Grayson, *Assyrian Rulers of the Early First Millennium I,* 138, 180, 181. The MA king Tukulti-Ninurta I called himself king of Babylon, Sumer, and Akkad, and sun god of all people. Grayson, *Royal Inscriptions,* 1:108, no. 713. MA: king of kings and lord of lords. Grayson, *Assyrian Rulers of the Early First Millennium I,* 90. Asshur-nasir-apli (Asshurnasirpal) gave himself the most titles: king of the universe, unrivaled king, king of the four compass points, sun god of the people, chosen by the gods, destructive weapon of the gods, beloved and favorite of the gods, valiant man, marvelous shepherd, chief herder, warrior, lion, hero, capturer of hostages, victorious over all lands, praiseworthy, exalted, important, magnificent, foremost, virile. Grayson, *Assyrian Rulers of the Early First Millennium I,* 194, 239, 263, 264, 281, 296, 298.

178. Salmanu-ashared (Shalmaneser) III bragged that after conquering Urartu, he killed eighteen thousand men, looted and burned all the palaces, took all the horses, mules, and donkeys as booty, and drove the women of the land in front of his army. Shamshi-Adad V claimed to have conquered, looted, and destroyed a city, taking thirty thousand prisoners, including the defeated king's palace women, sons, and daughters. Livingstone, *Court Poetry and Literary Miscellanea,* 46, no. 17.14–24; 108, no. 41.9–10,r.1. MA and LA kings destroyed the land around the cities they conquered. Many sowed salt over the fields, making them useless for growing crops. Grayson, *Assyrian Royal Inscriptions,* 1:60, no. 119. Sharrukin (Sargon) II bragged that besides destroying the cities, he destroyed dams, pastures, and grain supplies, burned crops, and cut down the trees and burned them. Saggs, *Might That Was Assyria,* 95, 260.

179. Adad-nerari I, Tukulti-Ninurta I, and Tukulti-apil-Esharra I. Grayson, *Assyrian Royal Inscriptions,* 1:61, no. 393; 103, no. 689; 119, no. 773. Grayson, *Assyrian Rulers of the Early First Millennium I,* 15. The MA kings destroyed and burned captured cities, but did not brag about killings, except military ones, or torture, as did the LA kings.

180. Asshur-nasir-apli (Asshurnasirpal) II. Grayson, *Assyrian Rulers of the Early First Millennium I,* 150: wives and daughters; 199: palace women and daughters; 217: girls as tribute; 218: ten women singers; 343: women musicians; 211, 218, 252, 261: king's female relatives with large dowries. It is unclear whether the unmarried women with large dowries were taken for actual marriage or for their dowries and then killed or taken as slaves. Salmanu-ashared IV received as tribute the daughter of the king of Damascus "with her enormous dowry." Kuan, *Neo-Assyrian Historical Inscriptions,* 115.

181. Flaying means cutting the skin off a living person, causing incredible pain and slow death. Kings hung up the skins on the walls of the conquered city. Impalement involved thrusting a stick up through the body of a person, then fixing it upright in the ground while the person slowly and painfully died. Grayson, *Assyrian Rulers of the Early First Millennium I,* 134, 198–99, 201, 242, 261 (flaying), 210, 220, 250, 260 (impalement). King Sharrukin (Sargon) II impaled his own cavalry officers if they did not report for urgent duty on time. He impaled them in front of their household and put their sons and daughters to death. Parpola, *Correspondence of Sargon II,* 22, no. 22. The first king to burn captives alive was Tukulti-Ninurta I, who thus killed all the inhabitants of a cult center. Grayson, *Assyrian Royal Inscriptions,* 1:103, no. 693.

182. Saggs, *Might That Was Assyria,* 109–16. Elam had been a vassal of Assyria and a buffer state between Assyria and the emerging might of Persia. When Elam decided to support Persia,

Asshur-bani'apli (Asshurbanipal) completely destroyed Elam. He even took their gods (statues) and the bones of their former kings to Asshur. He deported the remaining people, ruined their fields, and took all their animals. He left Elam empty and desolate, but ripe for the Persians to move in. Asshur-bani'apli also besieged Babylon, where his brother was king. The famine in Babylon was so bad that people were reputed to have eaten their own children. Arab tribes had supported Babylon. Asshur-bani'apli took one Arab prince, who became his vassal, and made him king over all the Arabs. Later this king was involved in an anti-Assyrian blockade of the western trade routes. Asshur-bani'apli went after him into the desert, plundered the tribes, and seized their wells. After capturing the king, he brought him back to Nineveh, where he humiliated him in public.

183. Liverani, "Deeds of Ancient Mesopotamian Kings," in *Civilizations of the Ancient Near East,* ed. Sasson, 4: 2353–55, 2358, 2361, 2365.

184. Grayson, *Assyrian Royal Inscriptions,* 1:82 (Salmanu-ashared). Grayson, *Assyrian Rulers of the Early First Millennium I,* 88 (Asshur-bel'kala), 132 (Asshur-dan II), 193–309 (Asshur-nasir-apli [Asshurnasirpal] II). The mutilation of war captives put a visible sign on their bodies of the might of their conqueror and their status as captives. However, Saggs suggests that few war captives were actually blinded or mutilated, only some of their leaders, since the blind and maimed would have little value as workers or slaves (*Greatness That Was Babylon,* 217–18).

185. Liverani, "Deeds of Ancient Mesopotamian Kings," 2361.

186. Saggs, *Greatness That Was Babylon,* after 266, fig. 46a: the use of the vise is clear; the second form of torture involved the victim in a horizontal position in the air, his wrist and ankles tied to pegs in the wall. An Assyrian soldier stood behind each victim doing something to the top of his back. This could represent the insertion of a tool to flay or remove the skin from the living victim. Parpola and Watanabe, *Neo-Assyrian Treaties and Loyalty Oaths,* 47, figs. 13 (rape), 14 (bones). Reynolds, *Babylonian Correspondence of Esarhaddon,* 160, no. 192: in this letter a threat of decapitation, including hanging the head on someone else's neck, was used in a non-military context. Roaf, *Cultural Atlas of Mesopotamia,* 185: impalement of captives on walls of Lakhish (relief, palace of Sennakherib, Nineveh). Ivan Starr, *Queries to the Sungod,* 56, fig. 21: drawing by Botta of one section of Nineveh palace relief, depicting Assyrian conquest of city in Media, showed thirteen naked men impaled outside the city wall. A. Leo Oppenheim, *Ancient Mesopotamia,* following p. 208, fig. 8 (heads). Fales and Postgate, *Imperial Administrative Records,* Part II, Frontispiece (pile of heads). A Livingstone, *Court Poetry and Literary Miscellanea,* 83, no. 34.20, and fig. 28 (head on neck), 68, fig. 24 (detail of head in tree from banquet scene). Roaf, 190 and Seibert, plate 70b: banquet scene (alabaster, NW palace of Asshurbanipal, Nineveh). Albenda, in *La Femme dans le Proche-Orient Antique,* 17–20 (deportees). Dietrich, *Babylonian Correspondence of Sargon and Sennacherib,* 124, fig. 17: drawing of relief of Babylonian women deportees, one woman and child riding a donkey and two Assyrian soldiers with five heads (reign of Sennakherib). Starr, *Queries to the Sungod,* 117, fig. 38: deportees, men in front, women following (reign of Sennakherib); 249, fig. 50: deportees, mostly women and children (reign of Asshurbanipal); 242, fig. 49: another relief depicted Assyrian soldiers looting and demolishing a captured town. Lanfranchi and Parpola, *Correspondence of Sargon II, Part II,* 117, no. 156: report to the king on the condition of deportees stated that they were weak, sick, and worn out by crossing the mountains; 170, fig. 33: men and women depportees mixed (reign of Sennakherib).

187. Pfeiffer, *State Letters of Assyria,* 45–46, no. 45; 29–30, no. 33. Parpola, *Correspondence of Sargon II,* 21–22, no. 21. Dietrich, *Babylonian Correspondence of Sargon and Sennacherib,* 99–100, no. 112.

188. Livingstone, *Court Poetry and Literary Miscellanea,* 120, no. 50.21.

189. Nahum 3:1, 7, 19. NRSV (modified). A. Kirk Grayson suggests that the fall of Assyria was caused by greed, embodied in a system of tax and tribute that took all the assets to the capital and

destroyed the economies of the outlying provinces of Assyria as well as those of vassal states, causing the empire outside of the capital to become very weak ("Assyrian Rule of Conquered Territory in Ancient Western Asia," in *Civilizations of the Ancient Near East*, ed. Sasson, 2:967).

Part Four: Khatti

1. Asia Minor, also called Anatolia, today forms the Asian part of Turkey. Hittite pottery was found at Kanish from 2000 BCE. The institutional structures and offices of kings, elders and assemblies, cult, priests, and the military existed by 1650. Amélie Kuhrt, *The Ancient Near East: C. 3000–330 B.C.*, 1:240. J. G. Macqueen describes the political and economic links between the proto-Hittites and OA I period (*The Hittites and Their Contemporaries in Asia Minor*, 19–21). In the Old Hittite (abbreviated OH) period, Khattusha, in central Asia Minor, was rebuilt after its destruction in protohistoric wars. Johannes Lehmann, *The Hittites*, 183, 185. The OH army conquered Babylon in 1595. At the height of its power, the Hittite empire included Asia Minor, northern Mesopotamia, Syria, and the Hurrian kingdom of Mitanni. The Late Hittite empire ended at the time of the Trojan war with Greece (about 1200). Hittite documents mentioned the Akhiya[wa], whom some scholars have identified with the Mycenean Greeks. Kuhrt, *Ancient Near East*, 1:237–38, 2:410–16. A few partially Hittite city-states survived in Syria and Asia Minor after 1200. Michael Roaf, *Cultural Atlas of Mesopotamia and the Ancient Near East*, 139 (map of Hittite empire).

2. Gary Beckman, "Royal Ideology and State Administration in Hittite Anatolia," in *Civilizations of the Ancient Near East*, ed. Sasson, 1:530–31, 533, 536, 538. Hittite kings and queens were not deified until after their deaths, when a cult was established. Kuhrt, *Ancient Near East*, 1:277, 280. Harry A. Hoffner, Jr., "Legal and Social Institutions in Hittite Anatolia," in *Civilizations of the Ancient Near East*, ed. Sasson, 1:563. Hittite kings identified with the god of justice and with the god of war. Richard H. Beal, "Hittite Military Organization," in *Civilizations of the Ancient Near East*, ed. Sasson, 1:545–48. The army had a chariot corps, infantry, and small cavalry. *Ancient Near Eastern Texts*, ed. Pritchard, 210–11. Hittite towns were fortified, locked, and guarded at night. The Hittites used bronze weapons, although they had iron, which was heavy and cumbersome. In Hittite art, the patron god or goddess was depicted holding his or her arms around the king and holding the king by the wrist, a gesture that denoted control and authority over the person held. Hoffner, 564, fig. 4. The same gesture is found in ancient Greek art.

3. Beckman finds Hittite society feudal in relation to its vassal states, but not internally, since it lacked the more complex chain of authority found in medieval feudalism ("Royal Ideology and State Administration in Hittite Anatolia," 542). Perhaps it is better to call it "direct feudalism," since tenants received feudal lands directly from the king to whom they owed military service.

4. Kuhrt, *Ancient Near East*, 1:232–36. Although cuneiform had been predominantly used for Semitic languages, it was sufficiently flexible to express Hittite, an Indo-European language. Hittite had no grammatical feminine pronouns (such as English "she" and "her") but a combined masculine/feminine for animate entities and neuter for inanimate objects. In English, "who" and "what" are not gender-specific: "who" denotes an animate subject, and "what" denotes an inanimate object. The feminine has to be deduced from the context, personal name or Sumerian gender marker. Jaan Puhvel, "*Genus* and *Sexus* in Hittite," in *Sex and Gender in the Ancient Near East*, ed. Parpola and Whiting, 547–48.

5. In the protohistory of Khatti, law was influenced by the large community of Old Assyrians who lived and worked in the early capital of Kanish and used Old Assyrian law in their courts and business transactions.

6. E. Neufeld, *The Hittite Laws*, 99–100. Harry A. Hoffner, Jr., *The Laws of the Hittites: A Crit-*

ical Edition, 3–5. City courts were located in the city gates. The king's court was held in the gate of the royal palace in the capital.

7. Martha Roth, *Law Collections from Mesopotamia and Asia Minor,* 213–14. Neufeld, *Hittite Laws,* 70–75, 111–15. The earliest extant copies of the Hittite Laws date from about 1500. Other copies found at Khattusha were from the period of the Hittite empire (abbreviated HE). The late HE recension with additional reforms is dated between 1350 and 1200. After detailed analysis, Hoffner finds manuscripts A and M to be OH, J to be early HE, and B and PT to be late HE (*Laws of the Hittites,* 229–30, 239, 245, 262). Some of the extant tablets date from the time they were written; others are copies of earlier laws made by later scribes.

8. Hoffner, *Laws of the Hittites,* 1. Neufeld, *Hittite Laws,* 97.

9. There were unwritten proto-Hittite customary laws. Many of these laws were collected and written down by the first OH king, Khattushilish I (1650). The first revision took place in the reign of King Telepinush (about 1500). *Cambridge Ancient History* I/2, 820–21. The revision formula, "formerly the law was x, now it is y," recalls the law reforms of the Sumerian king Uruinimgina, about one thousand years earlier. HtL 7, 9, 19b, 25, 57–59, 63, 67, 69, 81, 92, 94, 101, 119, 121, 129, 166–67. The changes in criminal penalties were noted in the laws. Fines were generally lowered. HtL 7, 9, 19b, 25, 57–59, 63, 67, 69, 81, 94, 101, 119, 129. Former corporal and capital penalties were replaced by fines. HtL 92, 101, 121, 166–67.The form of most of the laws was conditional. Hoffner, "Legal and Social Institutions of Hittite Anatolia," in *Civilizations of the Ancient Near East,* ed. Sasson, 1:555–56.

10. HtL 28. Hoffner, *Laws,* 37–38. Roth, *Law Collections,* 221. *Ancient Near Eastern Texts,* 190. The Hittite term was "marriage price," denoting the price a groom and his family paid for him to marry. In Assyria, it was "bride-price," connoting the sale of the bride. In Sumer and Babylonia, the premarriage transfer of property by the groom was called "marriage gifts."

11. HtL 29 and 30. Hoffner, *Laws,* 39–40. Roth, *Law Collections,* 221. *Ancient Near Eastern Texts,* 190.

12. HtL 27. Hoffner, *Laws,* 36–37. Roth, *Law Collections,* 220–21. This law contains an enigmatic clause: "they shall burn her personal possessions." Hoffner suggests that this might have been part of the funeral rites (*Laws,* 182). The manuscripts vary as to whether she had children or a son.

13. HtL 34, 36. Hoffner, *Laws,* 42–43, 185–86. Hoffner (pp. 42–43) and *Ancient Near Eastern Texts* (p. 190) have "no one shall change her social status." The same phrase occurs in both laws. In 34, it refers to the wife of the slave; in 36, to his son-in-law. In these laws the marriages between slave and free person fulfilled the requirements for legal marriage. Roth thinks that the free persons became slaves for life (*Law Collections,* 221–22).

14. HtL 31–33. Hoffner, *Laws,* 40–42. Roth, *Law Collections,* 221. *Ancient Near Eastern Texts,* 190. What the laws regarded as important in slave marriages was whether the marriage price was paid and by whom. Hoffner, "Legal and Social Institutions," 559–60.

15. HtL 26. Hoffner, *Laws,* 34–35. Roth, *Law Collections,* 220, 238 n. 21. *Ancient Near Eastern Texts,* 190. Some manuscripts say that the woman refused her husband. A lacuna in the text suggests that the husband had to give her more than just payment for childbearing. There are many gaps in the text of the second part of this law, which, if filled in, could alter the meaning.

16. HtL 176b, 177. Hoffner, *Laws,* 140–41. Roth, *Law Collections,* 234–35. *Ancient Near Eastern Texts,* 195. HtL 177 stated that the price of an augur, an interpreter of the flights of birds, was twenty-five sheqels, and the price of an unskilled woman or man was twenty sheqels, twice what a skilled artisan cost in the preceding law. The discrepancy indicates that the two laws had different times of origin and that prices had gone up. F. Imparati, "Private Life among the Hittites," in *Civilizations of the Ancient Near East,* ed. Sasson, 1:579.

17. HtL 158. Hoffner, *Laws,* 126–27, n. 412. Roth, *Law Collections,* 233, 239 n. 49. *Ancient Near Eastern Texts,* 195. One late HE manuscript had only two months' work for the women. In

that case, men would have earned 500 per month and women 300 per month. Elsewhere, Hoffner suggests that the work was different, that the harvest work of men was reaping and threshing and the work of women was milling the grain ("Legal and Social Institutions," 560). Yet even in this situation, it is still quite possible that the laws prescribed inequality in wages. Certainty is not possible without further evidence. HtL 24 (wages of slave men and women). In some laws, the wage was based on the time the person worked, and in others there was a set wage for the job itself. HtL 24, 150, 158 (time), 42, 160, 161, 200b (job).

18. HtL 171. Hoffner, *Laws*, 136–37. Roth, *Law Collections*, 234. *Ancient Near Eastern Texts*, 195. The text is fragmentary and unclear as to what the mother was supposed to do with the son's garment. The law indicates that women had some choice in deciding to whom they would leave their dowry. But in other laws, the dowry automatically went to their sons. Hoffner notes that this did not apply to royal mothers and children (*Laws*, 217).

19. HtL 1–2. Hoffner, *Laws*, 17. Roth, *Law Collections*, 217. Killing in a quarrel had intent, but not premeditation. Hoffner, *Laws*, 163. The text itself did not indicate whether the persons were given up to servitude or to death. The literal meaning of the word translated "persons" was "heads." HtL 174 prescribed the penalty for killing another person in a fight: one slave. These laws were probably from different times and sources.

20. HtL 3–4. Hoffner, *Laws*, 18. Roth, *Law Collections*, 217. Hoffner (p. 18 n. 10) and Roth (p. 238 n. 6) note that the amount of the fine was extremely high. It could be a scribal error in the text. The amount for a male victim is missing.

21. HtL 43–44a. Hoffner, *Laws*, 51–52. Roth, *Law Collections*, 223. Roth's translation is "one person"; Hoffner translates it as "a son." The evidence is insufficient to decide the question of intent, which could have been either simply to cross the river or to kill the man.

22. HtL 6. Hoffner, *Laws*, 20. Roth, *Law Collections*, 217–18. *Ancient Near Eastern Texts*, 189. In the OH version, the penalty was three acres or 12,000 square meters. If the corpse was found in open country, where no one owned the land, the officials drew a line with a three-mile radius around the spot. If there was a village within three miles, it had to pay compensation. This would have included all the inhabitants of the village. If there was no village within three miles, the heir of the murder victim forfeited his claim. Hoffner, *Laws*, 171–72.

23. HtL 7–9. Hoffner, *Laws*, 21–24. Roth, *Law Collections*, 218.

24. HtL 10–12. Hoffner, *Laws*, 24–26. Roth, *Law Collections*, 218–19.

25. HtL 13–16. Hoffner, *Laws*, 26–28. *Ancient Near Eastern Texts*, 189. There is some confusion about the fine for an offender who bit off a nose. Hoffner (*Laws*, 27 nn. 37–39) and Roth (*Law Collections*, 238 nn. 10–11) suggest that these were scribal errors and that the figures intended were thirty and fifteen sheqels. HtL 14 and 16 specified "male or female" slaves.

26. HtL 17-18. Hoffner, *Laws*, 28–29. Roth, *Law Collections*, 219–20. *Ancient Near Eastern Laws*, 190. See LL fragments d–f. SLEx 1–2. LH 209–14. MAL A 50–52.

27. HtL 19–21. Hoffner, *Laws*, 29–30. Roth, *Law Collections*, 220. Hoffner, "Legal and Social Institutions of Hittite Anatolia," in *Civilizations of the Ancient Near East*, ed. Sasson, 1:556.These are examples of vicarious punishment. The law did not state how a Hittite court could acquire jurisdiction over a foreign offender living in a foreign land. However, there were four extradition clauses in the treaty between Khattushilish I and Ramses II, pharaoh of Egypt. *Ancient Near Eastern Texts*, 200–201.

28. HtL 35. Hoffner, *Laws*, 43. *Ancient Near Eastern Texts*, 190. Roth, *Law Collections*, 222, 239 n. 26. The overseer was added in a late HE manuscript. The herder and overseer were not called slaves. The enslavement of the woman was temporary.

29. HtL 197. Hoffner, *Laws*, 155–56. Roth, *Law Collections*, 237. *Ancient Near Eastern Texts*, 196. See MAL 12–13. Deuteronomy 22:23–24 (city, did not cry out), 25–27 (country, cried out and no one heard).

30. HtL 189. Hoffner, *Laws*, 149. Roth, *Law Collections*, 236. The word *hurkel* is usually trans-

lated as "abomination," a legal term for a capital crime. Hoffner and Roth translate it as "an unpermitted sexual pairing." The same term was used for the forms of bestiality that were punished by death. Bestiality with a cow, a sheep, a pig, or a dog was a capital offense. HtL 187, 188, 199. In each case the offender was brought to the gate of the palace, but could not be tried before the king, as in other capital cases, because his impurity would contaminate the king. The king could impose or remit the death penalty. The cow, sheep, pig, and dog were ancient agricultural animals that had become sacred, representing gods. The death penalty was imposed for sacrilege, rather than for illicit sexual acts. HtL 200a. Bestiality with a horse or mule was not punished. These animals were relative latecomers and were not deified.

31. HtL 190, 191b, 195 (abominations), 194, 200a (not incest). Hoffner, *Laws,* 150–54. Roth, *Law Collections,* 236–37.

32. HtL 196. Hoffner, *Laws,* 155. Roth, *Law Collections,* 237. Putting the slaves to death would penalize their owner.

33. HtL 197b, 198. Hoffner, *Laws,* 155–56. Roth, *Law Collections,* 237. HtL 197b was part of a law on rape. The location of the act, in the woman's house, made the offense adultery. The law reverted to tribal custom, allowing the husband who caught them in the act, to kill his wife with impunity.

34. HtL 44b, 102, 111, 170, 176a, 198. Raymond Westbrook (*Studies in Biblical and Cuneiform Law,* 82), Hoffner (*Laws,* 189), and Roth (*Law Collections,* 230) state that the delegation of the case to the king's court indicated that sorcery was a capital offense. Anyone who failed to report the crime was punished by the penalty of the case, which was death. Telepinush, Edict 50. See LH 2 (man), MAL 47 (man or woman), Exodus 22:18 (woman)—all received the death penalty.

35. HtL 24. Hoffner, *Laws,* 32–33. Roth, *Law Collections,* 220, 238 n. 15. *Ancient Near Eastern Texts,* 190.

36. HtL 57–71, 81–83: theft of animals; 91–92: theft of bees; 96–97, 101–4, 108, 124: theft of grain, plants, vines, and trees; 119–20: theft of tame birds; 121–26, 129–31, 142: theft of farm tools and implements). Penalties were based on a number of factors: the age, sex, and training of animals, whether fattened, pregnant, or castrated. The penalty for theft of vines depended on whether the vineyard was fenced. These laws provide a glimpse into the agricultural dimension of Khatti.

37. HtL 126. Hoffner, *Laws,* 114–16. Roth, *Law Collections,* 231. The bronze weapon has been translated as "spear" (Hoffner and Roth) and "lance" (Neufeld, *Hittite Laws,* 37). In one Hittite ritual, the king and queen knelt before a spear, as before a sacred object. O. R. Gurney, *The Hittites,* 154. Theft of it may have challenged religious as well as royal authority.

38. HtL 166–67. Hoffner, *Laws,* 133–34. See Deuteronomy 22:9; Leviticus 19:19 (single sower, two different kinds of seeds).

39. HtL 43 (homicide), 197b–98 (adultery). Hoffner, *Laws,* 155–57. Roth, *Law Collections,* 237. There is a clause in the second law that involves putting something on someone's head. According to Hoffner, the husband placed a veil on his wife's head in reaffirmation of their marriage (*Laws,* 226). Hoffner, "Legal and Social Institutions of Hittite Anatolia," in *Civilizations of the Ancient Near East,* ed. Sasson, 1:558.

40. HtL 173a. Hoffner (*Laws,* 138) and Roth (*Law Collections,* 232) translate the penalty for disobeying the judgment of the king: the offender's "house will become a heap of ruins." The word "house" denotes the offender's family and other household members who would be killed, and only secondarily, if at all, the physical destruction of buildings. Since death was the penalty for the lesser offense, disobeying a magistrate, one can presume that it was also the penalty for the greater offense, disobeying the king.

41. HtL 173b. Hoffner, *Laws,* 138–39. Roth, *Law Collections,* 234. The exact nature of the clay jar penalty is much debated by scholars. Hoffner states that the nature and magnitude of the offense clause affected the meaning of the penalty clause (pp. 219–20). The penalty of putting

the slave into a clay pot could have been a form of humiliation and behavior modification if the slave's act was minor insubordination. If the offense was serious rebellion, the penalty could have been a form of execution: sealing the offender in the jar or burying him or her alive.

42. HtL 189–91, 195: incest, 44b, 111, 170: witchcraft. These were capital crimes which engendered pollution. In situations when the defendant had incurred pollution, the case could still be tried by the king's court, but the defendant could not enter the presence of the king, lest he or she pollute the king.

43. HtL 166–67. Both laws used the plural "they," implying some form of state jurisdiction. As penology developed in ancient civilizations, it was common to substitute animal sacrifice for human sacrifice, as in the OH revision of this law. Blood was still necessary to overcome pollution, but animal blood sufficed.

44. HtL 92, 121. Hoffner, *Laws*, 91, 110–11. The OH penalty for theft of a plow was similar to the penalty for sowing above. In this law the oxen were not put to death, since the crime of theft did not incur pollution. The penalties in these two laws used a principle of similarity or context (not the principle of *talion*).

45. HtL 1–6, 44a: homicide, 7–18: assault and battery, and 19–21: kidnapping.

46. HtL 93–95: burglary, 98–100: arson, and 101–3: theft, were punished by compensation. HtL 95 and 99 prescribed corporal mutilation of the nose and ears when a burglar or arsonist was a slave, plus compensation. In both laws, a slave owner who refused to pay compensation forfeited the slave.

47. The following laws contained fines that were increased in the late HE revision. HtL 6: free Hittite man or woman killed outside of Khatti, penalty in land increased, fine added; 7–8: blinded or knocked out tooth of free person: forty sheqels reduced to twenty, or twenty if accident; of a slave: ten raised to twenty, or ten if accident; 9: head injury: six reduced to three; 10: substitute worker, medical bills, and fine: six raised to ten, or two if slave; 13–14: bit off nose: forty reduced to thirty for free person, three raised to fifteen for slave; 16: tore off ear: twelve for free person, three raised to six for slave; 17: cause miscarriage of free woman, ten raised to twenty; 18: cause miscarriage of slave, five raised to ten. When the king revised the laws, he eliminated his own share of the fines for head injury and impurity, which reduced the fines by half. HtL 9, 25.

48. HtL 6: woman victim of murder; 24: help escaped male or female slave. The earlier OH version of many of the laws distinguished between male and female slaves who were victims of assault, even though the penalty for injuring either was the same. The revision did not make this distinction.

49. Penalties for slave offenders: HtL 93, 97 (fine of six sheqels), 101, 121, 132, 143 (fine of three sheqels), 95, 99 (mutilation of nose and ears), 170 (death). In HtL 95 and 99, the slave's owner paid compensation.

50. HtL 10. Roth, *Law Collections*, 218–19.

51. Kings composed annals of the events of their reigns beginning with the protohistoric king Anitta and continuing with the OH king Khattushilish I, the HE king Murshilish II, and the late HE king Tudkhaliyash IV. Kuhrt, *Ancient Near East*, 1:232–36. Most of the documents found at Khattusha date in the late HE period. Other sites provide a few letters and religious texts. The documents were written in many languages, including Hurrian, Akkadian, and Sumerian. Roth, *Law Collections*, 213. Beckman, "Royal Ideology and State Administration in Hittite Anatolia," in *Civilizations of the Ancient Near East*, ed. Sasson, 1:529, 539. Only the royal bureaucracy continued to use cuneiform writing, and their clay tablets survived. Ordinary documents were written on wood, which disintegrated. Hoffner, "Legal and Social Institutions of Hittite Anatolia," in *Civilizations of the Ancient Near East*, ed. Sasson, 1:555, 560. Macqueen notes that the majority of the population lived in agricultural villages, where society was still patriarchal, governed by male heads of households (*Hittites and Their Contemporaries in Asia Minor*, 74–75).

52. Hoffner, "Legal and Social Institutions," 560–62. The form of the exculpatory oath was: I did x and not y. If this is not the truth, "may the gods destroy me." A similar oath formula is found in the Hebrew Bible in Ruth 1:17; 2 Samuel 3:35. The royal bodyguard played a role in royal criminal trials. They brought in the defendant(s) under guard. The chief guard transmitted the case to the king. The guards stood armed during the trial. No one was permitted to go between the defendant and the guards. Hans G. Güterbock and Theo van den Hout, *The Hittite Instruction for the Royal Bodyguard,* 22–29, column 3:30–40.

53. Hoffner, "Legal and Social Institutions," 561. Kuhrt, *Ancient Near East,* 1:273–74. The king's son wrote to the provincial magistrates, accusing them of not following his father's instructions and becoming servants of the rich by eating and drinking with them in their households instead of listening to the complaints of the poor. OH "Instructions for Magistrates." HE "Instructions for District Governors." The clause against giving judgments for family members suggests an awareness of conflict of interest. Today judges would recuse themselves from such cases.

54. Hoffner, "Legal and Social Institutions," 561. HE "Instructions for District Governors." Imparati, "Private Life among the Hittites," in *Civilizations of the Ancient Near East,* ed. Sasson, 1: 577. Treaty between King Shuppiluliumash I of Khatti and King Hukkana of Hayasha. The text also mentioned sex with a brother, sister, or female cousin as illicit, but did not state the penalty for these.

55. Beckman, "Royal Ideology and State Administration in Hittite Anatolia," in *Civilizations of the Ancient Near East,* ed. Sasson, 1: 531, 536–37. Hoffner, "Legal and Social Institutions," in ibid., 1:564. "Great Queen" meant above all other queens, "empress." Hittite kings had harems filled with concubines and slave women for their sexual pleasure. Queens were different; they were depicted with their husbands on reliefs. Imparati, "Private Life among the Hittites," in ibid., 1: 578.

56. Trevor Bryce, *The Kingdom of the Hittites,* 96–98. Beckman, "Royal Ideology and State Administration," 537. Kuhrt, *Ancient Near East,* 1:240–41, 279. This office existed before the OH period. The first king used his relationship to the Tawananna to legitimize his claim to the throne. Lehmann, *Hittites,* 211. The relationship between the king as high priest and the Tawananna as head of the cult is unclear, although it was probably complementary. If it had been one of rivalry or conflict, the situation would have generated documents. However, lack of documentation cannot be taken to prove anything in the history of the ancient Near East. When a king prayed or someone else prayed for him, it was for the king, the queen, the princes, and the land. Macqueen, *Hittites and Their Contemporaries in Asia Minor,* 145, no. 135: relief showing King Tudkhaliya IV and Queen Sharruma leading worship together. Susana B. Murphy, "The Practice of Power in the Ancient Near East: Sorceresses and Serpents in Hittite Myths," in *Sex and Gender in the Ancient Near East,* ed. Parpola and Whiting, 436.

57. Hoffner, "Legal and Social Institutions of Hittite Anatolia," in *Civilizations of the Ancient Near East,* ed. Sasson, 1:561, 565. Kuhrt, *Ancient Near East,* 1:251–52, 254, 261, 267–68. King Shuppiluliumash I married a Kassite and sent his son to Egypt, but he was murdered on the way. Macqueen, *Hittites,* 46–47, 111. King Tudkhaliyash I married the Hurrian Nikalmati. J. G. Macqueen, "The History of Anatolia and of the Hittite Empire: An Overview," in *Civilizations of the Ancient Near East,* ed. Sasson, 2:1093: text of two letters from the Egyptian queen. King Khattushilish III married Pudukhepa. Henry Hoffner, Jr., "The Treatment and Long-Term Use of Persons Captured in Battle," in *Recent Developments in Hittite Archaeology and History,* ed. Yener and Hoffner, 64. His sister, Mashana'uzzi, was married to a vassal king. Theo van den Hout, "Khattushilish III, King of the Hittites," in *Civilizations of the Ancient Near East,* ed. Sasson, 2:1108. Marriages with vassal kings were sometimes made part of the treaty between king and vassal state. When the late HE city-state of Tabal was conquered by Assyria, Sargon (Sharrukin) II deposed the king, but gave the throne to the king's son and gave him an Assyrian princess in

marriage to obtain his loyalty. Macqueen, *Hittites,* 50, no. 26: picture of Khattushilish III taking his daughter to Pharaoh Ramses II.

58. Van den Hout, "Khattushilish III, King of the Hittites," 1110–12; 1111: rock relief of libations. Johan de Roos, "Hittite Prayers," in *Civilizations of the Ancient Near East,* ed. Sasson, 3:2004–5. Imparati, "Private Life among the Hittites," in ibid., 1:571. Gabriella Frantz-Szabó, "Hittite Witchcraft, Magic, and Divination," in ibid., 3:2015. *Ancient Near Eastern Texts,* 393–94: prayers of queen Pudukhepa. Letters may have been sent to the queen because the king was physically weak. She had joint seals with her husband and her son. Beckman, "Royal Ideology and State Administration in Hittite Anatolia," in *Civilizations of the Ancient Near East,* ed. Sasson, 1: 537 and 537, fig. 2: seal impression of Pudukhepa and son, King Tudkhaliash IV.

59. *Ancient Near Eastern Texts,* 358–61. "The Festival of the Warrior God." While the king and queen performed the rites, there were singers, dancers, musicians, and other functionaries performing their parts of the liturgy. Hoffner, "Legal and Social Institutions of Hittite Anatolia," in *Civilizations of the Ancient Near East,* ed. Sasson, 1:564. There are reliefs depicting the king and queen worshiping together. Kuhrt, *Ancient Near East,* 1:236.

60. *Ancient Near Eastern Texts,* 208–11, 399. "Prayer of Arnuwandas and Asmu-Nikkal Concerning the Ravages Inflicted on Hittite Cult-Centers." The priests were always listed first. The "mothers-of-the-god" were second once, and third twice. The other offices in this list were the "holy priests" and the "anointed." There was another list of lower temple personnel: musicians, singers, bakers, cooks, and gardeners. The "mothers-of-the-god" exercised an official religious office. The city or the border guards provided their rations. Gregory McMahon includes them with the priests ("Theology, Priests, and Worship in Hittite Anatolia," in *Civilizations of the Ancient Near East,* ed. Sasson, 3:1990–91). Hoffner, "Legal and Social Institutions," 657: women priests and singers. Macqueen, *Hittites,* 127, nos. 114–16: rock reliefs from Yailikaya show women priests (reign of Tudkhaliyash IV).

61. Jared Miller, "The *katra/i*-women in the Kizzuwatnean Rituals from Hattusa," in *Sex and Gender in the Ancient Near East,* ed. Parpola and Whiting, 423–24, 427.

62. *Ancient Near Eastern Texts,* 348–49: "Purification Ritual," 2, 4. Billie Jean Collins, "Ritual Meals in the Hittite Cult," in *Ancient Magic and Ritual Power,* ed. Meyer and Mirecki, 78–88.

63. *Ancient Near Eastern Texts,* 349–50: "Ritual against Impotence," by "Pissuwattis, the Arzawa woman who lives in Parassa." The ritual used the first person, suggesting that the author herself performed the ritual. After she consecrated the sheep, others killed it, cut it up, cooked it, and selected the special parts. The remainder of the text is missing. Miller, "*katra/i*-women," 425. Hoffner, "Legal and Social Institutions," 1:565: Anniwiyani and Ayatarsha.

64. *Ancient Near Eastern Texts,* 350–51: "Ritual against Domestic Quarrel." Hoffner, "Legal and Social Institutions," 567.

65. *Ancient Near Eastern Texts,* 347: "Ritual to Counteract Sorcery." The Hittite archives in Khattusha contained works on magic in Babylonian and Hittite, but none in Aramaic, Persian, or Greek. Frederick Cryer and Marie-Louise Thomsen, *Witchcraft and Magic in Europe: Biblical and Pagan Societies,* 91–92.

66. *Ancient Near Eastern Texts,* 346: "Ritual for the Purification of God and Man." The animals were oxen, cows, ewes, and goats. A ditch had been dug from the altar to the river.

67. Kuhrt, *Ancient Near East,* 1:270–71, 274–76, 279. Natural death contaminated those who were physically close to the deceased, such as family members.

68. Puhvel, "*Genus* and *Sexus* in Hittite," in *Sex and Gender in the Ancient Near East,* ed. Parpola and Whiting, 548–49. *Ancient Near Eastern Texts,* 351–54: "Evocatio" and "Soldier's Oath."

69. Beal, "Hittite Military Organization," in *Civilizations of the Ancient Near East,* ed. Sasson, 1: 547–48. *Ancient Near Eastern Texts,* 353–54: "The Soldiers' Oath." Hittite women covered their heads, a symbol of male dominance.

70. Beal, "Hittite Military Organization," 550.

71. Hoffner, "Legal and Social Institutions," 567. The story, although written in Hittite, was about a couple in a faraway land, so it is not absolutely certain that it reflects Hittite misogynism.

72. *Ancient Near Eastern Texts*, 208–9: "Instructions for Temple Officials," 5–6, 10, 14. The temple officials were not to "divide" what was given to, and therefore belonged to, the god. This tabu extended to meat, bread, and wine.

73. Lehmann, *Hittites*, 276–77: purification ritual.

74. Hoffner, "Legal and Social Institutions," 558–60, 566. Imparati, "Private Lives among the Hittites," 575. There are fewer extant documents about nonroyal lives because marriage contracts and household documents were generally written on wood, which decomposed. Hoffner, 558–59, figs. 1–2: OH vase painting of wedding preparations, fig. 3: relief on vase of couple alone, the groom removing the floor-length veil of the bride.

75. Hoffner, "Legal and Social Institutions," 567. Imparati, "Private Lives among the Hittites," 579–85. Archaeologists have found evidence in Anatolia of spinning and weaving: spindle whorls and loom weights. Every other ancient Near Eastern culture, as well as the Greek, made spinning and weaving the symbolic role of the woman. In Khatti women did spin and weave, but the foremost symbolic role of women in Khatti was grinding grain with a millstone. Harry A. Hoffner, "Treatment and Long-Term Use of Persons Captured in Battle," in *Recent Developments in Hittite Archaeology and History*, ed. Yener and Hoffner, 69. Beckman, "Royal Ideology and State Administration in Hittite Anatolia," 530. Since the millstone symbolized women's work, some Hittite kings humiliated their war captives by making them work at milling. Estate lists contain the number, sex, and age bracket of the persons and the animals in the estate. Hittite scribes held the same rank as officials of the royal court. Pearce, "Scribes and Scholars of Ancient Mesopotamia," in *Civilizations of the Ancient Near East*, ed. Sasson, 4:2266. This does not mean women scribes were given such a high rank.

76. The decree releasing debt-slaves was written in both the Hurrian and Hittite languages. Hoffner, "Legal and Social Institutions," 566: Annals of king.

77. Kuhrt, *Ancient Near East*, 1:242, 256. Annals of King Murshilish II, who did not attack the city. Lehmann, *Hittites*, 184. The proto-Hittite king was Anitta (about 1750).

78. Murphy, "The Practice of Power in the Ancient Near East: Sorceresses and Serpents in Hittite Myths," in *Sex and Gender in the Ancient Near East*, ed. Parpola and Whiting, 433–35, 442.

79. Beckman, "Royal Ideology and State Administration in Hittite Anatolia," 533–35. Succession according to edict of Telepinush: (1) prince of first rank, son of king; (2) son of second rank; (3) if no male heir, then the husband of first rank daughter.

80. King Telepinush, Edict 49. Roth, *Law Collections*, 237. Telepinush ruled from about 1525 to 1500 BCE. The option of choosing compensation also went back to primitive tribal society, in which the family of the murderer could pay "blood money" to the "avenger of blood," the representative of the victim's family who had been chosen to resolve the case. Hoffner, "Legal and Social Institutions," 556. According to King Telepinush's Edict 49, the victim's heir had the right to avenge, but could choose compensation instead of blood revenge.

81. *Ancient Near Eastern Texts*, 207–8: "Instruction for Palace Personnel." When a hair was discovered in the king's water, the water bearer was sent to undergo an ordeal, and, when found guilty, was executed. Edict of King Telepinush. Kuhrt, *Ancient Near East*, 1:247. The practice was revived in the empire. Hoffner, "Legal and Social Institutions," 564–65. *Ancient Near Eastern Texts*, 207–8, "Instructions for Temple Personnel," 2–3.

82. *Ancient Near Eastern Texts*, 353–54: "The Soldiers' Oath," 3.1–10.

83. *Ancient Near Eastern Texts*, 207–10: "Instructions for Temple Officials," 2–3, 5–6, 8, 10, 14, 18–19. These "instructions" were written as a mixture of apodictic and conditional laws. The execution of all the extended family members of a slave would have caused a large economic loss to the slave owner. The temple probably could sustain such a loss because it regularly received fresh supplies of war captives to be temple slaves. Hoffner, "Treatment and Long-Term Use of Persons

Captured in Battle," in *Recent Developments in Hittite Archaeology and History*, ed. Yener and Hoffner, 63. An individual slave owner could not.

84. Imparati, "Private Life among the Hittites," in *Civilizations of the Ancient Near East*, ed. Sasson, 1:574–75. Hittites depended on children for support in old age and for performance of religious rites after their death to help them in the afterlife.

85. Bryce, *Kingdom of the Hittites*, 98. King Khattushilish I. Beckman, "Royal Ideology and State Administration in Hittite Anatolia," 1:537–38. Hoffner, "Legal and Social Institutions," 1:565. The stepmother was from Kassite Middle Babylonia. Lehmann, *Hittites*, 193–94, 227–30. Van den Hout, "Khattushilish III, King of the Hittites," in *Civilizations of the Ancient Near East*, ed. Sasson, 2:1109.

86. Murphy, "Practice of Power in the Ancient Near East," in *Sex and Gender in the Ancient Near East*, ed. Parpola and Whiting, 441. Frantz-Szabo, "Hittite Witchcraft, Magic, and Divination," in *Civilizations of the Ancient Near East*, ed. Sasson, 3:2008. The king was Murshilish II. Hoffner, "Legal and Social Institutions," 563, 565, 568. She was the widow of king Shupiluliuma I. The OH king Khattushilish I called his wife a "snake," which carried the innuendo of witchcraft. Hittite kings were afraid of the magical powers of their queens. Sorcery engendered pollution in the royal family. After getting rid of the offender and undergoing a purification ritual, it was imperative that the offender never return to the state. The border guards were so instructed under pain of criminal punishment. *Ancient Near Eastern Texts*, 210–11. Westbrook, *Studies in Biblical and Cuneiform Law*, 82.

87. Imparati, "Private Life among the Hittites," 575–76. In the laws, it was a crime for a man to assault a pregnant woman causing miscarriage.

88. Miller, "*katra/i*-women in the Kizzuwatnean Rituals from Hattusa," in *Sex and Gender in the Ancient Near East*, ed. Parpola and Whiting, 428–30.

89. *Ancient Near Eastern Texts*, 208: "Instructions for Temple Officials," 5–6.

90. *Ancient Near Eastern Texts*, 207–8: "Instructions for Palace Personnel"; Instructions for Temple Officials," 2–3.

91. Telepinush, Edict 50. Roth, *Law Collections*, 237–38. *Ancient Near Eastern Texts*, 207–8: "Instructions for Temple Officials." Another form of the death penalty in the OH period was cutting the throat and hanging the body in the city gate. Bryce, *Kingdom of the Hittites*, 98. Hoffner, "Treatment and Long-Term Use of Persons Captured in Battle," 62, 67–69.

92. Edict of Telepinush, in Kuhrt, *Ancient Near East*, 1:247–48. Hoffner, "Legal and Social Institutions," 557. Witchcraft was a capital crime in most ancient Near Eastern legal systems. See LH 2, MAL A 47, Exodus 22:18.

Photo Credits

1. L. M. Tetlow
2. HIP/Art Resource, NY
3. National Museum of Archaeology, Baghdad, Iraq
4. National Museum of Archaeology, Baghdad, Iraq
5. National Museum of Archaeology, Baghdad, Iraq
6. Erich Lessing/Art Resource, NY
7. Erich Lessing/Art Resource, NY
8. Erich Lessing/Art Resource, NY
9. Museum, University of Pennsylvania, CBS 16665
10. Erich Lessing/Art Resource, NY
11. Réunion des Musées Nationaux, Art Resource, NY
12. Erich Lessing/Art Resource, NY
13. National Museum of Archaeology, Baghdad, Iraq
14. Museum, University of Pennsylvania, B 16229
15. HIP/Art Resource, NY
16. National Museum of Archaeology, Baghdad, Iraq
17. Erich Lessing/Art Resource, NY
18. Erich Lessing/Art Resource, NY
19. National Museum of Archaeology, Baghdad, Iraq
20. National Museum of Archaeology, Baghdad, Iraq
21. Erich Lessing/Art Resource, NY
22. National Museum of Archaeology, Baghdad, Iraq
23. Erich Lessing/Art Resource, NY
24. Erich Lessing/Art Resource, NY
25. Werner Forman/Art Resource, NY

Bibliography

Abusch, I. Tzvi. *Babylonian Witchcraft Literature*. Brown Judaic Studies 132. Atlanta: Scholars Press, 1987.

Abusch, Tzvi, John Huehnergard, Piotr Steinkeller, eds. *Lingering Over Words: Studies in Ancient Near Eastern Literature in Honor of William L. Moran*. Harvard Semitic Studies 37. Atlanta: Scholars Press, 1990.

Albenda, Pauline. "Woman, Child, and Family: Their Imagery in Assyrian Art." In *La Femme dans le Proche-Orient Antique*, edited by Jean-Marie Durand, 17–21. Compte rendu de la xxxiii Rencontre Assyriologique Internationale (Paris, 1986). Paris: Editions Recherche sur les Civilisations, 1987.

Allison, Penelope, ed. *The Archaeology of Household Activities*. London: Routledge, 1999.

Amiet, Pierre. *Art of the Ancient Near East*. New York: Abrams, 1980.

Aruz, Joan, ed. *Art of the First Cities: The Third Millennium B.C. from the Mediterranean to the Indus*. The Metropolitan Museum of Art. New Haven: Yale University Press, 2003.

Asher-Greve, Julia M. *Frauen in altsumerischer Zeit*. Bibliotheca Mesopotamica 18. Malibu, Calif.: Undena, 1985.

———. "Decisive Sex, Essential Gender." In *Sex and Gender in the Ancient Near East:* Proceedings of the 47th Rencontre Assyriologique Internationale, Helsinki, July 2–6, 2001, edited by S. Parpola and R. M. Whiting. Compte rendu, Rencontre Assyriologique Internationale 47. Helsinki: Neo-Assyrian Text Corpus Project, 2002.

———. "The Oldest Female Oneiromancer." In *La Femme dans le Proche-Orient Antique*, edited by Jean-Marie Durand, 27–32. Compte rendu de la xxxiii Rencontre Assyriologique Internationale (Paris, 1986). Paris: Editions Recherche sur les Civilisations, 1987.

Bahrani, Zainab. *Women of Babylon: Gender and Representation in Mesopotamia*. London: Routledge, 2001.

Barton, George R., ed. and trans. *The Royal Inscriptions of Sumer and Akkad*. American Oriental Society. New Haven: Yale University Press, 1929.

Batto, Bernard Frank. *Studies on Women at Mari*. Baltimore/London: Johns Hopkins University Press, 1974.

Beal, Richard H. "Hittite Military Organization." In *Civilizations of the Ancient Near East,* edited by Jack M. Sasson, 1:545–54. New York: Scribner, 1995.

Beard, Mary, and John North, eds. *Pagan Priests: Religion and Power in the Ancient World.* Ithaca, N.Y.: Cornell University Press, 1990.

Beaulieu, Paul-Alain. "King Nabonidus and the Neo-Assyrian Empire." In *Civilizations of the Ancient Near East,* edited by Jack M. Sasson, 2:969–80. New York: Scribner, 1995.

———. *The Reign of Nabonidus: King of Babylon 556–539 B.C.* New Haven: Yale University Press, 1989.

Beckman, Gary. "Royal Ideology and State Administration in Hittite Anatolia." In *Civilizations of the Ancient Near East,* edited by Jack M. Sasson, 1:529–43. New York: Scribner, 1995.

Behrens, Hermann, Darlene Loding, and Martha T. Roth, eds. *DUMU-E2-DUB-BA-A: Studies in Honor of Ake Sjöberg.* Occasional Publications of the Samuel Noah Kramer Fund 11. Philadelphia: University Museum, 1989.

Ben-Barrak, Zafira. "The Queen Consort and the Struggle for Succession to the Throne." In *La Femme dans le Proche-Orient Antique,* ed. Jean-Marie Durand, 33–40. Compte rendu de la xxxiii Rencontre Assyriologique Internationals (Paris, 1986). Paris: Éditions Recherche sur les Civilisations, 1987.

Bennett, Patrick R. *Comparative Semitic Linguistics.* Winona Lake, Ind.: Eisenbrauns, 1998.

Ben Zvi, Ehud, and Michael H. Floyd, eds. *Writings and Speech in Israelite and Ancient Near Eastern Prophecy.* Society of Biblical Literature Symposium Series 10. Atlanta: Society of Biblical Literature, 2000.

Biran, Avraham. "Tell Dan—Five Years Later." *Biblical Archaeologist* 43 (1980): 168–82.

Black, Jeremy A., and W. J. Tait. "Archives and Libraries in the Ancient Near East." In *Civilizations in the Ancient Near East,* edited by Jack Sasson, 4:2197–2210. New York: Scribner, 1995.

Bottéro, Jean. *Everyday Life in Ancient Mesopotamia.* Translated by Antonia Nevill. Baltimore: Johns Hopkins University Press, 1992.

———. *Mesopotamia.* Translated by Zainab Bahrani and Marc Van De Mieroop. Chicago: University of Chicago Press, 1992.

———. *Religion in Ancient Mesopotamia.* Translated by Teresa Lavender Fagan. Chicago: University of Chicago Press, 2001.

Bottéro, Jean, Elena Cassin, and Jean Vercoutter, eds. *The Near East: The Early Civilizations.* Translated by R. F. Tannenbaum. London: Weidenfeld & Nicolson, 1965.

Bottéro, Jean, Clarisse Herrenschmidt, and Jean-Pierre Vernant, eds. *Ancestor of the West.* Translated by Teresa Fagan. Chicago: University of Chicago Press, 2000.

Brinkman, J. A. "The Babylonian Chronicle Revisited." In *Lingering Over Words: Studies in Ancient Near Eastern Literature in Honor of William L. Moran,* edited by I. Tzvi Abusch, John Huehnergard, and Piotr Steinkeller. Harvard Semitic Studies 37. Atlanta: Scholars Press, 1990.

———. "Mesopotamian Chronology of the Historical Period." Appendix in *Ancient Mesopotamia: Portrait of a Dead Civilization*, by Leo Oppenheim, 335–47. Chicago: University of Chicago Press, 1977.

———. *A Political History of Post-Kassite Babylonia (1158-722 B.C.)*. Analecta Orientalia 43. Rome: Pontificium Institutum Biblicum, 1968.

———. *Prelude to Empire: Babylonian Society and Politics, 747-626 B.C.* Philadelphia: The Babylonian Fund, University Museum, 1984.

———. "Twenty Minas of Copper." In *Language, Literature and History: Philological and Historical Studies Presented to Erica Reiner*, edited by Francesca Rochberg-Halton. New Haven: American Oriental Society, 1987.

Bryce, Trevor. *The Kingdom of the Hittites*. Oxford: Clarendon, 1998.

Buss, Martin J. "The Distinction Between Civil and Criminal Law in Ancient Israel. In *Proceedings of the Sixth World Congress of Jewish Studies* I. Jerusalem: Jerusalem Academic Press, 1977.

Butzer, Karl. "Environmental Change in the Near East and Human Impact on the Land." In *Civilizations of the Ancient Near East*, edited by Jack M. Sasson, 123–52. New York: Scribner, 1995.

Cagirgan, G., and W. G. Lambert. "The Late Babylonian Kislimu Ritual for Esagil." *Journal of Cuneiform Studies* 43 (1991): 89–106.

The Cambridge Ancient History. Edited by I. E. S. Edwards et al. Cambridge: Cambridge University Press. Volume 1, part 1, 3rd ed., 1970; part 2, 3rd ed., 1971. Volume 2, part 1, 3rd ed., 1973; part 2, 3rd ed., 1975. Volume 3, part 1, 2nd ed., 1982; part 2, 2nd ed., 1991.

Cameron, Averil, and Amélie Kuhrt, eds. *Images of Women in Antiquity*. Detroit: Wayne State University Press, 1983.

Carena, Omar. *History of the Near Eastern Historiography and Its Problems: 1852-1985*. Alter Orient und Altes Testament 218. Neukirchen-Vluyn: Neukirchener Verlag, 1989.

Charpin, Dominique. "The History of Ancient Mesopotamia: An Overview." In *Civilizations of the Ancient Near East*, edited by Jack M. Sasson, 2:807–30. New York: Scribner, 1995.

Charpin, Dominique, F. Joannes, S. Lackenbacher, and B. Lafont, eds. *Archives épistolaires de Mari* I/2. Archives Royales de Mari 26. Paris: Editions Recherche sur les Civilisations, 1988.

Chirichigno, Gregory C. *Debt-Slavery in Israel and the Ancient Near East*. Journal for the Study of the Old Testament: Supplement Series 141. Sheffield: Sheffield Academic Press, 1993.

Civil, Miguel. "New Sumerian Law Fragments." In *Studies in Honor of Benno Landsberger on His Seventy-Fifth Birthday*, edited by Hans G. Güterbock and Thorkild Jacobsen, 1–8. Chicago: Chicago University Press, 1965.

———. "On Mesopotamian Jails and Their Lady Warden." In *The Tablet and the*

Scroll: Near Eastern Studies in Honor of William W. Hallo, edited by Mark Cohen, D. Snell, and D. Weisberg, 72–78. Bethesda, Md.: CDL Press, 1993.

Cohen, Mark, D. Snell, and D. Weisberg, eds. *The Tablet and the Scroll: Near Eastern Studies in Honor of William W. Hallo.* Bethesda, Md.: CDL Press, 1993.

Colbow, Gudrun. "Priestesses, either Married or Unmarried, and Spouses without Title: Their Seal Use and Their Seals in Sippar at the Beginning of the Second Millennium BC." In *Sex and Gender in the Ancient Near East:* Proceedings of the 47th Rencontre Assyriologique Internationale, Helsinki, July 2–6, 2001, edited by S. Parpola and R. M. Whiting, 85–90. Compte rendu, Rencontre Assyriologique Internationale 47. Helsinki: Neo-Assyrian Text Corpus Project, 2002.

Cole, Stephen W. *Nippur in Late Assyrian Times: C. 755-612 BC.* State Archives of Assyria Studies 4. Helsinki: Neo-Assyrian Text Corpus Project, 1996.

Cole, Stephen W., and Peter Machinist. *Letters from Priests to the Kings Esarhaddon and Assurbanipal.* State Archives of Assyria 13. Helsinki: Neo-Assyrian Text Corpus Project, 1998.

Collins, Billie Jean. "Ritual Meals in the Hittite Cults." In *Ancient Magic and Ritual Power,* edited by Marvin Meyer and Paul Mirecki, 77–92. Leiden: Brill, 1995.

Collon, Dominique. *Ancient Near Eastern Art.* Berkeley/Los Angeles: University of California Press, 1995.

———. *First Impressions: Cylinder Seals in the Ancient Near East.* Chicago: University of Chicago Press, 1987.

Cooper, Jerrold S. *The Curse of Agade.* Johns Hopkins Near Eastern Studies. Baltimore: Johns Hopkins University Press, 1983.

———. *Presargonic Inscriptions.* American Oriental Society Translation Series 1; Sumerian and Akkadian Royal Inscriptions. New Haven: American Oriental Society, 1986.

———. "Third Millennium Mesopotamia." In *Women's Earliest Records: From Ancient Egypt and Western Asia,* edited by Barbara S. Lesko, 47–51. Atlanta: Scholars Press, 1989.

———. "Virginity in Ancient Mesopotamia." In *Sex and Gender in the Ancient Near East:* Proceedings of the 47th Rencontre Assyriologique Internationale, Helsinki, July 2–6, 2001, edited by S. Parpola and R. M. Whiting, 91–112. Compte rendu, Rencontre Assyriologique Internationale 47. Helsinki: Neo-Assyrian Text Corpus Project, 2002.

Crawford, Harriet. *Sumer and the Sumerians.* Cambridge: Cambridge University Press, 1991.

Cryer, Frederick, and Marie-Louise Thomsen. *Witchcraft and Magic in Europe: Biblical and Pagan Societies.* Philadelphia: University of Pennsylvania Press, 2001.

Curtis, J. E., and J. E. Reade, eds. *Art and Empire: Treasures from Assyria in the British Museum.* New York: Metropolitan Museum of Art, 1995.

Dalley, Stephanie. *Mari and Karana.* London/New York: Longman, 1984.

Dalley, Stephanie, and J. N. Postgate, *The Tablets from Fort Shalmaneser*. Oxford: British School of Archaeology in Iraq, 1984.

Dandamayev, M. A. "State and Temple in Babylonia in the First Millennium." In *State and Temple Economy in the Ancient Near East*, edited by Edward Lipinski, 2:589–95. Leuven: Department Orientalistiek, 1979.

Diakonoff, I. M. "A Babylonian Pamphlet from about 700 BC." In *Studies in Honor of Benno Landsberger on His Seventy-Fifth Birthday*, edited by Hans G. Güterbock and Thorkild Jacobsen, 343–49. Chicago: University of Chicago Press, 1965.

———. "Some Remarks on the 'Reforms' of Urukagina." *Revue d'Assyriologie et d'Archéologie Orientale* 52 (1958): 1–15.

Dietrich, Manfried, ed. *The Babylonian Correspondence of Sargon and Sennacherib*. State Archives of Assyria 17. Helsinki: Helsinki University Press, 2003.

Donbaz, Veysel, and Benjamin R. Foster, *Sargonic Texts from Telloh in the Istanbul Archaeological Museum*. Philadelphia: University Museum, 1982.

Donbaz, Veysel, and A. Kirk Grayson. *Royal Inscriptions on Clay Cones from Ashur now in Istanbul*. Royal Inscriptions of Mesopotamia, Supplements 1. Toronto: University of Toronto Press, 1997.

Dossin, Georges. *Correspondance de Samsi-Addu et de ses Fils*. Archives Royales de Mari 1. Paris: Imprimerie Nationale, 1950.

Dougherty, Raymond Philip. *Archives from Erech: Time of Nebuchadrezzar and Nabonidus*. Goucher College Cuneiform Inscriptions 1. New Haven: Yale University Press, 1923.

———. *Archives from Erech: Neo-Babylonian and Persian Periods*. Goucher College Cuneiform Inscriptions 2. New Haven: Yale University Press, 1933.

Driver, Godfrey R., and John C. Miles. *The Assyrian Laws*. Oxford, 1935. Repr., Aalen: Scientia Verlag, 1975.

———. *The Babylonian Laws*. 2 vols. Oxford: Clarendon, 1952, 1955.

Durand, Jean-Marie. *Archives épistolaires de Mari* I/1. Archives Royales de Mari 26. Paris: Éditions Recherche sur les Civilisations, 1988.

Durand, Jean-Marie, ed. *La Femme dans le Proche-Orient Antique*. Compte rendu de la xxxiii Rencontre Assyriologique Internationale (Paris, 1986). Paris: Éditions Recherche sur les Civilisations, 1987.

Du Ry, Carel. *Art of the Ancient Near and Middle East*. New York: Abrams, 1978.

Edzard, Dietz Otto. *Gudea and His Dynasty*. Royal Inscriptions of Mesopotamia. Early Periods 3/1. Toronto: University of Toronto Press, 1997.

———. "The Sumerian Language." In *Civilizations of the Ancient Near East*, edited by Jack M. Sasson, 4:2107–2116. New York: Scribner, 1995.

Ehrenberg, Erica, ed. *Leaving No Stones Unturned: Essays on the Ancient Near East and Egypt in Honor of Donald P. Hansen*. Winona Lake, Ind.: Eisenbrauns, 2002.

Ellis, Maria de Jong, ed. *Essays on the Ancient Near East in Memory of Jacob Joel*

Finkelstein. Memoirs of the Connecticut Academy of Arts and Sciences 19. Hamden, Conn.: Archon Books, 1977.

———. "An Old Babylonian Adoption Contract from Tell Harmel." *Journal of Cuneiform Studies* 27 (1975): 130–51.

Eyre, Christopher. "The Agricultural Cycle, Farming, and Water Management." In *Civilizations of the Ancient Near East,* edited by Jack M. Sasson, 1:175–90. New York: Scribner, 1995.

Fales, Frederick M. *Aramaic Epigraphs on Clay Tablets of the Neo-Assyrian Period.* Studi Semitici Nuovo Serie 2. Rome: Università degli Studi *"La Sapienza,"* 1986.

———. *Assyrian Royal Inscriptions: New Horizons.* Rome: Istituto per l'Oriente, 1981.

Fales, Frederick, and J. N. Postgate. *Imperial Administrative Records, Part I.* State Archives of Assyria 7. Helsinki: Helsinki University Press, 1992.

———. *Imperial Administrative Records, Part II.* State Archives of Assyria 11. Helsinki: Helsinki University Press, 1995.

Falkenstein, Adam. *The Sumerian Temple City.* Monographs on the Ancient Near East 1/1. Malibu, Calif.: Undena, 1974.

Farber, Walter. "Witchcraft, Magic, and Divination in Ancient Mesopotamia." In *Civilizations of the Ancient Near East,* edited by Jack M. Sasson, 3:1895–1910. New York: Scribner, 1995.

Foster, Benjamin. "Notes on Women in Sargonic Society." In *La Femme dans le Proche-Orient Antique,* ed. Jean-Marie Durand, 53–61. Compte rendu de la xxxiii Rencontre Assyriologique Internationals (Paris, 1986). Paris: Éditions Recherche sur les Civilisations, 1987.

———. "Western Asia in the First Millennium." In *Women's Earliest Records: From Ancient Egypt and Western Asia,* edited by Barbara S. Lesko, 141–43. Atlanta: Scholars Press, 1989.

———. "Western Asia in the Second Millennium." In *Women's Earliest Records: From Ancient Egypt and Western Asia,* edited by Barbara S. Lesko, 213–14. Atlanta: Scholars Press, 1989.

Frame, Grant. *Rulers of Babylonia: From the Second Dynasty of Isin to the End of the Assyrian Domination (1157–612 BC).* Royal Inscriptions of Mesopotamia. Babylonian Periods 2. Toronto: University of Toronto Press, 1995.

Francke, Sabina. "Kings of Akkad: Sargon and Naram-Sin." In *Civilizations of the Ancient Near East,* edited by Jack M. Sasson, 2:831–42. New York: Scribner, 1995.

Frantz-Szabó, Gabriella. "Hittite Witchcraft, Magic, and Divination." In *Civilizations of the Ancient Near East,* edited by Jack M. Sasson, 3:2007–20. New York: Scribner, 1995.

Frayne, Douglas. *Old Babylonian Period (2003–1595).* Royal Inscriptions of Mesopotamia. Early Periods 4. Toronto: University of Toronto Press, 1990.

———. *Sargonic and Gutian Periods (2334–2113 BC)*. Royal Inscriptions of Mesopotamia. Early Periods 2. Toronto: University of Toronto Press, 1993.

———. *Ur III Period (2112–2004 BC)*. Royal Inscriptions of Mesopotamia. Early Periods 3/2. Toronto: University of Toronto Press, 1997.

Frymer-Kensky, Tikva. "Gender and Law: An Introduction." In *Gender and Law in the Hebrew Bible and the Ancient Near East*, edited by Victor Matthews, Bernard Levinson, and Tikva Frymer-Kensky, 17–24. Journal for the Study of the Old Testament Supplement 262. Sheffield: Sheffield Academic Press, 1998.

———. *In the Wake of the Goddesses*. New York: Free Press, 1992.

———. "Tit for Tat: The Principle of Equal Retribution in Near Eastern and Biblical Law." *Biblical Archaeologist* 43 (1980): 230–40.

Fuchs, Andreas, and Simo Parpola. *The Correspondence of Sargon II. Part III. Letters from Babylonia and the Eastern Provinces*. State Archives of Assyria 15. Helsinki: Helsinki University Press, 2001.

Garbini, Giovanni. *The Ancient World*. New York: McGraw-Hill, 1966.

Gelb, I. J. "The Ancient Mesopotamian Ration System." *Journal of Near Eastern Studies* 24 (1965): 230–43.

———. "Household and Family in Early Mesopotamia." In *State and Temple Economy in the Ancient Near East*, edited by Edward Lipinski, 1:1–98. Leuven: Department Orientalistiek, 1979.

Geller, M. J. "A New Piece of Witchcraft." In *DUMU-E2-DUB-BA-A: Studies in Honor of Åke Sjöberg*, edited by Hermann Behrens, Darlene Loding, and Martha T. Roth. Occasional Publications of the Samuel Noah Kramer Fund 11. Philadelphia: University Museum, 1989.

Gera, Deborah. *Warrior Women: The Anonymous* Tractatus de Mulieribus. Bibliotheca Mesopotamica Supplement 162. Leiden: Brill, 1997.

Gero, Joan M., and Margaret W. Conkey, eds. *Engendering Archaeology: Women and Prehistory*. Oxford: Blackwell, 1991.

Glassner, Jean-Jacques. "Women, Hospitality and the Honor of the Family." In *Women's Earliest Records: From Ancient Egypt and Western Asia*, edited by Barbara S. Lesko, 71–90. Atlanta: Scholars Press, 1989.

Goetze, Albrecht. "Tavern Keepers and the Like in Ancient Mesopotamia." In *Studies in Honor of Benno Landsberger on His Seventy-Fifth Birthday*, edited by Hans G. Güterbock and Thorkild Jacobsen, 211–15. Chicago: University of Chicago Press, 1965.

Good, Edwin M. "Capital Punishment and Its Alternatives." *Stanford Law Review* 19 (1967): 947–77.

Gordon, Edmund. *Sumerian Proverbs: Glimpses of Everyday Life in Ancient Mesopotamia*. Philadelphia: University Museum, 1959.

Grayson, Albert Kirk. *Assyrian Royal Inscriptions*. 2 vols. Wiesbaden: Otto Harrassowitz, 1972, 1976.

———. "Assyrian Rule of Conquered Territory in Ancient Western Asia." In *Civ-*

ilizations of the Ancient Near East, edited by Jack M. Sasson, 2:959–68. New York: Scribner, 1995.

———. *Assyrian Rulers of the Early First Millennium I (1114–859 BC).* Royal Inscriptions of Mesopotamia. Assyrian Periods 2. Toronto: University of Toronto Press, 1991.

———. *Assyrian Rulers of the Early First Millennium II (858–745 BC).* Royal Inscriptions of Mesopotamia. Assyrian Periods 3. Toronto: University of Toronto Press, 1996.

———. *Assyrian Rulers of the Third and Second Millennia BC (to 1115 BC).* Royal Inscriptions of Mesopotamia. Assyrian Periods 1. Toronto: University of Toronto Press, 1987.

———. *Babylonian Historical-Literary Texts.* Toronto Semitic Texts and Studies. Toronto: University of Toronto Press, 1975.

Greenfield, Jonas C. "Some Neo-Babylonian Women." In *La Femme dans le Proche-Orient Antique,* ed. Jean-Marie Durand, 75–80. Compte rendu de la xxxiii Rencontre Assyriologique Internationals (Paris, 1986). Paris: Éditions Recherche sur les Civilisations, 1987.

Greengus, Samuel. "A Textbook Case of Adultery in Ancient Mesopotamia." *Hebrew Union College Annual* 40–41 (1969–70): 33–44.

———. "Legal and Social Institutions of Ancient Mesopotamia." In *Civilizations of the Ancient Near East,* edited by Jack M. Sasson, 1:469–84. New York: Scribner, 1995.

———. "Old Babylonian Marriage Ceremonies and Rites." *Journal of Cuneiform Studies* 20 (1966): 55–72.

Gurney, O. R. *The Hittites.* Baltimore: Penguin, 1954.

Gurney, O. R., and Samuel N. Kramer. "Two Fragments of Sumerian Laws." In *Studies in Honor of Benno Landsberger on His Seventy-Fifth Birthday,* edited by Hans G. Güterbock and Thorkild Jacobsen, 13–19. Chicago: University of Chicago Press, 1965.

Güterbock, Hans G., and Theo van den Hout. *The Hittite Instruction for the Royal Bodyguard.* Oriental Institute of the University of Chicago Assyriological Studies 24. Chicago: University of Chicago Press, 1999.

Güterbock, Hans Gustav, and Thorkild Jacobsen, eds. *Studies in Honor of Benno Landsberger on His Seventy-Fifth Birthday.* Oriental Institute of the University of Chicago Assyriological Studies 16. Chicago: University of Chicago Press, 1965.

Haldar, Alfred. *Who Were the Amorites?* Leiden: Brill, 1971.

Hallo, William W. *Early Mesopotamian Royal Titles: A Philologic and Historical Analysis.* American Oriental Series 43. New Haven: American Oriental Society, 1957.

———. "Nippur Originals." In *DUMU-E2-DUB-BA-A: Studies in Honor of Ake Sjöberg,* edited by H. Behrens, Darlene Loding, and Martha T. Roth. Philadelphia: University Museum, 1989.

———. "Sumerian Historiography." In *History, Historiography and Interpretation: Studies in Biblical and Cuneiform Literature*, edited by H. Tadmor and M. Weinfeld. Jerusalem: Magnes Press, 1983.

———. "Women of Sumer." In *The Legacy of Sumer*, edited by Denise Schmandt-Besserat. Bibliotheca Mesopotamica 4. Malibu, Calif.: Undena, 1976.

Hallo, William W., and William K. Simpson. *The Ancient Near East. A History.* New York: Harcourt, Brace, Jovanovich, 1971.

Halpern, Baruch, and Deborah W. Hobson, eds. *Law, Politics, and Society in the Ancient Mediterranean World.* Sheffield: Sheffield Academic Press, 1993.

Hansen, Donald P. "Art of the Early City-States." In *Art of the First Cities: The Third Millennium B.C. from the Mediterranean to the Indus*, 21–42. Metropolitan Museum of Art. New Haven: Yale University Press, 2003.

Harris, Rivkah. *Ancient Sippar: A Demographic Study of an Old-Babylonian City (1894–1595 B.C.).* Istanbul: Nederlands Historisch-Archaeologisch Instituut, 1975.

———. *Gender and Aging in Mesopotamia.* Norman: University of Oklahoma Press, 2000.

———. "Independent Women in Ancient Mesopotamia?" In *Women's Earliest Records: From Ancient Egypt and Western Asia*, edited by Barbara S. Lesko, 145–56. Atlanta: Scholars Press, 1989.

Heimpel, Wolfgang. *Letters to the King of Mari.* A New Translation with Historical Introduction, Notes, and Commentary. Winona Lake, Ind.: Eisenbrauns, 2003.

Heltzer, Michael. "The Neo-Assyrian *Šakintu* and the Biblical *Sōkenet* (I Reg. 1, 4)." In *La Femme dans le Proche-Orient Antique*, ed. Jean-Marie Durand, 87–90. Compte rendu de la xxxiii Rencontre Assyriologique Internationale (Paris, 1986). Paris: Editions Recherche sur les Civilisations, 1987.

Henshaw, Richard A. *Female and Male: The Cultic Personnel.* Allison Park, Pa.: Pickwick Publications, 1994.

Hicks, Jim. *The Empire Builders.* New York: Time-Life, 1974.

Hoffner, Harry A., Jr. "Legal and Social Institutions of Hittite Anatolia." In *Civilizations of the Ancient Near East*, edited by Jack M. Sasson, 1:555–69. New York: Scribner, 1995.

———. *The Laws of the Hittites: A Critical Edition.* Documenta et Monumenta Orientis Antiqui 23. Leiden: Brill, 1997.

———. "The Treatment and Long-Term Use of Persons Captured in Battle." In *Recent Developments in Hittite Archaeology and History*, edited by A. Yener and H. Hoffner. Winona Lake, Ind.: Eisenbrauns, 2002.

Hout, Theo van den. "Khattushilish III, King of the Hittites." In *Civilizations of the Ancient Near East*, edited by Jack M. Sasson, 2:1107–20. New York: Scribner, 1995.

———. *The Purity of Kingship.* Documenta et Monumenta Orientis Antiqui 25. Leiden: Brill, 1998.

Imparati, Fiorella. "Private Life Among the Hittites." In *Civilizations of the Ancient Near East,* edited by Jack M. Sasson, 1:571–86. New York: Scribner, 1995.

Jacobsen, Thorkild. "An Ancient Mesopotamian Trial for Homicide." In *Studia Biblica et Orientalia,* vol. 3, *Oriens Antiquus,* 130–50. Analecta biblica 12. Rome: Biblical Institute Press, 1959.

———. "An Ancient Mesopotamian Trial for Homicide." In *Toward the Image of Tammuz.* Harvard Semitic Studies 21. Cambridge, Mass.: Harvard University Press, 1970.

———. *Philological Notes on Eshnunna and Its Inscriptions.* Assyriological Studies 6. Chicago: University of Chicago Press, 1934.

———. "Primitive Democracy in Ancient Mesopotamia." *Journal of Near Eastern Studies* 2 (1943): 159–72.

Jas, Remko. *Neo-Assyrian Judicial Procedures.* State Archives of Assyria Studies 5. Helsinki: Neo-Assyrian Text Corpus Project, 1996.

Jastrow, Morris, Jr. *Aspects of Religious Belief and Practice in Babylonia and Assyria: American Lectures on the History of Religions.* Ninth Series, 1910. Repr., New York: Benjamin Blom, 1971.

Jeyes, Ulla. "The Naditu Women of Sippar." In *Images of Women in Antiquity,* edited by Averil Cameron and Amélie Kuhrt. Detroit: Wayne State University Press, 1983.

Kang, Shin. *Sumerian Economic Texts from the Drehem Archive.* Chicago: University of Illinois Press, 1972.

Kataja, L., and R. Whiting. *Grants, Decrees, and Gifts of the Neo-Assyrian Period.* State Archives of Assyria 12. Helsinki: Helsinki University Press, 1995.

King, Karen L., ed. *Women and Goddess Traditions.* Studies in Antiquity and Christianity. Minneapolis: Fortress, 1997.

King, L. W. *The Letters and Inscriptions of Hammurabi, King of Babylon.* Vol. 3. London: Luzac & Co., 1900.

Klein, Jacob. "The Birth of a Crownprince in the temple: A Neo-Sumerian Literary Topos." In *La Femme dans le Proche-Orient Antique,* ed. Jean-Marie Durand, 97–106. Compte rendu de la xxxiii Rencontre Assyriologique Internationals (Paris, 1986). Paris: Éditions Recherche sur les Civilisations, 1987.

Kramer, Samuel N. *History Begins at Sumer.* 3rd ed. Philadelphia: University of Pennsylvania Press, 1981.

———. "Poets and Psalmists: Goddesses and Theologians." In *Legacy of Sumer,* edited by Denise Schmandt-Besserat, 13–16. Malibu, Calif.: Undena, 1976.

———. *The Sacred Marriage Rite.* Bloomington: Indiana University Press, 1969.

———. *The Sumerians: Their History, Culture, and Character.* Chicago: University of Chicago Press, 1963.

———. "The Woman in Ancient Sumer: Gleanings from Sumerian Literature." In *La Femme dans le Proche-Orient Antique,* ed. Jean-Marie Durand, 107–12.

Compte rendu de la xxxiii Rencontre Assyriologique Internationals (Paris, 1986). Paris: Éditions Recherche sur les Civilisations, 1987.

Kraus, F. R. *Ein Edikt des Königs Ammi-saduqa von Babylon.* Studia et Documenta ad Iura Orientis Antiqui Pertinentia 5. Leiden: Brill, 1958.

Kuan, Jeffrey Kah-Jin. *Neo-Assyrian Historical Inscriptions and Syria-Palestine: Israelite/Judean-Tyrian-Damascene Political and Commercial Relations in the Ninth-Eighth Centuries B.C.E.* Hong Kong: Alliance Bible Seminary, 1995.

Kuhrt, Amélie. *The Ancient Near East: C. 3000–330 B.C.* 2 vols. London: Routledge 1995.

———. "Nabonidus and the Babylonian Priesthood." In *Pagan Priests,* edited by Mary Beard and John North. Ithaca, N.Y.: Cornell University Press, 1990.

———. "Non-Royal Women in the Late Babylonian Period." In *Women's Earliest Records: From Ancient Egypt and Western Asia,* edited by Barbara S. Lesko, 215–39. Atlanta: Scholars Press, 1989.

Kupper, J. R. *Correspondance de Bahdi-Lim.* Archives Royales de Mari 6. Paris: Imprimerie Nationale, 1954.

Kupper, J. R., ed. *La Civilisation de Mari. Compte rendu,* Rencontre Assyriologique Internationale 15. Paris: Les Belles Lettres, 1967.

Kwasman, Theodore, and Simo Parpola. *Legal Transactions of the Royal Court of Nineveh, Part 1.* State Archives of Assyria 6. Helsinki: Helsinki University Press, 2000.

Lafont, Bertrand. "Les Filles du Roi de Mari." In *La Femme dans le Proche-Orient Antique,* ed. Jean-Marie Durand, 113–123. Compte rendu de la xxxiii Rencontre Assyriologique Internationale (Paris, 1986). Paris: Éditions Recherche sur les Civilisations, 1987.

Lambert, W. G. "The Language of Mari." In *La civilisation de Mari,* edited by J. R. Kupper. Compte rendu, Rencontre Assyriologique International 15, Liege, 1966. Paris: Les Belles Lettres, 1967.

———. "Goddesses in the Pantheon: A Reflection of Women in Society?" In *La Femme dans le Proche-Orient Antique,* ed. Jean-Marie Durand, 125–30. Compte rendu de la xxxiii Rencontre Assyriologique Internationale (Paris, 1986). Paris: Éditions Recherche sur les Civilisations, 1987.

Lanfranchi, Giovanni, and Simo Parpola. *The Correspondence of Sargon II.* Part II. State Archives of Assyria 5. Helsinki: Helsinki University Press, 1990.

Leemans, W. F. *Legal and Economic Records from the Kingdom of Larsa.* Studia ad Tabulas Cuneiformas Collectas A. SBL 1(2). Leiden: Brill, 1954.

Lehmann, Johannes. *The Hittites.* Translated by J. Maxwell Brownjohn. New York: Viking Press, 1977.

Leichty, Erle. "Esarhaddon, King of Assyria." In *Civilizations of the Ancient Near East,* edited by Jack M. Sasson, 2:949–58. New York: Scribner, 1995.

Leick, Gwendolyn. *The Babylonians.* London: Routledge, 2003.

Lesko, Barbara S., ed. *Women's Earliest Records: From Ancient Egypt and Western Asia.* Brown Judaic Studies 166. Atlanta: Scholars Press, 1989.

Levine, Louis. *Two Neo-Assyrian Stelae from Iran.* Toronto: Royal Ontario Museum, 1972.

Lipinski, Edward, ed. *State and Temple Economy in the Ancient Near East.* 2 vols. Orientalia Lovaniensia Analecta, 5–6. Leuven: Department Orientalistiek, 1979.

————. *Studies in Aramaic Inscriptions and Onomastica.* Orientalia Lovaniensia Analecta 1. Leuven: Leuven University Press, 1975.

Liverani, Mario. *Akkad: The First World Empire.* History of the Ancient Near East 5. Padova: Sargon, 1993.

————. "The Deeds of Ancient Mesopotamian Kings." In *Civilizations of the Ancient Near East,* edited by Jack M. Sasson, 4:2353–65. New York: Scribner, 1995.

Livingstone, Alasdair. *Court Poetry and Literary Miscellanea.* State Archives of Assyria 3. Helsinki: Helsinki University Press, 1989.

Loding, Darlene. *Ur Excavations: Texts IX, Economic Texts from the Third Dynasty.* London: British Museum and University of Pennsylvania, 1976.

Luuko, Mikko, and Freta Van Buylaere, eds. *The Political Correspondence of Esarhaddon.* State Archives of Assyria 16. Helsinki: Helsinki University Press, 2002.

Macqueen, James G. *Babylon.* London: Robert Hale Ltd, 1964.

————. "The History of Anatolia and of the Hittite Empire: An Overview. In *Civilizations of the Ancient Near East,* edited by Jack M. Sasson, 2:1085–1106. New York: Scribner, 1995.

————. *The Hittites and Their Contemporaries in Asia Minor.* Rev. ed. London: Thames & Hudson, 1986.

Maisels, Charles K. *The Emergence of Civilization.* London: Routledge, 1990.

————. *The Near East: Archaeology in the 'Cradle of Civilization.'* London: Routledge, 1993.

Malamat, Abraham. *Mari and the Early Israelite Experience.* The Schweich Lectures. London: British Academy, 1984.

Malul, Meir. *The Comparative Method in Ancient Near Eastern and Biblical Legal Studies.* Alter Orient und Altes Testament 227. Neukirchen-Vluyn: Neukirchener Verlag, 1990.

Matthews, Roger. *The Archaeology of Mesopotamia: Theories and Approaches.* London: Routledge, 2003.

Matthews, Victor, Bernard Levinson, and Tikva Frymer-Kensky, eds. *Gender and Law in the Hebrew Bible and the Ancient Near East.* Journal for the Study of the Old Testament Supplement 262. Sheffield: Sheffield Academic Press, 1998.

Mattila, Raija. *Legal Transactions of the Royal Court of Nineveh II.* State Archives of Assyria 14. Helsinki: Helsinki University Press, 2002.

————. *The King's Magnates: A Study of the Highest Officials of the Neo-Assyrian Empire.* State Archives of Assyria Studies 11. Helsinki: Neo-Assyrian Text Corpus Project, 2000.

Mayr, R. "The Depiction of Ordinary Men and Women on the Seals of the Ur III Kingdom." In *Sex and Gender in the Ancient Near East.* Proceedings of the 47th Rencontre Assyriologique Internationale, Helsinki, July 2–6, 2001, edited by S. Parpola and R. M. Whiting, 359–66. Compte rendu, Rencontre Assyriologique Internationale 47. Helsinki: Neo-Assyrian Text Corpus Project, 2002.

McCarter, P. Kyle, Jr. *Ancient Inscriptions: Voices from the Biblical World.* Washington, D.C.: Biblical Archaeology Society, 1996.

McMahon, Gregory. "Theology, Priests, and Worship in Hittite Anatolia." In *Civilizations of the Ancient Near East,* edited by Jack M. Sasson, 3:1981–96. New York: Scribner, 1995.

Melville, Sarah C. *The Role of Naqia/Zakutu in Sargonid Politics.* State Archives of Assyria Studies 9. Helsinki: Neo-Assyrian Text Corpus Project, 1999.

Meyer, Marvin, and Paul Mirecki. *Ancient Magic and Ritual Power: Religions in the Graeco-Roman World.* Leiden: Brill, 1995.

Meyers, Eric M., ed. *The Oxford Encyclopedia of Archaeology in the Near East.* Oxford: Oxford University Press, 1997.

Michalowski, Piotr. *Letters from Early Mesopotamia.* Society of Biblical Literature Writings from the Ancient World 3. Atlanta: Scholars Press, 1993.

————. *The Lamentation over the Destruction of Sumer and Ur.* Mesopotamian Civilizations 1. Winona Lake, Ind.: Eisenbrauns, 1989.

————. "Round About Nidaba: On the Early Goddesses of Sumer." In *Sex and Gender in the Ancient Near East.* Proceedings of the 47th Rencontre Assyriologique Internationale, Helsinki, July 2–6, 2001, edited by S. Parpola and R. M. Whiting, 413–22. Compte rendu, Rencontre Assyriologique Internationale 47. Helsinki: Neo-Assyrian Text Corpus Project, 2002.

————. "Royal Women of the Ur III Period." *Journal of Cuneiform Studies* 31 (1979): 171–76.

Michalowski, Piotr, and C. B. F. Walker, "A New Sumerian 'Law Code.'" In *DUMU-E2-DUB-BA-A: Studies in Honor of Åke Sjöberg,* edited by Hermann Behrens, Darlene Loding, and Martha Roth. Occasional Publications of the Samuel Noah Kramer Fund 11. Philadelphia: University Museum, 1989.

Miller, Jared. "The *katra/i*-women in the Kizzuwatnean Rituals from Hattusa." In *Sex and Gender in the Ancient Near East:* Proceedings of the 47th Rencontre Assyriologique Internationale, Helsinki, July 2–6, 2001, edited by S. Parpola and R. M. Whiting. Compte rendu, Rencontre Assyriologique Internationale 47. Helsinki: Neo-Assyrian Text Corpus Project, 2002.

Moscati, Sabatino, et al. *An Introduction to the Comparative Grammar of the Semitic Languages.* Porta Linguarum Orientalium. New series 6. Wiesbaden: Otto Harrassowitz, 1964.

Nemet-Nejet, Karen Rhea. *Daily Life in Ancient Mesopotamia.* London: Greenwood Press, 1998.

———. "Women in Ancient Mesopotamia." In *Women's Roles in Ancient Civilizations,* edited by Bella Vivante, 85–114. Westport, Conn.: Greenwood Press, 1999.

Neufeld, E. *The Hittite Laws.* London: Luzac, 1951.

Nijhowne, Jeanne. *Politics, Religion, and Cylinder Seals: A Study of Mesopotamian Symbolism in the Second Millennium B.C.* British Archaeological Reports International Series 772. Oxford: British Archaeological Reports, 1999.

Nissen, Hans J. *The Early History of the Ancient Near East: 9000–2000 B.C.* Translated by Elizabeth Lutzeier. Chicago: University of Chicago Press, 1988.

Nissen, Hans J., Peter Damerow, and Robert Englund, eds. *Archaic Bookkeeping: Writing Techniques of Economic Administration in the Ancient Near East.* Translated by Paul Larsen. Chicago: University of Chicago Press, 1993.

Nissinen, Martti. *Prophets and Prophecy in the Ancient Near East.* Edited by Peter Machinist. Society of Biblical Literature Writings from the Ancient World 12. Atlanta: Society of Biblical Literature, 2003.

———. *References to Prophecy in Neo-Assyrian Sources.* State Archives of Assyria Studies 7. Helsinki: Neo-Assyrian Text Corpus Project, 1998.

———. "Spoken, Written, Quoted, and Invented: Orality and Writtenness in Ancient Near Eastern Prophecy." In *Writings and Speech in Israelite and Ancient Near Eastern Prophecy,* edited by Ehud Ben Zvi and Michael H. Floyd. Society of Biblical Literature Symposium Series 10. Atlanta: Society of Biblical Literature, 2000.

Oates, Joan. *Babylon.* London: Thames & Hudson, 1979.

Oates, Joan, and David Oates. *Nimrud: An Assyrian Imperial City Revealed.* London: British School of Archaeology in Iraq/The British Academy, 2001.

O'Callaghan, Roger T., S.J. *Aram Naharaim.* Analecta Orientalia 26. Rome: Pontificium Institutum Biblicum, 1948.

Olmstead, A.T. *The Assyrians in Asia Minor.* Manchester: Manchester University Press, 1923.

———. *History of Assyria.* New York: Scribner, 1923.

Oppenheim, A. Leo. *Ancient Mesopotamia: Portrait of a Dead Civilization.* Edited by Erica Reiner. Rev. ed. Chicago: University of Chicago Press, 1977.

Ornan, Tallay. "The Queen in Public: Royal Women in Neo-Assyrian Art." In *Sex and Gender in the Ancient Near East.* Proceedings of the 47th Rencontre Assyriologique Internationale, Helsinki, July 2–6, 2001, edited by S. Parpola and R. M. Whiting, 461–77. Compte rendu, Rencontre Assyriologique Internationale 47. Helsinki: Neo-Assyrian Text Corpus Project, 2002.

Parpola, Simo. *The Correspondence of Sargon II.* Part I, *Letters from Assyria and the West.* State Archives of Assyria 1. Helsinki: Helsinki University Press, 1987.

———. *Letters from Assyrian and Babylonian Scholars.* State Archives of Assyria 10. Helsinki: Helsinki University Press, 1993.

Parpola, Simo, and Kazuko Watanabe. *Neo-Assyrian Treaties and Loyalty Oaths.* State Archives of Assyria 2. Helsinki: Helsinki University Press, 1988.

Parpola, Simo, and R. M. Whiting, eds. *Sex and Gender in the Ancient Near East: Proceedings of the 47th Rencontre Assyriologique Internationale, Helsinki, July 2–6, 2001.* Compte rendu, Rencontre Assyriologique Internationale 47. Helsinki: Neo-Assyrian Text Corpus Project, 2002.

Parr, P. A. "Ninhilia: Wife of Ayakala, Governor of Umma." *Journal of Cuneiform Studies* 26 (1974): 90–111.

Pearce, Laurie. "The Scribes and Scholars of Ancient Mesopotamia." In *Civilizations of the Ancient Near East,* edited by Jack M. Sasson, 4:2265–78. New York: Scribner, 1995.

Perrot, Michelle, ed. *Writing Women's History.* Translated by Felicia Pheasant. Oxford: Blackwell, 1992.

Pfeiffer, Robert H. *State Letters of Assyria.* New Haven: American Oriental Society, 1935. Repr., New York: Kraus, 1967.

Pinnock, Frances. "The Iconography of the Entu-Priestesses in the Period of the Ur III Dynasty." In *Intellectual Life of the Ancient Near East,* edited by Jiri Prosecky. Papers Presented at the 43rd Rencontre assyriologique internationale, Prague, July 1–5, 1996. Academy of Sciences of the Czech Republic. Prague: Oriental Institute, 1998.

Poebel, A. "The Assyrian King List from Khorsabad." *Journal of Near Eastern Studies* 2 (1943): 56, 86–88.

Pollock, Susan. *Ancient Mesopotamia: The Eden That Never Was.* Cambridge: Cambridge University Press, 1999.

Postgate, J. N. *Early Mesopotamia: Society and Economy at the Dawn of History.* London: Routledge, 1992.

Potts, Daniel T. *The Arabian Gulf in Antiquity.* Oxford: Oxford University Press, 1990.

Pritchard, James B., ed. *Ancient Near Eastern Texts Relating to the Old Testament.* 3rd ed. Princeton, N.J.: Princeton University Press, 1969.

———. *The Ancient Near East in Pictures.* 2nd ed. Princeton, N.J.: Princeton University Press, 1969.

———. *The Ancient Near East: Supplementary Texts and Pictures Relating to the Old Testament.* Princeton, N.J.: Princeton University Press, 1969.

Prosecky, Jiri, ed. *Intellectual Life in the Ancient Near East.* Papers Presented at the 43rd Rencontre assyriologique internationale. Prague, July 1-5, 1996. Academy of Sciences of the Czech Republic. Prague: Oriental Institute, 1998.

Radner, Karen. *Die Neuassyrischen Privatrechtsurkunden als Quelle für Mensch und Umwelt.* State Archives of Assyria Studies 6. Helsinki: Neo-Assyrian Text Corpus Project, 1997.

Radner, Karen, and Heather Baker, eds. *The Prosopography of the Neo-Assyrian Empire.* Volumes 1–3. Helsinki: Neo-Assyrian Text Corpus Project, 1998-2003.

Ranke, Hermann. *Babylonian Legal and Business Documents*. Philadelphia: University of Pennsylvania Press, 1906.

Reade, Julian. *Assyrian Sculpture*. Cambridge, Mass.: Harvard University Press, 1999.

———. *Mesopotamia*. London: British Museum Press, 2000.

———. "The Royal Tombs of Ur." In *Art of the First Cities: The Third Millennium B.C. from the Mediterranean to the Indus*, 93–108, 120–34. Metropolitan Museum of Art. New Haven: Yale University Press, 2003.

———. "Was Sennacherib a Feminist?" In *La Femme dans le Proche-Orient Antique*, ed. Jean-Marie Durand, 139–45. Compte rendu de la xxxiii Rencontre Assyriologique Internationals (Paris, 1986). Paris: Éditions Recherche sur les Civilisations, 1987.

Reisman, David. "Iddin-Dagan's Sacred Marriage Hymn." *Journal of Cuneiform Studies* 25 (1973): 185–202.

Renger, Johannes. "Interaction of Temple, Palace, and 'Private Enterprise' in the Old Babylonian Economy." In *State and Temple Economy in the Ancient Near East*, edited by Edward Lipinski, 1:249–56. Orientalia Lovanensia Analecta 5. Leuven: Departement Orientalistiek, 1979.

Reynolds, Frances. *The Babylonian Correspondence of Esarhaddon*. State Archives of Assyria 18. Helsinki: Helsinki Universitiy Press, 2003.

Richardson, M. E. J. *Hammurabi's Laws*. Sheffield: Sheffield Academic Press, 2000.

Roaf, Michael. *Cultural Atlas of Mesopotamia and the Ancient Near East*. New York/Oxford: Facts on File, 1990.

Rochberg-Halton, Francesca, ed. *Language, Literature and History: Philological and Historical Studies Presented to Erica Reiner*. American Oriental Studies 67. New Haven: American Oriental Society, 1987.

Rollin, Sue. "Women and Witchcraft in Ancient Assyria." In *Images of Women in Antiquity*, edited by Averil Cameron and Amélie Kuhrt, 34–45. Detroit: Wayne State University Press, 1983.

Römer, W. H. *Frauenbriefe über Religion, Politik und Privatleben in Mari*. Archives Royales de Mari 10. Paris, 1967.

Roos, Johan de. "Hittite Prayers." In *Civilizations of the Ancient Near East*, edited by Jack M. Sasson, 3:1997–2006. New York: Scribner, 1995.

Roth, Martha. *Babylonian Marriage Agreements: 7th–3rd Centuries B.C.* Alter Orient und Altes Testament 222. Neukirchen-Vluyn: Neukirchener Verlag, 1989.

———. "The Dowries of Women in the Itti-Marduk-Balatu Family." *Journal of the American Oriental Society* 111 (1991): 19–37.

———. "Gender and Law: A Case Study from Ancient Mesopotamia." In *Gender and Law in the Hebrew Bible and the Ancient Near East*, edited by Victor Matthews, Bernard Levinson, and Tikva Frymer-Kensky, 173–84. Journal for the Study of the Old Testament Supplement 262. Sheffield: Sheffield Academic Press, 1998.

———. "Homicide in the Neo-Assyrian Period." In *Language, Literature, and History,* edited by Francesca Rochberg-Halton, 351–65. New Haven: American Oriental Society, 1987.

———. "*Ina amat DN, u DN2 lishlim.*" *Journal of Semitic Studies* 33 (1988): 1–9.

———. *Law Collections from Mesopotamia and Asia Minor.* Society of Biblical Literature Writings from the Ancient World 6. Atlanta: Scholars Press, 1997.

———. "Marriage and Matrimonial Prestations in First Millennium B.C. Babylonia." In *Women's Earliest Records: From Ancient Egypt and Western Asia,* edited by Barbara S. Lesko, 245–55. Atlanta: Scholars Press, 1989.

———. "Mesopotamian Legal Traditions and the Laws of Hammurabi." *Chicago-Kent Law Review* 71 (1995): 13–37.

———. "The Neo-Babylonian Widow." *Journal of Cuneiform Studies* 43 (1991): 1–26.

———. "'She Will Die by the Iron Dagger': Adultery and Neo-Babylonian Marriage." *Journal of the Economic and Social History of the Orient* 31(1988): 186–206.

———. "The Slave and the Scoundrel: A Sumerian Morality Tale." *Journal of the American Oriental Society* 103 (1983): 275–82.

Rothman, Mitchell S., ed. *Uruk Mesopotamia and Its Neighbors.* Santa Fe: School of American Research Press, 2001.

Roux, George. "The Great Enigma of the Cemetary at Ur." In Jean Bottéro, *Everyday Life in Ancient Mesopotamia.* Baltimore: Johns Hopkins University Press, 1992.

———. "Semiramis: The Builder of Babylon." In Jean Bottéro, *Everyday Life in Ancient Mesopotamia.* Baltimore: Johns Hopkins University Press, 1992.

Sack, Ronald H. *Cuneiform Documents from the Chaldean and Persian Periods.* London: Associated University Presses, 1994.

———. *Neriglissar—King of Babylon.* Alter Orient und Altes Testament 236. Neukirchen-Vluyn: Neukirchener Verlag, 1994.

Saggs, H. W. F. *Babylonians.* Peoples of the Past 1. Norman: University of Oklahoma Press, 1995.

———. *Civilizations Before Greece and Rome.* New Haven: Yale University Press, 1989.

———. *The Greatness That Was Babylon.* London: Sidgwick & Jackson, 1988.

———. *The Might That Was Assyria.* Rev. ed. New York: St. Martin's, 1984.

Saporetti, Claudio. *The Status of Women in the Middle Assyrian Period.* Translated by Beatrice Boltze-Jordan. Monographs on the Ancient Near East 2/1. Malibu, Calif.: Undena, 1979.

Sasson, Jack M., ed. *Civilizations of the Ancient Near East.* 4 vols. New York: Scribner, 1995.

Schmandt-Besserat, Denise. "An Ancient Token System: The Precursor to Numbers and Writing." *Archaeology* 39 (1986): 32–39.

————, ed. *The Legacy of Sumer*. Bibliotheca Mesopotamica 4. Malibu, Calif.: Undena, 1976.

Schüssler Fiorenza, Elisabeth. *In Memory of Her: A Feminist Theological Reconstruction of Christian Origins*. New York: Crossroad, 1983.

Sefati, Yitschak, and Jacob Klein. "The Role of Women in Mesopotamian Witchcraft." In *Sex and Gender in the Ancient Near East:* Proceedings of the 47th Rencontre Assyriologique Internationale, Helsinki, July 2–6, 2001, edited by S. Parpola and R. M. Whiting. Compte rendu, Rencontre Assyriologique Internationale 47. Helsinki: Neo-Assyrian Text Corpus Project, 2002.

Seibert, Ilse. *Women in the Ancient Near East*. New York: Abner Schram, 1974.

Snell, Daniel C. *Life in the Ancient Near East: 3100–332 B.C.E.* New Haven: Yale University Press, 1997.

Snell, Daniel, and Carl H. Lager, *Economic Texts from Sumer*. New Haven: Yale University Press, 1991.

Sommerfeld, Walter. "The Kassites of Ancient Mesopotamia: Origins, Politics, and Culture." In *Civilizations of the Ancient Near East*, edited by Jack M. Sasson, 2:917–30. New York: Scribner, 1995.

Starr, Ivan. *Queries to the Sungod*. State Archives of Assyria 4. Helsinki: Helsinki University Press, 1990.

Steele, Francis R. "The Code of Lipit-Ishtar." *American Journal of Archaeology* 52 (1948): 425–50.

Stein, Gil, and Mitchell Rothman, eds. *Chiefdoms and Early States in the Near East*. Monographs in World Archaeology 18. Madison, Wis.: Prehistory Press, 1994.

Steinkeller, Piotr. *Sale Documents of the Ur III Period*. Freiburger Altorientalische Studien, 17. Stuttgart: Franz Steiner Verlag Wiesbaden, 1989.

————. *Third Millennium Legal and Administrative Texts in the Iraq Museum, Bagdad*. With Hand Copies by J. N. Postgate. Mesopotamian Civilizations 4. Winona Lake, Ind.: Eisenbrauns, 1992.

Stol, Marten. "The Care of the Elderly in the Old Babylonian Period." In *The Care of the Elderly in the Ancient Near East*, edited by Marten Stol and Sven P. Vleeming. Studies in the History and Culture of the Ancient Near East 14. Leiden: Brill, 1998.

————. *Letters from Yale*. Altbabylonische Briefe im Umschrift und Übersetzung 9. Leiden: Brill, 1981.

————. "Private Life in Ancient Mesopotamia." In *Civilizations of the Ancient Near East*, edited by Jack M. Sasson, 1:485–502. New York: Scribner, 1995.

Stol, Marten, and Sven P. Vleeming, eds. *The Care of the Elderly in the Ancient Near East*. Studies in the History and Culture of the Ancient Near East 14. Leiden: Brill, 1998.

Stone, Elizabeth C. "Adoption Texts from Nippur." In *Adoption in Old Babylonian Nippur and the Archive of Mannum-mesu-lissur*, edited by Elizabeth C. Stone and David I. Owen. Winona Lake, Ind.: Eisenbrauns, 1991.

Stone, Elizabeth C., and David I. Owen, eds. *Adoption in Old Babylonian Nippur and the Archive of Mannum-mesu-lissur.* Winona Lake, Ind.: Eisenbrauns, 1991.

Tadmor, H., and M. Weinfeld, eds. *History, Historiography and Interpretation.* Studies in Biblical and Cuneiform Literature. Jerusalem: Magnes Press, 1983.

Thompson, R. Campbell. *Late Babylonian Letters.* London: Luzac, 1906.

Tinney, Steve. *The Nippur Lament: Royal Rhetoric and Divine Legitimation in the Reign of Isme-Dagan of Isin.* Philadelphia: Publications of the Babylonian Fund, 1996.

Uchitel, A. "Women at Work: Weavers of Lagash and Spinners of San Luis Gonzago." In *Sex and Gender in the Ancient Near East.* Proceedings of the 47th Rencontre Assyriologique Internationale, Helsinki, July 2–6, 2001, edited by S. Parpola and R. M. Whiting, 621–31. Compte rendu, Rencontre Assyriologique Internationale 47. Helsinki: Neo-Assyrian Text Corpus Project, 2002.

Van De Mieroop, Marc. *The Ancient Mesopotamian City.* Oxford: Clarendon, 1997.

———. *Cuneiform Texts and the Writing of History.* London: Routledge, 1999.

———. "Gifts and Tithes to the Temples in Ur." In *DUMU-E2-DUB-BA-A: Studies in Honor of Ake Sjöberg,* edited by H. Behrens, Darlene Loding, and Martha T. Roth. Occasional Publications of the Samuel Noah Kramer Fund 11. Philadelphia: University Museum, 1989.

———. *A History of the Ancient Near East.* Oxford: Blackwell, 2004.

———. "An Inscribed Bead of Queen Zakatu." In *The Tablet and the Scroll: Near Eastern Studies in Honor of William W. Hallo,* edited by Mark Cohen, D. Snell, and D. Weisberg. Bethesda, Md.: CDL Press, 1993.

———. *Society and Enterprise in Old Babylonian Ur.* Berliner Beiträge zum Vorderen Orient 12. Berlin: Dietrich Reimer Verlag, 1992.

———. "Women in the Economy of Sumer." In *Women's Earliest Records: From Ancient Egypt and Western Asia,* edited by Barbara S. Lesko, 53–66. Atlanta: Scholars Press, 1989.

van der Toorn, Karel. "From the Oral to the Written: The Case of Old Babylonian Prophecy." In *Writings and Speech in Israelite and Ancient Near Eastern Prophecy,* edited by Ehud Ben Zvi and Michael H. Floyd. Atlanta: Society of Biblical Literature, 2000.

Van Driel, G. "Care of the Elderly in the Neo-Babylonian Period." In *The Care of the Elderly in the Ancient Near East,* edited by Marten Stol and Sven Vleeming, 161–93. Leiden: Brill, 1998.

Van Seters, John. *In Search of History.* New Haven: Yale University Press, 1983.

Veenhof, Klaas. "Old Assyrian and Ancient Anatolian Evidence for the Care of the Elderly." In *The Care of the Elderly in the Ancient Near East,* edited by Marten Stol and Sven Vleeming, 119–60. Leiden: Brill, 1998.

VerSteeg, Russ. *Early Mesopotamian Law.* Durham, N.C.: Carolina Academic Press, 2000.

Villard, Pierre. "Shamshi-Adad and Sons: The Rise and Fall of an Upper Mesopotamian Empire." In *Civilizations of the Ancient Near East,* edited by Jack M. Sasson, 2:873–84. New York: Scribner, 1995.

Vivante, Bella. *Women's Roles in Ancient Civilizations.* Westport, Conn.: Greenwood, 1999.

Walters, Stanley D. "The Sorceress and her Apprentice." *Journal of Cuneiform Studies* 23 (1970): 27–38.

Westbrook, Raymond. "The Female Slave." In *Gender and Law in the Hebrew Bible and the Ancient Near East,* edited by Victor Matthews, Bernard Levinson, and Tikva Frymer-Kensky, 214–38. Sheffield: Sheffield Academic Press, 1998.

———. *Studies in Biblical and Cuneiform Law.* Cahiers de la Revue Biblique 26. Paris: Gabalda, 1988.

Westenholz, Joan Goodnick, ed. *Seals and Sealing in the Ancient Near East.* Proceedings of Symposium Held September 2, 1993. Jerusalem: Bible Lands Museum, 1995.

Whiting, Robert M. "Amorite Tribes and Nations of Second Millennium Western Asia." In *Civilizations of the Ancient Near East,* edited by Jack M. Sasson, 2:1231–1242. New York: Scribner, 1995.

Whittaker, G. "Linguistic Anthropology and the Study of Emesal as (a) Women's Language." In *Sex and Gender in the Ancient Near East.* Proceedings of the 47th Rencontre Assyriologique Internationale, Helsinki, July 2–6, 2001, edited by S. Parpola and R. M. Whiting, 633–44. Compte rendu, Rencontre Assyriologique Internationale 47. Helsinki: Neo-Assyrian Text Corpus Project, 2002.

Wilcke, Claus. "Care of the Elderly in Mesopotamia in the Third Millennium B.C." In *The Care of the Elderly in the Ancient Near East,* edited by Marten Stol and Sven Vleeming, 23–57. Leiden: Brill, 1998.

Winter, Irene J. "Women in Public: The Disk of Enheduanna, the Beginning of the Office of *EN*-Priestess and the Weight of Visual Evidence." In *La Femme dans le Proche-Orient Antique,* ed. Jean-Marie Durand, 189–201. Compte rendu de la xxxiii Rencontre Assyriologique Internationals (Paris, 1986). Paris: Éditions Recherche sur les Civilisations, 1987.

Wiseman, D. J. *Chronicles of Chaldean Kings (626–556 B.C.) in the British Museum.* London: Trustees of the British Museum, 1956.

———. *Nebuchadrezzar and Babylon.* The Schweich Lectures. The British Academy. Oxford: Oxford University Press, 1985.

Wright, G. Ernest. *The Bible and the Ancient Near East.* Garden City, N.Y.: Doubleday, 1961.

Yaron, Reuven. *The Laws of Eshnunna.* 2nd ed. Jerusalem: Magnes Press, 1988.

Yener, K. Aslihan, and Harry A Hoffner, Jr. *Recent Developments in Hittite Archaeology and History: Papers in Memory of Hans G. Güterbock.* Winona Lake, Ind.: Eisenbrauns, 2002.

Index of Personal Names

A'abba, 247, 248
Abda, 20, 38, 253
Abi-eshu, 264
Abi-Simti, 22, 246
Abidala, 156, 292
Abikhali, 153
Abilikhiya, 156, 157, 290
Abirakhi, 156, 158, 292
Abirami, 151, 288
Abishamshi, 89
Abiyakhiya, 156, 292
Abshalim, 123
Adad-guppi, 104
Adad-talli, 292
Adda-ti, 152, 291
Addu-duri, 87, 269
Agargarutu, 272
Agatima, 29
Akalam, 38, 253
Akbara, 153
Akhakha, 123
Akhassunu, 83
Akhatabisha, 147, 155-57, 159, 162, 292-94
Akhati'imma, 156, 293
Akhatitabat, 156, 292-93
Akhatum, 75, 78, 83, 87, 121
Akhitalli, 152, 291
Akhu'a, 292
Alhapimepi, 54, 154, 156, 292
Alibashti, 28
Alitum, 78

Amadugga, 88, 269
Amakata, 29
Amalal, 250
Amanili, 23, 246
Amar-Sin of Ur, 10, 22, 246, 252
Amasukkal, 76
Amat-Kurra, 158
Amat-Shamash, 82, 90, 92-94
Amat-Sin, 22, 246
Amata, 106, 276
Ammisaduqa of Babylonia, 93, 263, 265
Ana'a, 37
Anadalati, 152
Anitti, 195
Anniwiyani, 192, 305
Apillatum, 245
Apirtum, 78
Arbail-khammat, 158
Arbail-sharrat, 156, 158, 292-93
Arnabum, 82
Arzakiti1, 92
Asa, 292
Ashag, 28
Ashmu-Nikkal, 191-92, 305
Ashume'eren, 20, 38, 245, 253
Ashumiyalibur, 89
Ashusikidilgir, 20, 37, 253
Atalia, 147
Attar-palti, 152
Aya-kala, 251
Aya-la, 88
Aya-reshat, 265

Aya-talik, 265
Ayatarsha, 192, 305
Azzari, 194
Azzia, 195

Ba'altiyabati, 158
Babaya, 156, 293
Babu-gamilat, 159
Badia, 157
Bakhlatum, 88
Bakisha, 292
Balta, 106, 276
Banat-Emashmash, 155
Bani, 157, 293
Banitu, 147
Banitu-ayali, 292
Banitu-banat, 106, 276
Banitu-teresh, 152, 290
Banna, 292
Bara'irnun, 21, 38, 253
Baramezida, 30
Baranamtara, 20, 22, 23, 28, 37, 253
Barsipitu, 153
Bazitu, 292
Bekhi, 89
Belassuna, 93-94
Beletum, 266
Belissunu, 251
Bellilitum, 107, 277
Beltani, 22, 82, 270
Beltiremanni, 76
Beltiya, 78
Beltum, 125, 147
Bi'a, 292
Bililutu, 152, 290
Bita, 157, 293
Bunanitum, 109
Busasa, 276
Busuku, 157
Buza, 122

Damiqtum, 81
Damkhurasi, 85, 268

Daqqatum, 31
Dimtur, 20, 245
Dingirbuza, 28
Dukshatum, 87
Dumqaya, 292

Eanatum, 237
Eanisha, 22, 23, 37, 246
Eduqidiru, 156, 293
Ekallatani, 92
Eli-eressa, 79, 82
Elmeshum, 78
En-anatuma, 25, 247, 250
En-anedu, 24, 25, 247
En-kheduanna, 7, 23, 24, 39, 246-47, 254
En-makhgalana, 247
En-megalana, 25
En-menana, 24, 247
En-nigaldi-Nanna, 104
En-ninsunzi, 15, 24
En-nirgalana, 10, 23, 24, 241, 246, 247
En-nirzianna, 10, 24, 247
En-shakiag-Nanna, 25, 247
Enmetena of Lagash, 237, 244
Ennilas, 28
Ennimami, 28
Erishti-Aya, 81-82, 88, 266, 269
Erishti-Shamash, 83
Esaggilu, 159
Esagil-ramat, 107
Esharra-khammat, 150, 289

Gabia, 293
Gansamannu, 20
Geme-Abzu, 28
Geme-Ashar, 253
Geme-Bau, 245, 253
Geme-Enlila, 22, 246
Geme-ezida, 28
Geme-Lama, 25, 29, 37, 253
Geme-Nanna, 28
Geme-Nanshe, 245

Geme-Ninlila, 22, 23, 37, 246
Geme-Sin, 22, 30
Geme-tarsirsir, 245
Gudea of Lagash, 20, 23, 25, 33, 252
Gula-rishat, 156, 292

Hammurabi of Babylon, 47, 53-73, 74,
    79, 80, 82-3, 85, 112, 243, 256-264,
    273, 280

Ibbi-Sin of Ur, 10, 22, 246
Igidingirnaesu, 28
Iltani, 80, 82, 89-90, 94, 251 n.109, 266,
    270
Ilushakhegal, 93
Ina-Eulmashbanat, 79
Inanna-amamu, 79
Indibi, 153
Inib-sharri, 86, 268
Inibshina, 75, 84, 88, 264, 269
Inim-Aya, 79
Innasaga, 29
Ishagani, 28
Ishdumkin, 22
Ishme-Dagan of Isin, 247, 252
Ishtapariash, 196
Ishtar-lamassi, 121-22, 279
Ishtar-ummi, 31, 36
Issar-remanni, 156, 292
Istar-tappi, 84
Izamu, 84

Kabal-aya, 152, 159
Kabta, 104
Kakkua, 293
Kali, 159
Khaditum, 123
Khala-Baba (or Bau), 23, 32, 246
Khalalamma, 23, 246
Khaliyatum, 82
Khambusu, 156, 292-93
Khamizirum, 92
Khamzaba, 292
Khanna, 107

Khantawiya, 195
Kharra, 292
Khatala, 121
Khattushilish, 196, 304
Khazala, 87, 156, 293
Khazzikannum, 92
Khekunsig, 37, 254
Khesamanu, 38, 253
Khitubarra, 292
Khuda, 156, 293
Kiru, 86-87, 268-69
Kittumshimkhiya, 91
Ku-Bau (or Ku-Baba) of Kish, 7, 20,
    239, 245
Kubatum, 37, 246, 253
Kulla, 106, 159
Kunshimatum, 21, 125, 280
Kuriakhiti, 254
Kuritum, 78
Kurra-dimri, 161

Lamashi, 158, 293
Lamassani, 79, 90
Lamassatum, 122, 254, 279
Lamassi, 80, 122, 270
Lassakhitu, 292
Lateggiana, 153
Libbalisharrat, 148, 150, 289
Lipit-Ishtar of Isin, 15-18, 243
Lipushia'um, 247
Lirishgamlum, 254
Liwir-Esagila, 82
Liwirmitashu, 21
Lugalanda of Lagash, 245
Lugalzagisi of Uruk and Umma, 244

Mannashi, 80
Mannasi, 93
Manuttum, 92
Marat-Eshtar, 95
Marquikhita, 156, 293
Mashana'uzzi, 304
Mashtigga, 192
Mattatum, 94

Mattu, 77
Megirimta, 38, 253
Mekubi, 75, 264
Mellatum, 266
Menbara'abzu, 20, 245
Mesa, 157
Metug, 28
Milkikhaya, 155
Mishaga, 245
Muballitat, 153, 291
Mukhadditum, 78
Mullissu-abu'usri, 155
Mullissu-duru'usur, 156, 292-93
Mullissu-kabtat, 155
Mullissu-khammat, 154
Mullissu-khasina, 156, 292
Mullissu-mukannishat-Ninua, 147
Mullissu-ummi, 156, 292
Munawwirtum, 81
Musa'itu, 158

Nabu-kudurri'usur I of Babylonia, 98,
    104, 272
Nabu-kudurri'usur (Nebukhadrezzar)
    II, 227, 230, 273, 277-78
Nabu-naid (Nabonidus) of Babylonia,
    104, 273, 275
Nabu-ramat, 156
Nadbata, 289
Naga, 157, 293
Nagikha, 84
Nakkartum, 79
Nanna-lamassi, 31
Nanna-lurshi, 157, 293
Nanna'ummi, 31, 32, 251
Nannaya-belbiti, 277
Nannaya-da, 156, 292
Nannaya-khussini, 109
Naqia, 148-49, 151, 154-55, 287-89
Naram-Sin of Akkad, 24
Naramtum, 86, 268-69
Nidintumbelit, 106, 276
Niditum, 251

Nikalmati, 190, 304
Nikaluzzi, 194
Ninagrigsi, 28
Nin-alla, 21, 23, 38, 246
Ninana, 29
Nin-banda, 20, 22, 37, 253
Nindada, 28, 36
Nindubsar, 28
Ningudka, 29
Nin-inimgina, 246
Ninkagina, 29
Ninkala, 21, 22, 23, 246
Ninkare, 28, 29
Nin-khedu, 21, 23, 246, 254
Ninkhilia, 21, 37, 245
Nin-khilisu, 20
Ninkinda, 37, 253
Ninmelam, 21
Nin-metabare, 23, 246
Nin-niginesi, 23, 246, 254
Ninshatapada, 24, 247
Ninshesh, 28, 29
Nintu, 30
Nin-Tur, 20, 245
Ninturturmu, 23, 246
Ninukkine, 29
Ninurani, 28
Ninusu, 20
Nizatia, 28
Nubanda, 22, 246
Nubta, 109, 277
Nungal, 33, 252
Nurusheli, 253
Nutuptum, 22, 31

Pakalam, 38, 253
Pissuwattis, 192
Puabi of Ur, 20, 245, 254
Pudukhepa, 191, 304-05
Pushki, 156
Putushisu, 156, 292

Qibidumqi, 159
Qikhila, 87

Rama-Ya, 157, 293
Ramti, 292
Ribatum, 78, 81, 266
Rim-Sin of Larsa, 22, 53, 246, 247, 280, 286
Rim-Sin-Shalabastashu, 22, 254
Rimuttu, 157, 293
Rubatum, 27
Rumatum, 95-96
Ruttum, 265, 266

Sabitu, 76
Sagburru, 26
Saggilramat, 157
Saggilu, 159
Salentu, 156, 292
Sammu-ramat, 148, 151, 288
Samsi, 150, 156, 289, 292
Sanakratum, 83
Sargon (Sharrukin) I of Akkad, 7, 23, 240, 245, 251
Shadditu, 151
Shagshag, 20, 22, 245
Shallurtum, 78, 265
Shamakhtum, 266
Shamshi-Adad I of Asshur, 53, 84, 124-25, 238, 267, 280
Sharkalisharri of Akkad, 245
Sharra'igiziabzu, 28
Sharrukin (Sargon) II
Sharruma, 304
Shat-Adad, 122, 279
Shat-Sin, 28
Shatira, 28
Sherua'eterat, 150, 289
Shibtu, 84-85, 88, 89, 268
Shimatum, 86-87, 95, 268-69
Shu'am, 20, 245, 253
Shu-Sin of Ur, 8, 10, 21, 22, 37, 246
Shulgi of Ur, 7, 10, 21, 26, 37, 241, 242, 245, 246, 248, 249, 262
Shulgi-simti, 7, 22, 240, 245, 246
Shumshani, 24, 247

Shuqurtum, 246
Siatum, 23, 246
Sikkuti, 106
Simat-Enlil, 23, 246
Simat-Ishtar, 22, 37, 246
Simqi-Issar, 156
Sin-akhe'eriba (Sennakherib), 264, 272
Sin-magir of Isin, 22
Sukkitu, 292
Sumulael of Babylonia, 80, 265
Surratum, 82, 266

Tabata, 107
Tadin-Istar, 22
Takilat-Arbail, 158
Talampalanigrisha, 247
Taliya, 124
Tappiya, 78
Taramkubi, 120
Taramsagila, 82-83
Taramulmash, 94
Taramuram, 10, 21, 23, 241, 246
Taribatum, 81
Tashlultum, 20, 245, 253
Tashmetum-sharrat, 288
Telepinush, 179, 185, 196
Tiamat-bashti, 22, 37, 253
Tirutu, 159
Tizpatum, 87, 269
Tulid-Shamshi, 25, 28, 248
Tutanapshum, 21, 24, 247
Tutasharlibish, 7, 20, 37, 240, 245, 253

Ummeda, 30
Ummi, 156, 292
Umumtabat, 85
Ununi, 156, 292
Uquputu, 156, 292
Ur-Bau of Lagash, 21, 32, 38
Ur-Nammu of Ur, 7, 10-14, 21, 23, 26, 241, 242, 245, 249
Ur-Nanshe of Lagash, 19, 38, 237, 244
Urkisharrat, 109
Urkittutashmanni, 156

Uru-inimgina of Lagash, 8-10, 22, 24, 25, 240, 241, 245, 251, 253, 262

Waqartum, 79

Yaba, 147
Yakhilatum, 81, 94
Yakhmama, 268
Yamama, 84
Yaqarakhe, 156, 292
Yaqira, 157, 293
Yasmakh-Addu, 257

Yatar-aya, 85, 268

Zabibe, 150, 289
Zanka, 28
Zarpi, 152, 290
Zaza, 165
Zedekiah of Judah, 111
Zibezibe, 122
Zimri-Lim of Mari, 84, 88, 237, 267-68, 271
Ziplantawi, 197
Zunana, 91

Index of Places

Adab, 6
Akkad, 6, 7, 20, 23-24
Aleppo, 84
Asshur, 53, 83, 119-20, 152

Babylon, 48, 53-54, 104, 146, 148, 159
Borsippa, 32

Eridu, 6
Eshnunna, 47, 48-52, 53, 83-84

Girsu, 6

Harran, 59

Isin, 6, 15-18, 21, 24-25, 31, 35, 38

Kanish, 120-123, 177, 279
Karana, 83, 88-91, 94
Khattusha, 178, 189
Kish, 6-7, 20, 26, 38

Lagash, 6, 8-10, 20-23, 26, 29, 38
Larsa, 6, 8, 24-25, 31, 34-35, 48, 53

Mari, 21, 23, 58, 83-84, 89-92, 95-96, 125

Nimrud (Kalkhu), 100, 152, 155
Nineveh, 53, 100, 148, 152, 154-55, 158-59, 169, 175
Nippur, 6, 11, 28, 35, 38, 159, 162

Shuruppak, 6
Sippar, 6, 11, 24, 74, 79-83, 92-93, 264

Terqa, 85, 87-88, 280

Umma, 21, 29, 37-38
Ur, 6-7, 10-14, 20-24, 29, 37-38, 99, 104, 159
Uruk, 6-7, 23-24, 26

Index of Subjects

abortion, 137-38, 174, 198

abuse of power, 9, 161

adoption, 56, 81-2, 106, 78, 264-65, 276

adultery, 9, 13, 14, 32, 34, 36, 41, 51, 63, 64, 65, 69, 71, 95, 111-12, 135-36, 184, 244, 261-62, 282, 284

Amorites, 7-8, 22, 31, 33, 34-5, 37, 42, 48, 53, 97, 83, 114, 124, 130, 171-73, 209-11, 240, 251, 263, 267, 279

assault and battery, 13, 19, 41, 50, 62, 113, 135, 181-82,187, 202-3

battery causing miscarriage, 17-19, 132, 133, 173, 182-83, 263, 303

blasphemy, 135, 144, 174, 193, 198, 283

bribery, 74

child sacrifice, 166, 175, 296

collective punishment, 64, 140, 160, 175, 186, 196-99, 200-202, 206-7, 297

corporal mutilation, 9, 33, 42, 68, 70, 72, 73, 97, 112, 132, 135, 139, 141, 165, 169, 171, 174-75, 186, 187, 197, 199, 202, 212, 242, 262-63, 284, 298, 303

cuneiform, 5, 8, 54, 178, 280, 299

death penalty/capital punishment, 12, 13-14, 17-18, 36, 51, 52, 60, 63, 64-66, 67, 68-69, 71, 73, 96-97, 112, 114, 124, 130, 135, 139, 165, 169, 174-75, 186, 199, 201, 206, 215, 217, 257, 261-63, 274, 279, 282, 286, 302, 307

deport/deportation, 126, 146, 156, 161, 170, 171, 287

distraint, 32, 50, 85, 113

divorce, 11-12, 18, 27-28, 35, 49, 56, 58, 66, 76, 93, 96,104, 113, 122, 124, 129, 260, 173, 180, 188

dowry, 11, 16, 27, 30, 35, 40, 41, 57, 76-77, 82, 86, 109, 129, 180, 188, 209, 250, 267, 279, 297, 301

false accusation, 12-13, 14, 17, 41, 62, 66, 69, 91-92, 96, 132, 140, 143, 160, 201, 244, 262, 282

flogging, 63, 72, 134, 139, 143, 162, 174, 214, 283

harem, 85, 125, 142-46, 151, 161, 168, 174, 268, 284, 287, 290, 304

honor/dishonor, 65, 69, 71, 72, 262, 265

human sacrifice, 38-39, 254

impale, 34, 68, 71, 114, 138, 261, 297

incest, 60-61, 64, 113, 183-84, 188, 201, 262, 284, 303

inherit, 16, 101-2, 109, 111, 121, 128, 279-80

justice, 11, 15, 19-20, 40, 54-55, 177, 207, 210, 258, 299

kezertum, 268

kidnap, 49, 52, 69, 91, 113, 183, 207-10, 242, 262, 303

kulmashitu, 83, 94, 154, 259-60, 267

literacy, 75-76, 84, 89, 159-60, 201, 264, 267

marriage, 11, 15, 27, 41, 48-49, 55-56, 76, 100, 102, 115, 121, 127, 151, 155-56, 173, 179-80, 188, 194, 201, 242, 256, 259, 273, 283

marriage contracts, 11, 27, 48, 49, 56, 76, 93, 102, 113, 110, 121, 271, 179, 275, 306

marriage gifts, 11, 15, 27, 35, 41, 48, 49, 52, 55-57, 86, 100, 179-80, 209, 256, 280-81, 300

marriage price/bride price, 127, 155-56, 179-80, 194

marriage settlement, 103, 110, 115

midwife, 29, 267, 282, 285

murder/homicide, 13, 35-36, 41, 50, 64, 71, 113, 130 160-61, 165, 181-82, 187, 196, 200-201, 244, 282, 295, 301, 303

music/musician, 25-26, 33-39, 40, 80, 154, 168, 195, 254, 270, 291

naditu priest, 25, 56, 58, 79, 80, 81, 82, 83, 88, 91, 93-94, 105, 111, 243, 246, 248, 259-60, 262, 265-67, 276

negligence, 17, 51-52

oath, 63, 96, 136, 304

oblate, 154-55, 292

penalty of the case, 18, 63, 69, 243-44, 262

perjury, 13, 63, 69, 113, 124, 242, 279

pledge, 31-32, 64, 73, 78, 91, 109, 113, 129, 130, 133-34, 151, 158, 160, 174, 251, 283, 290, 293-94

political marriage, 10, 21, 75, 86-87, 98, 102, 111, 125, 147, 190, 208

pollution, 60-62, 64, 68, 175, 186, 188, 193, 201-2, 217, 261, 303

polyandry, 9, 241

polygyny, 16, 22, 49, 77, 121, 172, 213, 241, 268

private jurisdiction, 69, 126, 130, 140-41, 166, 171, 185-98, 202, 206

procure, 136-37

prophet, 88-89, 106, 155, 276, 292

prostitute/prostitution, 16, 78, 106, 109, 134, 162, 244, 249, 277, 283, 268

purity/purification, 68, 94, 105-6, 142-43, 154, 193-94, 197-200, 202, 217, 249, 261, 266, 276, 290, 295, 305-7

qadishtu, 25, 37, 83, 243, 246, 248, 259-60, 267, 269, 278-79, 282, 285

rape, 12, 19, 31, 41, 49-50, 52, 60, 69, 113, 130-32, 135-36, 140, 168, 170, 173, 183, 188, 201, 242, 251, 256, 262, 282

ration lists, 30, 31, 89, 248, 250-51, 269

real property, 17, 28-29, 30, 58-59, 90, 92-93, 106, 113, 151, 153, 157, 158, 180

repudiation of relationship, 19, 41, 68, 70

res judicata, 29, 92, 250, 270

restitution, 18, 33, 52, 96

river ordeal, 12-13, 96-97, 136, 209, 261-62, 282

robbery, 63-64, 69, 113, 202, 262

sacred marriage, 26, 248

sacrilege, 113, 134, 139, 199, 201, 302

sagittu, 105, 111, 276

scribe, 151, 154, 159-60, 162, 167, 264-65, 268, 290, 293-94, 296, 306

seals, 37, 81, 84-85, 88-89

sekretu, 259-60, 262, 268

shakintu, 152-53, 155, 158, 159, 160, 162, 164, 290-91, 293, 295

shepherd, 15, 177, 258, 297

shugitu, 83, 259, 267, 271

slavery, 6, 7, 11, 12, 13, 14, 16-18, 28-29, 32, 33, 50, 51, 59-60, 67, 69, 79, 83, 101, 107-9, 113, 152, 153, 156-58, 162, 170, 180, 185-88, 240, 243, 248-49, 251, 257, 259, 262-64, 271, 276-77, 286, 290, 292, 300, 303, 306-7

strike the cheek, 72, 263

support, 16-18, 30, 77, 78, 107, 121, 128, 214, 244, 279, 307

talion, 62, 68, 70-71, 73, 173-74, 207, 262-63

tavern keeper, 20, 29-30, 40, 49, 51, 67, 69, 74, 81, 250

Tawananna, 190, 196-98, 304

theft, 9, 18, 32, 50, 65-66, 70, 109, 113, 138-39, 144, 154, 164, 185, 187, 257, 262, 274, 284

torture, 168, 170

treason, 113, 163

trespass, 9, 51, 257

ugbabtu priest, 25, 81, 88, 94, 122, 154, 243, 248, 259, 262, 266, 279, 291, 293

veil, 26-27, 130, 137, 140, 193, 268, 282, 305

vicarious punishment, 68, 71, 73, 131, 133-34, 140, 144, 160-61, 174, 181, 202, 214, 282, 284, 301

weavers, 76, 84, 192, 250, 255

wet nurse, 30, 67, 68, 89, 109, 262, 267

widow, 9, 27, 30, 56-57, 64, 77-78, 104, 123, 127-28, 259, 281

wise women, 26

witchcraft/sorcery/magic, 64, 94-95, 96, 101-2, 109-10, 112, 113, 137, 162-63, 165, 174, 184-86, 188, 193, 197, 199, 201, 249, 271, 283, 274, 289, 294-95, 303, 305-7

women high priests, 23-25, 39, 98-99, 104

women priests, 6, 7, 9, 15, 22, 23-25, 34, 39-40, 57-58, 79-81, 154, 172, 191-92, 209, 243, 248-49, 253-54, 260, 262, 305